# When Biology Became Destiny

## Women in Weimar and Nazi Germany

Edited by Renate Bridenthal,
Atina Grossmann, and Marion Kaplan

Monthly Review Press
New York

The painting on the jacket is reprinted with the permission of the Viking Press. It is from *Charlotte: Life or Theater? An Autobiographical Play* by Charlotte Salomon, translated from the German by Leila Vennewitz, introduced by Judith Herzberg (New York, 1981).

Charlotte Salomon was a Jewish woman born in Berlin in 1917. A serious student at the Berlin art academy, she was forced to flee Nazi Germany in 1939 to live with her grandparents in southern France. There she created 769 paintings depicting the story of her life, her longings, anxieties, and despair. When she finished, she entrusted her work to a French neighbor, saying "C'est toute ma vie." She was deported to Auschwitz where she died in 1943. Her art work is preserved in the Jewish Historical Museum in Amsterdam.

*Burgess*
*HQ*
*1623*
*.W475*
*1984*
*copy 1*

Copyright © 1984 by Renate Bridenthal, Atina Grossmann, and Marion Kaplan
All rights reserved

*Library of Congress Cataloging in Publication Data*
Main entry under title:

When biology became destiny:

Bibliography: p.
1. Women—Germany—History—20th century—Addresses, essays, lectures. 2. Germany—Politics and government—1918–1933—Addresses, essays, lectures. 3. Germany—Politics and government—1933–1945—Addresses, essays, lectures. 4. Right and left (Political science)—Addresses, essays, lectures. I. Bridenthal, Renate. II. Grossmann, Atina. III. Kaplan, Marion A.
HQ1623.W475 1984 305.4'0943 84-18969
ISBN 0-85345-642-9
ISBN 0-85345-643-7 (paper)

Monthly Review Press
155 West 23rd Street
New York, N.Y. 10011

Manufactured in the United States of America

10 9 8 7 6 5 4 3 2 1

Dedicated to our mothers,
who were there

Irene               Erika               Grete

# Contents

## Part 2
### Women in Nazi Germany

# Acknowledgments

Many people have helped, supported, and encouraged us in the three years we have been engaged in this project. Meredith Tax first persuaded us to do it after a panel the three of us had presented at "The Scholar and Feminist" conference at Barnard College in April 1981. Alexandra Weinbaum early on helped us to conceptualize the project. Meredith Tax, Marilyn Young, Ellen Ross, and other members of the New Feminist Library Board have heartened us and offered helpful criticism. We have also enjoyed working with our contributors and we have learned from them. We are enormously indebted to the members of our German Women's History Study Group—Bonnie Anderson, Jane Caplan, Amy Hackett, Deborah Hertz, Claudia Koonz, Mary Nolan, and Joan Reutershan—for their careful reading of our introduction, for catching some of our worst errors, and for their intellectual and moral support. Susan Lowes at Monthly Review Press has been helpful and considerate. In many ways, then, this has been a collective experience, not the least part of which was the enormous inspiration and joy that the three of us drew from each other, as friends and colleagues engaged in a collective endeavor. Finally, thanks to Jay Kaplan, Frank Mecklenburg, and Hobart Spalding, who were stoically patient as the demands of this book piled more responsibilities on their shoulders and gave them less companionship in return. And thanks to Ruth Kaplan, who was not only patient about her mother's commitments, but lightened and enlivened many of our meetings as well.

# A Note to Our Readers

The essays on German history collected here discuss the politicization—and political manipulation—of women's and family issues as well as of women's experience: biology made into destiny and the resistance to that destiny. We focus on a period of intense political upheaval and economic restructuring: the rationalization of the German economy during the 1920s, the Great Depression of the early 1930s, the Nazi triumph, the coming of World War II, and the Holocaust.

Our motivations for putting this book together were both political and personal. We were propelled by our own histories as activists and scholars from the late 1960s onward, as feminists and historians emerging from the student movement and the New Left. We conceived of the book during the early Reagan years, when economic crisis and political reaction shrank the resources for social welfare and sharpened the "politics of reproduction" debate. It seemed to us that, ironically, the right managed to politicize the "personal" even more militantly and successfully than had the left or the women's movement. Feminists and leftists were retreating into defending the right to "private choice," while the New Right and the Moral Majority were arguing forcefully that sex and procreation, abortion and contraception, women's wage labor and the maintenance of the family were public and political issues subject to state regulation. Seeking a "usable past," we looked back to German history where those issues were dramatically, unequivocally, and in the end horrifically decided.

We intended the book as a contribution to the debate on how feminists and the left—and leftist feminists in particular—could respond to the New Right's assault on women's reproductive rights, their economic gains, and on the liberal welfare state (such as it was) in general. Since that time, the Supreme Court has reaffirmed legal abortion, but the "right to choice" for women has been accompanied by a limited access to that choice, along class and race lines. The problems we face today—from the personal need to juggle the temptations and demands of work, friends, lovers, and families to the political task of confronting a government bent on asserting imperial dominance abroad while cutting services at home—have in many ways proven more problematic and intractable than the ideological and political impact of the New Right.

We did not want to make facile or potentially misleading comparisons, but as scholars we have been asked about the historical lessons of German fascism often enough that we agreed that it would be important to provide broad access to the information in this book. Our readers will ask more questions and continue the discussions about the contemporary relevance of the material we present here. A close look at the history addressed in this volume alerts us to the dangers signaled by well-financed, well-organized movements in command of the latest propaganda techniques that, then and now, mobilize around such code words as "pro-family," "abortion," "homosexuality," "pornography," "patriotism," and "military strength." We want to stress that Nazism did not arrive full blown, with promises of war and gas chambers. It came slowly, step by step, draped in the protective coloring of love for country, strong medicine to combat unemployment, and, most importantly for our purposes, a pledge to restore the traditional family and relieve women of their "double burden."

In a sense, therefore, we are asking in this book our own feminist version of the classic and unavoidable questions that all historians ask of German history: What went wrong? What were the ruptures and continuities between the Weimar Republic and Nazi Germany? How was it possible for the promise of Weimar to be so quickly destroyed and Adolf Hitler to become chancellor? How was Auschwitz possible? We are particularly haunted by those questions because we also carry the baggage of German-Jewish families and identities. Our study of German history is always shadowed by our knowledge of the end of this particular story; it is a history that we or our families have experienced very directly. One of us was born in Germany and escaped as a young child; the other two are children of refugees. Our families have given us a sense of the extremes of German history in this period: the intoxication of Weimar in the 1920s, the heady sense of possibility, the feeling of being new women and men in the (brave) new world of post-World War I, post-Wilhelmine Germany despite the continuing harshness of daily life; and then the shock of Weimar's collapse, the Nazis' expulsion of the Jews, and finally genocide. We carry with us a continuing obsession with that history, with the need to know why, and perhaps with a heightened sensitivity to the danger signals that our readers may recognize in this book.

The articles included here speak directly to the multiple and ambivalent ways in which women are both agents and victims of history, and of how women's experience is powerfully mediated and structured by class and racial/ethnic identities. Some of us address dangers implicit in a feminism that celebrates separate spheres and differences between the sexes, glorifies motherhood and women's bodies, but remains beholden to the demand to preserve family and national community. Others suggest that one lesson to be learned from this history is that a narrow and elitist women's movement that expects to participate in the administration of a socially unequal and hierarchical society will succumb to—and sometimes embrace—programs detrimental to women's freedom and to human rights in general. All of the contributions show the constant tension between the commitment to individual freedom and the demand for state intervention. They indicate how central the negotiation of the double burden is for women's experience at home and in the workplace, as well as in determining state policy regarding population control, social welfare, and women in general. We are struck by the continuing dilemma of the need for protection and security versus the assertion of independence and freedom. The articles point to the dangers in arguing for women's rights on the basis of innate female characteristics, even if this argument is used to support pacifism and international understanding. They document the limitations of German feminism and socialism—in particular, their inability to move beyond traditional notions of the family, race, and class.

It seems to us as editors that the work in this book revises certain notions current among historians of German feminism about its affinity to "liberalism." We see instead a movement that defies comfortable categorization. On the one hand, the German women's movement stressed duty more than rights, and so was perhaps more "conservative" than its Anglo-American counterpart; but on the other hand, its stress on the "protection of mothers" *(Mutterschutz)* took it much further in asserting that the personal is political and in accepting that the "private" is "public." German feminism was strongly nationalist, but it also nurtured a small but important pacifist minority. We also address the controversial question of German feminists' relationship to the rise of fascism. How do we evaluate their responsibility? Indeed, we present clashing interpretations of the term "feminist," and of German feminism's relationship to Nazi rule.

Women's and family issues, such as population policy, family survival, sexual segmentation of the wage labor force, unequal political representation, legal discrimination, housework, contraception, abortion, and sexual relations occupied a central and critical space in the political discourse during both the Weimar and Nazi eras. Debates on sexuality, the "New Woman," and population policy—especially the decline in the birth rate and the rise in the rate of abortion—marked political life during the Weimar period. Women's work in both production and reproduction was central to the aims of all political parties and of the state. Nazi Germany formulated and enforced the most comprehensive population policy ever attempted by any European state.

Thus, gender was an extraordinarily salient category throughout the period addressed in this volume. Indeed, its significance increased in the Nazi period because so much of Nazi rhetoric claimed that the government held population policy considerations paramount and promised the restoration of family, sexual morality, and a disciplined, well-socialized workforce. Nazi policy depended on a biological notion of "asocial" elements poisoning the body politic, which owed much to the Weimar focus on social hygiene, eugenics, and motherhood. Finally, even as Jewish women found that their identity as Jews, rather than as women, dominated their fate and their actions, the fact of their being women remained an important (and heretofore neglected) factor in how they experienced their fate. In sum, the essays show the centrality of women and women's history to any historical analysis of the Weimar and Nazi periods.

In our introduction, we place gender within the context of the social, political, and economic development of Germany from the Empire to the Third Reich. The integration is not seamless; it is full of jagged cracks and difficult transitions. But that accurately reflects the current relationship of women's history to the historical canon. We also recognize that even the women's history that we are trying to integrate into German history is, in itself, incomplete. We have not included essays, for example, on women's cultural history, lesbian history, or the history of women in the organized left—although we have recently learned of new projects in these areas—and that, too, reflects the newness of the field. We are satisfied if we have shown the way toward a gender analysis of this turbulent era.

# When Biology Became Destiny

# Introduction:
# Women in Weimar and Nazi Germany

Political discontinuities in the history of Germany have been sharp. Between 1871 and 1945 Germany saw three different forms of government: a monarchy until 1918, a republic until 1933, and a dictatorship until 1945. In all of those decades there were feverish struggles among various groups for power, for shares in the social wealth, and for autonomy.

## Imperial Germany and World War I

After Germany's unification in 1871, the dynamic expansion of the economy continually brought new forces onto the scene, each influencing the political complexion of the era. Industrialists disliked the favoritism bestowed on the landowning military elites and merchants chafed at the tariffs that hurt overseas trade. Further, the working class, organized in trade unions and the Social Democratic Party (Sozial Demokratische Partei Deutschlands; SPD); whose program was based on a Marxist analysis of class struggle, insisted on its right to both economic protection and political representation. It refused to accept the carrot and stick approach of the government of Imperial Chancellor Otto von Bismarck. The "carrot" was a state-supported old-age and health insurance program, part of a tradition of state intervention in social and population policy intended to "steal the thunder" of the socialists. The "stick" was the outlawing of the SPD between 1878 and 1890 and the prospect of this happening again.

Women, too, wanted political and economic advancement. The women's movement, composed of two distinct and sometimes antagonistic parts, embodied the class polarization of German society. By 1894, after several attempts at cooperation had failed to breach an ever widening rift, the German women's movement had confirmed class and ideological divisions that were to endure. In that year, a bourgeois wing, led by Helene Lange (and, later, Gertrud Bäumer) consolidated itself into the Federation of German Women's Associations (Bund Deutscher Frauenvereine; BDF). A proletarian women's movement, led by Clara Zetkin, was organized under the aegis of the Social Democratic Party. The BDF demanded improved legal status for women, better education and professional and career opportunities, sexual hygiene (incorporating notions of health and moral reform), improved conditions for working women, and, in 1902, female suffrage. Before then, the SPD had been the only party consistently to support the vote for women. Social Democratic women believed in class over gender solidarity, emphasized the importance of women's integration into the work world, but nevertheless built a strong and separate women's movement.

Although they were bitter political enemies, both movements shared a commitment to women's traditional roles in the family and to ideals of female duty, service, and self-sacrifice. Their feminism, like that of women in most other nations, was time and culture-bound. It consisted of an amalgam of woman-oriented concerns, internalized patriarchal values, and a peculiarly German deference to the whole community, whether perceived as the class or the nation. By analyzing the variety of ideas and methods through which women within and outside these movements tried to gain greater control over their lives (as Hackett, Kaplan, Bridenthal, and Meyer-Renschhausen do in their essays), we can examine this feminism as an ongoing process rather than as a strict ideology. For example, while both the bourgeois and socialist women's movements aimed at better integration of women into the world of wage labor, they both also accepted the ideology of "separate spheres" for women and men and tolerated (for different reasons) woman's "double burden," her dual responsibility in the workplace and at home. Neither group challenged the primacy of the family and motherhood for women, even though the socialists saw productive labor as a path to women's emancipation (following the ideas of August Bebel, in his 1879 book *Women and Socialism*) and the middle-class women wanted higher education and careers for women. Although demanding a general improvement in the rights and welfare of women, neither group placed the same emphasis on political equality as did their Anglo-American sisters.

The 1890s saw a further proliferation of women's groups, despite legal restrictions against women's political activities in most of the German states that lasted until 1908. While the Social Democratic Party, fully legal since 1890, moved toward a more revisionist theory and practice, its own women's movement continued to develop a range of programs. At the same time, small, vocal groups advocating a "new morality" emerged. They emphasized such issues as birth control, suffrage, and the abolition of state-regulated prostitution. In 1905 a new and radical society was organized as the Federation for the Protection of Motherhood (Bund für Mutterschutz). In this book, Hackett describes the feminist activist and pacifist Helene Stöcker, who became its outspoken leader. Even within the BDF there were more radical women, such as Marie Stritt, who tried to push for a more aggressive feminism. By 1908 however, the defeat of a motion to demand the legalization of abortion signaled that conservatives had won control over the BDF.

The social conflict over shares of the national product and over political power, which had been sharpening ominously in the last decades of the nineteenth century, was shelved during the national effort of World War I. With the declaration of war in 1914, Emperor William II pronounced a political truce in the Reichstag (or parliament) and requested united support for the government: "When it comes to war," he said, "all parties cease and we are all brothers." Both the SPD and the middle-class feminist movement joined in the great burst of patriotic fervor that greeted the outbreak of war and felt themselves included (if not mentioned) in this national *Burgfrieden,* or "truce in the fortress." Indeed, this led to a split in the SPD.

The war brought new roles for working- and middle-class women. The former joined the industrial labor force *en masse,* standing in for the men in the trenches. For the first time they worked at male jobs at higher—though still not equal—wages. The middle-class women's movement gained a new legitimacy and visibility as it mobilized to attend to catastrophic social conditions. Their hitherto unappreciated experience with volunteer social work took on new importance as they organized relief work at home. Women's heightened visibility on the home front undermined the sexual division of labor and traditional skill hierarchies, and the *Burgfrieden* even witnessed the cooperation of socialist and bourgeois feminists on the local level.

The war dragged on much longer than anyone had imagined in 1914. The truce between the classes began to unravel and tension between the sexes increased. World War I was a new kind of war. Civilians felt intense deprivation and yet had to support the war by working harder and longer and by increasing their volunteer efforts. For women, the winter of 1916–1917—"the turnip winter" of mass starvation—was a turning point. War dislocations, food scarcity, and high prices led to urgent calls for peace. Furthermore, by 1916 an increasingly unpopular military dictatorship controlled the country. As early as April 1915, the more radical wing of the bourgeois women's movement acted on its pacifist principles and met with other international women's groups in The Hague. A similar breach followed among the socialists: the core of the future Independent Social Democratic Party (Unabhängige Sozialdemokratische Partei Deutschlands; USPD) and the Communist Party (Kommunistische Partei Deutschlands; KPD) met in Zimmerwald, Switzerland, in 1917 to announce their opposition to the war. Some socialist women, including such prominent national leaders as Clara Zetkin and Luise Zietz, split with the party. Those hostile to the war joined the more radical socialist opposition. As the war bogged down, so did the "truce in the fortress."

When it became clear that Germany would lose the war, rebellion and pressure for revolution mounted. The military advised Emperor William II to abdicate. It also urged the leaders of the Reichstag, in which the SPD was the largest element, to proclaim a republic that would negotiate a peace treaty. This "revolution" happened on November 9, 1918. Friedrich Ebert, head of the SPD, assumed leadership of the caretaker government. At the same time, workers' and soldiers' councils, which had begun to form as early as the spring of 1917 (inspired partly by the Russian Revolution) demanded a different form of "power by council": constant democratic involvement and accountability of the delegates to their constituencies. They challenged the party bureaucracy as well as the established trade union hierarchies. In particular, they differed with the Ebert government over the issue of socialism. The most radical members of the councils saw the revolution against the monarchy as an opportunity to overthrow capitalism as well, while the majority of Social Democrats believed the time for such a move was not yet ripe. Two complementary alliances dealt with the radicals. On the day the Weimar Republic was proclaimed, General Groener of the Army Supreme Command offered Ebert his support in keeping "law and order," an offer that Ebert accepted in return for the guarantee of an orderly demobilization. A week later the industrialist Hugo Stinnes made an agreement with Carl Legien, head of the General German Trade Union Confederation (Allgemeiner Deutscher Gewerkschaftsbund), to recognize the unions (rather than the workers' councils) as the chief representatives of labor and as bargaining partners, in return for union commitment to the principle of private property. The first agreement allowed Ebert to order the armed repression of radical uprisings in the first few months of 1919 and the second effectively put a stop to any moves toward socialism. Thus, when the National Assembly was elected on January 19, 1919, the SPD emerged as the strongest party, with over one-third of the votes, and the main issues of the revolution had already been decided: the new government was to be republican but not socialist; political equality was proclaimed but economic inequality remained.

The trade unions proceeded to make long-coveted economic gains in welfare reforms and in wages and hours. Nevertheless they remained at the mercy of a united front of employers, who retained their grip on the economic levers upon which so much depended: reparations payments (once the peace treaty had been signed), investments, and taxes. The last of these financed the redistributive schemes that substituted for socialist revolution—but which would quickly be cut back. Ultimately, all social groups were dissatisfied. Capital regretted its concessions. Labor felt its fundamental powerlessness. Agriculturalists and the middle class felt excluded by the employer-worker agreements. The limits on democratization left many dissatisfied, while others felt democratization had gone too far. The civil service, judiciary, and military, holdovers from the Imperial era, remained uncommitted and indeed often actively disloyal to the Republic. Thus, while the revolution of 1918 marked a significant discontinuity in German history, it carried a burden of continuity that had great political weight.

### The Weimar Republic

In January 1919 the National Assembly began its deliberations in the town of Weimar, Goethe's birthplace, far from the revolutionary climate of Berlin and steeped in a respected Enlightenment tradition associated with the great poet. The new parliamentary Republic had to deal with the victorious allies and cope with imminent economic breakdown. Its first act was to fashion a constitution that was soon hailed as one of the most democratic in the world. It featured an upper and a lower house, adult suffrage—including women for the first time—proportional representation, and extensive civil liberties and social welfare guarantees. It also guaranteed equal rights and responsibilities for citizens of both sexes, and promised protection of the family and decent work and housing for all Germans. In Article 48, the president was given emergency powers to set aside the basic law of the land, a provision that became crucial after 1930. (It was used over 250 times in later years by men who neither supported the Weimar Republic nor democracy.) Parallel to the new constitution, the government also maintained a large body of Imperial law, such as the criminal code of 1871, which outlawed abortion and restricted access to birth control, and the civil code of 1900, which restricted women's rights in marriage and divorce.

The new constitution raised expectations that it could not possibly fulfill without the fundamental social and economic changes that its authors were unwilling to make. This contradiction set the stage for the many debates during the Weimar Republic about the role of the state in social welfare and about the conflict between individual rights and social duties. These debates were articulated in the Reichstag by the major political parties, although tiny splinter parties, encouraged by the constitution's representational system, also thrived in the tense political atmosphere of the day. The major Weimar parties included (from left to right): the Communist Party (Kommunistische Partei Deutschlands; KPD), whose voting strength was around 10 percent between 1924 and 1930 and rose a bit thereafter; the Independent Social Democratic Party (Unabhängige Sozialdemokratische Partei; USPD), which polled 5 million votes and occupied 84 of 452 Reichstag seats in 1920 but ceased to exist after 1924; the Social Democratic Party, which remained the largest party until 1932, but hit its peak of 38 percent of the vote in 1919; the Catholic Center Party (Zentrum), which participated in every coalition government until 1932; the Democratic Party (Deutsche Demokratische Partei; DDP), a small liberal party that had a delegate in every cabinet between 1919 and 1931 but dwindled to under 1 percent of the vote by 1932; the German People's Party (Deutsche Volkspartei; DVP), reluctant supporter of the Republic, which represented business and industry and was also in every cabinet from 1920 to 1931; the German National People's Party (Deutschnationale Volkspartei; DNVP), an ultraconservative, militarist, and anti-Semitic party, which represented mainly big industry and the Prussian estate owners and opposed the very existence of the Weimar Republic; and the National Socialist German Workers' party (Nationalsozialistische Deutsche Arbeiterpartei; NSDAP, or Nazi Party), which emerged as the second largest party in 1930, and in 1932 received almost twice as many votes as the SPD. By the end of the Republic a profusion of parties vied for the voter; further, there had been twenty-one cabinets between 1919 and 1932, reflecting—and increasing—the divisions in the society.

The influence of the Russian Revolution and "Yankee" culture also produced tensions and divisions. The example of Russia, which had pioneered social legislation to provide protection for mothers and children and had decriminalized abortion and homosexuality, inspired German sex reformers and Communists but sparked concern among some middle-class feminists who worried about the future of the family as an institution. In fact, the lifting of censorship after the fall of the Empire had an immediate and, for some, frightening cultural impact. There was an upsurge of sexually explicit films and literature. Magnus Hirschfeld's Institute for Sexual Science (Institut für Sexualwissenschaft) in Berlin made the German capital the international center of sexology and of the Sex Reform movement. Journalists and other writers responded to the arrival of the "Yankees" on European shores with an intense fascination that paralleled their reaction to Bolshevism. Americanism was exemplified by Henry Ford and his assembly line, and by an apparently more egalitarian "Girl *Kultur*," which included changes in dress, hair, make-up, and sexual behavior, and the promise of companionate marriage.

On the other hand, the war produced experiences and images of horror that intensified male demands for the soothing and procreative qualities they expected of women. Indeed, the war had widened the gap between women and men, who had experienced it so differently. Men continued to cherish the peculiar camaraderie of the trenches, and a "stab in the back" legend grew. According to this myth, the war was lost on the home front, rather than by the army, because of subversion by Jews, Communists, Social Democrats—and also women. Demobilization removed thousands of women from their wartime jobs and retracked others into lower paying "female" areas. By creating unemployment and job competition, demobilization intensified the antagonism between the sexes. Furthermore, fears of demographic disaster followed the sky-rocketing "homecoming divorces" and the perception that many "surplus" women, denied husbands by the slaughter of war, would not produce babies to replace a lost generation. In spite of these tensions, women were expected to bind the nation's wounds with their nurturing qualities. They had to mediate men's re-entry into the family and work.

At the same time, women at first made remarkable political gains. They voted in great numbers in the first National Assembly elections, and almost 10 percent of the delegates were women. Some women gained other political positions: veterans of the working-class women's movement won new, if limited, importance in the SPD and KPD; veterans of the middle-class women's movement found places in the new government ministries, especially in the social welfare bureaucracy or within the social work occupations that were just beginning to achieve professional status. Over time, however, women's political participation declined steadily. Economic and political tensions poisoned postwar public life. Bloody revolutionary and counter-revolutionary activity continued for many years, and women played a decidedly subordinate role in such extra-parliamentary politics, tending the wounded or the home fires.

The Treaty of Versailles, which forced Germany to accept a huge reparations burden, exacerbated domestic tensions. Territorial concessions meant a loss of 10 percent of the prewar population, 15 percent of the arable land, most of the colonies, foreign investments, fleet, and railroad stock. The leaders of the new republic—rather than those who had begun and lost the war—signed the treaty, and the new government was saddled with the responsibility for having accepted what it could not, in fact, have refused. The political right quickly labeled the SPD leadership as traitorous and spoke of its having "stabbed Germany in the back."

This was the beginning of a rightist campaign that lasted throughout the life of the Republic, and that continued to heap scorn on the government for Germany's difficulties and to ridicule democracy as "un-German." The right proclaimed militant nationalism, coupled with anti-Semitism, as its hallmark. It denigrated women's rights, seeing the assumption of nontraditional roles by women as "un-German" as well. In 1920 an attempted coup (the Kapp Putsch), led by extreme nationalists and militarists, threatened to destroy the young Republic. It was resoundingly defeated by a general strike among workers, but the army-supported, right-wing paramilitary forces, which had sprung up after the war, still ran rampant, bent on undermining the Republic and killing leftists. Leftist paramilitary groups often met them head on. Street violence and political assassinations were commonplace. As early as January 1919, after the defeat of an uprising (Spartacist Rebellion) by the young KPD (founded only two weeks earlier), rightists murdered two of its leaders, the brilliant theoretician and organizer Rosa Luxemburg and her close colleague Karl Liebknecht. A string of assassinations of prominent government officials and leftists, including Germany's first Jewish Foreign Minister, Walter Rathenau, followed. The forerunner of the Nazi Party, the German Workers' Party, was growing. On the left, diehard revolutionaries fought to advance socialism, most notably in a 1920 uprising in the industrial Ruhr region. The authorities meted out far sterner punishments to them than to those on the right, and their activity ceased sooner.

Women, while absent from these armed encounters, were nevertheless dramatically present in male fantasies and public discourse. To right-wing paramilitary (Free Corps) fighters, the proletarian "Red nurses" who stood ready to bandage and assist leftist militants symbolized the decadence of the new Germany. To the Communists, women often seemed potentially dangerous class traitors, "soft" on struggle and liable to lure men away from it. This ancient tendency to transform women into symbols conveyed women's illusory responsibility in the face of their actual political impotence. In short, women—much like Jews—were blamed for losing the war and for profiting from Germany's decline and their recent, visible entry into political and cultural life made such scapegoating easier.

A major economic issue of the postwar period was who would pay the costs of the war. Industry refused to take on the burden, either through taxation or through loans to the government. It threatened to "strike," or refuse to invest, a move that would have led to a recession. When Germany defaulted on its debts in 1923, France occupied the Ruhr region in order to force further payment. Helpless, fearing a "flight of capital," and having to support the costly passive resistance against the French, the government resorted to printing money. It thus triggered runaway inflation, so that by November 1923 the mark was valued at 4.3 trillion to the dollar. While this action underlined the fact that Germany would not be forced to pay reparations, it created a domestic disaster that shaped the remaining years of the Republic.

Economically, it greatly hurt organized labor, whose trade union treasuries were decimated and whose membership was halved when unemployment touched 1.5 million during the winter of 1923–1924. A weakened labor movement looked increasingly to the state, an uncertain ally at best, to mediate conflicts with capital and to legislate social policy.

The middle class, comprised of owners of small enterprises, distributors, large and small, and professionals, lost its economic base. People dependent on fixed incomes, such as pension and personal savings, were reduced to penury, with women—particularly widows—suffering disproportionately. Those peasants and estate owners who were in debt gained somewhat since they were able to pay back their loans with cheapened money. The big industrial capitalists gained the most, benefiting from the bankruptcies of smaller businesses—a process which concentrated capital in fewer hands—and from lowered real wages, which made German exports more competitive.

Inflation turned the moral universe upside down, so that the traditional values of thrift, saving, and delayed gratification suddenly became meaningless, even counterproductive. Housewives bought bread with wheelbarrows full of worthless paper money. The scathing caricatures of artists like George Grosz depicted rich speculators, impoverished solid citizens, prostitutes prowling the streets, and proper daughters of the middle class forced to go to work. Traditional class distinctions blurred as young women of the middle and working classes rubbed elbows in the female job ghettos of the burgeoning service sector. Traditional moral distinctions between respectable and indecent women blurred as sexual taboos seemed to loosen to the point of demoralization. It appeared as though the shaky Weimar Republic was unraveling even before it had established itself.

The Weimar Republic was not, however, in crisis for its entire fourteen years. For a short period in the mid-1920s the government and economy appeared to stabilize. U.S. loans and a long-term repayment schedule—the Dawes and Young plans of 1924 and 1929 respectively—aided the economic recovery. Currency stabilized, the economy grew, and despite an endemic unemployment rate averaging 12 percent, it seemed to those who had incomes that a halcyon period had arrived.

The effects in the political sphere were immediate. The SPD lost its dominant position in the government, replaced by a centrist coalition of conservative and liberal middle-class parties under Gustav Stresemann. This shift to the right was a more accurate reflection of the actual constellation of forces than was the original Weimar coalition, which was created at a time when fear of revolution had temporarily prompted business interests to cooperate with labor. Now, with the unions weakened, even the eight-hour day was lost to the "necessities" of reconstruction.

Industry invested in new machinery and tried to rationalize production on a wide scale. This involved a complex of processes that included mechanization, the standardization of interchangeable parts, which were assembled on a moving belt, and a concomitant breakdown of the work process into smaller tasks requiring less skill. It created a labor force of un- or semi-skilled workers, themselves now more like interchangeable parts, who were closely supervised according to "rational" time-motion studies that made them appendages to a paced machine. Women comprised a significant proportion of this new assembly-line proletariat. As Annemarie Tröger's article shows, they were psychologically tested for suitability and "handled" by "scientific management" to get the utmost out of their labor. And those firms that could not afford such drastic reorganization quickly succumbed to those that could, further concentrating capital, increasing the number of cartels, and adding to the power of the banks, through which the new investment was channeled.

The rationalization of production thus deskilled labor, restructured, and—in certain cases—rigidified the sex-segregated labor market, while also undermining traditional hierarchies of skill. In addition, hard times forced more married women into the labor market. Since one man's spouse was often another man's scab, this led to tension around women's right to employment. Heated debates took place about married women's right to work (they were called "double earners") and about the future of family life. Again women were blamed for conditions beyond their control. The fact was that rationalization did not significantly increase the proportion of women in the paid labor force. What it did was to reorganize the labor market so as to tighten, even institutionalize, the modern sexual division of labor. Women may have seemed to be in the vanguard—on assembly lines, in mechanized offices, behind department store sales counters, and in the expanded social welfare bureaucracies—but they rarely displaced men.

In this volume the article by Renate Bridenthal and Claudia Koonz shows that shifting structures of production and a more highly differentiated production process tended to push women even further toward the bottom of the skills-and-pay pyramid than before. Only a few women, who had gained experience in the prewar and wartime bourgeois women's movement, won high government positions. By the late 1920s, the BDF counted thirty-eight women in responsible adminstrative posts, all in education and welfare. About thirty women sat in the Reichstag. In addition, the opening of the universities to women in 1908 had produced a small corps of professionals who now began to come into their own. By and large, however, "progress" for women in this era was dubious indeed. The majority still worked at traditional tasks, either as domestic servants or as unpaid workers in the household or family enterprise. Women often moved in and out of factory or office work, depending on shifts in the economy and in their own life cycles. Trade unions fought the resulting instability only weakly, paying lip service to the equality of women in the labor force but rarely standing up for it in practice. Employers of domestic servants also combated irregular female work patterns but in a different way. In her article on "professional" housewives, Bridenthal shows how they tried to create and keep a stable workforce of domestic servants by marshaling the traditional ideology of women's place in the home.

Rationalization affected even those women still engaged in traditional forms of paid and unpaid labor. It implied a reordering of people's private lives to meet the new industrial pace and rhythms. At least as a metaphor, rationalization extended from the factory and office to public institutions and political life and into the home, even into the bedroom. The term was used to describe developments in many areas, including the birth rate, sexual behavior, housework, and design and architecture. Rationalization was supposed to help women better manage the double burden of work and family through new labor- and time-saving devices and through the introduction of efficient time-and-motion-coordinated patterns of work organization. Even sexual techniques and birth control were not spared from attempts to "rationalize" the most private of human activities.

Social observers of all political persuasions—from journalists and sociologists to government experts and political leaders—detected the emergence of a "new woman" and a "new family" in the 1920s. Indeed, Weimar culture did produce a certain heady and intoxicating sense of freedom in the big cities, especially for some intellectual and professional women. But the development of the "new woman" represented a phenomenon both broader and more complex than the images of the flapper or the sexy saleslady convey. The "new women"—who voted, used contraception, obtained illegal abortions, and earned wages—were more than a bohemian minority or an artistic convention. They existed in office and factory, bedroom and kitchen, just as surely as—and more significantly than—in café and cabaret. Their confrontation with the rationalized workplace, their heightened visibility in public places, and their changing sexual and procreative options preoccupied population experts and sex reformers. And it was this "new woman" who was to become a symbol of degeneracy and modern "asphalt culture" in Nazi propaganda. In fact, the bourgeois women's movement also joined in bemoaning the supposed sexual laxity of the times, urging closer supervision of morality. A generation gap opened up between younger women and older middle-class feminists who expected women to make better (and more "serious") use of their new rights and saw the younger generation as flighty, materialistic, and individualistic.

Indeed, the Weimar years were a period of crisis in population and family policies and a transitional era in defining new ideas about women and family. In many ways policies directed toward family and population later developed by the Nazis, which are described by Gisela Bock in her article, were designed to reestablish boundaries and reassert definitions that had become blurred. This was to happen both in the workplace and in private life, where contraception, abortion, and venereal disease collapsed rigid distinctions between respectable women and prostitutes. The article by Elisabeth Meyer-Renschhausen poignantly describes a victim of these changing distinctions.

The period from 1925 to 1928 witnessed some major efforts to establish social welfare and population policies, and saw the achievement of certain gains long demanded by the SPD and the middle-class women's movement. Women parliamentarians decisively influenced some of this legislation, especially in the areas of youth welfare, control of venereal disease, and maternity benefits for women workers. In 1926 and 1927 the state governments of Saxony and Prussia set up marriage counseling centers designed to encourage sound and healthy marriages and to discourage the procreation of the "unfit" or "unhealthy." These distinctions predated, but foreshadowed, the Nazis' particular application of racial hygiene, described in Bock's essay. Antiabortion laws were reformed but not abolished. In 1927 unemployment insurance became a right rather than a welfare benefit. Maternity benefits were integrated into workers' health insurance. The bourgeois women's movement won the passage of a law to combat venereal disease that transferred authority over prostitutes from the police to health officials and made it a crime to transmit venereal disease knowingly (see Meyer-Renschhausen's article).

All of these gains were ambivalent, however, and did little to meet the needs of all workers. The maternity benefits sought to encourage healthy and devoted childraising but only applied to full-time workers. The venereal disease law proved unenforceable except insofar as it could be used to prosecute nonmedical people who treated sexual and reproductive problems; it thus became another step in the professionalization of medicine and the general bureaucratization of society. Such reforms marked a more sophisticated degree of state intervention into people's everyday lives, which meant, for example, that while more people—especially women—were covered by health insurance, more people also relied on state services.

Relative stabilization did bring with it an explosion of cultural innovation. The work of the Bauhaus school of architecture, for instance, sought to develop a new style of housing and decoration that was functional as well as beautiful and that could be used by the masses of workers as well as by the privileged who had traditionally patronized art. The new Weimar culture was fascinated with "modernity," eager to break with a stultifying Imperial past. It was in many ways a culture of former outsiders: of Jews, socialists, and some women, of people who wanted to move Germany into the modern democratic era as well as into the community of Western culture. Republican Germany thus became a major battleground between the modern movement and the forces of tradition in literature, the theater, the visual arts, and architecture. Right-wing nationalists attacked Jews for being in the forefront of this new and daring movement. Jews were indeed prominent among novelists, journalists, critics, cartoonists, theatrical producers, and Expressionist poets, and many were important figures in the cinema and light entertainment. They owned the leading liberal newspaper and publishing houses. In short, although they comprised under 1 percent of the German population, they seemed ubiquitous in those areas where traditional values were being challenged. To the political right, the rich and vital urban culture (which owed a great deal to Jews) seemed like a modern Babylon.

In this culture, women stood at the nexus of the "morality question." They were simultaneously seen as guardians of morality and as the chief agents of a "culture of decadence." They were both stars of the cinema and its major audience. In the developing consumer industries, women manufactured, sold, and consumed new items, thus becoming representative of a new pleasure-seeking consumerism. While the "new woman" did not signal female emancipation or the collapse of patriarchy, she did represent—to some—a moral crisis. The definition of the female in the Weimar period included images of women as victim, threat, and salvation. Thus the "new woman" captured the imagination of progressives who celebrated her, even as they sought to discipline and regulate her, and of conservatives who blamed her for everything from the decline of the birth rate and the laxity of morals to the unemployment of male workers.

All sorts of anxieties were embodied in this symbol, and for political parties, government agencies, doctors, and social workers, real women became objects to be manipulated in an attempt to defend against such anxieties. One such attempt was the campaign to establish Mother's Day as a national holiday, detailed by Karen Hausen below. On the ideological plane, the campaign addressed insecurities about women's nurturant qualities by celebrating their selflessness and caring. On the economic plane, it deliberately created a new market for small businesses—in this case, florists and confectioners. Mother's Day therefore served multiple purposes: it enhanced profit through induced gift-giving, it glorified motherhood without providing any material benefits, and it added weight to the insistence that women were primarily creatures of their biology. It also promoted a hierarchy of value that distinguished between socially and racially desirable families "rich in children" that would strengthen the *Volk* and large "asocial" families that would be a drain on it.

### The Depression and the Onset of Nazism

The period of relative stabilization that allowed this culture— alternately experienced as threatening and exhilarating—to flourish was short lived. Even before the New York stockmarket crash in 1929, the German economy was showing signs of weakness. As early as 1928 investments fell significantly and unemployment began to rise again, thereby reducing effective demand. When the U.S. banks called in the short loans that had been contracted under the Dawes Plan, invest- ment slowed still more. The worldwide nature of the Depression shrank trade, reducing the international market for German-produced exports. This created still more unemployment, which in turn further reduced the domestic market. And so the vicious downward spiral continued until it bottomed out at over 6 million registered unem- ployed in 1932, an average of one out of five workers.

Since heavy industry was hit before the predominantly female con- sumer industry, and since many women did not work at the insured jobs that showed up in the official unemployment statistics, it may have seemed as though women were not affected as much as men. This fueled a campaign against "double earners," which was supported by all the parties except the KPD. But as with the fear of women replacing men in "rationalized" production processes, this proved to be a dis- torted—if politically powerful—perception. In many ways, as Atina Grossmann's article indicates, women—whether employed, unem- ployed, or never employed—bore a particular burden in this period of political anxiety and social dislocation.

Monopolization sharpened the crisis, because the largest companies chose to ride out the storm by curtailing production rather than by lowering prices. This caused unemployment to spread to those indus- tries that produced capital goods. It also forced many of the artisans and tradespeople who had flourished during the stabilization period into bankruptcy. They watched their incomes fall by about 50 percent and saw their futures as self-employed independents seriously threatened. For the economically strongest, on the other hand, it was an opportunity to win control over even more capital, so that the long- term trend toward cartelization received yet another boost. The work- ing class and lower middle class were sent reeling.

The Depression also produced a surge of anti-Semitism. As during the inflation of 1923, Jews suffered essentially the same deprivations as the rest of the population. The impact on Jewish-owned businesses was uneven, as it was on businesses in general. Jewish merchants and professionals, however, were subjected to Nazi-sponsored economic boycotts and Jewish salaried workers suffered from discriminatory hiring and firing. In the case of Berlin, where one-third of all Jews lived, the number of Jews on welfare doubled between 1925 and 1931. The Jewish economic decline from the bourgeois prosperity of the Imperial era was accelerated by the Depression. The fate of Jewish women followed a parallel course: Marion Kaplan's article shows how the League of Jewish Women (Jüdischer Frauenbund) shifted the emphasis of its occupational training programs from social work, nursing, and teaching to domestic service—if only for the duration of the Depression, as they hoped.

The most telling impact, however, was political. The Depression, and the policies adopted to combat it, brought a sharp shift to the right. The SPD had not participated in the six cabinets between the end of 1923 and June 1928, when they returned with Hermann Müller heading a new coalition government. It was to be the last parliamentary government in Germany for fifteen years. Ironically, the very party that had been so unfairly blamed for the Versailles "Treaty of Shame" had to preside over the beginning of the Republic's collapse during the Depression. Two years later Müller resigned when the SPD refused to approve a potentially unpopular reduction of unemployment benefits. In the midst of economic chaos, the Center Party's Heinrich Brüning took Müller's place as chancellor. Brüning called a fateful election in September 1930 in which Nazi Party seats in the Reichstag increased from 12 to 107 and Communist strength increased from 54 to 77, signaling tense political polarization.

The demise of SPD influence, the weakening of the trade unions, the stalemate in the Reichstag, and the pressures of unemployment meant that big industry and big agriculture now ruled openly under Brüning, who quickly earned the name of "Hunger Chancellor." The president of the organization of Prussian estate landlords became minister of agriculture; I. G. Farben, one of Germany's largest conglomerates, furnished the finance minister. Brüning governed without the consent of parliament, using the emergency powers as provided by Article 48 of the Constitution. He proceeded to dismantle most of the labor legislation (attempting to lower prices and wages) and further curtailed social insurance. He thereby broke the Weimar compromise between capital and labor. In December 1931 a more draconian decree allowed employers to break contracts and push wages back by as much as 10 to 15 percent, to January 1927 levels. Brüning's successor, Franz von Papen, carried "deregulation" even further. In September 1932 his administration allowed companies that hired new employees to cut their wages by up to 50 percent.

Deflationary policies neither halted the pace of unemployment nor revived the economy. The pioneering comprehensive unemployment insurance program, organized in 1927, provided for twenty-six weeks of support, including health benefits, and then moved the worker onto the relief rolls. It was not prepared for the massive demands that were being made on it and by 1932 its funds were exhausted. Working women, especially if they were married, felt the legal restrictions of eligibility before most others. Women were more likely to lose their insurance benefits, more likely to have to wait longer for their benefits to begin (due to stricter means tests for women), and more likely to drop out of the labor market completely.

In other ways, too, the Depression affected women more intensely than men. Emergency decrees cut health insurance benefits and lifted rent controls, measures that particularly affected women in their capacity to organize for the family's survival. The economic crisis set off a national debate about entitlements and priorities. Women stood in the center of that debate, although they very rarely participated directly. Women were the primary users and beneficiaries of the social services; they were the first to suffer when these were withdrawn. On the other hand, as in wartime, they were also expected to "take up the slack" when these services were no longer available. Furthermore, population policy concerns occupied center stage as the government sought to enforce social discipline and to regulate the birth rate by cracking down on the massive number of illegal abortions. Doctors, eugenicists, and politicians debated sterilization as a cost-efficient measure to reduce social welfare costs and eliminate potential "asocial ballast." The campaign to legalize abortion in 1931, described by Grossmann, marked one of the few instances when women of the middle and working classes joined in an attempt—albeit a futile one—to oppose cutbacks and protest government control over women's bodies.

By the early 1930s the government had been paralyzed by Brüning's constant invocation of emergency decrees, while the deepening Depression had intensified political polarization. The working class was split between Socialists and Communists, and the gap between both of these and a fearful middle class widened. German capitalists would support only those governments that were friendly to their own ambitions and sharply curbed labor's strength. As organized labor became increasingly militant, a growing Communist Party called for stronger measures.

The moment had come for the Nazi Party to make its contribution to the crisis. Nazi paramilitary units, consisting of former army veterans and unemployed young men, tore into union offices, destroyed their files and their printing presses, and beat up staff members. Many of these "Brown Shirts," as they came to be called, harbored diffuse and contradictory anticapitalist as well as anti-left and anti-Semitic sentiments, but this in no way inhibited their attacks on the labor movement. Nazi thugs also terrorized Jews and people whom they viewed as their political opponents. As in the period after the failed revolution, the authorities were lenient in their punishment of Nazis, and the left was forced to organize its own defense. Some urban working-class districts fell into a state of virtual civil war. The Nazis were provoking the kind of chaos from which they claimed to want to save Germany. At the same time, the "Harzburg Front" (of 1931) brought together prominent industrialists, bankers, right-wing leaders, and the Nazis in a political alliance to defeat the Republic.

The women's movement, like most groups, was rent by similar, although considerably less violent, forces. For example, Kaplan's article shows how estrangement set in—often all too easily—between Jewish and non-Jewish members. Also, Bridenthal and Meyer-Renschhausen demonstrate that in attempting to bridge class differences through gender solidarity (in the cases of the organized housewives or the issue of prostitution, respectively), the women's movement often crashed against the social rock of economic inequality and conflicting interests. Bridenthal details why, by 1932, the right wing of the BDF (the rural and urban housewives' associations which were the two largest member organizations in the BDF) withdrew from the more moderate majority.

In the presidential elections of March and April 1932, Adolf Hitler, head of the Nazi Party, with four hundred thousand stormtroopers at his call, ran for office in a bitterly polemical campaign. He succeeded in forcing the aged incumbent, World War I hero General Hindenburg, into a runoff election. Although Hindenburg won—19.4 million votes to Hitler's 13.4 million and the KPD candidate Ernst Thälmann's 3.7 million—Hitler had demonstrated considerable popularity at the polls, an important bargaining point in gaining the support of industrialists. Women voted in great numbers for Hindenburg, rather than for Hitler or Thälmann. Hindenburg, despite his conservative background, appeared in this context as the candidate of the center. After the election, none of the governments supported by Hindenburg's presidential decrees (Brüning until May 29, 1932; Franz von Papen, June to December 1932; Kurt von Schleicher, December 1932 to January 1933) were capable of instituting policies to alleviate the Depression, much less to end it.

In the parliamentary elections of July 1932 the Nazi Party won 37 percent of the vote, the most it was to garner in a free election; much of this was achieved by the bullying described above, although it is not to be denied that Hitler enjoyed a broad popular base of support. On the left, the Socialist Party lost its position as the largest political party in the Reichstag, receiving only 21 percent of the vote, while the Communist Party won 14 percent. The remaining votes were shared by a number of small parties. The center did not hold; the left and right gained at its expense. Contrary to some myths about massive female support for the Nazis, it seems clear that most women resisted this polarization. Again, they were less volatile, voting in higher numbers for the older parties.

Adolf Hitler was well known to the extreme right, but had been unable to make political headway beyond it until the calamity of the Depression. His political acumen and energy, his use of modern propaganda techniques, his programmatic opportunism, and especially the excesses of his uniformed stormtroopers helped his party's rise from an insignificant fringe group founded in 1920. Following his failed putsch in 1923, Hitler had spent a year in prison writing *Mein Kampf (My Struggle)*, which became the party bible. But, as we have seen, the Depression was the catalyst for his dramatic but legal seizure of power. In particular, the Nazis successfully blamed contradictory forces for the economic crisis. On the one hand, they pointed the finger at the capitalists; on the other hand, they blamed the Socialists and "Socialism"—the Nazis' name for the Social Democratic Party's reformist policies. They raised the spectre of Communism to frighten the German middle classes into following their lead. They also blamed the Treaty of Versailles on the "treasonous" Socialists who had signed it. In addition, Jews, who could be found among capitalists as well as Socialists and Communists, were blamed for virtually every misery.

"Degenerate" women also came in for their share of blame. The Nazis accused them of undermining the home front during the war, led astray by what they called "Marxist, Jewish, cosmopolitan women's rights advocates," and of deserting their domestic and childrearing responsibilities in favor of stealing men's jobs and seeking urban adventure.

Hitler and his followers preached their own version of a class-consensus society, one based on racial mythology. The Nazi Party promised renewed nationalism and *völkisch* solidarity in place of class divisions. It promised orderly families and healthy children in place of double earners and illegal abortions. To Germans, the term *Volk* (literally, a folk, people, or nation) carried with it a host of conservative symbols. To them it meant a racial unity, a shared history, fate, and consciousness. As used by the Nazis, it took on mystical proportions and was used to subordinate individuals to the party (which claimed to represent the *Volk*) and to expel "undesirables"—Jews and other "parasites"—accused of living off scarce resources and of being a danger to the body politic. To the Nazis, only "Aryans"—a term for allegedly superior Caucasians—belonged to the "racial community" or *Volksgemeinschaft.* Jews and "asocials"—all seen as undesirables— were to be ostracized and excised from the *Volk.* Thus internal social conflict was to be resolved by creating a romanticized vision of the *Volk* as one big family from which "aliens," such as Jews and "traitors" (like Socialists and Communists), were somehow (the method was not yet fully clear) to be removed. The remaining Germans were to be convinced to act for the good of the whole rather than selfishly. The basic unequal ownership of property, deemed to be an organic formation of the valued *Volk,* was, however, to be left intact. By creating an exclusive *Volk* (defined in a way that disciplined the masses), the state could circumscribe more narrowly the population for which it was responsible—for example, in the area of social welfare. Further, the Nazis could justify their imperialist ventures by arguing that a healthy, productive, and prolific *Volk* needed more *Lebensraum* (living space). The women of the *Volk,* as described by Bock, were to be recruited to wage a "battle of births" which would both substantiate the need for more space and provide the people needed for that expansion. This "superior" *Volk* looked eastward, where "inferior" people would be forced to give up their land and where Germans would find markets and raw materials.

The Nazi formulas, perhaps because they were so contradictory, succeeded in attracting a mass following even among formerly hostile groups. Strange bedfellows crept under the Nazi blanket. The middle class as a whole joined in numbers disproportionate to its share of the population. The lower middle classes—bewildered by inflation and economic depression and fearful of socialism and of being further declassed—were also strong supporters. The Nazis also gained support from the educated and propertied upper middle class—many wealthy urban Protestants gave Hitler the veneer of respectability he sorely needed. The Nazis also had support in the Protestant countryside and in small towns. There were others, too: the desperate unemployed, some leftists disillusioned with failed agendas, and new voters among young people who feared for their future livelihoods.

Women, despite their apparently more moderate voting patterns, were not exempt from the enthusiasm. While Nazi propaganda exaggerated women's adulation of Hitler, in fact many women saw in him a solution for very real problems. The middle-class women who supported the Nazis often did so for the same reasons as the middle-class men. In addition, they expected the Nazis to implement their promise of gender-separate spheres of activity. For women this meant home and family, as well as the "female" worlds of teaching or social work.

The Nazis manipulated this ideology cynically during their period in power. Koonz describes women in the Nazi Party, recruiting for it and planning to run a separate women's sphere within it. Koonz—and also Tröger, in her discussion of Nazi labor policies—show that the hope some women had of gaining influence within a Nazi state that would truly protect motherhood and the family and enforce morality was a delusion. Moreover, women were blind to—or woefully ignorant of—the ruthlessness of the state in which they wanted to share responsibility.

## The Nazi State

The failure of the final and short-lived minority governments to end or even alleviate the Depression cleared the way for the last-ditch candidate; behind-the-scenes intrigues led President Hindenburg to name Hitler as chancellor on January 30, 1933. The election of March 5, five weeks later, was the first and the last to be held in Nazi Germany. Even under the repressive conditions then in force, the Nazi Party failed to gain a majority of the vote. A week earlier, a fire in the Reichstag had given Hitler the pretext he needed to suspend civil liberties, freedom of the press, and the right to *habeas corpus.* This was a signal for many Communists and Socialists to flee or go underground; many were nevertheless arrested. Proclaiming a "Red threat," the Nazis prohibited rival parties from meeting and intimidated voters with beatings and bullying. After the March elections the Nazis suppressed all the state governments and, through intimidation, violence, and political bargaining, forced an "Enabling Act" through the Reichstag that gave dictatorial powers to Hitler, destroyed the party system, and voided the Weimar Republic's constitution.

In April the Secret Security Police Forces (Gestapo) rooted out any remaining opposition. In the same month, four laws affecting the civil service, legal, medical, and teaching professions, as well as students, provided the basis for eliminating "undesirable" elements, be they Communists, Socialists, liberals, or Jews. The Nazis also instituted a systematic campaign against female "double-earners," beginning by removing them from better paid civil service positions. Only women over the age of thirty-five could be civil servants, and then only at fixed lower salaries. This particularly affected women doctors, who had just begun to establish themselves in the social health and welfare apparatus. The Nazis also introduced a 10 percent quota for female university students. On May 10, 1933, "un-German, decadent, Jewish, Marxist" books were burned on public pyres. The library of Magnus Hirschfeld's pioneering Institute for Sexual Science was sacked, as were many others. By the end of May the Nazis had shut down the emerging network of birth control and sex counseling clinics in large German cities, smashed the working-class sex reform organizations, which had provided members with contraception, and forced physicians sympathetic to sex reform into exile. By July the provision of marriage loans for the "fit"—significantly, as part of the Law for the Reduction of Unemployment—and the program of coercive sterilization in the Law for the Prevention of Hereditarily Diseased Offspring marked the institutionalization of the Nazi's selective population policy that Bock describes in her article. Also by July, Heinrich Himmler, the head of the elite stormtroopers (SS, or "Black Shirts") had acquired the unprecedented power that culminated in his takeover of the national state police. This led to the further arrest, torture, or murder of many Socialists and Communists.

A year later, on June 30, 1934, during the "Night of the Long Knives," the Nazis turned against their own paramilitary in order to win over the regular army and assure their conservative right-wing supporters that they would discipline their unruly troops. The SS murdered over two hundred leaders of the SA ("Brown Shirts"). Those who had believed that a return to normalcy was possible were finally convinced of the ruthlessness of the Nazi system. This act marked the end of random lawlessness and the beginning of rational state terror. By the end of the summer, approximately fifty concentration camps stood in place.

In a process called *Gleichschaltung* (literally, synchronization), the Nazis imposed authoritarian forms on all existing associations. The "leadership principle" required unfailing obedience to one's superior in a hierarchical chain of command emanating from Hitler himself. *Gleichschaltung* forced associations to expel their Jewish members and to merge with specially devised central state or party agencies. The Nazis pressured countless women, young people, farmers, and shopkeepers, including many previously unorganized, to join the new Nazi organizations. Schools and churches were also expected to conform to Nazi ideology and practice.

In 1933 the BDF dissolved itself rather than face *Gleichschaltung.* Historians and feminists continue to debate the meaning of that action. Was this self-dissolution a courageous act of defiance or an act of passive resignation? These questions require detailed analysis, and, as the articles in this book indicate, opinion remains divided. Bridenthal and Hausen show that, cautious though the BDF might have been in its adherence to ideas of family and nation, numerous member groups still found it too feminist; some even welcomed the Nazis eagerly. Some women's organizations affiliated with the BDF, like the Federation of Women Doctors or the housewives' associations, showed a remarkable lack of resistance to the Nazi demand that they purge their Jewish members. The BDF itself at first hoped to preserve its organizational autonomy, even at the price of sacrificing Jewish members, but finally chose to dissolve rather than be merged into the Nazi women's organizations and thereby lose all organizational integrity. Some German historians have argued that the damage had already been done: the movement was already split, weakened by disappointment and by a sense of betrayal at the unfulfilled promises of the Weimar Republic. In addition, it was sympathetic to Nazi appeals to motherhood, racial hygiene, social health, and eugenics, which had always been central concerns of the middle-class women's movement. On those "reproductive" issues, no well-developed alternative discourse existed, in contrast to genuine counterpositions on the issues of women's wage labor, political participation, or access to higher education. There was a general consensus among feminists and non-feminists as to the desirability of motherhood for all women, and on the family as the germ cell of the nation, class, or *Volk*. The lack of a competing conceptual framework certainly contributed to the middle class's vulnerablity to Nazi family ideology. The articles in this volume show the hegemony of that discourse on social health and eugenic hygiene, on duty and glorified motherhood. They thus shed light on why the "great fortress" of German feminism—as it was described by Clifford Kirkpatrick in his *Women in Nazi Germany* (1938)—failed to resist Nazism in any meaningful way.

Some women, especially the younger ones, were positively enthusiastic about the new regime. They welcomed a national "renewal" and "mobilization" that would tear them—safely—out of the narrowness of their conventional female lives. Koonz conveys the spirit of these pro-Nazi women, many of whom still fondly recall their sense of freedom from parental authority and their camaraderie with other women in the League of German Girls (Bund Deutscher Mädel). To them the Nazis seemed to promise escape from wage labor and marital drudgery, *not* preparation for a future of "*Kinder, Küche, Kirche*" (children, kitchen, church). By 1939 women were represented by two major Nazi organizations with a total of about 3.3 million members under male leadership and direction. They were thus simultaneously marginal and central to Nazi policies.

The Nazis' new organizations of work and leisure cut across class boundaries, but they did not make them disappear. On the contrary, the purpose of masking classes in this way was to mute the conflict between them by weakening working-class organizations, particularly political parties and trade unions. Businessmen and the landed aristocracy were unaffected, as were the civil service and the army. They had to show loyalty, but they remained relatively free to pursue their own interests. For Jews, however, it was different. Bands of Nazis marched through the streets calling for their death, and the government passed laws making them second-class citizens, excluding them from the professions and limiting their numbers in the universities. In April 1933 stormtroopers enforced a boycott of Jewish businesses. In 1935 the Nuremberg race laws forbade marriages and other forms of sexual relationship between Jews and "Aryans." By 1939 unofficial harassment of Jewish businesses, and official "Aryanization" of those that remained, brought an end to Jewish economic life in Germany. In effect, Jews were forced out of public life; those who could, emigrated. Kaplan's article depicts the disappointed hopes of those Jewish women who had worked within and in cooperation with the BDF from 1907 to 1933. She points to the pain they experienced as a result of rejection by their "Aryan sisters," and to the steps they took to respond to persecution.

Apart from these immediate brutal attacks on their perceived enemies, the Nazis had few programs and little idea of how they would fulfill their contradictory promises. Their economic program went through two main phases. The first was that of crisis management. By 1937, through a deft combination of state planning and cooperation with private enterprise, unemployment had been virtually wiped out, though some of the decrease was due to statistical sleight-of-hand, such as not counting those women who had been fired and forced to return to their "proper" place in the home. Through public employment in highway and home construction and through rearmament—in defiance of the Versailles Treaty—the German economy recovered to the point where it became the envy of other still depressed economies.

How was this miracle wrought? Industry gained confidence as trade unions were dismantled and workers incorporated into the new state-organized and controlled Labor Front (Deutsche Arbeitsfront). Tax inducements led to investment in construction and defense. Perhaps most important of all, workplace reorganization restored total employer control and used the political/social vocabulary of "leader" *(Führer)* and "follower." Finally, as noted before, social insurance was reduced and welfare payments made liable to a means test.

Germans—as defined in the Nuremberg laws—were wooed with marriage and home ownership loans. State social services were replaced with an older concept of charity—to be carried out by women "volunteers" who were often pressured into the work. Furthermore, a pervasive propaganda campaign put the euphoric edge on material recovery.

Much as they waged the battle for full employment, the Nazis also waged a "battle for births." This time, however, the soldiers were women. Debate continues over the effects of these early population policy measures. What was the cause of the slight but indisputable rise in the birth rate from 1933 to 1935? First of all, was it significant, given that it merely returned to pre-Depression levels while the trend toward the two-child family continued? Was it due to pro-natalist measures, to antiabortion and anticontraception measures, or to both? How important was the loss of pro-contraception doctors and of medical and lay sexual reformers? How much can be attributed simply to the end of the Depression and the increase in previously delayed marriages and childbearing, now that couples could benefit from marriage loans? These issues still have not been resolved. We can say with certainty, however, that the Nazi regime's accomplishments in the areas of protection of motherhood and of women workers fell far behind the social welfare reforms of the Weimar Republic, and carried an additional racist agenda as well. Women were expected to play a crucial role in enacting racial policies: by marrying racially and eugenically correctly, bearing healthy children, policing their children's behavior, enforcing neighborhood social segregation, carrying out consumer boycotts, and generally acting as the nation's racial conscience. One historian has noted: "The Nazi regime's policies toward women were in fact policies toward the family, policies toward the whole population. They constituted the *only* new and comprehensive social policies which the regime implemented in the 1930s. Thus, the position of women in Nazi Germany was one of the broadest political significance."[1]

In 1936 the second phase of the Nazi economic program began with a Four Year Plan that imposed greater party control over the economy. Its stated goal was to expand *Lebensraum* by forcibly acquiring properties in the east. It meant war. War plans, however, cost money. Where was it to come from without incurring a new inflationary spiral and greater budget deficits? The Nazis' answer was financial manipulation. By taking control of the National Bank, the Nazis centralized the nation's financial system and gained access to credit. The party secretly forced loans from savings banks, to be repaid out of expected war booty. A wage freeze and state control over the use of raw materials and over the direction of investments diverted production from consumer goods to armaments. The party set up its own companies and forced private enterprises to invest in them. It used expropriated Jewish capital as another source of funds. In sum, heavy industry was supported more generously than it had been by any previous government.

In this volume, Tröger shows some of the ways in which this Nazi manipulation of the economy affected women. There were continuities with pre-Nazi labor management schemes, especially "scientific" techniques to intensify labor productivity. Many contradictory rationales channeled women into the dreariest and most poorly paid jobs at a time when new machinery and technology were revolutionizing the labor process. Under Nazi state auspices, "experts" used biology to explain every twist and turn of changing labor policy with regard to women, ultimately relying on a supposed maternal instinct to keep women from being fully committed to the permanent labor force and from seeking long-term improvements of their status within it. Middle-class women were never required to work, although drafting them was discussed from time to time. A major share of new workers were either prisoners of war or semi-conscripted (lured and forced laborers)—there were 7.5 million of these by 1944. Despite this influx of foreign labor, the number of women in the labor force rose between 1933 and 1939, from 11.6 million to 14.6 million. In part this was the result of a critical change in the marriage loan legislation in 1937. Women were no longer required to give up their jobs to qualify for the loans; quite the reverse, they were only available if the bride continued to work. The government continued to cajole and prod "well-bred" women of the *Volk* into childbearing—although with minimal results. In 1938, a change in the marriage laws allowed a man to divorce his wife if the marriage was childless. Daycare centers, closed during the early years of Nazi rule, were reopened. The Weimar trend toward smaller families and increased numbers of women, particularly married women, in the workforce continued and indeed was reinforced.

Bock's article shows how racist and sexist notions influenced population policy and assisted in the general task of social control. The vision of a racially unified and strong—because genetically sound—people led to ruthlessly coercive measures, including involuntary sterilization and strict enforcement of prohibitions against abortion. In short, state control over reproduction was instituted on an unprecedented scale. There is a continuity here with the popularity (and respectability) of eugenics and racial hygiene under the Weimar Republic. But now state and party policy, determined by Nazi men, decided who was or was not to bear children. A nation with scarce resources, needing a cost-effective, efficient military machine, could brook no drag on its mobilization. Nazi decisions, ostensibly scientific, were clearly political. Unwanted "types" were to be removed quite literally through surgery on the body politic. Women's bodies thus became a domestic battleground, the home front in the most basic sense of the word. The same pseudoscientific racism was later used to "explain" euthanasia and the outright murder of "asocial elements." Like the "scientific managers" the Nazis employed to help in production, "genetic engineers" assisted in the realm of reproduction. Despite its archaic vocabulary, Nazism employed the most modern methods.

As war came closer the attack on the Jews who still remained in Germany intensified. Beginning in November 1938 terror and violence increased dramatically. On November 9, 1938—known as "Crystal Night," because of all the shattered glass—stormtroopers initiated "spontaneous" attacks on Jews, their businesses and synagogues. They brutally rounded up thirty thousand Jewish men and sent them to concentration camps. Arson ruined or destroyed over one thousand synagogues. By the outbreak of the war, about three hundred thousand German Jews, or two-thirds of the pre-1933 Jewish population, had managed to flee Germany, but the rest—many of whom were elderly and female—remained trapped inside. They were systematically dispossessed and ghettoized. Ultimately they, along with millions of other European Jews, were deported to concentration and extermination camps.

In Germany the main winners of the massive rearmament campaign were the arms and chemical industries. While they lost some independence of decision-making and while some branches of industry, such as consumer goods, suffered relative to heavy industry, industry as a whole reaped huge profits. Whether or not individual industrialists contributed directly to the Nazi Party or approved of all its policies, the fact remains that collaboration paid off handsomely. The middle strata of small producers and tradespeople, many of whom had enthusiastically welcomed what they thought to be a fresh approach to their economic woes, became victims of the orientation toward arms production. Agriculture won a temporary reprieve, but ultimately it too lost out to the war industries.

Military victories were needed to fulfill the many economic and political promises of the regime. Even before war broke out, the Nazis, banking on the disunity of the allied powers, achieved one foreign-policy success after another. By 1936 they had reorganized the military, rearmed, remilitarized the Rhineland, and were planning to annex Austria. Hitler then allied with Mussolini, the fascist dictator of Italy, and together they entered the Spanish Civil War on the fascist side. In March 1938 Hitler marched into Austria. To the amazement of Germany's General Staff, the former and future allies did not respond. At Munich in September 1938, Britain and France bowed to Hitler's demand to dismember Czechoslovakia. After signing a nonaggression pact with the Soviet Union in August 1939, Hitler invaded Poland. Finally the West responded and World War II began.

After the first easy victories in Eastern Europe and France, the war did not go smoothly for the Germans. Allied bombing raids on German civilian targets began in 1942, after German attacks on London and Coventry. Indeed, in a dramatic reversal of the experience of World War I, it sometimes seemed that the battlefront was safer than the home front. The tide turned definitively against the Nazis after their invasion of the Soviet Union and their defeat at Stalingrad in the winter of 1942–1943. When the Allies, after some delay, opened a second front on Germany's European flank, the pressure doubled. By 1944 the German people confronted heavy air raids, evacuations from the cities, food shortages, a black market, and severe losses at the front. Once

again, women became the organizers of survival, adept at finding food
and shelter in the devastated cities. Women also suffered intensified
exploitation at the workplace, often working sixty hours a week, including night work. The war massively intensified the old "double burden"
for working women.

When the war began so did the mass killings of Jews. At first the
killing was uncoordinated, but after January 1942 Nazi leaders inaugurated the "final solution," a plan for the systematic destruction of
European Jewry. Historians have noted that even after the war effort
began to go badly, the Nazis continued to drain their resources in order
to expedite the slaughter. The scale and cold-bloodedness of the
Holocaust destroyed two-thirds—about 6 million—of the prewar Jewish population of Europe. And there were indications that criteria
other than race—for example, fitness and ability to work—were applied as well: the Nazis murdered seventy thousand "mentally retarded" and "incurably ill" in Germany itself. The list of victims goes on
and on, including, among others, millions of European civilians and
prisoners of war, leftists and resistance fighters, the Polish intelligentsia, political commissars in the Soviet army, gypsies, and homosexuals.
In this carnage, the question has been posed, were women's experiences different from those of men? Sybil Milton's essay addresses this
issue, focusing on the persecution of German-Jewish and German
women.[2]

The Nazis enforced their obsession with categorization and murder-
ously efficient labeling of the "deviant" through the vast network of
labor, concentration, and extermination camps, where inmates were
divided by categories such as "Jewish," "political," "criminal," "homosexual," and "asocial." For example, the women's concentration camp
at Ravensbrück, one of those described below by Milton, had separate
barracks for "politicals" and "Jews," though a political Jew was inevitably categorized as a Jew. This camp provided labor for many German
firms. Ninety-two thousand women were killed through overwork,
torture, and, finally, systematic liquidation. The sheer listing of
women's camps has its own ghastly effect, but Ruth Nebel's memoir,
published here, stuns us with the experience of one concentration
camp survivor.

Most German civilians tolerated these horrors passively. They later
claimed that they had not known about them, although some lived at
the very edges of concentration camps and others had heard reports
from soldiers back from the front. However, pockets of resistance did
exist, organized by Communists or by those few brave individuals who
did their part in sabotaging the Nazi war industries and sheltering the
hunted. Whether politically motivated or inspired by an internalized
moral code, these resisters knew they could be killed for their convic-

tions—and many were. Adequate data for an interpretive essay remain slight, but new questions are being asked of existing material, including how exactly we should define "resistance," and what forms are gender-specific. Should resistance be seen on a continuum from absenteeism and contrary or oppositional behavior to a more consciously illegal or fighting stance? Or does such a broad definition debase the meaning of the term for those who risked more daring acts?

In any event, women participated all along that spectrum. Heroic stories of resistance fighters usually portray men, with women providing a support network. But in this volume, we reprint the oral history of Katharina Jacob, who operated the tools of resistance: typewriters and mimeograph machines that produced forbidden leaflets. Working-class women slowed down on the job, and middle-class women could not be mobilized into the workforce. Most women refused to have large families. Whatever the motivation, personal or political, women's recalcitrance hindered the smooth functioning of the war machine and made it impossible to achieve a total mobilization of "Aryan" labor for total war. Some women gave food or other support to Jews, political fugitives, and slave laborers, and a few hid and saved the persecuted. Caring for the children of resisters was a form of resistance peculiar to women; needless to say, however, caring for their own children prevented many from participating in the struggle more fully. Yet it was an important service: children of resisters might be killed or removed to state institutions to be raised as little Nazis, a fate worse than death to many committed antifascists.

In May 1945, Allied forces occupied Germany and ended the Nazis' "Thousand Year Reich." Within three years Germany was divided into two different and often antagonistic states. An enduring image of postwar Germany is one of women standing in the ruins, engaging in a national clean-up campaign devoted to rebuilding family and nation, and forgetting the very recent past. As the men straggled home from POW camps, energetic women swept away the rubble and buried memories of horror and brutality that in Germany still remain to a great extent unaddressed and unexamined. These stolid women cleaning up—doing "women's work"—marked the end of an era in which biology—whether defined by sex or race—so clearly became destiny.

## Notes

1. Tim Mason, "Women in Germany, 1925–1940: Family, Welfare and Work. Part I," *History Workshop* 1 (April 1976): 87.
2. Joan Ringelheim, a philosopher, has undertaken an oral history project to document a gender analysis of the Holocaust. For further reading see Joan Miriam Ringelheim, "The Unethical and the Unspeakable: Women and the Holocaust," *Simon Wiesenthal Center Annual*, vol. I (1984): 69–87; Esther Katz and Joan M. Ringelheim, eds.,

*Proceedings of the Conference on Women Surviving the Holocaust* (New York: Institute for Research in History, 1983). Also, see Vera Laska, ed., *Women in the Resistance and in the Holocaust: The Voices of Eyewitness* (Westport Conn.: Greenwood Press, 1983).

# Part 1
## Women in the Weimar Republic

# Beyond *Kinder, Küche, Kirche:*
# Weimar Women in Politics and Work

## Renate Bridenthal and Claudia Koonz

*The Weimar Republic, with its new constitution promising legal equality to women, seemed to many in Germany to presage a new age. In fact, however, Renate Bridenthal and Claudia Koonz show that the continuity of the socioeconomic structure diminished the impact of most of women's new political freedoms. Furthermore, class interests divided women almost as much as men, as voting patterns showed. The advancement of capitalist development, with its new technology and work processes—dubbed "rationalization"—created new forms of sex segmentation in the labor market, driving increasing numbers of women into low-skilled, low-paid jobs, while only an elite few made gains in the professions. The same advancement impoverished sections of the middle class, which could not compete. Women of those strata became hostile to the Republic, which they felt had betrayed them. Economic processes thus hindered women from transcending class and party conflicts, except in a few areas of social reform and reproductive rights. And yet, with no gains in the latter, women's double burden weighed at least as heavily as before. The result was that gender-specific class interests deformed and crippled the organized women's movement, customary male dominance discouraged politically active women, and constitutional equality remained largely on paper.*

It is a commonplace that the National Socialist assumption of power in Germany in 1933 was to a large extent made possible by a clever manipulation of irrational fears provoked by the economic, social, and political tensions of the time. More than once since the Frankfurt School's famous study on authority and the family it has been suggested that the authoritarianism of the German family contributed to the susceptibility of the population to the siren call of the leadership principle and that threats to the traditional structure of society, especially the family, made people fearful and desperate enough to see a saviour in Hitler.[1] Certainly his call for women to return to hearth and home found a responsive audience. The *Kinder, Küche, Kirche* (children, kitchen, church) issue in Nazi propaganda implied that women were deserting their homes, their children, and their morality, challenging men's authority by asserting their independence and by flooding the labor market to such an extent that honest fathers of families *(Familienväter)* found themselves without "work or bread," to use the compassionate terms of the otherwise objective 1933 census.[2] Carl Gustav Jung, in his pamphlet *Die Frau in Europa (The Woman in Europe)*, was only one of the more distinguished spokesmen for the widely held view that women's emancipation was responsible for endangering not only the institution of marriage but also the whole spiritual balance between the masculine and feminine principles.[3]

The traditional view of liberal historians proceeds on many of the same assumptions, though it appears to welcome the "progress" women made during the years of the Weimar Republic. David Schoenbaum, in *Hitler's Social Revolution,* draws the common picture when he writes of "the economic liberation of thousands of women sales clerks . . . an ever increasing contingent of women doctors, lawyers, judges and social workers . . . thousands of women in shops, offices, and professions in competition with men. . . . The campaign against the democratic Republic was a repudiation of the equality of women."[4]

If liberation had been proceeding apace, it is not difficult to understand why men would react against it. But how do we account for the fact that women voted for Hitler as enthusiastically as men, and in general preferred the conservative parties, which had for decades opposed women's emancipation, over liberals and socialists who promised equality for women? Prevailing opinion holds that with these legal changes, and with equalized employment and educational opportunities, the status of women improved dramatically. If this were so, why did the *Kinder, Küche, Kirche* appeal of Nazi propaganda not deflect their votes? A U.S. journalist asked incredulously after the 1931 elections: "Why does she [the German woman] vote for a group that intends to take the ballot from her? Why does she support antifeminism? How are we to account for the fact that in nine cities where the sexes voted separately last autumn, more women than men voted for the Nazis?"[5]

German women did not merely lose the fight for equality; they joined the opposition. How do we account for this enigma? Was there something dubious about these new options? We will show that the conservatism of Weimar women must be seen in the context of the fraudulence of their supposed emancipation. Despite the rhetoric

about women's emancipation, patriarchal ideology continued to domi-
nate all institutions of German economic and political life.

*1*

German women received the right to vote as part of that spate of
reforms commonly termed the "November Revolution" of 1918. They
voted for the first time in the National Assembly elections two months
later. When the Weimar constitution was drafted, women were assured
that "women and men have basically the same rights and duties," and
promised that all discrimination against women in the civil service
would end.[6] Prior to November 1918, only the Socialists had advocated
woman suffrage as an official party demand. But once the reform became law, all political parties hastily inserted planks on the "woman
question" into their platforms, issued numerous pamphlets to attract
the new voters, and included women in lists of candidates for office. No
politician publicly opposed woman suffrage. Even the leader of a
women's organization opposed to women's rights quickly dropped her
crusade and ran for election to the National Assembly.[7] Overt hostility
toward women disappeared from official party statements, as women
were welcomed into the public sphere. A survey of Communist,
Socialist, Liberal, Conservative, and National Socialist parties reveals
the limitations of women's victory.

Judging from the first elections, women responded enthusiastically
to their newly granted right. Nearly 80 percent of all eligible women
voters cast their ballots in 1919—a percentage slightly higher than that
of the eligible male voters.[8] Nearly 10 percent of the National Assembly delegates were women and between 5 and 10 percent of the state
legislators elected shortly thereafter were women.[9] Most contemporaneous observers believed this immediate acceptance of women
into political life augured well for the future of women's rights.

Such an auspicious beginning would lead, they predicted, to legal
reforms, widespread social legislation, wage equalization, improved
protection for women workers, and increased educational opportunities for women and girls. As one Social Democrat put it: "We have
voted, we have sent women to all levels of local and state government,
and we have helped to write the Constitution. . . . We have created the
necessary foundation upon which we can build that equality which
alone will make us free."[10] Non-Socialist women were also optimistic.
"A new Golden Age dawns! The outlines of a new German realm become clear. And we will help build it!" exclaimed a journalist in a
popular middle-class women's magazine.[11]

The right to vote was not regarded as an end, but as the means by which women could work toward complete equality. After 1918 women could continue their fight for emancipation within the political structure instead of outside it. Rights, therefore, became linked with new responsibilities;[12] demands became transformed into duties.[13] Socialists had always welcomed women into their ranks and vigorously opposed any autonomous women's organization. Now liberals and conservatives also incorporated women into their party organizations and the women agreed it was time for women to cease being "equal righters" *(Frauenrechtlerinnen)* and to become party members.[14] This did not mean that these women intended to end their struggle for equal rights, but it did indicate that they were convinced this struggle could best be waged from within the party structure.

This optimism proved to be unfounded. Despite the frequent praise of the emancipated German woman, the progress of women's rights was disappointing. Judicial decisions upheld women's legal inequality in family law and property rights. Wages, job security, and working conditions continued to be more favorable for men than for women. Even sweeping legislation to protect mothers and improve health care for children failed to pass in the Reichstag. The "woman question" continued to be one of the most controversial topics of the 1920s, but the economic and legal status of women did not improve. As one psychologist commented in 1932, "The fact that there is a woman here and there has not altered the status quo in the slightest."[15]

Perhaps most disillusioning to proponents of emancipation was the fact that women's participation in the political process did not increase after 1919. Quite to the contrary, in each election until the Great Depression fewer eligible women bothered to vote at all, and fewer women appeared among the Reichstag delegates.[16] Although most of the leaders from the women's movement joined the Democratic Party and Socialists had long advocated women's rights, German women in general did not heed their call and voted instead for those parties that had for so long opposed women's rights. This trend was established in the earliest elections of Weimar and did not change thereafter. For example, the women's vote affected the 1928 Reichstag in the following ways: it increased the delegates of the Catholic Center Party by twelve, those of the Nationalists by nine, and those of the right liberals by two; it decreased the delegates of the Democratic, Socialist, Economic, and Nazi parties by one to four, and of the Communists by eight (see Table 1).[17]

The explanation for women's persistent loyalty to conservative parties can be found in the reactions of politicians to their new women constituents. Before we examine the responses of various parties, several generalizations about all parties may be considered. Both male and

Table 1
Impact of the Women's Vote on 1928 Reichstag Elections

| Party | Total Delegates Elected | Estimated Delegations Based on Male Vote Only | Loss or Gain Due to Female Vote |
|---|---|---|---|
| Catholic Center | 62 | 50 | + 12 |
| National Fatherland | 73 | 64 | + 9 |
| People's | 45 | 43 | + 2 |
| Democratic | 25 | 26 | − 1 |
| Social Democratic | 153 | 157 | − 4 |
| Economic | 23 | 24 | − 1 |
| Communist | 54 | 62 | − 8 |
| National Socialist | 12 | 16 | − 4 |

Source: Gertrud Bäumer, *Die Frau im Deutschen Staat* (Berlin: Junker u. Dünnhaupt, 1932), p. 45.

female politicians hoped that women would one day participate equally in politics. But women politicians would not be the same as men. Women could bring into political life special feminine concerns and ideals. They were more able than men to stand above party squabbles and strive for distant objectives. Both men and women agreed that further reforms were necessary to realize women's equality in public life. However, no one imagined that motherhood would cease to be the major concern of all normal women. Special legislation should protect women factory workers who were forced to work for wages; "exception women" in the professions were not to be hindered by sex discrimination; expanded social legislation would encourage more women to devote themselves exclusively to homemaking. Women, idealists predicted, would retain their separate identity, but be treated equally.

### The Socialist Parties

As Marxists, both Communists and Social Democrats saw capitalism as the cause of women's special oppression. While reforms within the dominant capitalist system might ameliorate some conditions, no satisfactory emancipation of women could, Marxists believed, occur until the ultimate triumph of socialism. Similarly, the inferior place of women within the family was attributed to private property and not to cultural norms or vague entities like the male ego. It followed from these assumptions that for women to achieve true emancipation, they must join the ranks of socialists and fight for the overthrow of capitalism. Marxists called bourgeois women who organized in exclusively women's groups "female parasites," and looked suspiciously upon women comrades who devoted too much attention to the potentially divisive woman question.[18] The woman socialist's job was to convince other women to fight for a socialist state, shoulder to shoulder with men.

After World War I, German Communists split with the majority Social Democratic Party (as well as with the short-lived Independent Social Democratic Party) because they believed revolution to be the priority of the day. According to the Communist priorities of 1919, barricades and street fighting seemed more important than electoral politics. Not surprisingly, Communist leaders cared little about attracting the "woman vote" and ignored the woman question altogether in their revolutionary appeals. Even after Rosa Luxemburg and Karl Liebknecht were murdered in an unsuccessful uprising in January 1919, the Communist Party (Kommunistische Partei Deutschlands; KPD) directed its energy toward violent revolution and not toward electioneering for women's votes. Of the millions of pamphlets and leaflets distributed by the KPD in 1919, none mentioned women's issues.[19] Later, as the revolution failed to materialize in the mid-1920s, the party recruited women voters and included large percentages of women as Reichstag candidates. "Agitation among women" had appeared on an earlier agenda, but this issue was removed from the discussion until the third party congress in February 1920.[20] Comrade Marz, who introduced the subject, assured her audience that it was understood that party agitation among women would not rest "on any sort of exclusively women's interests," but would aim at encouraging "proletarian women to join their male class comrades in the fight for communist goals."[21] This type of disclaimer did not, it should be noted, accompany the debates about agitation among other special groups, such as soldiers, youths, and peasants. But, despite women's promises to subordinate their concerns, the woman question was especially divisive throughout the Weimar years.

Unlike the Communists, the moderate socialists realized they had to attract women voters from the very beginning of the Weimar Republic. From the earliest postwar days women's issues appeared in party literature and women candidates were placed on Socialist ballots. The Social Democrats, Independent Socialists, and Communists each urged women to eschew the other Socialist parties. However, despite this rivalry there was very little difference among the three parties where the woman question was concerned. All socialists demanded guarantees of the woman's right to work; protective legislation and improved factory inspection; increased maternity and health-care benefits; the granting of full legal status to out-of-wedlock children; the establishment of day care facilities; better social welfare protection for families with insufficient incomes; and, finally, cooperation between men and women comrades. Seeing the partriarchal family as protective of women, the left-wing parties attacked capitalism for eroding strong family ties. Thus, party leaders quietly dropped rhetoric about equal pay for equal work in favor of demands for protective legislation. When Communists and Socialists supported reforms to outlaw the legal disadvantages suffered by children born out of wedlock and to liberalize divorce and antiabortion laws, they argued their case in terms of strengthening and humanizing the family. Schemes for collective kitchens and laundries or child care centers did not appear in lists of Marxist proposals. Potential contradictions in women's "double burden" in production and reproduction were minimized and women were encouraged to assume party responsibilities in addition to work in factory and family.[22]

Although the Communist Party did not begin its campaign to attract women voters until several years after the beginning of the Weimar Republic, when it did, it relied on the same techniques of membership recruitment and voter mobilization as the Social Democrats. Organizations for women workers, proletarian girls' clubs, educational courses in homemaking and political theory, consumer cooperatives, lectures or reading evenings, and weekend outings comprised the major activities for members and supporters. Although the female vote never exceeded the male vote for any socialist party, the ratio of women members to men members improved in the Social Democratic party after several years of organizing. In 1924 women comprised 15.8 percent of the Socialist party; by 1928 this percentage had risen to 21.1 percent, and in 1930 it was 23 percent.[23] It was mainly in the urban areas where women comprised an increasing proportion of party members—in rural areas the ratio of men to women was as high as fifty to one.[24]

As women increased their constituencies, they received a decreasing share of party offices, party budgets, and influence. Invariably requests for these were circumvented or denied. With each election, fewer Socialist and Communist women were sent to the Reichstag; fewer party offices were held by women.[25]

On several occasions (usually in the semiprivacy of party meetings or in the pages of *Die Genossin* [*The Comrade*], the newsletter for leading party women) SPD women did protest their poor representation. When they did, Socialist men (and sometimes women too)[26] usually responded with accusations that women had not yet been successful in marshaling women workers to the cause of socialism. Often they even blamed the failure of so many Socialist reforms on the granting of woman suffrage. It was the conservative women's vote, they asserted, that prevented the socialist parties from obtaining a majority in the Reichstag.[27] Sometimes the women countered this charge:

> You accuse us of not correctly utilizing the ballot. . . . The big brother
> scolds us, the little sister. If, in the 38 years during which we have worked
> [for socialism], we had encountered a little more practical socialism
> within the family, then women might have a little more love and under-
> standing for socialism. . . . The guilt belongs with big brother. Before you
> did not think it worthwhile to bother enlightening the inferior woman.
> Now we all must suffer.[28]

Neither Socialists nor Communists integrated their positions on
women's oppression into the general framework of party ideology. No
party pamphlet or newspaper addressed to the general reader discussed women's oppression. Even an exhortation to Communist men
telling them to send their women to party meetings appeared in the
women's pages of the party paper.[29] Of the twenty-five to thirty-six
books listed as suggested reading for Communists in the 1920s, none
mentioned women (although four were written by Luxemburg and
three by Clara Zetkin).[30] Similarly, an annual Socialist publication, *Our
Program in Word and Picture*, never mentioned women—except in
one picture that urged, "Women, organize yourselves!"[31] Socialist journals, pamphlets, and newspapers were addressed to men. Contrary to
Socialist appeals about marching shoulder to shoulder, the women's
organizations were regarded merely as useful auxiliaries.

Socialists and Communists understood that the woman question
could become an extremely divisive issue. Occasionally someone
would comment on the fact that "between men and women erupts an
abrasive fight over bread and work,"[32] but these discussions were
dropped at once. Socialist theory dictated that antifeminism stemmed
from male workers' insufficient understanding of capitalism—their true
enemy. Hostility toward women indicated some form of dissatisfaction
(however crude) with the capitalist system. Rather than directly attacking this false consciousness, Socialists sought to redirect it against the
capitalist system. The parallel with Socialists' views on anti-Semitism is
striking in this respect.[33] The Marxist parties did not want to eliminate
antifeminism; they wanted to use it. Their rhetoric was designed
primarily to attract women voters, which was not necessarily the same
as emancipating women.

### Liberal and Conservative Parties

The nonsocialist parties, of course, campaigned vigorously to attract
the "woman vote." Their appeals stressed protection for women workers and mothers, improved educational opportunities for women, and
increased social services to aid families with many children. To a
greater extent than the Socialists, bourgeois politicians stressed the
importance of legal reforms to implement the equality of women in the
family and in professions.[34] Liberal and conservative women promised

to infuse German public life with a new idealism, and male politicans welcomed this promise with enthusiasm. What the nation needed, according to this analysis, was not a socialist or economic revolution, but rather a spiritual revolution. At best what they wanted could be termed a "reformation" and, at worst, "counterrevolution." In any case, women of the center and right believed they had a very special role to play in the reconstruction of Germany. Both men and women would have to change their traditional attitudes to encourage women to contribute to public life. But this new outlook did not mean that women were to abandon their feminine nature or concerns. Quite the contrary, they were encouraged to assert their femininity and play a leading role in pressing for domestic reform. After four years of wartime propaganda that urged women to maintain morale on the home front and that built up women's self-esteem, this message was already a familiar one in 1918–1919. The nonsocialist parties simply redirected this basic appeal away from the defense of the fatherland and toward the victory of their own parties. As with the left-wing parties, the center and right wing stressed one message to woman voters: "We need you." But these parties added, "Without you Germany will collapse and fall into the chaos of Socialism."

One nationalist poster addressed its appeal to the rural women: "TO THE DEAR, GERMAN COUNTRY GIRLS! You wonderful, energetic, brave German country girls with healthy red cheeks and fresh, pious hearts—we are counting on every one of you!"[35] A conservative woman, Clara Viebig, called on women to fight socialism: "We do not want civil war—whether we live in villas or huts!"[36] Democratic Party leader Gertrud Bäumer reminded her readers, "The Revolution called us into political life; but now we are also called on to oppose the Revolution."[37] Right-wing liberal Clara Mende urged bourgeois women to plunge themselves into politics in order to defeat the "women's troops" of the socialist parties.[38]

The nonsocialist parties had a distinct advantage in recruiting women. They could capitalize on women's self-image as housewives and mothers. Socialists had to re-form women's view of themselves from "wife" to "worker" before their propaganda could be fully effective. Bourgeois propaganda emphasized the importance of women within traditional roles—upgrading the status of "feminine" responsibility rather than expanding or changing the roles. This propaganda, rooted in the gender-specific ideology of "separate spheres," had unfortunate consequences in the Weimar Republic. Even before Ludendorff's accusation about the "stab in the back", women had begun to blame themselves for the low morale on the wartime home front.[39] The brave young men who faced death in the trenches, sang "German Honor, German Women," wrote one author,[40] while women at home could not stop disorder, black marketeering, or lawlessness. Although soldiers' contempt for the home front was certainly widespread, it was absurd to scapegoat women for the defeat. It is surprising that women seemed so susceptible to the charge. Perhaps women realized that the war that had killed over 2 million soldiers had indeed provided women with unprecedented access to previously "masculine" positions, jobs, and educational opportunities. Comfortable assumptions about women's "natural" character dissolved as millions of German women excelled at physically and mentally demanding tasks. Feelings of guilt about this short-lived liberation may well have made them vulnerable to accusations that they had somehow failed in their "feminine" responsibilities.

Democrat Marianne Weber was horrified that just before the surrender, "minor shoplifting went unpunished; no one had any respect for rationing. Cunning, selfishness, vile profiteering, dishonor, shameless hoarding, and swindling permeated all circles."[41] She uttered not a word about the responsibility for the outbreak of the war or about the conditions created by the blockade; instead, she heaped recriminations on herself and other women at home for not preventing this "spiritual decay"! This was to be a persistent motif throughout the Republic. Women, disappointed with the new government, would wonder wherein they had failed or what remained for them to do in order to achieve that putative utopia, "The New Germany." While it may inflate the ego to be praised for "spiritual" superiority, the theory is a pernicious one. However flattering, it is futile to accept responsibility for a phenomenon over which one has no control. Germany's malaise in the 1920s was not created by women; nor would it be overcome by their efforts—spiritual or otherwise.

The obstacles to creating a spiritual revolution or reformation may have been formidable, but women of the center and right were undaunted because the tasks assigned to them were already so familiar. The wife of Friedrich Naumann (who founded the German Democratic Party) listed the priorities for women in the New Germany: (1) Avoid depopulation; (2) maintain national unity; (3) make the people's state *(Volksstaat)* a pleasant place for all; (4) improve public school education; (5) maintain Germanic traditions and high health standards; (6) feel oneself to be a German citizen.[42]

The Catholic Center Party belatedly welcomed new women voters and expressed the hope that women's new status would aid the national effort to attack decadence. In fact, the party platform linked demands for protection of the woman and family with a call "forcefully to oppose any degenerate art and all avant-garde literature . . . [we must] allow women free opportunity to cooperate . . . utilizing the full capabilities of the feminine nature."[43] Although the Catholic Center Party sent only a few women delegates to the Reichstag during the Weimar Republic, it remained the most successful in attracting women's votes.[44] The right-wing liberal German People's Party also insisted that women's political activity was the natural consequence of their newly elevated status as wives and mothers. Katarina von Kardorff railed against the "irrational and emotional" Weimar constitution, which had been written by men. She called on German women to attack male values and protect democracy. "Women by nature reject dictatorship and injustice more than men do."[45] Nationalist politicians explicitly recognized that housework must be accorded new status if women were to remain satisfied with their traditional role. "The irreplaceable value created by the work of housewife and mother must be socially and economically recognized."[46]

The major parties of the center and the right believed that traditional laws (such as liabilities against children of unmarried parents and strict enforcement of laws against abortion) combined with support for a father's rights within the family would provide stability in a social world that seemed to be rapidly slipping from their control. Instead of guaranteeing equality to women who chose to live outside this structure, they sought to make motherhood more attractive. Thus, *Kinder, Küche, Kirche* was upgraded from a responsibility to a calling through home economics courses, homemaker helper programs, and social work projects. In this way, politicians of the center and right endeavored to make traditional roles attractive to a new generation by underwriting the father's authority and the mother's responsibility within the family.

Whatever lip service these parties paid to ideals of women's emancipation, this underlying conservatism showed through. One of the most dramatic examples of this hypocrisy may be found in a Democratic Party pamphlet of 1919, which suggested themes for local campaign posters. After some general appeals for "peace, solidarity, and unity" came a second set of appeals to the "family father." Recalcitrant men who still opposed woman suffrage were told, "You do not need to fear the loss of your position in your home: remain just who you were and who you will be! But bring your daughter and your wife along with you to vote. As odd as it may seem, you *should* discuss politics with them. . . . You must become their political educator!" The next set of suggestions was directed at women voters, who were reminded that "your vote is your own business. No one—either in your family or where you work—ought to tell you how to vote."[47]

Within each of the center and right-wing parties, women did press for more far-reaching changes. As in the socialist parties, women requested more party funds for their activities and greater recognition of women's issues from the party as a whole. "You rely too strongly on the loyalty of the woman," warned one Democratic woman in 1927. "We need publicity, literature, and funds for educational activities just like all other groups."[48] Catholic women wished that their party would devote more attention to moral, educational, and religious issues.[49] Katarina von Kardorff warned in 1930 that she might form a "Mother's League" if the People's Party did not accord more importance to women's demands.[50] Anna Mayer, lawyer and member of the liberal People's Party, complained that many legal reforms were essential if women were to become equal citizens.[51] Nationalist women assured their male colleagues that "we do not want to be a party within a party," but added, "women do need their own special forum to discuss the issues which concern them."[52]

Despite the requests for greater attention to women's issues, the percentages of women in Reichstag delegations from liberal and conservative parties did not increase during the Weimar Republic. The Democrats' 1920 delegation included 9 percent women in 1920 and declined to 7 percent in 1930; Catholic Center representation dropped from 6.3 percent in 1919 to 4.6 percent in 1924 and rose to 5.9 percent in 1930; The People's Party delegation included 4.5 percent women in 1919 and 3.5 percent in 1930; the Nationalist representation included 7 percent women in 1919, 2.6 percent in 1928, and 7.3 percent in 1930.[53] While these percentages were not as high as similar statistics for liberal and socialist parties, representation of women at state and local levels was far lower—typically under 1 percent.[54] Moreover, German women displayed little concern about the relative absence of women on the ballots and persisted in their preference for the parties of the right. These parties emphasized the primacy of the family and encouraged women to participate in politics in order to preserve and enhance their status within their traditional role.

2

The ethos of *Kinder, Küche, Kirche* was further reinforced by developments in German economic life. Modernization, usually held to be a progressive, liberating force for women, appears on closer scrutiny to have been a retrogressive, constricting force.

*Labor-Force Participation*

To begin with, the much-vaunted increase of women in the German labor force was itself partly a statistical delusion. The first postwar census (1925) showed 35 percent of all women to be working, an increase of 5 percent over 1907. Less remarked upon was the increase in the proportion of men working: 6.6 percent, to include 68 percent of the total male population. Thus, while there was a somewhat larger relative increase in the proportion of women working, within the framework of a generally expanding workforce the change was not spectacular. Before the war, women made up 34 percent of the working population; after the war, 36 percent[55]—hardly a great leap forward. Three million more women entered the workforce, but so did four million more men. Women's presence was felt more because it had never really been accepted in the first place and because inflation and depression made jobs scarce and competitive.

Some of the upsurge in women's work was due to the imbalance in population caused by the war and was considered temporary. In 1925 there were 32.2 million women to 30.2 million men, or 1,072 women to 1,000 men, a differential that, it was hoped, would be reduced by the time of the next census (1933).[56] The participation of women in the workforce was not seen as being on an upward trajectory, but was expected to decline as women got busy replacing the "lost" population.[57] The falling birthrate was anxiously watched as were the suspiciously high figures for miscarriages reported by sickness insurance agencies.[58] Women were not supposed to be working or independent; they were supposed to be producing babies.

A second statistical misinterpretation is due to the fact that the census of 1925 gave women more latitude in defining their status. They could now register as gainfully occupied full time if they considered their main subsistence to derive from participation in the business of the head of household. This immediately accounted for one-third of the reported female working population, or 4.1 million women, only half of whom had reported themselves in this category before the war.[59] Part of the reason was definitional and part was real: with the impoverishment of the small establishment, hired help was let go and wives took over more of the work. As "helping dependents," however, they were working harder than ever and they had no control over the property mutually acquired with their husbands.

Most of the remaining 7.4 million gainfully occupied women were wage earners, whom the Revolution of 1918 had promised equal pay for equal work and for whom special legislation was enacted regarding night work, midday breaks, and maternity leave.

A good way of looking at all of these 11.5 million economically productive women is by economic sectors, not only because the census material is organized that way, but because such a division is useful for an analysis of change. Agriculture, industry, distribution, and services are not only contemporaneous activities. The development of each in relation to the others indicates change along a historical continuum. Keeping in mind that the period of the Weimar Republic was itself a moving point along a longer line of national industrialization, we can look at the place of women in each sector and analyze their changing role in at least this one case of rapid capitalist development.

## Agriculture

Nearly half of all the working women in the Weimar Republic were in agriculture; most of them were peasant wives, that is, helping dependents, on whom the war, the blockade, and postwar reconstruction had placed a very heavy burden. Industrialization in the late nineteenth century had drawn men out of the country, leaving women to do more and more of the farm work, a trend intensified by male absence during World War I, so that in 1925 there were actually more women than men working in agriculture.[60] In the second period of the Republic, however, when the rationalization of industry and some aspects of agriculture intensified, women were drawn into the former and pushed out of the latter. By 1933, men again dominated agriculture and even the total female population in the countryside fell disproportionately, leading to complaints of a "lack of women" *(Frauenmangel)*, while the rest of the nation worried about its "surplus of women" *(Frauenüberschuss)*.[61]

What this means is that when the family farm became more labor-intensive relative to other sectors of the economy, women assumed an increasing share of the work. Peasant wives suffered the most, since the eight-hour day and regulated wages now made hired help unprofitable and put a greater burden on the family, creating conditions that probably did not endear the Republic to peasant women. Many maids were let go. However appealing city lights may have been to the young women who left the country, it should be remembered that it was mainly economic pressure that forced their departure.[62] Meanwhile, the peasant woman toiled in field and garden, did the dairying and poultrying that brought her an independent income for household expenses, and carried out her normal household duties. A cross section of the Württemberg peasant economy showed the wife working an average of 12 percent more hours a year than her husband and 40 percent more than the hired help, while it was reckoned that she consumed only 80 percent of the food needed by an adult male.[63] Even before the war, the peasant wife had begun to murmur: she chafed against the "raw despotism" of her husband who, she complained, seemed to care more for his cattle and fields than for his wife, treated her like a dog or a baby-producing machine, and rarely appreciated her until she was dead.[64]

As modern techniques began to penetrate agricultural life in the second half of the Weimar period, they tended to displace the woman rather than give her a new and more prestigious role. Thus, when dairying and poultrying became big businesses with state subsidies, they became male-dominated. Women were forced to turn for every household need to their husbands, whose income before had been reserved for farm maintenance and taxes. This new situation caused

family friction and, on the part of women, an increasing sense of dependence and frustration. Their daughters had no incentive to stay and
become like their mothers. Many, like their lesser cousins, the maids,
left for the city.[65]

Furthermore, women literally lost ground as heads of farms. In 1907
they made up 14 percent of the independent heads of farm households;
in 1925, this had slipped to 12 percent; by 1933, it was down to 10
percent.[66] Moreover, most of their farms were tiny: women owned
about half the miniplots under one hectare and a diminishing proportion of larger farms. With inflation and depression, the smallest ones
were absorbed by the middle-sized ones, reducing the number of
female owners.[67]

Nor did women come to occupy an important place in the new
agricultural ventures. They held only one-sixth of the management
positions in 1925 and only one-twelfth in 1933.[68] Prewar optimists
about women's future in agriculture gave way after the war to more
cautious prognosticators. A women's vocational guide for agricultural
professions stressed the teaching of home economics and suggested
gardening as a career, provided that candidates not set their sights
much higher than gardener's aide. It acknowledged the fact that males
were preferred in large-scale poultrying or dairying; smaller enterprises were more likely to welcome women, of whom they also expected domestic services. It concluded by reminding women that, in
general, management positions were closed to them since men resented female supervisors.[69]

*Industry*

If half the agricultural working population was female, only one-
third, and later only one-fourth, of the industrial working population
was female, another indication of the reduced role women played in
the modernizing sectors. Urban nonworking wives of industrial laborers became dependent on their husbands for the income needed to
purchase essential items they might once have produced, such as food
and clothing. They lost their economic indispensability, a condition
whose psychological effects are only now being explored in depth. On
the other hand, the wife of a worker whose income did not provide the
basic necessities had to work for wages in order to buy them. If she had
small children, she usually did piecework at home, which often meant
crowding an already overcrowded city apartment and working for the
most exploitative rates of all. If she worked in a factory, her life became
divided, introducing the familiar split from which many women still
suffer, with all its attendant guilt for not being at home all day.

In addition, much of the legislation designed to protect women was a
sham. The eight-hour day did not account for work taken home at night

by underpaid women workers. Midday breaks were curtailed because women preferred to leave earlier in the evening in order to prepare dinner for their families—and were grateful for the right to do so. Maternity-leave policy was consistently violated by women who could not afford six unpaid weeks. The result was job instability, since women had to report pregnancy to their employers. There was also a suspiciously high rate of miscarriages, as reported by firms and insurance agencies.[70]

The war brought women of all the belligerent countries into industry, but Germany sustained the largest proportional increase and generally maintained, though did not enlarge, this increase during the postwar years.[71] In March 1917, women first outnumbered men at work and their number grew until the end of the war.[72] Defense-related needs brought them into industries that had never employed them before: for example, Krupp, which hired no women in 1913, reported 28,302 of them by 1918; and roughly three-fifths of the metal industries in Rhineland Westphalia introduced women for the first time during the war. Other fields, such as chemicals, opened wider, and even some closed crafts, such as the printing trades and locksmiths, admitted women for the first time. In light industry women predominated by up to 75 percent in many plants during the war and in those of heavy industry they often reached 25 percent.[73] Social work expanded to meet the needs of fatherless families and the bourgeois women of the organized feminist movement rushed to help with food distribution, job information, housing, and child care.[74] Behind the lines, women did the traditional sewing, cooking, and nursing for the army, but they also freed men for the front by getting into the heaviest work, such as construction of munitions dumps, road building, dynamiting, setting up barbed wire, and so on. A communications division uniformed in blue almost became an official news corps of the army, but the war ended before its formation. Insufficient statistics prevent any clear picture of the extent of female participation in the war effort, but it seems clear that while some sex barriers to work were dropped, most of the new jobs were unskilled and did not promise much in the way of professional advancement for women.[75]

Backlash was evident as early as the winter of 1917 when the war ministry, preparing demobilization, established guidelines for women to relinquish their jobs to returning veterans. Demobilization set the tone for later arguments used especially during the Depression that women competed with men for work. With the worsening economic situation of the early 1920s, tension between the sexes over jobs increased. Women were either sent home (which might mean back to the country), or released into the economic custody of their returning husbands or fathers or brothers, or placed in domestic service, or retrained in some traditionally feminine line like sewing.[76] Those who kept their jobs suffered a revived discrimination in wages. The socialist-backed demand for equal pay for equal work, written into some contracts immediately after the revolution, was gradually retracted beginning in 1920, when male-dominated unions adjusted to capitalist realities. Wage differentials between men and women settled around 30 to 40 percent. This was an improvement over prewar levels, which had been 50 to 60 percent, but disappointed the proponents of women's equality, who now had to settle for merely a reduced inferiority.[77]

Although the unions bitterly fought home industry, the old standby for women who had to work, it proved ineradicable.[78] The most exploitative of all wage labor, since it drew on the vulnerable group of mothers, invalids, and pensioners and since it placed the costs of overhead such as rent and utilities on the worker, home industry was nevertheless a *sine qua non* of many a household. The government's and the unions' attempts to suppress this source of income encountered bitterness and suspicion on the part of many women who had already been deprived of their factory jobs.[79]

What ultimately made female employment seem threatening to men was the extensive rationalization of industry after 1925. Generally this meant standardization of parts, and serial or flow production, that is, improved movement of the product along assembly lines. Intensive mechanization was more rare, since the amount of available capital was limited. The breakdown of work into small, simple, mechanical, repetitive tasks made the hiring of cheap, unskilled labor possible, and women were the most available source. They did not, however, actually displace men in most cases. What happened was that industries that already employed women expanded. Most affected were those industries that had rationalized even earlier and whose products now came into greater demand, such as the electro-technical, chemical, paper, and duplicating industries, and metalware manufacturing. These had employed women on a fairly large scale for some time, ostensibly for their patience, precision, and dexterity—arguments rarely advanced on behalf of female surgeons—but in fact for their low wages as unskilled and docile labor.[80]

After 1925, consumer industries grew in Germany. The chemical industry developed soaps, perfumes, and cosmetics, enlarging the branches that employed women. Those of men, largely in factory maintenance and transport, remained about the same. Similarly, the amount of electrical products made mainly by women, such as bulbs, telegraph and telephone equipment, wires, and radios, grew faster than the items produced mainly by men in the heavy-current industry, such as turbines and transformers.[81] The clothing and food industries, which traditionally employed many women, expanded, as did the proportion of women in them—again because the kind of work they did was related to production, which increased; men, however, worked in the more unchanging areas of plant and delivery.[82] Only in optics and precision tools and in the manufacture of metal wares did the development of standardized parts actually displace men, but to a very small degree.[83]

As noted earlier, the proportion of men in the labor force also increased. Of the 1.5 million new jobs added in the period from 1925 to 1933, 77 percent were taken by men.[84] Their jobs came from gains in construction and in the development of heavy industries, such as iron and steel and auto manufacture, as well as in the machine industry. Thus, the picture of women streaming into assembly-line jobs while men were pounding the pavement looking for work gave a superficially persuasive but fundamentally misleading impression. The actual proportion of women in the labor force did not so much rise as shift. In some cases, rationalization even worked against women. For example, textiles, traditionally the most female-dominated field, began to languish in the face of competition from new synthetic fibers such as rayon, in which men predominated.[85] Contrary to the commonly held views, loudly voiced during the Depression, women were not displacing men. Rather, they were themselves displaced, moving out of agriculture and home industry into factories where they were more visible as a workforce and more likely to provoke resentment. "Women's work" became a scapegoat.

Meanwhile, the federal employment-counseling offices adjusted to the increased availability of unskilled jobs for women by steering girls away from learning a skill, since fewer apprenticeships were available to them than to boys. A government representative resorted to prejudice to help the counselors cope with the situation:

> We will have to revise our one-sided emphasis on artisan and trade skills for girls in favor of semi-skilled work. . . . Many a girl with mediocre or weak intelligence will prefer a semi-skilled trade, in which she will find greater satisfaction than in a skilled trade whose requirements are too difficult. . . . The skilled trades can use only lively and intelligent people . . . less-talented girls will be happier with simple assembly work.[86]

No reference was made to simple-minded boys.

Rationalization was pernicious in other ways too. The speedup on the assembly line, a new form of industrial brutality, resulted in many cases of physical and nervous exhaustion.[87] The accident rate was higher for women than for men. Most of the factory inspection reports attributed this to women's greater carelessness, nervousness, and distractibility. One of them did note that in a metalware factory women worked at the lighter presses, which operated faster than the heavy ones worked by men, who could take time to be careful.[88] The same inspector did not, however, remember that fatigue also affected the women's performance, since most of them had two jobs, the other being housework and child care. More than half the female industrial workers were married and even unmarried women living alone or with their families were seldom relieved of domestic chores then as now.[89]

Rationalization in industry also encouraged bigness, and this trend cost women ownership or management positions even more than it did for men and just as it did in agriculture. In the clothing industry, for example, where the number of women nearly equaled that of men, the number of independent women, excluding those in home industry, dropped by one-third from 1925 to 1933, while that of men fell only one-eighth.[90] In the food and beverages industry, in which women were also heavily represented, the number of independent women fell 14 percent, while that of men dropped by only .5 percent.[91] The larger the establishment, the less likely was a women to hold a high position in management. This tendency, which had begun before the war, was accelerated by the mergers under the Weimar Republic. A test sample of industries in Baden, Hamburg, and Württemberg in 1925 showed that the percentage of female managers in industry had just about halved since the census of 1907, twice as steep a drop as the overall average.[92]

## Trade

In trade, the proportion of female shop owners declined from 1907 to 1925, though it picked up again to prewar levels by 1933.[93] However, the proportion of women heads of inns and taverns fell from 30 percent in 1907 to 25 percent in 1933, while that of men rose again after an initial drop, probably indicating the increase in large hotels under predominantly male ownership and management.[94]

Turning to white-collar work, we find it to have been the fastest growing area of female employment, though it had the lowest absolute number of women. Structural changes in the public and private sectors, such as the mushrooming of bureaucracies in government, in the political parties and unions, and in offices, and the development of the distributive sector created thousands of clerical and sales jobs. This, too, was related to rationalization, as the use of adding machines and typewriters derogated many aspects of office work to the level of simple mechanical tasks to be performed by low-paid, semiskilled female labor. Male white-collar jobs, being higher level, grew more slowly.[95]

Meanwhile, hordes of saleswomen streamed into the small shops and department stores, where an integral part of their job was to sell a product by seduction, symbolically, that is, through the use of feminine wiles.[96] Indeed, not until distribution and services developed fully did appearance and sexual role-playing come to be so important a part of women's work. One of the more pathetic medical cases to come to the attention of one of the few women doctors in Germany was that of a twelve-year-old girl whose face had been disfigured by tuberculosis and who, unaware that she was about to die, worried that the disfigurement would bar her from an office or sales job when she grew up—a problem surely not an obstacle for peasant women or industrial workers.[97]

Youth also became an essential part of the new working woman's equipment. Most clerks and salesgirls became obsolete by thirty, a condition that again did not hold true for their sisters in industry or agriculture.[98] Newspapers advertised for twenty-five-year-olds.[99] Businesses phased out older women rather than promoting them through the hierarchy. In 1925, less than 1 percent of the female white-collar workers held management positions, compared with 6 percent of the males. To put it another way, men held 95 percent of the top posts, though they constituted only three-fourths of the white-collar force. Women, who made up one-fourth of the total contingent, held only 5 percent of the top posts.[100] Many a girl who had had some enthusiasm for a career lost it once she realized that she had no future.

Social pressure to marry, in addition to lack of opportunity at work, led most young women to regard their jobs as temporary, a fact that made them hard to organize into unions. Filled with Cinderella fantasies encouraged by the media, they dreamed of marrying the boss rather than uniting against his exploitation of their labor and sex. Though they often worked extra-long hours for barely subsistence wages and had dependents such as aged parents or younger siblings, they scrimped to buy the fashionable clothes and cosmetics their proletarian sisters turned out on the assembly line.[101] Once married (though rarely to the boss), they did not return to work, since they usually allied themselves with someone from the same white-collar group—a male better paid than themselves. Here again we see women leaving the economy as it modernizes.

### Services and Professions

Agriculture occupied nearly half the female labor force, industry a third to a fourth, and the service and distributive sectors an eighth, the remainder being the women in the free professions. In the fields of health, education, and the arts, women who had access to higher learning did make some significant advances. A majority taught, and women comprised one-third of all teachers; they made up more than half in the health professions, though mostly as nurses; and they provided four-fifths of social welfare workers.[102] The number of women doctors multiplied by thirteen after the war and nearly doubled again before the

Nazi takeover; the number of female dentists and dental technicians had nearly as dramatic a rise, and the number of lawyers quintupled from 1925 to 1933. Certainly an impressive set of gains, one would think, even if they did involve only 6 percent of the total female working population.[103]

Yet looked at in another way, women's progress in the professions was somewhat less spectacular. For example, while about 30 percent of the teachers were women, this did not represent a rise in proportion over prewar levels. Only 7 percent headed schools and in fact they were losing ground. Men slowly took over the formerly private high schools and lyceums for girls, which had been founded and seen through their early financial crises by women.[104] Even before the war, there had been a widespread fear of the feminization of public education.[105] After the revolution, as the states took over more of the educational burden, male influence in the schools increased. Prussian legislation stipulated that in girls' schools, one-third of the faculties be men and one-third of the science work be done by them. A court decision of 1922 put women teachers on a salary schedule below that of men because "men teachers were contributing to the material restoration of Germany by training workmen, whereas the women were only making housewives."[106] In short, coeducation and state control increased the number of schools and the number of female and male teachers, but derogated the position of women in education relative to the prewar period.

The health professions underwent an interesting metamorphosis as the number of midwives declined by over 6,000 while the number of female doctors rose only 4,200 in the period from 1907 to 1933. Only 5 percent of all the doctors were women.[107] Of these, only half had an independent practice, compared with three-fourths of the male doctors; the rest were employed in clinics or hospitals or public health institutions. The majority of women in the health professions went into nursing. Professionalization seemed to be proletarianizing most women, though it allowed a few to achieve elite status.

Women made up less than .5 percent of lawyers in 1925 and this figure rose to 1.5 percent in 1933, for a grand total of 251 women lawyers—hardly an invasion of the field. Of these, two-thirds had their own practices, compared with 95 percent of the male lawyers, and most of them dealt with family law or protective factory legislation for women.[108]

In short, advances in the professions were indeed made over the prewar period, but one can hardly speak of the liberation of thousands of women in competition with men. Above and beyond social conditioning and the difficulties of combining family life with employment, sex prejudice effectively blocked many a career.

3

From the foregoing, it is possible to draw some clear conclusions regarding the position of women in the politics and economy of Weimar Germany.

No political party (with the possible exception of the Communists) undertook the task of reeducating women to accept full citizen status. Women voters were regarded much as American politicians might view the "ethnic vote." Their ballots were sought, but too large a participation in party leadership was not encouraged. Every party in the early years of the Weimar Republic made a great effort to include at least a few women in its upper echelons and regularly placed women's names on its list of candidates. In the most conspicuous positions, women comprised between 5 and 10 percent of elected or party offices, but at local levels the percentage of women fell away to between 1 and 2 percent. [109] This pattern contrasts sharply with many sociologists' predictions about the impact of political emancipation on participation. According to a common paradigm, women tend to be better represented in less important positions. As jobs increase in pay, responsibility, and status, the percentages of women decline. [110]

Thus, the Weimar example seems to provide us with a dramatic case of "tokenism." The effect of this situation was not to provide role models and thereby encourage more women to enter local political activities. Instead, as long-time leaders of the women's rights movement observed women in many conspicuous places, they relaxed their efforts at further change and turned their attention to national issues unrelated to the recruitment of additional women into public life. Meanwhile, opponents of women's participation in politics became alarmed at what they perceived to be an inundation of women into politics, and their intransigence against further reforms increased.

One effect of this top-heavy participation of women in the government was the recruitment of the most tractable leaders of the women's rights campaign into the political party structure; die-hard feminists, by contrast, preferred to work outside formal, male-dominated structures and found their influence dwindling. Women in responsible party offices proved to be pragmatic politicians rather than militant feminists. When party leaders refused to grant more funds or tabled motions related to women's issues, women leaders tended to accept such treatment without strong protest. Socialist women felt easily intimidated by accusations that they had not yet been sufficiently effective in recruiting more women party members; bourgeois women too often were mollified by promises that a subcommittee would investigate their demands. Similarly, when bills concerning legal rights of women failed to pass in a legislature, women delegates acquiesced and did not renew pressures for change. Not wishing to disrupt party or legislative harmony, women proved to be docile participants in the political process when it came to feminist issues.

All parties, in short, desired to attract the woman vote, but displayed considerably less enthusiasm about recruiting women into their party structures or about changing male attitudes. Discussions about the woman question did not appear in the pamphlets or newspapers addressed to the general (male) readership of any party. Although bourgeois parties emphasized women's role in a putative spiritual revolution and the socialist parties told women to view themselves as workers for the overthrow of capitalism, no party successfully integrated its rhetoric supporting women's rights into its theory or practice. Resentment toward women workers persisted and was even reinforced by the socialists' hesitancy to fight for equal pay for equal work. In the Liberal and Conservative parties as well, women's participation in the economy was encouraged only insofar as women did not overstep the bounds of their traditional interests. No political party endorsed measures that would upset the traditional supremacy of German men—in the economy, the family, or the government. Male politicians supported emancipation only as long as the status quo was not threatened. Women politicians sensed this limitation on the goodwill of their fellow party members. Consequently they were careful to reaffirm their desire not to disrupt the time-honored division of labor between men and women. In short, no politician in Weimar Germany challenged the ideal of separate but equal.

On the economic front as well, war and postwar developments did not provide an unambiguous improvement for women. Thus, the traditional picture of women's economic liberation must be seriously modified. Modernization of techniques and concentration of ownership reshuffled jobs so that women as a group were pressed increasingly into unskilled work with lessened responsibility or out of the economy altogether. They lost status and sometimes relative independence and probably a corresponding sense of competence and self-esteem. As women were recriminated against for abandoning their families, and suffered consequently from a sense of failure at home as well as at work, their socially induced feelings of inferiority were reinforced by low pay and lack of advancement.

In politics, however, the failure of major reforms and the reluctance of the parties to integrate women into their organizations cannot be attributed solely to male misogyny or female passivity. The right to vote and constitutional promises of equality between the sexes had come as part of the "revolution from above." In fact, the suffrage victory had come in 1918—when the women's movement was less active than it had been before war work claimed the full attention of its participants.[111] The right to vote had been given to women in the hope that women voters would help to ensure the defeat of Bolshevism and to provide a progressive, liberal image of Germany at the Paris Peace Conference. When the crisis of 1918–1919 subsided, so did loyalty to *all* of the Weimar reforms, which had been dictated by opportunism, not idealism. In this respect, the fate of women's emancipation shared the fate of the Weimar Republic itself. As the only major political party that had not participated in the foundation of the Weimar Republic, National Socialists did not bother to maintain even a hypocritical support for its values. Hitler, undeterred by the need to pay lip service to women's equality, stated his opposition to women in politics more boldly than did other politicians. But there can be no doubt that the prevailing attitudes in Weimar Germany presaged the practices of the Third Reich.

Despite much rhetoric about the rights of women, Germans did not envision a change in the traditional role of women. Women had as little reason as men to seek a basic transformation of their role. When women did enter the traditionally masculine occupations, they were neither paid nor treated equally. And no political solution to this problem appeared to be forthcoming. Without an appealing alternative, women persisted in their loyalty to the familiar *Kinder, Küche, Kirche* ethos and saw emancipation more often as a threat than as a blessing.

Thus, it should not surprise us that the women of the Weimar Republic failed to embrace their putative emancipation and even rejected it politically. Conservative politicians understood the appeal of tradition in times of uncertainty. They, unlike liberal and left-wing parties, could make political propaganda out of this anxiety. The home was to the German woman what the workshop or small business or farm was to the German man. It meant status, independence, respectability, and security. It was, in short, territory to be defended. Women's apprehensions about losing their traditional niche in society were akin to men's fears of "proletarianization." The Depression exacerbated the resulting tensions. Hitler told women that politics was a dirty business and not suited for them; that women should be honored in their homes, not exploited in the factory; that they should sew brown shirts and inspire their menfolk. Obviously, he struck a responsive chord: German women had come a long way—in the wrong direction.

## Notes

This is a revised version of an essay that appeared in *Liberating Women's History*, ed. Berenice A. Carroll (Chicago: University of Chicago Press, 1976).

1. *Studien über Autorität und Familie: Forschungsberichte aus dem Institut für*

*Sozialforschung*, introd. by Max Horkheimer; Schriften des Instituts für Sozialforschung, no. 5 (Paris: F. Alcan, 1936).

2. Germany, Statistisches Amt, *Statistik des deutschen Reichs* 453, pt. II, 6–7. Hereafter *Stat.d.d.R.*
3. Carl Gustav Jung, *Die Frau in Europa*, 3d ed. (Zurich: Rascher, 1948). It is interesting that this essay was reprinted in the post–World War II period.
4. David Schoenbaum, *Hitler's Social Revolution* (Garden City, N.Y.: Doubleday, 1966), p. 178.
5. Miriam Beard, "The Tune Hitlerism Beats for Germany," in John Weiss, ed., *Nazis and Fascists in Europe, 1918–1945* (Chicago: Quadrangle, 1969), p. 96. Karl Dietrich Bracher is among the recent historians who have puzzled over this apparent paradox. (Bracher, *The German Dictatorship* [New York: Praeger, 1970], pp. 86–87, 338–39).
6. Siegfried Berger, *Einführung in die Deutsche Reichsverfassung von 11. August 1919* (Berlin, 1927), p. 49. For an excellent summary of women's legal status in the Weimar Republic, see Emma Oekinghaus, *Die gesellschaftliche und rechtliche Stellung der Frau* (Jena: Fischer, 1925).
7. Related by Clara Mende, *Die deutsche Volkspartei zur Frauenfrage* (Berlin: Staatspolitischer, 1919), p. 5.
8. Gabrielle Bremme notes that this relatively low percentage of male voters resulted in part from bureaucratic problems in registering recently demobilized soldiers (Bremme, *Die politische Rolle der Frau in Deutschland* [Göttingen: Vandenhoeck und Ruprecht, 1956], p. 31). Maurice Duverger observed that this percentage of women voting in their first election was larger than that of women in other countries just after suffrage reform (Duverger, *The Political Role of Women* [Paris: UNESCO, 1955], pp. 56–60).
9. Gertrud Bäumer, *Die Frau im Deutschen Staat* (Berlin: Junker und Dünnhaupt, 1932), pp. 43ff.; Alois Kloeckner, *Die Zentrumsfraktion* (Berlin: Prussian Center Party, 1919), p. 10; Oekinghaus, *Die gesellschaftliche und rechtliche Stellung der Frau*, p. 125.
10. Clara Böhm-Schuch, "Die Politik und die Frauen," *Frauenstimmen aus der Nationalversammlung: Beiträge der sozialdemokratischen Volksvertreterinnen zu den Zeitfragen* (Berlin: SPD, 1920), pp. 16–17.
11. Käthe Schrey, "Advent 1918," *Deutsche Frauenzeitung, Illustrierte Familie Wochenschrift mit Modenzeitung* XXXII, 9, 1, November 30, 1918.
12. Clara Viebig, *Mütter und Frauen!* (n.d.), p. 1. This was a pamphlet published by the DVP in 1919 or 1920.
13. This was a fairly common theme in bourgeois publications. See, for example, *Die Frau*, 1918–19.
14. Marie Stritt, "Von der Frauenstimmrechtlerin zur Parteipolitikerin," *Die Staatsbürgerin, Monatsschrift des deutschen Reichsverbandes für Frauenstimmrecht*, VII:10/11, 30, January and February 1919. See also G. Bäumer, *Lebensweg durch eine Zeitenwende* (Tübingen: R. Wunderlich, 1933), p. 430.
15. Alice Rühle-Gerstel, *Das Frauenproblem der Gegenwart: eine psychologische Bilanz* (Leipzig: S. Hirzel, 1932), p. 387.
16. Fewer women voted as compared both with the percentage of eligible women voting in 1919 and with the percentages of eligible men who voted in each election. Bremme notes, however, that women tend to vote more sporadically than men. For example, in the "crisis" situations of 1919, 1930–33, and 1945 the percentages of women voting increased dramatically.
17. Bäumer, *Die Frau im Deutschen Staat*, p. 45. Hans Beyer investigates in greater detail the impact of woman suffrage on each of the Weimar parties (Beyer, *Die Frau in der politische Entscheidung* [Stuttgart: F. Enke 1932], pp. 34–41). For a com-

plete breakdown by sex and region of Weimar elections, see Duverger, *The Political Role of Women*, pp. 52ff.

18. G. G. L. Alexander, *Kämpfende Frauen: historische-materialische Studien* (Berlin: Neuer Deutscher Verlag, 1921), p. 32. For a concise, eloquent statement of the Socialist position, see Clara Zetkin, "Frauenreichskonferenz," of 1920. KPD, *Bericht* (Berlin, 1920), pp. 285ff.

19. KPD, *Bericht über den 2. Parteitag der Kommunistischen Partei (Spartakus) vom 20. bis 24. Oktober 1919* (Berlin, 1919), p. 29. Pamphlets and leaflets were, however, directed at soldiers, workers in special industries, and peasants.

20. KPD, *Bericht über den 3. Parteitag der KPD (Spartakus) am 25. und 26. Februar 1920* (Berlin: KPD, 1920), p. 57. No other item was dropped from the agenda.

21. Ibid., pp. 58–59.

22. Besides the official party platforms of each party, see Oda Olberg, "Polemisches über Frauenfrage und Sozialismus," in Wally Zepler, ed., *Sozialismus und Frauenfrage* (Berlin: P. Cassirer, 1919), pp. 38ff.; Luise Zietz, *USPD Protokoll über die Verhandlung des Parteitages in Leipzig vom 8. bis 12. Januar 1922 sowie über die zweite Reichsfrauenkonferenz, 1922* (Leipzig: A.G., n.d.), pp. 184ff.; *Protokoll der Reichs-frauen-Konferenz der USPD 29. und 30. November 1919* (Berlin: Freiheit, 1919), pp. 461ff.; KPD, *Bericht, 3. Parteitag*; A. Blos, *Frauenfrage, pp. 165ff.*; KPD, *Frauen Wacht auf!* (Berlin [1924?]), p. 8.

23. Werner Thönnessen, *Die Frauenemanzipation in Politik und Literatur der Deutschen Sozialdemokratie, 1863–1933* (Gelnhausen, 1958), pp. 120ff. Also noteworthy is the fact that the differential between male and female support for the SPD narrowed. In 1920, 25.4 percent of all males voted SPD as compared with 19.9 percent of the females. The statistics for 1930 are less complete, but in the districts that separated male and female votes, the differential had dropped to just under 3 percent. These observations are based on tables in Duverger, *The Political Role of Women*, p. 54.

24. Blos, *Frauenfrage*, 165, 180, 193.

25. The one exception to this rule was the Communist delegation of 1930, which included thirteen (17.1 percent) women. This compared very favorably with earlier representations of about 5 or 6 percent. Social Democratic representation declined from 13.3 percent in 1919 to 11.1 percent in 1930 (Bremme, *Die politische Rolle der Frau in Deutschland*, p. 124).

26. For example, see Luise Zietz's tirade against conservative Socialist women, *USPD Protokoll über die Verhandlungen des Parteitages in Leipzig*, pp. 187ff.

27. Even *Die Gleichheit* repeated this charge without criticism: "Without women's vote, progress would have already made greater strides" (*Die Gleichheit*, no. 14/15 [1922], p. 1). See also *Vorwärts*, August 22, 1931.

28. *Protokoll über die Verhandlungen des Parteitages der SPD, abgehalten zu Görlitz*, 1921, p. 189. Thönnessen discusses this issue in *Die Frauenemanzipation*, pp. 101ff.

29. *Tribüne der proletarischen Frau* in *Die Rote Fahne*, no. 4, November 10, 1920, p. 1. This particular admonition urges men to send their women to party meetings and tells them not to worry that the housework won't be completed. The women's improved morale will help them do their household chores in much less time.

30. These lists appeared in advertisements in party pamphlets and in printed editions of party protocols throughout the 1920s.

31. Among twenty portraits of party leaders, none was of a woman. *Unser Program in Wort und Bild* (Berlin, 1931), p. 17.

32. Matilda Wurm, "Die Frauenarbeit," report read at the USPD Convention, *Protokoll; Leipzig 8–12. Januar, 1922* (Leipzig, n.d.), p. 511.

33. For a discussion of Socialism and anti-Semitism, see Peter Pulzer, *The Rise of Political Anti-Semitism* (New York: Wiley, 1964), pp. 259–71; for a slightly different perspective, see Hannah Arendt, "Anti-Semitism," in *Origins of Totalitarianism* (New York, 1968).

34. The one exception to this was the Catholic Center party's reluctance to sponsor any reforms that would have undercut complete male supremacy within the family.

35. Leaflet no. 6, Evangelischer Frauenverein, Federal German Archive, Coblenz; Bestand nr. 34. Hereafter BA Koblenz.

36. Viebig, *Mütter und Frauen!*, p. 2.

37. Bäumer, *Lebensweg*, p. 360. "*Wir sind gerufen durch die Revolution. Aber wir sind auch gerufen gegen die Revolution.*"

38. Mende, *Die deutsche Volkspartei zur Frauenfrage*, p. 3.

39. Similar reactions in England are noted by Sandra Gilbert, "Soldier's Heart: Literary Men, Literary Women and the Great War," *SIGNS*, Spring 1983), pp. 422–450.

40. A von Zahn-Harnack, *Schriften*, pp. 18–19.

41. M. Weber, "Die besondere Kulturaufgabe der Frau" (1918), *Frauenfragen und Frauengedanken: Gesammelte Aufsätze* (Tübingen, 1919), p. 252. Also, Helene Lange, *Kampfzeiten II*, Entry for November 1918, p. 227. For wartime propaganda on this theme, see Ursula von Gersdorff, *Frauen im Kriegsdienst* (Stuttgart: Deutsche Verlags-Anstalt, 1969), pp. 107–78 *passim*.

42. Frau Fr. Naumann, *Was soll die Frau in der Politik?* (Berlin, 1918), p. 2.

43. "Aufruf und Leitsätze des Reichsausschusses (Frankfurt, December 30, 1918), quoted in Wilhelm Mommsen and Günther Franz, *Die Deutschen Parteiprogramme 1918–1930* (Leipzig and Berlin: B. G. Teubner, 1931), pp. 11–13.

44. Hans Beyer notes that while men had been dropping out of the Center party since before the war, women's votes more than compensated for this loss and maintained the Center as a leading party throughout the 1920s (Beyer, *Die Frau in der politische Entscheidung*, pp. 34ff). In 1919, 6.3 percent of Center delegates were women; in 1930, the percentage dropped to 5.9 (Bremme, *Die politische Rolle der Frau in Deutschland*, p. 124).

45. Quoted in Kardorff Nachlass, "Wir brauchen eine Mutterliga!" item 12, Folio 40. Kardorff called women the "tragic sex" because they had been misled by male values, and closed her speech with the appeal "Mothers of all the World, Unite!"

46. DNVP, "Grundsätze," quoted in Mommsen and Franz, *Die Deutschen Parteiprogramme*, pp. 60–71; see also p. 90. For a liberal statement of this view, see Dr. Jur. Anna-lise Schellwitz-Ueltzen, *Die Frau im neuen Deutschland* (Berlin: Staatspolitscher, 1920), pp. 7ff.

47. *Frauen-Flugschriften der Deutschen demokratischen Partei*, pamphlet (Berlin: Demokratischer, 1918).

48. Frl. Wittstock, organization meeting at Bad Eilsen, September 17 and 18, 1927, BA Koblenz, R 45 III/29 (27–9), item 31.

49. For a discussion of the Catholic women's movement, see Hilde Lion, *Zur Soziologie der Frauenbewegung (Die sozialistische und die Katholische Frauenbewegung)* (Berlin, 1932), pp. 78ff.

50. Kardorff Nachlass, "Wir brauchen eine Mutterliga!"

51. Anna Mayer, *Die Rechtsstellung der Ehefrau und der ehelichen Mutter* (Berlin: Staatspolitischer, 1921). This is pamphlet no. 9 in the series *Flugschriften der Deutschen Volkspartei*.

52. Frauenabteilung der Reichsgerschäftsstelle, *Winke für Frauenausschüsse* (Berlin, n.d.), p. 2; BA Koblenz, Zsg 1 - 42/46 (26).

53. Bremme, *Die politische Rolle der Frau in Deutschland*, p. 124.

54. Rühle-Gerstel, *Das Frauenproblem der Gegenwart*, pp. 287ff.

55. *Stat.d.d.R.*, 402:423 and 408:9.

|  | Female | | Male | |
|---|---|---|---|---|
|  | Total population | Gainfully occupied | Total population | Gainfully occupied |
| 1907 | 27,884,309 | 8,501,005 | 27,106,774 | 16,655,012 |
| 1925 | 32,213,796 | 11,478,012 | 30,196,823 | 20,531,288 |

56. *Stat.d.d.R.*, 408:8. Germany, Statistisches Amt, *Wirtschaft und Statistik* 5 (1925): 12 (Hereafter *W & S*). The differential came down to 1059/1000 in 1933—*W & S* 14 (1934): 159.

57. *Stat.d.d.R.*, 408:318–19, projected that in 1933, 34 percent of the female population would be working. Forced displacement of women after the Nazi takeover made this figure accurate. *W & S* 5 (1925), Sonderheft 2, p. 5, looking worriedly at the huge population of Russia, counted the German losses as between twelve and thirteen million: two million soldiers, three-quarter million civilians, three million unborn children, and seven million in lost territories, and calculated that the normal population of Germany should be seventy-five million rather than sixty-two-and-a-half million. Even so, it was the largest population in Europe, with Great Britain following with forty-four million and France and Italy with thirty-nine million each.

58. *W & S* 5 (1929), "Beiträge zum deutschen Bevölkerungsproblem," p. 29.

59. *Stat.d.d.R.*, 407:7.

60. *Stat.d.d.R.*, 221:205, 132*; 402:232; 453 (Pt. II): 36.

Agricultural working population

| 1895 | 2,730,216 | 5,315,225 |
|---|---|---|
| 1907 | 4,558,718 | 5,023,084 |
| 1925 | 4,969,279 | 4,793,147 |
| 1933 | 4,649,279 | 4,694,006 |

This shows male participation in absolute numbers steadily decreasing, women's increasing until 1933, when they, in turn, began their "flight from the country."

61. In the countryside, the ratio of females to males in 1933 was 1,002 to 1,000 and only 862 to 1,000 among the twenty-year-olds, indicating a high rate of emigration for young girls. The national average was 1,059 to 1,000 and in the big cities it was greater, with Berlin leading at 1,160 to 1,000—*W & S* 14 (1934): 160; 15 (1935): 197.

62. From 1925 to 1933, the total number of agricultural workers decreased by 12 percent, female workers alone by 22 percent—*W & S* 14 (1934): 632. The Chamber of Agriculture in Pomerania ascertained that from January 1, 1928, to June 30, 1929, about 20 percent of the *Mägde* from Eastern Pomerania emigrated (Max Sering, *Die deutsche Landwirtschaft unter volks- und weltwirtschaftlichen Gesichtspunkten* [Berlin: Reichsministerium für Ernährung und Landwirtschaft, 1932], p. 149).

63. The average number of hours a year worked by the peasant woman in Württemberg was 3,933, by the peasant man 3,554, by the hired help, 2,800 (Adolf Münzinger, *Der Arbeitsertrag der bäuerlichen Familienwirtschaft; eine bäuerliche Betriebserhebung in Württemberg* [Berlin, 1929], II, pp. 811–12, 835).

64. Ibid., pp. 809–10; Rosa Kempf, *Arbeits- und Lebensverhältnisse der Frauen in der Landwirtschaft Bayerns* (Jena: G. Fischer, 1918), p. 132.

65. Ibid., pp. 36, 133.

66. *Stat.d.d.R.*, 212:606–7; 410:70–71; 461:52–53.

Leading positions in agriculture
(owners, lessors, directors)

|  | Female | Male |
|---|---|---|
| 1907 | 403,400 | 2,526,093 |
| 1925 | 428,244 | 3,158,318 |
| 1933 | 313,878 | 2,710,682 |

Note that while male ownership also dropped in the second period of the Republic, it remained above prewar levels, while that of women fell below.

67. *Stat.d.d.R.*, 410:70–71; W & S 14 (1934): 444.
68. *Stat.d.d.R.*, 402:232; 453 (Pt. II): 36.

Managerial positions in agriculture

|  | Female | Male |
|---|---|---|
| 1925 | 1,577 | 8,248 |
| 1933 | 288[a] | 2,583[b] |

[a] Plus 52 unemployed: 14 percent
[b] Plus 180 unemployed: 6.5 percent

The *Stat.d.d.R.*, 211:207, commented on the drop in the number of female heads of agricultural institutions from 1895 to 1907, relating it directly to the development of dairy co-ops; Kempf, *Arbeits- und Lebensverhältnisse der Frauen*, p. 129, noted that the commercial development of agriculture tended to exclude women and jeopardized the peasant wife's relative independence.

69. Emma Stropp, *Die landwirtschaftlichen Frauenberufe; ein Wegweiser für die Berufswahl* (Gotha: Verlag Die Landfrau, 1919). Lily Hauff, *Entwicklung der Frauenberufe in den letzten drei Jahrzehnten* (Berlin: Puttkammer und Mühlbrecht, 1911), pp. 24–25, had expected educated women to make great headway in all these fields. Women's place in gardening underwent some dramatic changes from 1907 to 1933. From 1907 to 1925, the number of female gardeners dropped sharply, then picked up by 1933, though only to half the prewar level. The number of men in the profession climbed steadily. *Stat.d.d.R.*, 211 (Anhang): 53; 402:410; 470:35.

Gardeners

|  | Female | Male |
|---|---|---|
| 1907 | 26,833 | 121,404 |
| 1925 | 7,814 | 126,456 |
| 1933 | 13,701 | 164,949 |

70. These are recurrent themes in the reports of the factory inspectors (Germany, Arbeitsministerium, *Jahresberichte der Gewerbeaufsichtsbeamten und Bergbehörden*, 1919–34; hereafter *GAB*). In 1928, one factory in Berlin reported 148 live births to 724 "miscarriages," and in 1926 a factory inspector remarked that if the unsafe conditions of some factories were known, women would queue up to work in them, given their tendency to try to abort (*GAB* [1926] I:105; [1928] I:113). In Prussia, the ratio of live births to miscarriages completely reversed itself from 1916 to 1922: from 8 live births to 5 miscarriages it became 5 live births to 8 miscarriages (*GAB* for Prussia [1922]: 62).

As late as 1932, the criminal code still prohibited contraceptive devices; and abortion, permitted only for medical reasons, carried a penalty of six months to five years imprisonment for the patient and up to ten years for the doctor. Nevertheless, illegal abortions for those who could afford them were performed. The files of one doctor operating in a small town of 25,000 indicated that in one year he had performed 426 abortions, mostly on married women (Else Kienle, *Frauen: aus dem Tagebuch einer Ärztin* [Berlin, 1932], p. 25).

71. Antonina Vallentin, "The Employment of Women since the War," *International Labor Review* 25 (January–June 1932): 484; Helene Kaiser, *Der Einfluss industrieller Frauenarbeit auf die Gestaltung der industriellen Reservearmee in der deutschen Volkswirtschaft der Gegenwart* (Leipzig: Teicher, 1933), p. 22.

72. Harry Oppenborn, *Die Tätigkeit der Frau in der deutschen Kriegswirtschaft* (Hamburg: Hans Christians Druckerei und Verlag, 1928), p. 19.

73. Ibid., pp. 16–43; Ursula von Gersdorff, *Frauen im Kriegsdienst* (Stuttgart: Deutsche Verlagsanstalt, 1969), p. 25.

74. Oppenborn, *Die Tätigkeit der Frau*, pp. 44–52.

75. Von Gersdorff, *Frauen im Kriegsdienst*, p. 37.

76. *GAB* (1919) I:113.

77. Jürgen Kuczynski, *Die Geschichte der Lage der Arbeiter unter dem Kapitalismus* 18 (Berlin: Akademie Verlag, 1963): 223. In chap. 3, the author analyzes the wage differentials between men and women during the Weimar period and concludes that it tended to narrow during bad times, the inflationary twenties and the Depression, when men's real wages fell closer to subsistence level and thus to women's wages, while in good times, such as the period of relative stabilization, the differential tended to widen again as men's wages recovered.

78. Ibid., p. 230; *GAB* (1919) I:123.

79. *GAB* (Prussia, 1921) I:113.

80. Kaiser, *Der Einfluss industrieller Frauenarbeit*, p. 49; *W & S* 6 (1926): 792.

81. Robert Brady, *The Rationalization Movement in German Industry* (Berkeley: University of California Press, 1933), pp. 171–72, 240.

82. Ibid., p. 309.

83. Kaiser, *Der Einfluss industrieller Frauenarbeit*, pp. 100–05.

84. Brady, *The Rationalization Movement in German Industry*, p. 309.

85. Employment in the textile industry:

| | Female | Male |
|---|---|---|
| 1925 | 672,842 | 533,889 |
| 1933 | 586,077 (incl. unemployed) | 532,638 (incl. unemployed) |
| | 465,512 (employed) | 391,169 (employed) |

Note that while women's participation in the diminishing textile labor force dropped much more sharply than that of men, 13 percent compared with 0.2 percent, their rate of unemployment was considerably lower, so that actual employment of women dropped only 16 percent while that of men dropped 27 percent. This kind of phenomenon gave rise to the impression that women were displacing men on the job market, when actually the structural change underlying the crisis was going in the opposite direction *Stat.d.d.R.*, 402:236; 453 (Pt. II): 40.

86. Germany, Arbeitsministerium, "Die öffentliche Berufsberatung in Deutschland nach der Berufsberatungsstatistik von 1926/1927," *Reichsarbeitsblatt II* (1928), no. 15, pp. 253–57. There was one job available for every two male applicants who came for counseling and one for every three female applicants. Forty-three percent of the males were placed, 35 percent of the females.

87. Kuczynski, *Die Geschichte der Lage der Arbeiter unter dem Kapitalismus*, p. 238.

88. *GAB* (Prussia, 1922): 68.

89. Margarete Blum, *Neuzeitliche Arbeitsteilung zwischen Mann und Frau in Handel und Industrie* (Köln: Welzel, 1932), p. 41.

90. Independents in the clothing industry:

|  | Female | Male |
|---|---|---|
| 1925 | 298,867 | 316,714 |
| 1933 | 196,717 | 279,470 |

*W & S* 7 (1927): 576 and 14 (1934), Sonderblatt no. 24: 8.

91. Independents in the food and beverages industry:

|  | Female | Male |
|---|---|---|
| 1925 | 21,677 | 228,579 |
| 1933 | 18,481 | 227,327 |

*W & S* 7 (1927): 575 and 14 (1934), Sonderblatt no. 24: 8.

92. Percentage of employees in managerial positions:

|  | Wurttemberg | | Baden | | Hamburg | |
|---|---|---|---|---|---|---|
|  | Women[a] | Total[b] | Women | Total | Women | Total |
| 1925 | 18 | 20.8 | 15.4 | 17.2 | 27.5 | 18.3 |
| 1933 | 10.4 | 15 | 7.3 | 13.5 | 12 | 15.2 |

[a] Women in managerial positions as a percentage of all managers
[b] Managers as a percentage of all employees

*W & S* 6 (1926): 915. The census of 1907 already noted the inverse relationship of numbers of workers and heads of managers of firms on a sexual basis. *Stat.d.d.R.*, 211:207 remarked on the general tendency for the number of female clerks to increase more rapidly than that of male clerks while the number of female owners and managers fell more rapidly than that of males. The census of 1925 showed this to be a continuing trend. *Stat.d.d.R.*, 408:133–34:

Independents in industry and crafts

|  | 1907 | 1925 | % change |
|---|---|---|---|
| Female | 307,295 | 241,489 | − 21.4 |
| Male | 1,223,976 | 1,269,379 | 3.7 |

Meanwhile, the employment of women in home industry rose, while that of men fell.

Home industry

|  | 1907 | 1925 | % change |
|---|---|---|---|
| Female | 127,883 | 189,299 | 48 |
| male | 109,274 | 84,946 | − 22.3 |

In trade and commerce, the number of female independents increased, but considerably less than the number or proportion of male independents.

Independents in trade and commerce

|  | 1907 | 1925 | % change |
|---|---|---|---|
| Female | 224,879 | 265,863 | 18.2 |
| Male | 702,924 | 932,339 | 32.6 |

93. *Stat.d.d.R.*, 211:205; 408:124; 453 (Pt. II):46.

Independents in trade

|  | Female | Male | % Female |
|---|---|---|---|
| 1907 | 169,670 | 497,568 | 25 |
| 1925 | 200,112 | 736,074 | 21 |
| 1933 | 250,943 | 737,369 | 25.5 |

94. Ibid.

Heads of inns and taverns

|      | Female | Male    | % Female |
|------|--------|---------|----------|
| 1907 | 69,503 | 169,173 | 30       |
| 1925 | 63,297 | 131,564 | 32       |
| 1933 | 44,849 | 136,346 | 25       |

95. *Stat.d.d.R.*, 453 (Pt. II):7.

White-collar employees (to nearest thousand)

|      | Female    | Male      | % Female | % Total female work force |
|------|-----------|-----------|----------|---------------------------|
| 1907 | 493,000   | 2,818,000 | 14.9     | 5.8                       |
| 1925 | 1,446,000 | 3,996,000 | 26.6     | 12.6                      |
| 1933 | 1,695,000 | 3,818,000 | 30.7     | 14.8                      |

Note that men were affected more by the Depression, again leading to the impression that they were being displaced by women, when in fact men's and women's white-collar work were very different.
96. Blum, *Neuzeitliche Arbeitsteilung*, p. 17; Stephanie Herz, *Zur Typologie der kaufmännischen Angestellten* (Berlin: Druckerei des Studentenwerks e. V. 1931), p. 26.
97. Kienle, *Frauen*, p. 50.
98. Half the female clerks were under age twenty-five, compared with one-fourth of the males (Staffi M. Tarrasch, *Die weiblichen Angelstellten: Das Problem ihrer Organisation* [Heidelberg, 1931], pp. 15–16.
99. Herz, *Zur Typologie der kaufmännischen Angestellten*, p. 25.
100. *Stat.d.d.R.*, 409:139.
101. Herz, *Zur Typologie der kaufmännischen Angestellten*, p. 17, Frieda Glass, "Einkommen und Lebensbedingungen berufstätiger Frauen; nach einer Erhebung der Arbeitsgemeinschaft deutscher Frauenberufsverbände," *Jahrbuch der Frauenarbeit* 7 (Berlin: Verband der weiblichen Handels- und Büroangestellten, 1931): 24–45.
102. *Stat.d.d.R.*, 408:87, 93–94.
103. *Stat.d.d.R.*, 453 (Pt. II): 48–50; *W & S* 7 (1927): 576–77.
104. *Stat.d.d.R.*, 408:298; *W & S* 15 (1935), Sonderbeilage no. 14: p. 18; Hauff, *Entwicklung der Frauenberufe*, p. 44.

Teachers

|      | Female | Male    | % Female |
|------|--------|---------|----------|
| 1907 | 89,110 | 188,043 | 32       |
| 1925 | 97,675 | 211,066 | 32       |
| 1933 | 94,140 | 212,469 | 30       |

105. Kempf, *Arbeits- und Lebensverhältnisse der Frauen*, p. 137.
106. Hugh Wiley Puckett, *Germany's Women Go Forward* (New York: Columbia University Press, 1930), p. 199.
107. *Stat.d.d.R.*, 211:269–76; 408:308–9; *W & S* 15 (1953), Sonderblatt no. 14: 19.

Medical profession

|      | Doctors |        | Midwives | Nurses  |
|------|---------|--------|----------|---------|
|      | Female  | Male   |          |         |
| 1907 | 195     | 29.763 | 28,393   | 71,624  |
| 1925 | 2,572   | 45,332 | 23,452   | 117,128 |
| 1933 | 4,395   | 47,132 | 21,911   | 131,794 |

108. *Stat.d.d.R.*, 408:299; W & S 15 (1935), Sonderbeilage no. 14: 19.
109. Blos, *Frauenfrage*, pp. 133–36; Alois Kloeckner *Die Zentrumsfraktion in der Preussichen Landesversammlung* (Berlin, 1919), p. 10; Elisabeth Suersen, *Die Frau im Deutschen Reichs- und Landesstaatsdienst* (Mannheim, 1920); Bäumer, *Die Frau im Deutschen Staat*, pp. 43ff.
110. Duverger, *The Political Role of Women*, p. 123. For further discussion on this, see Rühle-Gerstel, *Das Frauenproblem der Gegenwart*, pp. 142, 251–65.
111. For an interesting array of opinions on why women were enfranchised, see DNVP, "Aufruf des Vorstandes, 27. December, 1918," in Mommsen and Franz, *Die Deutschen Parteiprogramme*, p. 19; Blos, *Frauenfrage*, pp. 97–99; Ruth Kohler-Irrgang, *Die Sendung der Frau in der Deutsche Geschichte* (Leipzig, 1942), p. 277; Konrad Meyer, *Wahlrecht und Wahlpflicht der Frau* (Magdeburg, 1918), pp. 2–9.

# Abortion and Economic Crisis: The 1931 Campaign Against Paragraph 218

## Atina Grossmann

*The persistent gap between constitutional promises of gender equality and family protection and the social reality of most women's lives was most clearly dramatized by the massive incidence of illegal abortions. Paragraph 218 of the Criminal Code, which punished abortion, an act many women considered necessary to their own and their families' survival, became the focus of intense political controversy throughout the Weimar period. In the piece that follows, Atina Grossmann shows how the campaign for the abolition of paragraph 218 became a central focus of the Sex Reform and Communist women's movements. The 1931 arrests of two physicians and Sex Reform activists on charges of having performed illegal abortions sparked a storm of protest from feminists, Communists, and Socialists. Under the leadership of the Communist Party, they organized an extraordinary coalition campaign for the legalization of abortion. A woman's right to control her own body was their key demand, and they justified the right to abortion in terms of social eugenic health and collective welfare. The struggle for legalization represented a conscious attempt by the left to use sexual politics as a lever to mobilize women across classes against the capitalist system. Its ultimate failure points to the problems of organizing a temporary alliance around a politics of reproduction that is motivated by divergent interests. Nevertheless, the resonance of this campaign revealed the centrality of these issues for any politics claiming to address women.*

You're going to be a lovely little mother
You're going to make a bunch of cannonfodder
That's what your belly's for
And that's no news to you

And now do not squall
You're having a baby, that's all.
>                                   —Bertolt Brecht[1]

Oh, I am a valuable thing,
Everybody cares about me:
The church, the state, doctors, judges—
For nine months,
But when those nine months are past . . .
Well, then I have to look out for myself.
>                                   —Kurt Tucholsky[2]

We want all children to be awaited with love,
they should be welcome guests at the table of life.
>                —Soviet People's Health Commissar Semaschko[3]

In 1931, Alice Lex-Nerlinger graphically represented a particular moment in the history of working-class struggle during the Weimar Republic.[4] Her "§218" is a product of, and tribute to, a mass campaign during the winter, spring, and summer of that crisis year when thousands of women demonstrated in the streets and gathered together in rallies and meeting halls to demand the right to abortion and birth control. They protested against unemployment, rising prices and taxes, a drastic housing shortage, and the Brüning regime's cutbacks in social services and women's rights. They demanded equal pay for equal work, social protection for mothers and children, and an immediate stop to the prosecution of two doctors, Else Kienle and Friedrich Wolf, who had been arrested in Stuttgart on February 19, 1931, on charges of having violated Paragraph 218, the law that made abortion a criminal act.

The image reflects, I think, an important and dual understanding of what women's power and liberation must mean. As a woman artist and left intellectual (today we might say "feminist"), Lex-Nerlinger spoke to women's need to control their own bodies, that is, to separate sexuality from procreation, to determine their own sexual satisfaction, and to decide when, if, and under what social and personal conditions they would bear children. As a socialist and member of the German Communist Party (KPD) since 1928, she saw the possibility for such control and self-determination only within the collective struggle of the working class for the overthrow of a capitalist social order tied to clerical reaction, militarism, and the subordination of women. In that sense, the poster expressed both the promise of the campaign that I will briefly describe here, its astonishing strength and resonance among masses of women, bourgeois as well as proletarian, Social Democratic, Communist, and politically unaffiliated; and also the limits and contradictions of a coalition movement around a women's issue organized within the context of larger overriding national and class concerns.

Lex-Nerlinger's women are active, strong, and united, pushing collectively with all their might against the §218 carved on an enormous cross, while the conventional icon of the long-suffering solitary woman, with kerchief and big belly, recedes pale and faceless into the background. The 1931 image stands in stark contrast to Käthe Kollwitz's poster, "Down with the Abortion Paragraph," produced in cooperation with the KPD in 1924—before the abortion issue had become the focus of mass agitation. While eloquently cutting through the pervasive bourgeois sentimentalization and glorification of the joys of motherhood and "the blessing of children" *(Kindersegen)*, the Kollwitz poster presents the classic figure of the "Woman in Need," *(Frau in Not)*, the proletarian woman in misery and despair clutching her hungry children to her pregnant belly. Dumb, passive, and helpless, she appears as the ultimate victim of the inhumanity and irrationality of capitalism. The young Hete, desperately seeking an abortion in the sensational anti-Paragraph 218 drama *Cyankali* (1929), by the Communist doctor and author Friedrich Wolf, speaks for her when she cries out: "We working women know much too little of those things that we should know about. Every day they hit us. And then no one will help us."[5]

Indeed, women's, particularly working-class women's, daily existence and ability to control their own lives was directly constrained by two sections of the German penal code. Paragraph 218, as amended and reformed by the Reichstag in 1926,[6] called for jail sentences for women who aborted their fetuses and for anyone aiding them. Those who performed abortions without the consent of the pregnant woman or for "commercial gain" faced indefinite penitentiary sentences. Only those terminations of pregnancy medically certified as strictly necessary were not considered abortions in the legal sense. Paragraph 184, Section 3, prohibited the advertising, publicizing, or display of contraceptive methods and devices because they were "objects intended for indecent use."[7]

Selectively and arbitrarily enforced, the paragraphs decreed what leftists and sexual reformers termed a *Gebärzwang*,[8] the tyranny of involuntary childbearing, for those women with neither the means to purchase expensive contraceptives nor the connections to doctors who might have encouraged their use. Masses of German women were therefore denied not only safe, legal abortions but also access to birth control information and technology. They were driven in ever increasing numbers, as many as 1 million a year[9] by 1931, to the dubious and often fatal[10] ministrations of "wise women" and back-alley abortionists, and to the blandishments of costly quack remedies, most of them ineffective and frequently harmful.

The victims of the paragraphs, the "Women in Need,"[11] as they were collectively labeled, became the objects of fierce debate as the political, legal, medical, and eugenic aspects of the abortion issue were discussed in the Reichstag, political parties, press, medical societies, and government ministries. Government authorities, population policy experts, and party politicians worried about the health, working ability, and regenerative capacities of the German *Volk*. They discussed possible incentives, such as parents' insurance *(Elternversicherung)*— which would be financed by a tax on the unmarried[12]—to restore the "joy of reproducing" *(Gebärfreudigkeit)* of the German wife and mother.[13]

The decline in the birth rate and "the suspiciously high rate of miscarriages, as reported by firms and insurance agencies,"[14] had been of consistent concern throughout the Weimar years, but public discussion and consciousness sharpened with the onset of economic crisis in late 1928 and 1929. The Reichstag Criminal Justice Committee began formulating a new criminal code in 1929, and Paragraph 218 quickly became a main point of contention. An expert Reichs Committee for Population Questions, convened in January 1930, was especially delegated to investigate and combat the "national scourge" *(Volksseuche)* of abortion.[15]

Women as a group remained marginal in the politics of the Weimar Republic, but the problem of women's reproductive work, dramatized by the abortion issue, came to occupy a critical place in the political discourse of depression Germany. For right and left both, the question was not women's reproductive freedom or individual right to determine their own lives, but rather the central function of their reproductive work as bearers and socializers of children and nurturers of the family unit. At stake was women's ideological role in legitimizing or threatening the social system and the moral and actual authority of the state and its laws, by their willingness and ability to reproduce the next generation, as well as their material function in preserving and reproducing the family—a position that becomes particularly critical in a time of political instability and economic crisis.

For the women themselves, however, the issue was posed as a question of survival and crisis management. The need to limit births became particularly urgent in the German Depression from 1929 to 1933. Women were expected to cope with and soothe the stresses and strains of shortages and unemployment, up to over 5 million by 1931, at the same time that they themselves were particularly hard hit by unemployment in traditionally female branches such as domestic service or the textile industry. Women were more likely to be cut off from unemployment insurance, received lower compensation due to an original wage differential, and in any case were more likely to be found as wage laborers in uninsured home industry or temporary jobs.[16]

The burden of reproductive work—childbearing, child raising, and housework—was exacerbated in the broad sense of physical and emotional labor required to manage an ever more precarious family existence. Women were forced, in a very material sense, to step in for the state in the social welfare sector so heavily cut back by the emergency decrees of Brüning's Catholic Center government. The crisis precipitated a general reprivatization of socialized reproduction such as maternal and infant care, medical care, canteen lunches or school lunch programs, which had previously been at least partially undertaken by the state or employer. Housework tasks such as the acquisition and preparation of foodstuffs, drugs, or articles of clothing which had previously been purchased ready-made, were now relocated into the private home. Under the force of unemployment and social service cutbacks, such reproductive work reverted to the responsibility of the individual woman in the private household.

In this sense one can perhaps speak of a reserve of reproductive labor that is forcibly activated during an economic crisis. Unlike workers in the production process, women in the household cannot go on strike or otherwise sabotage an intensification of the work required for their own and their families' survival. The state, drastically cutting back its own share of responsibility for reproduction, relied on the fact that women would indeed do at least the minimum amount of work necessary for family subsistence and reproduction.[17]

For many women, however, most of them proletarian, married, and already the mothers of several children,[18] the burdens and conflicts of their dual role in production and reproduction[19] became insupportable. Women sought to limit their offspring by all possible means, on pain of death, disease, and jail sentence, and not infrequently also by infanticide and suicide.[20] It was estimated that on the average, every German woman underwent an abortion at least twice in her lifetime; probably the figures for the working-class woman were considerably higher.[21] Else Kienle, writing from jail, described the women on whom she had performed abortions: "[Despite] the natural desire to carry her child and bring it into the world . . . she must recognize that she does not have the material basis for the care of a child."[22] One can think of abortion under these circumstances as a tactic in a reproductive strategy that will ensure the survival of the woman herself, as well as the family within which most women defined their identity and organized their subsistence.[23]

On a public political level, the mass violations of the abortion paragraph became the symbols of the bankruptcy of Weimar democracy and its promise of civil equality for the sexes and social justice and protection for the family.[24] The left, represented by the KPD and numerous progressive sexual reform groups, took as its slogan George Bernard Shaw's wry observation that a land that cannot feed its children does not have the right to demand children. Bolshevik Russia was constantly cited as a society in which, despite the legalization of controlled medical abortions, a comprehensive program of protection for mothers, working women, and children assured that population figures continually rose. The achievements of socialism in female emancipation, social welfare, and the encouragement of motherhood were contrasted not only to a "sterile" Germany but also to Mussolini's fascist Italy, where attempts to remove women from the workforce and return them to their "natural" roles as wives and mothers had produced only a minimal upturn in the low birthrate.[25]

Indeed the economic crisis not only produced an increased concern with population policy on the part of the state but also intensified intervention and activity by independent left and Communist sexual reform groups, which had always included the demand for the abolition of Paragraphs 218 and 184 in their programs. The first Reichs Congress on Population Policy was organized by the KPD-oriented Working Group of Social Political Organizations (ARSO) in February 1929.[26] The first Doctors' Course in Birth Control (and abortion techniques) was conducted in December 1928, by Helene Stöcker's[27] Committee for Birth Control with the active aid of doctors from the KPD and the Berlin Health Insurance League (Verband der Berliner Krankenkassen). Within one year, by the end of 1929, the Health Insurance League had established six Birth Control Counseling Centers in Berlin.[28] The first Reichs Congress of Working Women, in October 1929, raised the abolition of Paragraph 218 as a central demand of the Reichs Committee of Working Women. This committee came out of a Communist women's delegate and conference movement first organized in 1926 under the leadership of KPD Reichstag deputy Helene Overlach, with the express purpose of winning Social Democratic or unaffiliated—"indifferent" as they were called—women workers and workers' wives for the party, or at least one of its mass proletarian welfare or antirepression organizations such as the International Workers Aid (IAH), the Red Aid (Rote Hilfe) or later the Anti-Fascist League (Anti-Fa).

On New Year's Eve, 1930, Pope Pius XII issued an encyclical on Christian marriage that denounced sex without intent to procreate, urged the state to act on its responsibility to protect the weak and unborn, imposed an absolute prohibition on contraception and abortion, insisted on women's subordinate position within the family, and warned against the false freedom that was female emancipation. The Communist Party, consistent with its general response to increasing cultural reaction and political repression, interpreted the papal letter as a sign of the increasing fascisization of the bourgeoisie. The encyclical was seen as an attempt to force the production of "cannon fodder" for imperialist war against the Soviet Union as well as a reaction to growing contradictions within capitalism and increasing militancy among the working class, particularly women's recent active participation in strikes in the predominantly Catholic Ruhr and Upper Silesian districts.

The KPD, and especially the Communist women's movement, also saw the papal action as an effort to legitimize the Brüning regime's policies of reducing social services while attacking women's, particularly married women's *(Doppelverdiener)*, right to work and to social insurance. The response to this appeal to women's responsibility for home and reproduction was clearly articulated in Communist women's journals and conferences: "We women refuse to let ourselves be regarded as baby machines and then additionally to serve as slaves in the production process. . . . Our slogan is not 'back into the family,' but equal wages for equal work."[29]

The beginnings of what would become a broad coalition against Paragraph 218 and the prosecution of Drs. Wolf and Kienle were launched on January 28, 1931, when the Reichs Committee of Working Women met with representatives of the Sexual Reform organization, the Federation for the Protection of Mothers (Bund für Mutterschutz), led by Helene Stöcker, and the independent feminist Women's International League for Peace and Freedom[30] to plan a campaign against the encyclical and the assault on women's rights it represented. The coalition of Communist women's movement, Sex Reform, and independent feminist and pacifist groups produced an expanding movement that quickly attracted a great deal of publicity.

In a period in which the leaderships of the Social Democratic and Communist parties were attacking each other as the primary enemy, and the fabric of what remained of Weimar democracy was unraveling daily, the demand for reform of the abortion law united—in a unique and extraordinary fashion—liberal and radical lawyers, doctors and other intellectuals, Social Democrats, Communists, and thousands of women of all classes and many parties. Indeed, the campaign did not really take off until an alliance was forged between the KPD, the Communist women's movement, and parts of the feminist and autonomous Sex Reform movements. The alternative service network of birth control and sex counseling centers run by Communist- or socialist-affiliated sex-political organizations, such as the Reichs League for Birth Control and Sexual Hygiene established in 1928,[31] sponsored meetings and rallies where women were introduced to birth control methods and information with the admonition, "Better to prevent than to abort." Simultaneously, they were encouraged to join the fight against Paragraph 218 and for legal medical abortions.

On February 19, 1931, Dr. Else Kienle, director of a Reichs League counseling center, and Dr. Friedrich Wolf, physician, member of the Communist Party and author of the play *Cyankali*, which had been playing to full houses throughout the country, were arrested in Stuttgart. They were charged with seeking commercial gain by having performed abortions on more than one hundred women and providing the necessary medical certificates. Those were the heaviest charges possible under the provisions of Paragraph 218, and the enormous volume of police and government ministry documentation on the early activity of the abortion campaign supports the Communist contention that the arrests were a direct response from a state that felt itself threatened by such a mobilization of women during a crisis.

However, rather than breaking the momentum of the campaign and narrowing the issue to its legal and medical aspects, the arrests served to unleash a storm of protest. The "people's uprising *(Volkssturm)* against Paragraph 218," as Dr. Wolf put it, shifted the focus of attention from the Reichstag and courtroom to the public arena, dramatized the social and political implications of the issue, and turned the prosecutors into the publicly accused. Wolf's concluding call in *Cyankali*, "A law that turns 800,000 mothers into criminals every year is no longer a law,"[32] became the battle cry of a growing movement.

Within a few days, the women's coalition that formed against the encyclical grew to include a host of liberal, socialist, and communist groups—from the League for Human Rights to the Association of Socialist Physicians[33] to a celebrities committee including Albert Einstein, which called on women "in secure stations in life" and their doctors to speak out about their own experiences with abortion.[34] Doctors, lawyers, and journalists gathered in closed meetings to declare their common conviction that the paragraph no longer reflected popular opinion and should at the very least be reformed to allow a mixed socioeconomic and medical indication for an approved abortion.[35] Newspapers announced open readers' forums and sponsored rallies.[36] When the *Berliner Volkszeitung* polled its readers about keeping, abolishing, or reforming the law, 45,000 responses, most of them from working-class women, poured in within a few days. Only 150 favored keeping Paragraph 218.[37] The liberal bourgeois *Vossische Zeitung* reported that the arrests had pushed the abortion struggle to an "acute, virtually sensational stage."[38]

The massive mobilization of press, intelligentsia, and culture was a major component of the campaign. Performances of *Cyankali* were transformed into spontaneous demonstrations. The Piscator Collective went on nationwide tour with the play *Frauen in Not*, adapted from the Social Democrat Dr. Carl Credé's book, *Gequälte Menschen: §218 (Tormented People).*[39] Erich Weinert, Kurt Tucholsky, and Bertolt Brecht published poems.[40] Franz Krey's Red-One-Mark-Novel *Maria and the Paragraph,*[41] in which a young stenotypist survives a botched abortion (unlike the hapless Hete in *Cyankali*) and goes on to join the movement, was serialized to great success in Willy Münzenberg's *Arbeiter Illustrierte Zeitung*. Films such as *Kuhle Wampe*, shot in the summer of 1931, and workers' literature from the League of Proletarian-Revolutionary Writers[42] took up the theme of abortion as a metaphor for general class and sex oppression.

On International Women's Day, March 8, 1931, there were over 1,500 rallies and demonstrations throughout Germany; 3,000 women defied a ban on outdoor demonstrations and marched through the streets of Berlin shouting, "Down with the Brüning Dictatorship, Down with Paragraph 218, We Want Bread and Peace!"[43] Women took the floor at numerous regional congresses of the Delegate and Conference Movement to "speak bitterness" about too many and neglected children, and the horrors of illegal abortions.

The high point of popular agitation came on April 15 when over 15,000 people gathered in the Berlin sports stadium for a mass protest rally. The police report described a packed hall, walls and galleries draped with posters and banners, and it noted with particular consternation that "among the female guests, there were numerous well dressed and even elegantly dressed women and girls."[44] Drs. Wolf and Kienle reiterated their positions:

> We are opponents of abortion and supporters of birth control. We consider it irresponsible to bring yet more victims of hunger into a Germany of hunger, of housing shortages, and of chronic misery. . . . We know that our women and girls will once again joyfully give the gift of life to children, even in Germany . . . but in a free socialist Germany.[45]

For the Communist left and its women's movement, abortion was clearly a class issue. The restrictions on abortion were seen not so much as an encroachment on women's individual right to control their own bodies, but rather a particularly brutal and immediately personal form of sex-specific class oppression. A bourgeois woman could afford a discreet journey abroad, preferably to a Swiss clinic,[46] or a doctor's fee for the issuing of a medical certificate. She could afford to purchase the contraceptives that might make abortion unnecessary—after all, condoms, diaphragms, dutch caps, all manner of foam contraceptives, even IUDs were available.

And yet, the presence of so many "elegantly dressed" women at a KPD-sponsored protest meeting speaks to the fact that the paragraph was an example not only of class injustice but also of patriarchal oppression. Else Kienle was an uncomfortable ally and heroine for the KPD because she tended to emphasize that side of the question. Unknown and not a member of the Communist Party, Dr. Kienle remained in jail after public pressure had led to Wolf's speedy release on bail. She gained popular support and a place in the hearts of the Communist women's movement only after more than a month of incarceration, when she engaged in a bitter hunger strike that brought her near death and won her release. In her impassioned prison journal, she reflected, "As a woman, I stand against the man; as a woman I must defend women's cause against the law, against the court of men,"[47] and asked herself, "Of what use is suffrage to woman if she is still to remain a helpless baby machine?"[48]

Kienle identified with the peculiar form of feminism, so common to sexual reform and birth control activists, that celebrated women's unique and fundamentally different sensibility *(Sonderbarkeit)*. While assuming that female nature and sexuality could be truly fulfilled only in motherhood, it nevertheless insisted on women's right to sexual pleasure and control of their bodies.[49] Thea von Harbou, independent woman, screenwriter, and politically unaffiliated, articulated the feminist content of the campaign at a Mother's Day rally sponsored by non-Communist groups:

> Our main goal is to find a new form of preventing pregnancy and therefore to make the entire §218 unnecessary. Immediately, however, the Paragraph must fall because it is no longer morally recognized by women. It is no longer a law. We need a new sexual code because the old was created by men and no man is in a position to understand the agony of a woman who is carrying a child that she knows she cannot feed. This law derived from male psychology, which forces a woman into having a child, creates, even if not deliberately, constitutional inferiority of women in relation to men which serves as a bulwark against women's activity in economic and public life.[50]

The mainstream of bourgeois feminism, on the other hand, as represented by the Federation of German Women's Associations (Bund Deutscher Frauenvereine) and its journal *Die Frau (The Woman,)* held itself studiously aloof from the abortion controversy. In line with a general refusal to handle issues either in terms of class or sexuality, it maintained that such a question could be resolved only within the context of a women's and population politics that encouraged the health and preservation of the family.[51] Indeed, *Die Schaffende Frau,* (The Active Woman), a journal directed at the "new" professional woman, angrily accused the traditional bourgeois women's movement of a tendency to treat violators of the paragraph as victims of their own overdeveloped lustful desires.[52]

Abortion was then, as it is now, a complicated issue and within the broadly based coalition against Paragraph 218 there was a multitude of varied positions. At the height of the campaign, Berlin women doctors[53] called for striking the antiabortion law and for improved protection of mothers and children for two reasons: because coerced legislated motherhood was inconsistent with the "dignity of human rights and position of women within the state"; and in order to assure a "high quality offspring and the preservation and encouragement of the ethical power of the family to preserve the state."[54] They thus combined a feminist commitment to women's public equality with a faith in the dominant motherhood-eugenics consensus; abortion rights were defended as eugenic and family-stabilizing measures.

Abortion is after all, as we have learned in our own struggle for abortion rights and against sterilization abuse, not only a question of class discrimination and women's right to choose, but also one of population policy.[55] Certainly, the eugenic component was an important factor in the abortion, birth control, and Sex Reform movements. That it was the social responsibility of the unfit, including the syphilitic, alcoholic, tubercular—that is, a not insubstantial part of the impoverished proletariat—and the feebleminded not to reproduce themselves was the common conviction of many social reformers. Many people who defined themselves as progressives or socialists thought that the decision about an abortion was much too important to be left to the personal whims and perceived needs of an individual woman, and should be decided by expert professionals who could weigh the individual situation against the demands of the general welfare. For the women doctors, as for all the diverse groups and individuals involved and mobilized in the 1931 abortion campaign, the issue was complex and multifaceted: it involved questions of equal rights and civil liberties as well as social health and collective welfare; class justice for the proletariat as well as generalized concerns about the health of women and families across class lines; the professional prerogatives of doctors as well as medical and eugenic judgments. For many women—not least of all, the defendant Else Kienle—women's right to control their own bodies and resist patriarchal authority was also at issue.

One must differentiate very carefully when discussing the emancipatory content of this abortion campaign. The crucial questions relate to power, control, and access. Who has the right to decide whether an abortion should be performed, under what conditions and for what reasons; the woman herself, the doctor, the state and its intermediaries, committees of experts, or counseling centers?[56] Who is responsible for funding and with what provisions?

The KPD therefore presented a clearly emancipatory alternative when it categorically demanded the abolition of Paragraph 218 and all legislation regulating personal sexual behavior, and called for public sex education and counseling coupled with health insurance and municipal welfare financing of medically sound abortions and safe, effective contraception. With its analysis of women's dual oppression in production and reproduction (in turn divided into the "triple burden" of childbearing, childrearing, and housework), the party recognized that a woman's ability to control her own body was at least as much a prerequisite for her active participation in the class struggle as her integration into the social process of production.

Certainly, Communist population and sexual policies were limited and ambivalent. The KPD consistently supported complete de-criminalization at the same time that abortion restrictions were being reintroduced in the Soviet Union, a fact that was not lost on the opponents of abortion. The KPD also believed in the magic of motherhood and the tragedy of its denial, and it shared demands for improved protection and benefits for mothers, children, and the family with many other groups: conservative, Social Democratic, sexual reform, and feminist. Communists, however, assumed that in a socialist society on the model of Soviet Russia, not only adequate welfare but also the socialization of housework would create the preconditions for joyous and carefree childbearing, rendering abortion unnecessary.[57] The triple reproductive burden was to be lightened by a technological solution to the "petty slavery of housework" in the form of communal kitchens or laundries, but women remained responsible for childbearing and childrearing. The KPD's primary target was not the family or the sexual division of labor within the family, but the hypocrisy of bourgeois morality and social and economic conditions that threatened the well-being of the proletarian family.

Nevertheless, by raising the slogan "Your Body Belongs to You" (*Dein Körper Gehört Dir*)[58]—not usually found in the standard political, medical, or eugenic arguments for abortion—and by waging a lonely battle in the Reichstag for complete decriminalization of abortion and against the dismissal of married women employees, the KPD implicitly and rather nervously defended the individual woman's right to choose, even that of the non-working-class woman who might choose abortion for personal reasons not directly connected to dire material need. For many social reformers within the Communist left, it was the party's consistent and active position on the abortion issue that "gave us the feeling that we were on the right side."[59] The Communist left at least partially broke through the motherhood and eugenic consensus that extended into the ranks of left, feminist, and Sex Reform movements.[60]

The Communist Party understood that the abortion issue was absolutely critical to the lives of working-class women and indeed to the family as a whole, and was therefore an excellent tactical organizing tool. The creation of a highly visible coalition against Paragraph 218 and for the defense of Wolf and Kienle was consistent with the current Party line of "Go to the People" (*Heran an die Massen*), first articulated by Ernst Thälmann at the 1925 Party Congress in Frankfurt, which purged the "ultra-left" leadership of Ruth Fischer and Arkadi Maslow. The abortion struggle also offered a rare opportunity to practice effectively the "united front from below" tactic of the Sixth Congress of the Comintern, which had declared Social Democracy "social-fascist" but had also urged alliances with the working-class base of the SPD.

The campaign also came during a period when KPD organizations were attempting to unify the mushrooming autonomous Sex Reform and birth control groups under class-conscious Communist leadership.[61] In that sense, the politics of reproduction was never—the eternal dilemma of those of us who would unite Marxism and feminism—adequately integrated into Communist ideology. Rather, it was defined by the organizational needs of the party as a whole. Sexual politics was seen as a vehicle for attracting unaffiliated or SPD women, whose votes the party desperately needed,[62] or at the very least as a means of neutralizing women's antipathy to Bolshevism.[63] It was also a particularly pointed means of exposing the timid vacillatory politics of the SPD, which insisted on maintaining an abortion law on the books (if only as a protection for women against men who might try to escape their responsibilities by pressuring women into abortions), while allowing for all kinds of exceptions and extenuating circumstances.

The Bolshevization of the party ordered in 1925 had meant a switch from the traditional SPD-influenced community-based organization to a focus on the workplace. The abortion campaign represented an important exception to the Central Committee's policy of appealing to women as workers in the production sector. As a mass coalition action, the Wolf/Kienle Paragraph 218 struggle was considered part of Willy Münzenberg's "Alliance Politics" *(Bündnispolitik)* of linking up with special interest groups such as intellectuals, youth, or women, who were seen as both theoretically and organizationally marginal.[64] While causing uneasiness among orthodox cadres about possible dilution of the class issue, this focus on a mass protest coalition meant that the 1931 campaign appealed to women of all classes—not only as exploited workers but as women oppressed by their sex, not only in terms of their relation to production but in terms of their role in reproduction.

The abortion issue also offered female leadership an opportunity to gain importance and visibility outside the confines of the Delegate and Conference Movement. Helene Overlach, herself five months pregnant at the time, recalled that she fought for the right to be the party's main speaker at the huge April 15 rally. "This is after all a woman's question; I can do this better than a male comrade," she insisted, and won her point.[65]

The stress on the politics of reproduction, no matter how circumscribed or ambivalent, no matter how opportunistic at times, was, at least for the course of the campaign, central to KPD strategy and to the party's conception of the role of the working class within the state. It pointed to the possibility of mending the deadly split in socialist and communist women's politics, which always tried either to subsume the entire question of women's emancipation into her integration into productive wage labor or to ghettoize women's issues within a purely "mothers and children" realm. Precisely this strength, this moment of potential for a powerful mass women's movement, posed a fundamental and ultimately insoluble problem for the KPD. The party was constantly at pains to define the struggle around Paragraph 218 and around the entire matter of sexual reform and female liberation as a partial struggle, and it continually warned against the dangers of a separate women's movement. And yet, it had set into motion masses of women with no real means of organizing them and no structures into which they could be absorbed. The move into the cadre of the party where reproductive issues were once again subordinated was simply too long a leap.[66] The Delegate and Conference Movement, which might have provided a political home for women politicized in the abortion struggle, was slowly crumbling, partly because of lack of support from the party and also because its leader, Helene Overlach, who was ill after the birth of her child, could no longer assume as much work and responsibility.[67] The KPD feared precisely what it had helped to bring into existence—a strong and potentially autonomous women's movement.

The KPD's attempt, under the auspices of the International Workers Aid and the Working Group of Social Political Organizations, to build a proletarian movement for sexual reform also failed when the numerous lay organizations resisted "politicization" on Communist terms. A unity congress in June of 1931 fell apart with the KPD representatives crying "SPD betrayal" and accusing the other groups of being nothing more than fronts for birth control manufacturers and indiscriminate dispensers of contraceptives.[68] The KPD was in no position to continue the campaign. It was increasingly on the defensive, more and more divided between a rigid cadre politics and a mass propaganda directed by Münzenberg. Increasingly a party of the unemployed, it was reduced to helplessly protesting the dismantling of the Weimar Republic and its Social Democratic reforms; furthermore it lacked strong independent female leadership and a theory of reproduction. The party dropped its coalition policy and formed its own Unity Committee for Proletarian Sexual Reform,[69] isolating itself from the mass base of the birth control and abortion movement.

It was a familiar story in the final years of the Weimar Republic, and in that sense the campaign fell victim to the ever increasing polarization between the SPD and the KPD. Indeed, this was probably the last time that Communists and Social Democrats agitated together on the

# 80   When Biology Became Destiny

same platform. By June of 1931, the police noted with relief, there was a marked reduction in activity around Paragraph 218.[70]

The course and failure of the abortion struggle[71] must, I think, be analyzed on two distinct yet connected levels. Inasmuch as it was part of the general working-class movement, it shared its fate and was destroyed by the combined pressures of economic collapse, increasing political repression[72] and National Socialist strength,[73] and the disunity of the left. Inasmuch as it was a coalition of disparate groups converging around a particular women's issue, which had spoken to women's needs but not let them define its terms, the campaign could never articulate a clear strategy or provide a unified organization for a mass women's movement. The experience of the German struggle for birth control and abortion rights must, I think, point us toward the necessity and possibility of an autonomous, class-conscious women's movement.[74]

## Notes

This article is reprinted in a slightly revised version by permission of *New German Critique*, where it first appeared in Spring 1978. It originated as a paper at the 1977 American Historical Association Convention in Dallas, Texas, and owes much to the suggestions, criticism, and support of Renate Bridenthal, Marion Kaplan, Molly Nolan, and Harold Poor.

1. Bertolt Brecht, "Herr Doktor," in *Gesammelte Werke* 8 (Frankfurt/M., 1967), p. 382.
2. Kurt Tucholsky, "Die Leibesfrucht spricht," in *Gesammelte Werke*, vol. 3 (Hamburg, 1960), p. 983, translated as "The Embryo Speaks" by Harold Poor.
3. Quoted virtually in all KPD material on population policy.
4. Alice Lex-Nerlinger, 1893–1975, constructivist artist, joined the KPD and the Association of Revolutionary Artists in 1928. Her *Spritztechnik* work "§218" was confiscated by police at a Berlin art exhibit in 1931. It is now stored in the Märkisches Museum, Berlin, GDR.
5. Friedrich Wolf, *Cyankali*, in *Gesammelte Werke* 2 (Berlin, 1960): 134.
6. The 1926 text was only mildly changed from the Paragraphs 218 to 220 of the 1871 Criminal Code. The reformed single Paragraph 218 lessened the possible punishment for the aborting mother from penitentiary to jail and allowed the judge more latitude with the sentences.
7. One possible loophole was the 1927 Law to Combat Venereal Diseases (*Gesetz zur Bekämpfung der Geschlechtskrankheiten*), which encouraged the use of methods suitable for preventing venereal disease. However, the government consistently tried to prevent advertising of any methods or devices not directly and primarily intended to combat VD.
8. See, for example, Emil Höllein *Gegen den Gebärzwang: Der Kampf um die bewusste Kleinhaltung der Familie* (Berlin, 1927).
9. Observers on all sides agreed that illegal abortions had reached the proportions of a national scourge (*Volksseuche*), but statistics were hotly disputed. Whereas Wolf in 1929 still used the figure of 800,000 annual abortions, a year later the general consensus was that approximately 1 million (out of a total female population of 31.2 million) German women underwent abortions annually (*Frauenwelt*, Heft 9, May 3, 1930, p. 201). Official statistics were in any case notoriously inaccurate. When the

Ministry of Health *(Reichsgesundheitsamt)* sent out a questionnaire to hospitals on number and nature of interruptions of pregnancy performed or treated, the Berlin Charité reported that 91.2% of its cases resulted from criminal abortions, while a hospital in Catholic Münster insisted that 100% of the interrupted pregnancy cases treated were spontaneous miscarriages! *(Reichsgesundheitsblatt,* Heft 50, 1930, p. 925). Of course, hospital statistics, even under the best of circumstances, could only encompass that minority of cases that actually ended up in a hospital. An important source for abortion estimates was the so-called Grotjahn *Kartothek,* the 1927 medical records of a doctor in a rural town of 25,000. The doctor performed as many as seven procedures a day *(Die Frau,* Jg. 30, Heft 1, Oct. 1931, pp. 56–57). See Alfred Grotjahn, *Eine Kartothek zu Par. 218,* (Berlin, 1932).

10. Fatality and complication statistics were also the objects of bitter debate. Dr. Wilhelm Liepmann, a noted gynecologist and opponent of abortion, claimed as many as 40,000 deaths a year. The Social Democrat Dr. Julius Moses and the *Reichsgesundheitsamt* insisted that there were no more than 4,000 annual deaths *(Zeitschrift für Sexualwissenschaft,* 16, October 10, 1929, No. 5). KPD estimates ranged from 10,000 to 40,000 deaths, usually 10,000 to 12,000 annual fatalities with 50,000 cases of complications.

11. The Münzenberg women's journal *Weg der Frau* sponsored a huge art exhibition in Berlin in October 1931 called *"Frauen in Not"* at which numerous artworks attacking the Paragraph were exhibited and which was intended to draw attention to the "Fate of Woman as Mother, Worker, Unemployed Worker and Victim of outdated morality" *(Weg der Frau,* No. 4, September 1931, p. 7).

12. It is interesting to note that the model for such measures was Mussolini's fascist Italy, and that many of the material incentives for marriage and childbearing considered during the Weimar years were later put into effect by the National Socialist regime. See Gisela Bock's article in this volume.

13. The Prussian Ministry of Social Welfare issued a memorandum in October 1928, "The Birth Decline in Germany, Its Consequences and How to Combat It," in which it was recognized that "family limitation is often nothing more than dire necessity. . . the longing for children is still deeply rooted in men and women, even today; it is only repressed by circumstance" (Bundesarchiv Koblenz, hereafter BA, *Reichsgesundheitsamt* files, hereafter R86, File 2369/2).

14. Renate Bridenthal and Claudia Koonz, "Beyond *Kinder, Küche, Kirche:* Weimar Women in Politics and Work" reprinted in this volume.

15. BA R86/2369(2).

16. For detailed, easily accessible data on women's position in regard to unemployment and unemployment insurance, see the monthly reports *(Arbeitsmarktlage und Unterstützungsempfänger)* in *Proletarische Sozialpolitik* starting with Jg.1, Heft 4 (September 1928) and continuing through the final issue, Jg. 6, Heft 1/2 (Jan./Feb.1933). See also the excellent analysis by Marguerite Thibert, "Economic Depression and the Employment of Women," *International Labour Review* 27, No. 4 (April 1933): 443–70 and No. 5 (May 1933): 620–30. For a general discussion of women's economic position in the crisis, see Bridenthal and Koonz in this volume, and Bridenthal, "Beyond *Kinder, Küche, Kirche:* Weimar Women at Work," *Central European History* 6 (1973): 148–66; and Tim Mason, "Women in Germany, 1925–1940: Family Welfare and Work," *History Workshop* 1 (1976): 74–113 and 2 (1976): 5–32.

17. For provocative discussions of the material role of housework and reproduction, see Gisela Bock and Barbara Duden, "Arbeit aus Liebe—Liebe als Arbeit: Zur Entstehung der Hausarbeit im Kapitalismus," pp. 118–199; and Annemarie Tröger, "Die Dolchstosslegende der Linken: Haben Frauen Hitler an die Macht gebracht?" pp. 324–355, both articles in *Frauen und Wissenschaft: Beiträge zur Berliner Sommeruniversität für Frauen,* (Berlin, 1977).

18. The Grotjahn *Kartothek* noted that of 426 aborted women, only 74 were unmarried.

Sixty-eight were domestic servants, but there were also two police employees, the wife of a Reichswehr officer, and numerous wives of academics (*Die Frau*, Jg. 39, Heft 1, October 1931, pp. 56–57). Else Kienle said of her patients: "There was an enormous number of women with several children; there was hardly one who came with a first pregnancy" (*Weg der Frau*, Jg. 1, No. 1, June 1931, p. 2).

19. For a theoretical discussion of the dual role, see Renate Bridenthal, "The Dialectics of Production and Reproduction in History," *Radical America* 10, No. 2 (March–April 1976): 3–11.

20. The pages of the SPD *Frauenwelt*, the KPD-oriented *Weg der Frau*, and the KPD *Die Kämpferin* are filled with reports of suicides and women who try to gas or drown their children. Indeed suicide, often taking children along (for example in Piel Jutzi's 1929 film *Mutter Krausens Fahrt ins Glück*), was as much of a cultural motif in the presentation of the proletarian woman as was abortion, and the two were frequently connected. Dr. Roesle of the *Reichsgesundheitsamt* reported in the *Medizinische Wochenschrift*, No. 25 (June 21, 1929): "Germany has the highest female suicide rate in all Europe and probably the entire world" (cited in *Proletarische Sozialpolitik*, Jg. 2, H. 10, October 1929).

21. *Frauenwelt*, Heft 9 (May 3, 1930): 201.

22. Dr. Else Kienle, *Frauen: Aus dem Tagebuch einer Ärztin* (Berlin, 1932) p. 140.

23. See Tröger "Die Dolchstosslegende der Linken," for discussion of women's relationship to a familial "subeconomy" during times of economic crisis. For general discussion of reproductive strategies in the family economy, see Louise Tilly and Joan Scott, *Women, Work and Family* (New York: Holt, Rinehart and Winston, 1978).

24. Paragraph 109 of the Weimar Constitution guaranteed basically equal rights and responsibilities for male and female citizens. Article 119 assured the state's responsibility for the health, social protection, and encouragement of the family, and promised special equalizing benefits for large (*kinderreiche*) families.

25. The attack on and exposure of fascist population policy is especially well documented in *Referenten Material für die Volksaktion gegen §218 und Verteidigung Friedrich Wolfs* (Kampfausschuss, 1931).

26. *Proletarische Sozialpolitik* Jg.2, Heft 1 (January 1929), p. 29, and BA R86 2369/(1). The ARSO (Arbeitsgemeinschaft sozialpolitscher Organisationen) was established in April 1928 under the leadership of KPD Reichstag deputy Siegfried Rädel, and encompassed numerous groups such as the International Workers Aid (Internationale Arbeiterhilfe), Red Aid for political prisoners (Rote Hilfe), Red Girls and Women's Federation (Rote Frauen und Mädchen Bund), and the International Federation for the Victims of Work and War (Internationale Bund für die Opfer der Arbeit und des Krieges). *Proletarische Sozialpolitik* was the ARSO journal.

27. On Helene Stöcker, see Amy Hackett's article in this volume.

28. The counseling center activity of the left-oriented Berlin Health Insurance League was particularly important since most of the municipal counseling centers in Berlin did not offer adequate birth control services. Dr. Kurt Bendix, director of the League's counseling services, reported that 80.3% of the clients sought birth control advice, 4.4% sex counseling and only 2.5% were interested in the eugenically oriented marriage counseling offered by most government centers (Kurt Bendix, Report at the World League for Sexual Reform Congress, London, September 1929, reprinted in *Die Neue Generation* 10 [October 1929]: 282–86).

29. Second *Reichs* Women's Conference of the IAH in Halle, March 14–15, 1931. Resolution reported in BA, *Reichssicherheitshauptamt* files, hereafter R58 (BA R58/684).

30. See Lida Gustava Heymann and Anita Augspurg, *Erlebtes-Erschautes: Deutsche Frauen kämpfen für Freiheit, Recht und Frieden, 1850–1940* (Meisenheim am Glan, 1977) for an account of the activity of the Women's International League for Peace and Freedom. Both the Federation for the Protection of Mothers and the League for

Peace and Freedom had separated from the mainstream of the German middle-class women's movement because of their more radical positions on pacifism and sexual morality, including their stand against Paragraph 218. See Hackett and Koonz in this volume.

31. Numerous Sex Reform groups, encompassing a total membership of about 150,000, were attempting to unite during the period 1930 to 1931. For information on the Sex Reform organizations, see my article " 'Satisfaction is Domestic Happiness': Mass Working-Class Sex Reform Organizations in the Weimar Republic," in Michael N. Dobkowski and Isidor Wallimann, eds., *Towards the Holocaust: The Social and Economic Collapse of the Weimar Republic* (Westport, Conn., 1983): 265–93.

32. Wolf, *Cyankali*, p. 342. On the campaign, see also Hans Jürgen Arendt, "Eine demokratische Massenbewegung unter der Führung der KPD im Frühjahr 1931. Die Volksaktion gegen den Paragraphen 218 und gegen die päpstliche Enzyklika 'Casti Connubi'." *Zeitschrift für Geschichtswissenschaft* 19, no. 1 (1971): 213–23.

33. The Association of Socialist Physicians and the League for Human Rights, for example, cosponsored a meeting of over 2500, many of whom, it was expressly noted, were women (*Der Sozialistische Arzt*, 7, No. 3 (March 1931) :67–69).

34. The Committee for Self-Accusation Regarding §218 was led by Dr. Heinrich Dehmel and also included Ernst Toller, the screenwriter Thea von Harbou, and Margarete Kaiser, editor of *Die Schaffende Frau*. The call for self-denunciation was an old demand of the anarcho-syndicalist movement, which rejected the Communist and sexual reform organization tactics of parliamentary and electoral action. See Gerlind Lachenicht, "*Die Ideen der libertären Bewegung zur Veränderung im Bereich der individuellen Reproduktion, dargestellt am Beispiel des Frauenbundes in der Freien Arbeiter Union Deutschlands* (FAUD)" (unpublished Diplomarbeit, Free University of Berlin, 1978).

35. The International Jurists' Union (Internationale Juristische Vereinigung) and Helene Stöcker's Committee for Birth Control sponsored a joint meeting in the Prussian *Herrenhaus* for doctors, jurists, and journalists only, at which Friedrich Wolf, the Social Democrat Dr. Carl Credé, Dr. Roesle from the Ministry of Health, Kienle lawyer Alfred Apfel, and a politically wide spectrum of other noted doctors and lawyers appeared together on the same platform (BA R58/548/8, p. 134).

36. The Münzenberg *Welt am Abend* started an "Open Protest against Paragraph 218" on February 28, 1931 and sponsored numerous protest meetings (BA R58/548/8, p. 129). The *Berliner Volkszeitung* started its readers' forum on March 1, 1931, and also sponsored a mass "nonparty political" meeting on Mother's Day, May 10, 1931, at the Admiralspalast in Berlin (BA R58/548/8, p. 140).

37. *Die Neue Generation* 27, Heft 7/8/9 (July/August/September, 1931): 165–66.

38. *Vossische Zeitung* March 8, 1931, p. 2.

39. Carl Credé, *Gequälter Menschen, §218* (Berlin, 1930). Credé himself served time in jail for having performed illegal abortions. The third anti-Paragraph 218 play was Hans José Rehfisch's *Der Frauenarzt* (Berlin, 1928/29). The three authors reflected the different political tendencies that coalesced around the abortion issue: Wolf, a Communist; Credé, a eugenically oriented Social Democrat; and Rehfisch, a liberal bourgeois lawyer.

40. Weinert's poem was first written in 1929, Brecht's "Herr Doktor" in 1931, and Kurt Tucholsky's "Die Leibesfrucht spricht" in 1931. An earlier version of Tucholsky's under the pseudonym Theobald Tiger was published in *Die Kämpferin*, Jg. 1929, No. 2.

41. First published as Band 5, Rote Eine Mark Reihe, in 1931 with a foreword by Friedrich Wolf and immediately serialized in the *AIZ*; reprint Berlin, 1972.

42. For example, Rudolf Braune, *Das Mädchen an der Orga Privat* (Frankfurt, 1932; reprinted Berlin, 1975) and serialized in *Der Weg der Frau*, 1, and Willi Bredel, *Rosenhofstrasse*, Band 6, Rote Eine Mark Reihe (reprint Berlin, 1974).

43. *Die Kämpferin,* No. 5/6, 1931, p. 3.
44. BA R58/548/8, pp. 167–76. Lengthy police report written by Oberregierungsrat Dr. Hesse.
45. Friedrich Wolf, *Sturm gegen den Mordparagraphen 218: Unser Stuttgarter Prozess* (Kampfausschuss, Berlin, 1931), pp. 23–24.
46. Felix Halle, the KPD's legal specialist, noted that although abortions were illegal abroad as well, authorities were reluctant to prosecute well-heeled foreigners (*Proletarische Sozialpolitik,* 5, Heft 7, July 1932, pp. 205–210).
47. Kienle, *Frauen,* p. 21.
48. Ibid., p. 309.
49. For a discussion of the different tendencies in German feminism and a brief description of the so-called *Neue Ethik* movement and its relationship to sexual reform, see Richard Evans, *Feminism in Germany, 1894–1933* (Berkeley, 1976).
50. At a mass non-KPD speak-out, May 10, 1931, sponsored by the *Berliner Volkszeitung,* Kienle and her lawyer Alfred Apfel also spoke; a representative of the Berlin Archdiocese even attempted to defend the Church position on abortion to angry catcalls from an audience of over 2000! (BA R58/548/8, p. 140).
51. See, for example, Gertrud Bäumer, "Frauenprogramm: Neuer Aufbruch oder?" *Die Frau* 39, Heft 12 (September 1932): 730–32.
52. *Die Schaffende Frau: Zeitschrift für das moderne Frauentum,* ed. Margarete Kaiser, 2, Heft 2 (March 1931): 57.
53. The Berlin women doctors represented an important force within the medical profession. In 1929, 2,562 out of a total of 45,332 doctors in Germany were women, including 476 who practiced in Berlin (*Die Frau* Heft 5 [February 1931], 312). In the summer of 1930, they submitted a position paper to the Reichstag Committee on Criminal Justice maintaining that "it is our conviction that the will to motherhood cannot be coerced by legal paragraphs and threats of punishment; rather it is an innate female natural instinct which, though it can certainly be repressed by worry and need, will fully express itself again—all on its own—with the removal of adverse conditions" (*Die Frau* 37, Heft 10 [July 1930]: 600). The *Bund deutscher Ärztinnen* sent out a questionnaire to 2,761 women doctors in February 1931 directly after the Wolf/Kienle arrests. Approximately half of the questionnaires were returned and of those, almost 75%, mostly from urban areas, supported a change to a mixed social/medical indication. A slight majority favored recognition of a purely socioeconomic indication (*Weg der Frau* 2, No. 3 [March 1, 1932], 28; and *Die Frau* 39, Heft 5 [February 1932], 312). The action of the women doctors is particularly significant when one considers that most German doctors steadfastly held to the strictly anti-abortion position of the 1925 Leipzig Medical Convention.
54. *Die Frau* 38, Heft 7 (April 1931): 439–40.
55. See Allan Chase, *The Legacy of Malthus: The Origins of Scientific Racism* (New York, 1976), and Linda Gordon, *Woman's Body, Woman's Right: A Social History of Birth Control in America* (New York, 1977), for discussions of the connections and distinctions between population control and birth control. See also *Women under Attack* (New York: Committee for Abortion Rights and Against Sterilization Abuse, 1979).
56. Most of the government-sponsored marriage counseling centers were not intended to provide sex or birth control information but rather to offer eugenic advice and guidelines (*Ehetauglichkeit*) for couples planning marriage or children. See Reichsgesundheitsamt BA R86/2373 (2-4) on marriage counseling (*Eheberatung*).
57. The following quite astonishing story was proudly repeated at KPD women's conferences and printed in KPD publications: A delegate to the Second Reichs Working Women's Congress in Berlin, November 22–23, 1930, joins a women's delegation to the Soviet Union in December 1930. She comes home, totally impressed by the Soviet achievement in birth control and protection of mothers and children, and

reports: "I asked a doctor if he could not recommend a suitable birth control method to take home to the proletarian women in Germany where thousands of women are destroyed by the Paragraph and many hundreds of thousands physically harmed. The doctor gave me the following reply, 'Yes, comrade, I can tell you one sure-fire method. Make a revolution in Germany like we made in Russia in 1917 . . . then you too will be able to bear healthy children with the aid of expert medical attention'" (*Die Kämpferin*, No. 2 [1931]: 10). Also BA R134 (*Kommission für die Uberwachung der öffentlichen Ordnung*), /70/,p. 206.

58. The *Weg der Frau*, the Münzenberg women's journal spawned by the *Arbeiter Illustrierte Zeitung*, for example, began publication in June 1931 with a front-page interview with Dr. Else Kienle under the headline "Your Body Belongs to You" (*Weg der Frau*, 1, No. 1 [June 1931]: 1). Interestingly, the mass women's issue-oriented *Weg der Frau* began publication at just the same time that the more cadre-oriented *Kämpferin* began to narrow its abortion coverage to anti-SPD polemics.

59. Personal interview with Manes Sperber (Paris, February 1, 1978).

60. See Sheila Rowbotham, *A New World for Women: Stella Browne, Socialist Feminist* (London, 1977) for a highly suggestive discussion of the connection between social-ism and eugenics, and the failure of the Marxist left to offer a viable theoretical alternative to the tie between sexual reform and eugenics.

61. The KPD estimated that these so-called lay groups, that is nonmedical and not directly party-bound, had a total membership of 55,000 with the League for the Protection of Mothers (not to be confused with Federation for the Protection of Mothers; most of these groups had confusingly similar names as the police were wont to complain), the largest with 22,000 members (*Proletarische Sozialpolitik*, 4, Heft 7 [July 1931]: 233). A year later, the estimate had risen to 150,000 members (*Proletarische Sozialpolitik* 5, Heft 8 [August 1932]: 254).

62. The male/female differential among KPD voters was considerably larger than that for all other political parties and was frequently over 20%. See Gabrielle Bremme, *Die politische Rolle der Frau in Deutschland* (Göttingen, 1965), p. 73.

64. On Münzenberg and KPD politics, see Helmut Gruber, "Willi Münzenberg's Ger-man Communist Propaganda Empire 1921–1933," *Journal of Modern History* 38, No. 3 (September 1966): 278–97.

65. Personal interview with Helene Overlach, former KPD *Reichstag* deputy and KPD women's leader (*Reichsfrauenleiterin*), Berlin, GDR, January 11, 1977.

66. The KPD did, however, occasionally claim great success from the abortion cam-paign. Friedrich Wolf insisted that 352 new people joined the KPD in Stuttgart within ten days of his arrest! (*Sturm gegen den Mordparagraphen 218*, p. 23).

67. Personal interview with Helene Overlach.

68. BA R58/757/1, p. 46. See also Hans Lehfeldt, "Die Laienorganisationen für Gebur-tenregelung, *Archiv für Bevölkerungspolitik, Sexualethik und Familienkunde* 2 (1932):

69. BA R58/548/6, p. 52–65.

70. BA R58/548/8, p. 173.

71. Paragraph 218 is still on the books in the Federal Republic of Germany in a reformed but still restrictive version, and continues to excite controversy.

72. The emergency decree of March 28, 1931, had severely restricted the right to outdoor demonstrations. The KPD women's journal *Die Kämpferin* (the organ of the Delegate and Conference Movement) was banned in May 1931 for having published an anticlerical series, "The Pope Against Suffering Women" (*Der Papst gegen die notleidenden Frauen*) (No. 2 [1931]: 5–7; No. 7 [1931]: 11). It reappeared on June 15 in a new, larger, and yet more rhetorical format, strengthened in its social facism line by the fact that the ban had been ordered by the Social Democratic Prussian Minister of the Interior Grzesinski (No. 10, 1931).

73. The NSDAP had introduced a resolution in the Reichstag on March 12, 1930, calling

for penitentiary sentences for anyone attempting in any way to interfere with the "natural fertility" of the German *Volk.*

74. The contradictions of women's simultaneous centrality and marginality in the Paragraph 218 campaign are demonstrated by the very nature of the evidence that I have presented here and the type of source materials used. The women in the campaign, though they are massively documented and continually commented on, are for the most part anonymous. They appear as disputed statistics in debates about the consequences of abortion and the decline in the birth rate, as percentages in police reports on rallies and demonstrations, as prizes in the KPD numbers game for female membership, and as stylized figures in cultural products.

If we are truly to give character and content to the historical experience of the militant women in Alice Lex-Nerlinger's graphic, if we are to discover what moved them and what determined their political consciousness, we cannot simply rely on archival or printed sources. We must also turn—and we must hurry—to the exciting and illuminating techniques of oral history. There are women still alive who can tell us much that we need to know about the §218 campaign and the general relationship of the left in Weimar Germany to feminism and sexual reform.

Annemarie Tröger has for several years been directing the project "Oral History: A Charlottenburg (Berlin) working-class neighborhood in the Weimar Republic and under National Socialism."

# The Bremen Morality Scandal
## Elisabeth Meyer-Renschhausen

*As with the Paragraph 218 campaign, the dramatic scandal described in this case history of a young woman who was forcibly committed to a "prostitute's ward" and who died as a result of treatment for venereal disease created unexpected alliances between feminists and the working-class movement in the Communist and Social Democratic parties. But in contrast to the abortion struggle, this protest against a system that victimized women charged with prostitution—in a time of rapidly shifting sexual mores, this meant potentially any woman—even brought the Catholic Church and the moderate bourgeois women's movement into an alliance with the Socialists and Communists. Elisabeth Meyer-Renschhausen describes the complex ways in which sexual politics incorporated both sexual radicalism and moral purity, and thereby cut across traditional political divisions and created new, but problematic, alliances.*

### The Case

Late in 1926 a book entitled *Vom Leben getötet (Killed by Life)* triggered one of the biggest scandals of the Weimar era. The book was issued by Herder Verlag, a Catholic publisher, and edited by the head-mistress of an Ursuline convent.[1] It purported to be the diary-novel of a young woman who had died at the age of seventeen from the effects of a syphilis treatment. The book had been written by her mother.[2] This woman, the mother of five children, earned money by taking in washing and ironing, since the income of her husband, a shoemaker, was not sufficient for the family. The setting was the north German commercial city of Bremen.

The novel, written in an extraordinarily moving manner described how a young girl "from the underprivileged strata of society" had, during the early 1920s, become the victim of the morals police and the medical establishment. In the spring of 1923 the girl, Lisbeth Kolomak, then age fifteen, had run away with a girlfriend to Berlin, the Mecca of the 1920s.[3] The mother, Elisabeth Kolomak, fearing the possibility of a white slave traffic (forced prostitution), notified the police that the children were missing. After they had been found, destitute, in Berlin, they were summoned by the police in Bremen, who accused them of having maintained themselves in Berlin by means of prostitution. According to the mother's account, her daughter experienced this accusation and the ruthless language used by the male officers during questioning as demeaning, an exceptionally harsh form of "enlightenment."

The police summons prompted vicious gossip by the neighbors, whose suspicions, already aroused by the trip to Berlin, were confirmed. The daughter's "good reputation" was destroyed.[4] The parents tried to counteract that by forbidding their eldest child to leave the house. They did not allow her to resume training as a salesperson, and kept her at home to learn housekeeping. The mother took in additional washing and ironing, leaving most of the housekeeping for the eight-member family to the daughter. (The family also took in a boarder.) The daughter nonetheless had sufficient freedom to be able to go to dance halls with girlfriends and to form friendships with young men. The mother believed that the daughter should choose her future husband very carefully. She wanted to avoid repeating the error her parents had made by letting her marry the first reasonable prospect.

On several occasions a homeless girlfriend was permitted to stay overnight with the shoemaker's family. Considering the "normally" crowded conditions under which the Kolomaks lived in the small row house in Bremen, this meant that the two girls had to sleep in the same bed. It is therefore possible—as the mother assumed in the novel—that the daughter acquired her infection in this manner. One day the police fetched the girlfriend from the Kolomak house because she was suspected of having venereal disease. On the way to the police station, this young woman denounced Lisbeth as also being infected with venereal disease. The Kolomak daughter was then also fetched by the police. At the police station she was asked about her previous sex life—once again in a rude tone by male officials. The hearing, as well as the compulsory examination by the police doctor, another male, outraged and shamed the girl:

> At first we went quietly. Then when we had been out of my parents' house for hardly two minutes, the official became offensive. He wondered where I had gotten that coat and hat. After all, my father was just a poor shoemaker and could not afford to buy such a coat. I was astonished, first

about his use of *Du* [an intimate form of address] and secondly, I did not know what he meant. . . . We arrived at the stationhouse, where I stood facing three officials, each more mocking than the next: "So you seem to have earned well to be able to buy such things. . . . Where did you sleep? Which hotels? How much did you get paid?" . . . They shamed and mocked me. . . .[5]

The compulsory examination by the police doctor, which Lisbeth Kolomak found demeaning, showed that she did have venereal disease—though, since she was menstruating, she was examined only superficially. Along with other women who had been arrested, she was taken to the city hospital in an easily recognizable police car ("the Green Minna"). After a while, without her parents' having been informed or their legally required consent having been obtained, she was subjected to syphilis treatment.

The substances used on Lisbeth Kolomak—silver salvarsan and neo-arsphenamine—were relatively new chemical products. In medical circles they were touted as a "chemotherapeutic revolution" in the belief that for the first time there was now a really effective medication available for syphilis. Yet salvarsan was by no means free of controversy, particularly among experts. Many severe incidents of mutilation (particularly skin burns), as well as numerous deaths, had resulted from the treatment.[6] As described in the novel, the women brought in as prostitutes to the locked "police wards" of the hospitals were informed about the dangers of the medication and accordingly followed instructions for the salvarsan treatments precisely.[7]

Kolomak's mother tried in vain to get her daughter out of the hospital and into private treatment, particularly after she discovered that her daughter showed signs of kidney poisoning, presumably resulting from the medication. Since the daughter, as a minor, had been ordered to the hospital by the police, private treatment was not permitted. The stay at the hospital lasted approximately three months. Only when the skin rash typical of salvarsan poisoning appeared was the treatment interrupted, but the girl was not released, as a gonorrhea infection had been detected.[8] The venereal disease ward had been housed in barracks since its establishment during World War I, and therefore did not offer the best hygienic conditions. Therefore it may very well be, as the mother assumed, that the daughter acquired this infection on the ward.[9] After the salvarsan rash had abated, treatment was resumed. Lisbeth then started to run a fever and to vomit. This was initially erroneously diagnosed by an assistant doctor as flu and later as typhus.[10] Subsequently the girl vanished into an isolation ward and her mother could not reach her. Only after some time was she again permitted to see her daughter and, eventually, to take her home. A short time thereafter her child died.[11]

When the younger siblings were taunted at school about their sister's alleged "checkered past," Elisabeth Kolomak brought the teacher her daughter's diary, which the mother had revised while in a trancelike state, in order to spare the children further troubles. But she did not say a word about her work on the diary. The teacher found the diary impressive and passed it on to the magistrate who tried juvenile offenders. The magistrate had several copies typed up in order to circulate them among groups concerned with youth welfare. The head of the Catholic welfare organization concerned with "endangered girls" brought one of the copies to the headmistress of the nearby Haslünne Convent. The women found the portrayal of this typical conflict of the times impressive and decided to publish it in book form. The nuns invited the mother to the convent to test her truthfulness. After long hesitation Elisabeth Kolomak agreed to the publication of the diary-novel, without however daring to say that she had at least co-authored it.[12] While all the names and places were changed, it nonetheless soon became clear to the interested public that the case must have taken place in Bremen.

### Public Interest in the Case

Immediately after the book's publication, people from all quarters snapped it up, unanimously lauding and praising the deceased young author. When it then became known that the mother had written the diary, the astonishment about this piece of literature did not diminish; if anything, it increased.

Actually the laundress Kolomak (and her daughter) had accomplished something astonishing. In this novel, a "typical conflict of the times" was portrayed in a vivid, lively, and suspenseful manner by someone directly involved, namely the mother, a member of a socially disadvantaged class. The conflicts between the various value systems, which clashed harshly on both the public and private levels during the Weimar period, were portrayed with all the drama they had acquired for this particular young woman and her mother.

The book described how any young woman who, for whatever reason, struck the police as a possible prostitute could, by means of the police surveillance system and compulsory treatment in a hospital, be made into a social pariah, and thereby into a prostitute. Using the example of the girlfriend and other "police girls" on the ward, the book described how the police and welfare system could virtually force young girls who had come to their attention into prostitution. In the police ward of the hospital they were at the mercy of the doctors' rigorous "treatment methods."

The diary thereby took up a topic that had been one of the main concerns of the organized women's movement since the turn of the century. Since that time, the women's movement had vehemently directed its efforts against Section 361, subparagraph 6, of the penal code, which did not in fact forbid prostitution, but permitted it only under police supervision. The women's movement wanted the complete abolition of this paragraph since this system of "regulated prostitution" by no means curbed prostitution, but on the contrary furthered it. The institutionalization of a special class of prostitutes legitimized by the state promoted rather than curbed extramarital sex. Furthermore—and here the argument of the women's movement strikingly coincided with the portrayal in the novel—this paragraph and the police surveillance it provided for constituted a potential threat to every young woman. Ultimately anyone could arbitrarily be branded a prostitute by the police. The inescapable stigma thus created prostitutes.

During the 1920s, when the discussion and treatment of prostitutes had generally shifted from the level of morals to the realm of health policy, all young women—and only women—were potential victims of compulsory treatment in state hospitals, in just the way described in the diary-novel. Moreover, the book was published in December 1926, precisely at the time that the Law for Combatting Venereal Disease, by means of which the women's movement hoped to suspend the existing law (which targeted only young women) was up for passage in the Reichstag. From the point of view of the women's movement, the new law had been a compromise: Section 361, subparagraph 6, would be suspended only if the women's movement agreed to concessions concerning new regulations "for combating venereal diseases" desired by both the doctors and the politicians interested in health issues.

During the disputes concerning this legal reform, the issue had been whether licensed physicians were to be solely responsible for the treatment of venereal disease. The medical establishment had used the impetus behind this bill to combat the alternative healing practices that were still acceptable in 1926, such as, for example, naturopathy. This was explosive, because many people feared being exclusively at the mercy of the medical profession. There was also strong resistance from the ranks of licensed doctors who had serious doubts about the legitimacy of massive "chemical bombardments," such as those involved in salvarsan therapy. Professional practitioners had begun to cure syphilis with salvarsan in 1910, thereby ushering in the "triumph of chemotherapy." The opponents of salvarsan therapy, along with the heavily attacked natural healing practitioners, were accused of quackery and were thus silenced. Consequently and ironically, during the

Kolomak trial in Bremen, the former police doctor and *Völkisch* (nationalist-conservative) opponent of salvarsan, Dr. Dreuw, was able to publish only in the Communist newspaper, *Arbeiterzeitung*.[13]

It was the particular concern of the women's movement to use the new version of the law to get rid of the brothels, which, although forbidden by the state, existed everywhere. The degradation of women into purchasable commodities in such "public houses" had become a particular thorn in the eyes of feminists, who regarded these houses as the incarnation of contempt for women. Further, feminists noted that the local authorities' de facto toleration of brothels unmasked the state as the "chief procurer."

Bremen had now achieved a special rank in these discussions. Bremen insisted that it had no brothels; instead, it professed to have found a wonderful alternative to "pleasure houses" in the form of licensed prostitution.[14] Based on its "Helene Street" model, all officially approved ("registered") prostitutes in the city were compelled to rent lodgings in one lone street, which however had no official brothel keeper. The women's movement felt this "reform model" to be a blatantly cynical response to their efforts. In their polemic against state-promoted brothel practices, they had always attacked Bremen's Helene Street particularly vigorously.[15] Therefore, it was understandable that people paid attention when it turned out that the Kolomak novel described conditions in Bremen.

In view of the multiple conflicts that the diary-novel once again presented for debate, it was not surprising that both opposition parties in Bremen, the Social Democrats and the Communists, immediately took up the matter and, using the old arguments of the women's movement, started a massive attack on the system. Hence, the Communists in the City Parliament (Bürgerschaft) demanded (1) immediate reorganization of Bremen's morals police; (2) immediate hiring of ten female police welfare officials; (3) immediate changes in the kind of medical treatment that persons with venereal diseases received in the hospital; and (4) immediate placement of young people under the supervision of the youth welfare board rather than of the police.[16]

The almost unanimously favorable reviews of the book and the ensuing attacks by the left against Bremen's institutions are probably what prompted the men of the ruling parties to feel so offended about the blemished "honor of Bremen" that they started a massive counterattack.[17]

### The Mother's Punishment

The tables were turned, and precisely two years after the death of the daughter from salvarsan and just two days after the first reviews praising the book appeared in the Bremen newspapers, the mother's activities as a procurer were "revealed." As early as January 1, 1927, all local newspapers were obliged to present the police version: "The girl was a whore, the mother a procurer."[18]

Allegedly prompted by an anonymous tip, the police subsequently appeared at the shoemaker's house to search—in vain, of course—for concealed infantry rifles.[19] Then a neighbor who was not on good terms with Elisabeth Kolomak was bribed by the *Bremer Nachrichten* (the official newspaper of the administration) to present under her own name an opposite version of Lisbeth Kolomak's story entitled "Honor to the Truth" *(Der Wahrheit die Ehre)* in its January 19 issue. In this portrayal it seemed that both parents had known of the daughter's "goings-on," and that the daughter had earned her money as a prostitute, actively supported by the mother's activities as a procurer. In addition, it was asserted that the diary did not come from the daughter, but from the mother herself.[20]

This led to a discussion by the leaders of the city's parliamentary parties, to which the head of the Communist Party was not invited.[21] Thereupon, Faust, the Social Democratic editor who had benevolently championed the mother and her book in his newspaper, *Volkszeitung,* persuaded her—she had confidence in him—"to admit" that she herself, rather than her daughter, had written the diary.[22] To a large extent, people initially did not believe the mother's "confession" because they found it hard to imagine that she could have imitated her daughter's handwriting in such a deceptively childlike manner. Nevertheless, Elisabeth Kolomak unmasked herself as a "forger"; the result was that people became more willing to believe that she was a procurer. She had not expected this reaction, and fled to the convent, where the Bremen police, circumventing the legal process, soon arrested her. They put her in detention for an unusually long period of time (six weeks) on suspicion of "extensive procurement."[23] A feminist editor bitingly interpreted this procedure:

> She was supposed to be able to think over everything alone and in peace. For this reason, on January 28 she was taken into custody in another province without a warrant. She was placed in protective or investigative detention in police headquarters.
>
> Despite the woman's untroubled conscience, one can imagine that her calmness was somewhat shattered and that she felt insecure, even anxious, about a possible five-year incarceration and all its consequences for her children and herself. After all, she had already been through numerous hearings and investigations.[24]

Although most of the press in the country considered the long imprisonment unjust, the laundress was not released until February 20, 1927, after she had repeated her confession. The trial was finally held in June 1927 and lasted three days. The trial was not against the city of Bremen, the police, or the doctors; rather, it was against the mother of the salvarsan victim. Against her will, the well-informed public was excluded on the basis of "endangerment of morals." Kolomak was condemned on the basis of a statement by the star witness for the prosecution—the same girlfriend who, according to the book, had led Lisbeth Kolomak astray. Most of the other evidence was rather weak: two of the three young men retracted statements made to the police and stressed that they had not had an unfavorable impression of Lisbeth; only the star witness and the previously mentioned neighbor testified against her. Nevertheless, Kolomak was sentenced to eight months in prison.[25]

Not until 1928, when the affair had quieted down, was the laundress freed on the basis of a general amnesty covering offenses committed due to the impoverishment caused by the big inflation of 1923–1924. The mother's lawyer, a Center Party deputy known for his social commitment, had already suggested during the court proceedings that this law be used as a compromise solution, but his proposal had initially fallen on deaf ears. The belated amnesty—decided in quasi-secrecy—was, however, significant, and a strong indication that people were well aware of the injustice committed against the shoemaker's wife.

### The Meaning of "Treatment"

As critics noted, the medical report concerning the case, submitted on the demand of the Bremen City Parliament, was obtained only from those doctors who themselves were advocates of salvarsan therapy. Nevertheless, the report yielded a clear picture. The police had committed Lisbeth Kolomak to the hospital on the vague suspicion of her having syphilis.[26] She had denied having the infection and had asserted that she had never had sexual relations.[27] Particularly in syphilis cases, an infection is indeed possible without sexual relations. Since she had never signed the police report, it is at least possible that the police had expressed themselves somewhat more crudely than the girl had reported for the record and that she really was sexually inexperienced.

Some time after she had been brought in—and following a by no means completely harmless lumbar puncture—she was given a dosage of the medication[28] customary in Bremen but corresponding to the maximum dosage approved by the Ministry of the Interior solely for administration to strong adult men.[29] Many doctors, however, did not adhere to this limitation.[30] The high dosage for the young girl was justified thus: "As a person suffering from venereal disease, it had to be assumed that she could continue to be sexually active; hence for hygienic reasons a thorough treatment seemed to be indicated."[31] In other words, a young woman, brought to the doctors by the police and claimed by them to be "sexually active" outside of marriage—regardless of how many persons this activity involved or whether she earned money with it or whether the police made a mistake—was quasi-preventively bombarded with massive doses of a controversial medication, since in this manner the (male) doctors hoped to control "syphilis, the people's plague." This was done although the remedy had not yet been sufficiently tested, as even advocates of the medication admitted. An expert called in from Breslau confirmed that there was no agreement as to how or in which dosages salvarsan—or silver salvarsan or neoarsphenamine—would work. Moreover, syphilis was considered a disease that, even without treatment, could progress in extremely different ways, including spontaneous remission.[32] In other words, in many cases the seriousness of the disease did not justify the consequences of chemotherapy.

During the city's parliamentary debate about the case, none of the doctors completely denied that Lisbeth Kolomak's death could have resulted from the medication.[33] To be sure, people tried to wash their hands of the matter by continually speaking of the deceased as a "whore,"[34] a "fact" that had not, after all, been officially established by the court. In addition, confusion was created by adding that possibly she had died of poisoning from bismuth-genol (medication for gonorrhea), another new medicine. What the medical report had not noted was recalled by the assistant doctor in his testimony: that in fact Lisbeth Kolomak was one of the first to have been given sodium sulphate to "neutralize" the eczema resulting from salvarsan.[35] Therefore, it was not so far-fetched when the mother depicted the women on the locked ward as fearful of being used as guinea pigs for the medical profession.[36] Otherwise the extreme anxiety of the Bremen doctors about openly admitting an instance of malpractice can hardly be explained.[37] Any woman with venereal disease whom circumstance drove into the hands of the police could become the victim of these conditions; this did not, however, apply to young men. The Kolomak diary made an impression precisely because it showed how the young "new woman" with her somewhat "freer morality" could all too easily be caught in the wheels of the system. Particularly since World War I, large numbers of female youth no longer adhered to the traditional models of femininity and claimed greater personal freedom for themselves. At the same time, promiscuity, without necessarily involving prostitution, could lead to compulsory treatment in a locked ward on the pretext that it constituted a threat to the health of the *Volk*.

Evidently, what was really at issue was the deterrent nature of this kind of treatment; the issue of real help for sick people was at best secondary. In Bremen, this was indicated by the completely unhygienic conditions in the locked women's wards of the hospital and by the fact that like everywhere else, this section was far too small to actually accommodate all the young women suffering from venereal disease. People hoped to discipline "immoral females" by subjecting them to a treatment more like a punishment than a beneficial cure.[38] Men were subjected to such experiments only as soldiers during the war or as prisoners. Many women did not voluntarily submit to treatment because their anxiety about the negative side effects of salvarsan was too great. Therefore it was not the method of treatment that was at issue, since not all were cured, and certainly not the men. At issue was the continuation and reinforcement of the old double standard by new means.

### The Fight Against Male Standards of Morality

One of the first and oldest concerns of the German women's movement, in Bremen and elsewhere, was to attack this double standard and its restrictive effects on the freedom of movement of all women. As will be shown later, the extraordinary fact is that it was mainly the moral question that, despite all other differences, had always united the women's movement and continued to do so until the end of the Weimar era. Even during the 1860s and 1870s the bourgeois women's movement had established maids' lodgings *(Mägdeherberge)*, an organization—Friends of Young Girls (Freundinnen junger Mädchen)—and Train Station Missions for the Protection of Young Single Working Women Traveling Alone (Bahnhofsmission zum Schutze alleinreisender erwerbstätiger junger Frauen).[39] These services were supposed to protect young girls from marriage swindlers and the white slave traffic.

After the third meeting in 1898 in Hamburg of the Federation of German Women's Associations (Bund Deutscher Frauenvereine, founded in 1894 as an umbrella organization), the Association for the Protection of Youth (Verein Jugendschutz) was founded in Bremen. This organization aimed to "save" girls who had "fallen" for the first time from further corruption, through personal care and the provision of lodgings and employment opportunities. Simultaneously, this association instigated an initiative against "red light" bars and for effective protection for waitresses.[40]

In 1903 a branch of the more aggressive and radical International Abolitionist Federation (Internationale Abolitionistische Föderation) was founded in Bremen. In April 1909 this group, with its particularly active propaganda, succeeded in getting thirteen Bremen women's organizations with the most diverse political agendas to draw up a joint petition to the city parliament, requesting the repeal of Section 361, subparagraph 6, of the penal code as well as the application of the procurement paragraph (paragraph 180 of the penal code) to the public houses.[41] With the first demand the women wanted to eliminate the prostitution law. The law not only promoted immorality, but was senseless, since the definitions of prostitution were fluid and therefore not ascertainable. Instead of curbing venereal disease, the paragraph achieved the opposite. Attached to the petition was a ten-page rationale stating, among other things:

> On the basis of this regulation, the morals police can at any time arrest any woman, even on the most unfounded suspicion. For the woman erroneously taken into custody, however, arrest on suspicion of prostitution is always a detriment to her reputation, frequently also a detriment to her economic interest, not infrequently causing loss of employment (as a private tutor, for example). The regulation therefore constitutes a very serious danger to the entire world of working women, particularly to young single women in cities.[42]

In addition, the petition was directed against the brothels of Helene Street, which not only existed, contrary to the regulations of Section 180 of the penal code forbidding procurement in general and for profit in particular, but even existed "with the approval of the police and city authorities."[43] The women believed that this situation dangerously distorted "public respect for the law" as well as the "ethical consciousness of the population"; that it taught young men debauchery, and delivered them back to their families in a diseased condition.

This petition was signed by nearly all the women's organizations in Bremen at the time, ranging from Women Against Alcohol Abuse (Frauen gegen den Alkoholmissbrauch) to the Protestant Women's League (Evangelische Frauenbund), the Jewish Women's Association (Israelitischer Frauenverein), the Women's Auxiliary of the Kaiser Friederich Lodge (Schwesterbund der Kaiser-Friederich-Loge), the Bremen Association of Women Teachers (Verein Bremer Lehrerinnen), and the Association for the Protection of Mothers and Infants (Verein Mütter- und Säuglingsschutz).[44] The only concrete result was the fulfillment of a traditional demand of the women's movement— namely, the hiring of a "female police assistant" in Bremen—which took place that year, probably not by coincidence. As the feminists envisioned it, this female police assistant was to be particularly concerned with young women who had "fallen" for the first time, in much the same manner as was the Association for the Protection of Youth.[45] Certainly the symbolic success of this petition was important: after all, women of varying ideologies had agreed on a demand against the state and on the wording of a long petition.

The abolitionist movement, which had temporarily ceased its activities when the war broke out, stirred again in the year 1916. Women's rights champions were outraged about military ordinances that, in many parts of the country including north Germany, permitted the police, without real cause, to arrest any "civilian"—in other words, any woman—suspected of being capable of transmitting venereal disease and take her to the hospital for compulsory treatment.

After the war was over, the organized women's movement immediately renewed its campaign to abolish Section 361, subparagraph 6, along with other regulations dating from the year 1916. Particularly women like Marie Elisabeth Lüders, who had engaged in the welfare work of the women's organizations on a daily basis during World War I, were convinced that the repeal of state regulation was the *sine qua non* for the success of any welfare work as well as for the improvement of public morality.[46]

It turned out, however, that the feminists could achieve the elimination of Section 361, subparagraph 6, only by accepting—at least in part—the rhetoric of those men who, like most of their sex, did not intend the abolition of the prostitution paragraph, but were favorably disposed toward a law for combating venereal diseases. This law first came up for debate in the Reichstag in 1923 and was finally passed in 1927. The 1927 law decriminalized prostitution, at least officially, and shifted the supervision of persons suffering from venereal disease from the police to the health authorities. The criterion that permitted the authorities potentially to monitor the health of every woman was now no longer prostitution but "frequently changing sexual partners." But at the state level—as, for example, in Bremen—implementation of the law was to a large extent postponed or it was not enforced.

Utterly contrary to the women's original intentions, during the world economic crisis the law led to renewed, increased control over more women than ever before,[47] although in 1927 (after the long battle by the Bremen women's movement[48]) the brothel district, Helene Street, was abolished, at least officially. What the women's movement had feared during the early 1920s had happened: instead of leading to improvements, the law had become "a new punitive instrument in somewhat different garb."[49]

## The Disputes in Bremen:
### Prostitution and the Venereal Disease Law

Parallel to developments at the national level, the Bremen women had resumed their battle after the war. By mid-1919 they had gotten their female representatives in the Bremen National Assembly (Nationalversammlung) to submit a petition requesting the establishment of a welfare office for the rehabilitation of prostitutes. According to the women's expectations, these facilities would be financed by the state but under the direction "of women for women." They were to be as independent and self-sufficient as possible, and in particular were to work independently of other authorities.[50] This petition had been signed by almost all the women's organizations of Bremen, both political and nonpolitical. It was ignored by the National Assembly.[51]

In Bremen, too, as will be shown, it turned out that the police and medical doctors were particular opponents of this demand by the women's movement. The police did not want to give up their authority to regulate prostitution. In order to take the wind out of the women's sails, they simply changed the title of the only female welfare official employed by them to the "welfare officer" *(Pflegeamt)*.[52]

Granted, the feminists achieved the establishment of a welfare office by their petition, but only in a form that made it possible for men to drag out its actual establishment for another three years. Only in 1924 did the welfare office come into being, and then it had to share its two rooms with the Federation for the Protection of Mothers (Bund für Mutterschutz).[53]

In view of the anticipated Law for Combating Venereal Disease, the Bremen feminists tried again in 1926 to eliminate Helene Street once and for all. All thirty-two organizations of the City Federation of Women supported a petition submitted in the city parliament by Minna Bahnson of the Democratic Party; even Gesine Becker of the Communist Party vehemently advocated it.[54] A resolution by eight residents of Helene Street opposed the proposal. Justifying the petition, Minna Bahnson, one of the most active representatives of the Bremen Abolitionist Association, stressed that the Bremen women surely knew that prostitution could not be extinguished. But in contrast to the men on the medical commission, they refused to restrict their efforts to combating venereal diseases. On the contrary, their goal was "to protect thousands of girls in Bremen and all over Germany from the fate of being expelled from the human community."[55] Feminists argued that although the women from Helene Street stressed that they were there voluntarily, all ties to normal, respectable life were in fact blocked. In the final analysis, the prostitutes lived in Helene Street only because there they were able to purchase some protection "from our present police system."[56] Precisely on these points, Minna Bahnson, the Democrat, was strongly supported by Gesine Becker, the Communist. The Communists also believed that the women from Helene Street had drawn up their petition against the street's abolition because "the prostitutes of Helene Street are worn-out objects who are completely run down physically and no longer fit into respectable society, because they are 30, 35, 40, even 45 years old and no longer capable of an orderly life."[57] Anna Stiegler, a Social Democrat, argued similarly: while Helene Street was a relatively humane form of brothel, this did not change the fact that the state had taken on the role of "top pimp."[58] Although she too sympathized with the petition by the prostitutes from the brothel street, she favored its elimination:

> We are not of the opinion that these girls should be consigned to further ruin. If they have the will to return to bourgeois life, the road is paved for them by all the measures that have already been taken in Bremen in the form of the welfare office and the welfare home. Hence if they want to, they can find the way back.[59]

The social inevitability of prostitution was particularly stressed by the women of the left.[60] Young women received only 9.5 marks unemployment insurance per week; if their employment benefits had run out, they received 15 marks welfare relief for the entire month, half of which generally had to be set aside for rent. The petition stipulated that the dissolution of the brothel street would take place only after three-quarters of a year had passed so that the residents would have some time to adjust, but in fact the members of the women's movement did not think much of prostitutes. Minna Bahnson observed many "abnormal, asocial elements" among them,[61] and Anna Stiegler was infuriated that they seemed so proud of their "good bourgeois households," which the brothel street allowed them to establish.[62] Apart from that, the fury of the feminists was directed primarily against the unequal treatment of men and women by the state—the double standard that Helene Street so clearly represented. The petition by the thirty-two women's organizations was in fact accepted. Anna Stiegler successfully insisted on removing provisions for supplementary rehabilitative detention and on forming a female police force instead. In response to the Kolomak scandal, the women of Bremen managed in February 1927 to hold yet another large meeting and to produce a unanimous statement of intentions. This surely had something to do with the fact that on April 1, 1927, Helene Street was at least officially abolished and renamed Franke Street.

### Women's Response to the Kolomak Case

In the contest of the heated disputes about the Law for Combatting Venereal Disease, at both the national level and in Bremen, Elisabeth Kolomak's book attracted attention even before its publication in December 1926. An almost ecstatically favorable review of the "splendidly written diary novel" in *Die Frau*, the official organ of the Federation of German Women's Associations, had already appeared in the fall.[63] Later references to the affair in this publication were, however, extremely brief. The cause of this conspicuous brevity may be that the case had become a scandal and that in Bremen it had acquired a clear political coloration, especially since the Socialist and Communist parties had become advocates of Kolomak. Since the organized women's movement sought to present itself as politically neutral in order to safeguard its continued existence as a movement that cut across all political groupings, the editors of *Die Frau* probably refrained from further commentary concerning the matter.

Precisely those Bremen women who had been most involved in the question became skeptical when it seemed to be clear that the mother had assembled the diary. In the women's movement as a whole there were also varying opinions. The men governing Bremen had managed to win over to their side Sophie Dorothea Gallwitz, a frequent contributor to *Die Frau*. They were able to persuade her to present a portrayal of the incident from the point of view of the Bremen Senate and the police in the newspaper *Berliner Börsenblatt*, in which she characterized the mother as a procurer and the daughter as a whore.[64] Sophie Gallwitz was probably alone in exclusively condemning the mother, but it turned out that the feminist and committed abolitionist Minna Bahnson was also initially inclined to give greater credibility to the police version. In her portrayal in the Hamburg Housewives' Organization newsletter, she was, however, simultaneously certain that male notions of morality and a misogynist legal system served to facilitate such immorality among young people:

> If one considers the fact, however, that with this fourteen-year-old passionate instincts were awakened by immoral dealings, that she was seduced and systematically physically and mentally destroyed over a period of three years, and that there was and is no possibility of bringing to account even one of the men through whose hands this minor passed, and to whom she was an object of pleasure, then we women must blush with shame and fury about such laws and such loopholes of the law! . . . As soon as girls have accepted presents or money, this supposedly absolves these men of all responsibility, even absolves them of all pangs of conscience, and brands the girls "paid whores"![65]

In contrast, other women journalists tried to get at the root of the matter by visiting the mother at her home. The Social Democrat Clara Bohm-Schuch wrote:

> When I visited this woman who, despite her 42 years and five children, made a girlish impression, and asked her, "Did you know anything about Lisbeth's companion's lifestyle?" She responded, "I did not know it. If I had known it, I would have always had to be afraid that she would bring a baby home."[66]

The author drew the conclusion: "This answer is perhaps more proof against the indictment and conviction as a procurer than anything else."[67] Similarly, other women's magazines tried to understand the case from the point of view of concerned mothers who perforce were confronted with a new generation of girls and their modern desire for recreation. A convinced Christian wrote in a Leipzig magazine for housewives:

> She had not done anything much different from what unfortunately hundreds—no, what thousands of mothers do. She let her pretty young daughter go the route of amusement. . . . However, if one wanted to indict all mothers who had behaved as she did, the judges would never get out of court.[68]

The "radical wing" of the "bourgeois women's movement," mostly organized in the Women's International League for Peace and Freedom (Internationale Frauenliga für Frieden und Freiheit; WILPF) or the Federation for the Protection of Mothers, not only showed understanding for an overtaxed mother but, also sharply condemned the police vice squad, the doctors, and the state of Bremen.\* Auguste Kirchhoff, wife of a Bremen senator, and the legal expert Anita Augspurg were among those who expressed themselves in the magazine *Die Frau im Staat (The Woman in the State)*. Augspurg was outraged by the public reaction, especially in the media, after it had been discovered that the mother might have been the author of the diary:

> The question was no longer the destruction of a young . . . person, nor a scientific murder by salvarsan . . . nor the horrendous conditions typical for vice squads in all large and medium-sized cities; on the contrary, the question was: is the book "forged?" i.e., did the mother write the book instead of the daughter. If it was the mother, then from between the lines there emerged the clear general conclusion that a swindle was inevitably involved. Therefore, it is entirely in order that a young girl go to ruin as a result of police institutions, and it is allowable cheerfully to torture people to death in hospitals and to kill them by overdoses of salvarsan.[69]

### Social Welfare, Education, and Female Police: Weimar Disappointments

If the printed reactions of the women's movement were diverse, the practical responses were much more united. By January 16 several women from various women's organizations and political parties involved in social work published a statement referring to the frequently criticized "unfitting practices" among the vice squad and in the hospital. They demanded appropriate care for "persons in need of supervision" and finally appealed to doctors and educators to attend more carefully to the socialization of boys.[70]

---

\*Bremen, like Hamburg, was a separate province within the Republic; therefore it was both a city and a state.—Ed.

These women also pressured the local Commission for Women's Interests (Kommission für Fraueninteressen) to summon a coalition of all Bremen women's organizations "from the most extreme right to the extreme left"[71] to a large public meeting. The event attracted so many women that it had to be moved to a larger hall. Feminists had invited Josephine Erkens from Frankfurt, known from her article in *Die Frau* as the first German woman police commissioner to lecture on the demand for female police that the German women's movement had been discussing since 1925.

The meeting resulted in a resolution adopted with one dissenting vote (probably by Gesine Becker of the Communist Party, who opposed female police). The first demand was for a vocational school for all young girls in Bremen. Despite federal law to the contrary, such a facility for the continuing education of young women workers, young women living at home, and domestic servants did not yet exist. The women of Bremen had wanted this kind of school since the turn of the century. Like the early women's movement, they were convinced that young women would be less vulnerable to the "seductions of the system" if they had the benefit of a more general education. At the same time, they hoped that vocational training would make women's occupations more "skilled," and therefore better paid. Naturally, they thought that the teachers in the vocational schools would be women from their own ranks who would be able to educate the girls in the spirit of the women's movement.

The other demands were also not particularly new. The Youth Welfare Department (Jugendamt) was conceptually derived from the voluntary welfare work of the women's movement before World War I,[72] but its institutionalization at the state level after the war had not resulted in management positions for women. In Bremen, women therefore demanded that a woman should be hired as a department head on an equal basis with the director of the Youth Welfare Department. The demand to hire a female doctor with full-time responsibilities in the Youth Welfare Department for the examination of children, girls, and women was also a traditional feminist demand, since male gynecologists were considered particularly unacceptable in such functions. The women of Bremen demanded more female social workers for the Youth Welfare Department, "pedagogically and psychologically trained" women youth leaders in each department of the venereal disease wards in the hospital, and the credentialing of volunteer social workers as part of the welfare program. All social reform plans of the women's movement of the Weimar era were frustrated by the fact that all too few paid positions for women's projects and welfare institutions were even approved by the state. Trained women social workers and youth counselors were consequently the special hope of the movement, because they came from social work schools, which were direct products of the women's movement.[73]

During the 1920s the Bremen feminists were still entirely convinced of "their" school: they believed that female social workers were capable of significant accomplishments if only the state would hire them in sufficient numbers. Also at issue here was the feminists' insistence on the importance of these schools of social work for women. Astonishingly enough, women in the Weimar Republic had to fight even for the right to offer voluntary, unpaid, mostly religiously supported "labors of love" for women and youth suffering from venereal disease.

The last part of the resolution took up the demand for hiring female police; this seemed to be a gesture of resignation reflecting the lack of latitude granted the social welfare offices in comparison with the police. Moreover, this was a demand that had been taken over from the American and English women's movements. Although the Bremen women had not yet generally accepted female police in 1926, they were more willing to be convinced now.[74] They expected passage of the Law for Combatting Venereal Disease, which had been instigated by them, and were convinced that it would be enforced in the spirit of equality they had intended. They demanded female police as an instrument for dealing with "morally endangered" persons and those on the verge of getting into trouble. Also, female police should take over preliminary hearings of suspected and criminal women, adolescents, and children.[75] This too was nothing new. The same issues had been raised prior to World War I.[76] That even women from the Bremen left consented to this demand in January 1927 was due to the fact that the women's movement believed that female police should represent something completely different from male police. Female police should by no means support male police in their work, but should "supplement" them. This meant that the female police should not bring more women to court, but on the contrary should seek to avoid just that. The problems inherent in this demand were clear to the feminists. Anna Pappritz, one of the most active abolitionists, wrote:

> The danger cannot be dismissed out of hand that out of misbegotten zealousness the female police will strive to do the same thing as their male colleagues. . . . Their effectiveness ultimately should constitute a protection of the female population by bringing the endangered to the social welfare and not to the criminal justice system.[77]

In late February, a petition almost identical to the resolution of the Bremen women's organizations, now numbering forty-six, was submitted by Rita Bardenheuer of the Social Democratic Party to Bremen's city parliament, where it was dealt with on March 26.[78] If the women of the movement understood the demands for the expansion of vocational training for unskilled female workers as inextricably linked with those for more female welfare officials, female police, and a staff female doctor, the male parliamentarians did not see the connection at all. They tried to weaken the women's demands by subdividing them and did not even want to consider vocational training for all girls, so dear to the hearts of feminists.[79] Further, they denied the demand for female police.[80]

During the debate in the city parliament, it became clear, however, that the women did not confine themselves to influence at the parliamentary level. They used influence wherever they had it. Thus, Agnes Heineken, the director of the schools of the Women's Employment Association (Frauenerwerbsverein), of which vocational schools were also a part, and her women colleagues acquired a substantial number of copies of the Kolomak novel and discussed it during class. The mayor of Bremen could not get over his outrage:

> Is that really happening? Then I must grab myself by the head and ask how is such a thing possible! The domestic science school is a compulsory continuing education, state institution, hence I have the right to such a question.[81]

Thus, the women of the "official" women's movement had taken up the commitment of an ordinary woman, had included her in their domestic science classes, and had seized the opportunity for discussing the problems of women's lives and the goals of the contemporary women's movement, as exemplified by the novel. Possibly, this piece of "educational work" was more important than the women's demands, which remained for the most part unfulfilled.

The united front of women, which transcended parliamentary divisions when it came to issues of the movement for morality in Bremen in 1909, 1919, 1926, and 1927, as well as the novel by Frau Kolomak show that for the women of that era the question of prostitution was so much *the* sign of the system's contempt for women that they finally resorted to the somewhat desperate demand for female police. Women's notions concerning state financing of their social work projects were so unsatisfactorily addressed, especially in reference to prostitution, that feminists came to the following conclusion in 1932 when confronted with the world economic crisis:

> The world and all its institutions, creations, conditions, and connections that we see quaking and collapsing under our feet is a male world. And we women believe that a large part of its deterioration and convulsions is due to the fact that it is only a male world.[82]

At the parliamentary level the feminists therefore did not achieve much.[83] The system's frugal attitude toward such modest demands remains astonishing. At that time the "male state" believed that the social crisis could be controlled by subsidizing investments in battleships and road construction instead of approving modest funds for the "merely reproductive" realms, such as social work.

A novel such as that by Kolomak, "a woman of the people," is, however, inconceivable without the background of a thirty-year history of feminist efforts. That the novel could attract so much attention was due to the fact that it was published at precisely the right time—during the 1920s, when there were debates about the "new woman" and sexuality and discussion about the Law for Combating Venereal Diseases—and that the morality question as understood by the women's movement was the central issue of the era. In that sense, the novel perhaps achieved more than all parliamentary efforts by the women's movement in Bremen. The Bremen feminist Auguste Kirchhoff came to the following conclusion concerning the Kolomak affair: "This much is certain: a book that so touches the conscience of people and throws light on the inadequacy of existing conditions has fulfilled its mission, regardless of who wrote it."[84]

—Trans. Martha Humphreys; ed. Atina Grossmann

## Notes

1. M. I. Breme, ed., *Vom Leben getötet*, (Freiburg, 1926).
2. To what extent the novel was written by the mother or in fact was more or less the daughter's diary was never entirely clear.
3. Compare the "Compilation of the Records and Findings Concerning Elisabeth Kolomak by the Police" (hereafter "Compilation") in Bremen State Archives (hereafter StA B) 4:21–424.
4. Ibid., pp. 64ff., 74, 79f, 181.
5. Ibid., pp. 216f.
6. See also Proceedings of the Bremen city parliament (hereafter Proceedings) of 2/25/1927, speeches of Faust as well as the opinion by the Breslau spokesman for salvarsan, Dr. Jadassohn, M.D., in: StA B 4:21–422.
7. Breme, *Vom Leben getötet*, pp. 119, 232.
8. See StA B 4:21–422.
9. Breme, *Vom Leben getötet*, p. 232. See also StA B 3—M.1.w.2. No. 710.
10. Record of the interrogation of Dr. Muehle of 2/10/1927 in StA B 4:21–422, p. 3. The salvarsan treatment was later resumed, new manifestations of poisoning were again not properly recognized; as a consequence she died in June 1924.
11. Breme, *Vom Leben getötet*, pp. 232ff., StA B 3—P.1. a. No. 1080.
12. "Compilation," p. 4.
13. See also StA B 3—P.1.a. No. 1080 Quad 70.
14. See also "Über die sanitäre Überwachung der Prostitution in Bremen von Kreisarzt Dr. O. Weidanz," in *Zeitschrift zur Bekämpfung der Geschlechtskrankheiten* XV (1914): 88–103.
15. See also Anna Pappritz, *Herrenmoral* (Leipzig 1903).
16. Proceedings, January 14, 1927, p. 2.
17. Proceedings, pp. 105, 107; report of Dr. Neurtah in *Weser Zeitung*, January 6, 1927, and *Bremer Nachrichten*, March 10, 1927.

18. See all Bremen newspapers of January 8, 1927, including *Weser Zeitung.*
19. Auguste Kirchhoff, "Die bremischen Frauen und das Buch *Vom Leben getötet,*" *Die Frau im Staat* 4 (1927): 6ff., here p. 6.
20. *Bremer Nachrichten,* January 19, 1927. See also StA B 7:2007–86 92 (files of the government counsel, Dr. Hertl).
21. Proceedings, February 15, 1927, pp. 56 and 97.
22. Alfred Faust, Proceedings, February 15, 1927, pp. 100ff.
23. Kirchhoff, "Die bremischen Frauen."
24. Anita Augspurg, "Der vorläufige Abschluss," *Die Frau im Staat* 4 (1927): 7–9, here p. 8.
25. According to the police report, the Kolomak daughter admitted having had sexual relations on three occasions with three different men. Compare Compilation and StA B 4:21–424.
26. The findings vary: according to the police investigations (Compilation, p. 2), she was not brought in because of lues, but because of gonorrhea.
27. According to the case history in StA B 4:21–422.
28. See Proceedings, February 25, 1927, and Augspurg, "Der vorlaüfige Abschluss."
29. Communication, March 3, 1923, by the Minister of Interior, Berlin, to the state governments concerning the guidelines for the use of salvarsan preparations.
30. It was known that malnutrition after the war contributed to salvarsan intolerance. See report by Prof. Dr. Hahn in StA B 4:21–422.
31. Dr. Bischoff to Jadassohn on February 15, 1927, in StA B 4:21–422.
32. See opinion of the expert, Jadassohn, in ibid., p. 19.
33. Proceedings, February 25, 1927, p. 100.
34. Ibid., p. 89.
35. Record of the interrogation of Dr. Mühle, February 10, 1927, p. 2, in StA B 4:21–422.
36. Breme, *Vom Leben getötet,* p. 219.
37. Proceedings, p. 100.
38. See also Havelock Ellis, *Geschlecht und Gesellschaft* (trans. from English) (Würzburg, 1911); and Abraham Flexner, *Die Prostitution in Europa* (trans. from English) (Berlin, 1921).
39. *Nordwest* from the year 1884, pp. 369 and 390, among others.
40. Else Wex, *Staatsbürgerliche Arbeit deutscher Frauen 1865–1928* (Berlin, 1929), p. 49. See also StA B 4:21–409.
41. See "Der Abolitionist" II (1903), vol. 3, p. 28. These efforts, initiated by Josephine Butler and her women friends in England in 1867, were soon internationally recognized and combatted. See Judith Walkowitz, *Prostitution and Victorian Society: Women, Class and the State* (Cambridge, 1980).
42. Concerning the question of the regulation of prostitution by Felicitas Buchner, appended to the petition submitted by the 13 organizations to the Bremen Senate in April 1909, in StA B 4:21–412, p. 1.
43. Ibid., petition.
44. Ibid.
45. See Irmgard Jaeger, "Frauenfürsorgetätigkeit bei der Polizei," in Anna Pappritz, ed., *Einführung in das Studium der Prostitutionsfrage* (Berlin, 1919), pp. 200–20.
46. Marie Elisabeth Lüders, "Eine Forderung ohne Einschränkung," *Die Frau* 1920/21, pp. 53–55, here p. 55. Concerning welfare work in the women's movement during World War I, see also Irene Stoehr and Detel Aurand. "Opfer oder Täter? Frauen im 1. Weltkrieg," *Courage* 7 (1982), Vols. 11 and 12, pp. 43–50 and 44–51.
47. Gertrud Bäumer, "Reaktion in der Frage der Reglimentierung," *Die Frau,* 1932/33, pp. 81–86.
48. It was again introduced in 1939 by the National Socialists and still exists up to the present.

49. Lüders, "Eine Forderung ohne Einschränkung."
50. See Report of the Commission dated November 9, 1920, about the establishment of a welfare office (Proceedings, p. 3).
51. Report No. 3 of November 9, 1920, to the City Parliament of Bremen: Report of the Commission due to establishment of a welfare office, in *Verhandlungen der Bremischen Buergerschaft,* 1920, supplement to the records of the proceedings, p. 4.
52. Proceedings, 1920, of December 10, 1920, p. 640.
53. Compare also Proceedings, 1925.
54. Proceedings, 1926. Request submitted on March 19, 1926, p. 154. Debate on March 30, 1926 (pp. 213–24). I was not successful in locating the text of the resolution by the residents of Helene Street.
55. Ibid., p. 213.
56. Ibid.
57. Ibid. p. 218.
58. Ibid. p. 219.
59. Ibid.
60. The other 800–1,000 prostitutes were scattered throughout Bremen. Ibid., p. 220.
61. Ibid., p. 224.
62. Ibid., p. 219.
63. Dr. Agnes Wurmb, "Noch ein Tagebuch," *Die Frau,* 1926/27, pp. 132–34.
64. StA B 3-P. 1. a. No. 1080. This article was intended as a counter-portrayal to the one by Gabrielle Tergit entitled "Der Fall Machan-Kolomak," which was published in insert 1 of *Berliner Tageblatt,* February 16, 1927.
65. Minna Bahnson, *Vom Leben getötet,* in *Frau und Gegenwart* 8 (February 22, 1927): 2 and 4, here p. 2.
66. Clara Bohm-Schuch, in *Frauenstimme,* Beilage zum *Vorwärts,* August 4, 1927.
67. Ibid.
68. Dorothee Goebler, in *Für's Haus,* Leipzig, July 31, 1927.
69. Augspurg, "Der vorläufige Abschluss," p. 7.
70. *Weser Zeitung,* January 16, 1927.
71. Kirchhoff, "Die bremischen Frauen," p. 7. Also the source for the text of the resolution.
72. Agnes von Zahn-Harnack, p. 83. Youth welfare in particular derived from welfare for the "endangered."
73. See Dora Peyser and Alice Salomon, "Alice Salomon: Ein Lebensbild," in *Alice Salomon,, die Begründerin des sozialen Frauenberufs in Deutschland. Ihr Leben und Ihr Werk* (Cologne, 1958), pp. 9–121.
74. Minna Bahnson, *Frau und Gegenwart,* p. 4.
75. Ibid.
76. Concerning this, see my essays: "Von sittsamen Frauen und liederlichen Weibspersonen," *Courage,* February 1982, pp. 28–33; and "Der Männerhass der Polizeimatrone—Zur Sittlichkeitsbewegung," *Courage,* July 1983, pp. 41–46.
77. Ibid. Anna Pappritz, "Die Einrichtung der weiblichen Polizei," *Der Abolitionist,* August 1, 1927, pp. 55–57, here p. 56.
78. Proceedings, February 27, 1927, p. 56, and April 3, 1927, pp. 131ff.
79. Proceedings, April 30, 1926.
80. See *Die Frau* 37 (1929–30): 503.
81. Proceedings, May 25, 1927, p. 94.
82. Agnes von Zahn-Harnack, in *Nachrichtenblatt des Bundes deutscher Frauenvereine* 12 (1932), Vol. II, pp. 111ff.
83. See Claudia Koonz, "Conflicting Allegiances: Political Ideology and Women Legislators in Weimar Germany," *Signs* 1, No. 3 (1976): 663–83.
84. Auguste Kirchhoff, *"Vom Leben getötet"* in *Die Neue Generation,* April 1927.

*Left:* Bertha Pappenheim (1859–1936), founder of the League of Jewish Women. Photo courtesy of the Leo Baeck Institute, N.Y. (See article by Marion Kaplan.) *Below:* Women at the Ravensbruck Concentration Camp. Photo courtesy of the Leo Baeck Institute, N.Y. (See articles by Sybil Milton and about Katharina Jacob.)

*Top:* Red League of Women and Girls Against Paragraph 218, a Communist group, protests. Photo courtesy of Staats-Archiv Bremen. (See article by Atina Grossmann.)
*Bottom:* Women sewing Nazi flags. Photo courtesy of Landesbildstelle Berlin. (See article by Claudia Koonz.)

*Top:* League of German Girls, a Nazi youth group. Photo courtesy of Landes-bildstelle Berlin. (See article by Claudia Koonz.)

*Bottom:* Women pushing against Paragraph 218 carved on an enormous cross. Poster by Alice Lex-Nerlinger (1931); photo courtesy of Märkisches Museum, Berlin. (See article by Atina Grossmann.)

*Top:* Students in a home economics class of the Hanover Housewives' Association. Photo courtesy of 20 Jahre Hausfrauenvereinsarbeit in Hanover 1915–1935. (See article by Renate Bridenthal.)    *Bottom:* Children at Village School in the Warthegau being lectured on the laws of heredity. Photo courtesy of Hans Peter Bleuel, *Sex and Society in Nazi Germany* (Philadelphia and New York: J.B. Lippincott, 1973.) (See article by Gisela Bock.)

# Helene Stöcker:
# Left-Wing Intellectual
# and Sex Reformer

## Amy Hackett

*Helene Stöcker embodied many of the ideological complexities and ambiguities of pre-Nazi feminism and social reform. As leader of the Federation for the Protection of Mothers (Bund für Mutterschutz), she fought for a new "social morality": a definition of morality which addressed broader social concerns. As an advocate for women's rights, Stöcker went beyond the mainstream of the feminist movement, which she found too reluctant to deal with relationships between men and women. She attempted to reform these sexual relationships and to transform a society that she viewed as based on exploitation and on war. At the same time, she rejected affiliation with any political party, although she was sympathetic to the left in general and to the Bolshevik Revolution in Russia. Amy Hackett's article describes an extraordinary woman who is only now being recognized as the important intellectual and political force that she was. Stöcker's life exemplifies the 1970s feminist maxim that the "personal is political," and also helps us to understand an independent feminist of the left in this era of German history.*

Sex reformer and feminist, Nietzschean and pacifist, Helene Stöcker was first an intellectual. Engaged though she was in myriad causes, indeed often enough burdened by the mundane tasks of mobilizing for short-term reform or long-term revolution, Stöcker's activism was always informed by ideas. Some of these ideas now seem mutually contradictory, perhaps because our imaginations have suffered from knowledge of their subsequent history. Although Stöcker thought she had formed a coherent philosophy, in retrospect we may find her a problematic figure. Temperamentally and philosophically an individualist, despite her many affiliations, she resists easy classification. Certainly, however, she was one of Weimar Germany's conspicuous and critical "left-wing intellectuals," although here she was continuing a career well established during the Wilhelmine Empire.[1] Because Stöcker remains relatively unknown, and because her life and ideas are profoundly intertwined, this essay begins with a biography.

Helene Stöcker was born in Elberfeld, a Rhenish textile center, in 1869. As she recalled it from old age and exile, her upbringing seemed most remarkable in its piety.[2] To his ultimate regret, her father had abandoned missionary training to take over the family textile business. (Helene's great-grandfather had discovered artificial indigo blue.)[3] The Stöckers belonged to one of the few Calvinist congregations that had not joined in the official union with Lutheranism in 1817. The personal experience of Christian rebirth was central to their family piety, as were such outward manifestations as prayer and Bible-reading three times a day, accompanied by hymns with her father at the harmonium. Theater and dancing met with disapproval, and the home library was censored. (This did not protect Stöcker altogether; she counted the *Song of Solomon* as her introduction to the mysteries of sex.)

By her later account, Stöcker was not yet fourteen when, after much inner turmoil, she rejected her family's religion, notably its obsession with sin and damnation. Aware of the multiplicity of faiths, she worried how one could know the "correct" teaching. The oldest of eight children, all but one of them girls, Helene for a time envied two sisters who died as children, since her mother assured her that they were in heaven, having eluded the affliction of original sin. As Helene understood it, "we were not personally guilty" of this sin, "because it was, after all, something passed on . . . because of [which] we always did evil things, the more so the older we were."[4] Stöcker could not stop thinking and questioning—the purpose of human understanding, by her lights—and she could not find the faith that she felt her parents' religion demanded. She did, however, retain a lasting affection for the merciful Christianity of the Sermon on the Mount.

In 1892, Stöcker, aged twenty-two, arrived in Berlin, ostensibly to prepare for the teaching exam but in fact to educate herself as an advocate of women's causes. She had begun this mission in Elberfeld, where a lending library had introduced her to Bebel's treatise on women, among other works of philosophy and science. Stöcker's formal education was unremarkable: a standard middle-class girl's schooling, except that an eye ailment had—to her relief—saved her from the obligatory needlework. The escape from home was delayed by paternal opposition and by the birth of two siblings around the time of her graduation. The birth of Helene's only brother was followed by the long illness of her mother. All this meant heavy responsibility for the oldest girl and kept her at home until a younger sister could take over as mother's helper. Stöcker's zealous advocacy of birth control must have been influenced by this intimate view of maternal exhaustion.

In 1896, after four years of preparatory courses in the informal educational institutions that feminists had created in Berlin, Stöcker entered the university, where she studied literature, philosophy, and national economy. The noted professor of philosophy Wilhelm Dilthey, a favorite teacher, chose her to help edit the correspondence of the Romantic theologian Friedrich Schleiermacher, whose humanistic Christianity and support for female emancipation made him a sympathetic figure. Stöcker left the university and Berlin in 1899 because a key professor refused to accept women students, as was his prerogative before their presence in Prussian universities was officially sanctioned in 1908.

While a student, Stöcker met Alexander Tille, a professor of German at the University of Glasgow. In Berlin to pursue research on the Faust legend, he had left a wife and two young children at home. Stöcker first encountered Tille as the pseudonymous "Social Aristocrat" who had authored a book on her recent revelation: Friedrich Nietzsche. Stöcker characterized their exhilarating but tense relationship as "aesthetic," while Tille apparently complained that it was "ascetic." Soon after the professor returned to Scotland, Stöcker received a telegram notifying her of his wife's sudden death and imploring her to join him—at least as ersatz mother to his children. Thus Stöcker journeyed to Glasgow, where she also enrolled at the university.

Torn between intellectual and nurturing demands, Stöcker increasingly felt the conflict between love for the two children and a gnawing awareness that she and their father differed profoundly on their reading of Nietzsche, notably regarding the social question and women. While Stöcker leaned toward socialism, Tille espoused a Social Darwinism that sanctioned "social conditions under which those more gifted and fit by birth are richly nourished, while the less fit one is, the less he should have to eat, so that the unfit infallibly perish and cannot reproduce." Accordingly, Tille characterized the slums of East London as a "National Hospital" for so admirably disposing of social liabilities.[5] Perhaps hastened by anti-German demonstrations at the university, Tille left Scotland and academia for positions with the Alliance of German Industrialists and the Saarbrücken Chamber of Commerce, where he became an intimate of the steel magnate Baron von Stumm. Moreover, to use current rhetoric, Tille exhibited male chauvinist tendencies.

Clearly, this was a doomed relationship, yet Tille was the only man whom Stöcker had as yet even imagined as a husband. She also contemplated, as perhaps more ideal, "a couple of years of bourgeois marriage and then return[ing] to my work with a child." But the "current form" of marriage was "impossible," and she would consider a "free union as right only if it were a matter of more than pleasure"; nor would she want a child to bear the onus of illegitimacy. There remained her work. As Stöcker told the feminist to whom she confided her plight, and alluding to Nietzsche's Zarathustra, she wanted strength, not happiness.[6]

In Glasgow, Stöcker learned firsthand that women had a harder time than men being both parent and practicing intellectual. Henceforth she felt that her particular mission within feminism was to enable women to combine marriage, motherhood, and a career. In this aim she felt alienated from other German feminists—on both the left and the right—who seemed primarily concerned about women who had no husbands to support them, or who treated women as asexual or, if sexual, as victims of men. The "goal of the women's movement" was, for Stöcker, not just employment *(Broterwerb)*, but the creation of conditions that also made possible "home, love and parenthood."[7]

Stöcker left Glasgow within a year. She finished her studies in Bern, with a dissertation on the Romantic author Wilhelm Friedrich Wackenroder and eighteenth-century aesthetics.[8] Stöcker felt a great affinity for the Romantic period; two of her cultural heroines were Bettina von Arnim and Caroline Michaelis-von Schlegel-Schelling, a collection of whose letters she edited.[9]

In the Romantics, Stöcker found intellectual and spiritual ancestors. They had already discerned the essential elements of "modern love— or 'sexual' philosophy, as we today more soberly and scientifically, but perhaps *not* more aptly call it."[10] Romanticism's "great, wonderful, liberating, reconciling, world-beautifying, life-enriching lesson" was, for Stöcker, "that love is life, that life is love."[11] This love was not only spiritual, but in its perfect form a "unity of soul and senses."[12] The Romantics' unitary world view rejected the man as an ideal against which women must necessarily fall short. Valuing the sexes equally, the Romantics fashioned new ideals of humanity, such as the "androgyne," which united masculine and feminine on a higher plane. Like Stöcker and her comrades, the Romantics struggled against hypocrisy, false shame, and prudery. They understood that marriage transcended the legal institution, and thus demanded correction in case of a mistaken love object.

Caroline's peculiar attraction was "that she possessed to such a singular degree, the greatest of arts, the art of living." Stöcker found in her life a "total unity of feeling, thought and desire, and between thought and action." Such integrity was "to us today the only criterion of morality."[13] Instinctively, it seemed, Caroline led her life by the precepts spelled out in the philosophies of Schlegel, Schleiermacher, and Novalis. Her main weakness was also her virtue: "her unlimited capacity for love, which led her to think a life without love not worth living."[14] Finally, Caroline was herself a "Gretchen" figure, having found herself unwed and pregnant in a Mainz prison cell, sentenced for revolutionary activities, whence she was rescued by her marriage to August Wilhelm von Schlegel.

In 1901 Stöcker returned to Berlin to fight for her ideals. She supported herself as a free-lance writer and lecture-circuit feminist, as which she traveled as far as Russia and Rumania. Involved in various feminist organizations since she arrived in Berlin in the 1890s, she was by now an officer in several, particularly the left-wing Alliance of Progressive Women's Organizations (Verband fortschrittlicher Frauenvereine). Stöcker was, incidentally, a founding member of Germany's first woman suffrage organization in 1901, although she had relatively little faith—even for a German suffragist—that the ballot would accomplish much or that a majority vote should be the essence of democracy. But if men voted, so should women.

Stöcker's primary organizational involvement—as speaker, journal editor, and administrator—was with the Federation for the Protection of Mothers (Bund für Mutterschutz).[15] An organization with diverse members, whose leaders themselves had conflicting agendas, this federation was primarily Stöcker's vehicle from 1905 until her exile in 1933. In its infancy, it survived a dispute with Ruth Bré, herself an illegitimate child and propagandist for single motherhood as a remedy for women's allegedly innate maternal yearnings. Bré, who actually founded the organization in 1904, envisioned rural colonies for Germany's unmarried mothers: an estimated 180,000 a year. Influenced by *völkisch* theory, she also had in mind the breeding and rearing of healthy German stock.[16] In the end, the Federation worked more modestly toward establishing a network of counseling centers and maternity homes where needy women could go for emotional support and material aid, rather than succumbing to the desperation that too often led to infanticide or to the Christian Magdalene homes with their obligatory moralizing.

Because Stöcker believed that sexuality involved both sexes, she solicited men's involvement in her reform efforts. The Federation members included a complement of physicians and sexologists, some of whom grew impatient with Stöcker's harping on ethics and philosophy. In 1908 the organization's journal, originally named *Mutterschutz*, with the subtitle *Journal for the Reform of Sexual Ethics*, split in two: a separate *Sexual Problems* and Stöcker's *The New Generation*.[17] It should be emphasized, however, that Stöcker viewed herself as part of the scientific movement to study sex. Her journal regularly published articles and excerpts from the likes of Auguste Forel, Iwan Bloch,

Sigmund Freud, and Havelock Ellis. In 1911 Stöcker internationalized her efforts when, in conjunction with a large hygiene exhibition in Dresden, she founded the International Union for the Protection of Mothers and Sexual Reform. Germany's preeminence in the scientific study of sex, she explained, gave her own group the lead in this organization.[18]

This essay will not present a detailed history of the Federation for the Protection of Mothers, which suffered at least its share of infighting and splits. The most damaging, in 1910, degenerated into a series of libel suits involving Stöcker's alleged malfeasance in office and—ironically enough—charges and countercharges of extramarital sexual liaisons among its leaders. Stöcker had by then openly established a "free marriage" with Bruno Springer, a lawyer and fellow Federation enthusiast, with whom she lived until his death in 1931 (and to whose grave she continued to send flowers from exile). In this she was true to her principle—and, she thought, that of her organization—that the state had no business interfering in the intimate lives of women and men, at least until that union produced a child. And she and Springer remained childless.

It was Stöcker's fervent belief that ideas counted. Reading Nietzsche had, after all, changed her life. From him she had learned that "when we change [*umändern*], transvalue [*umwerten*] our ideas about things, we also change the things themselves—that we ourselves are the ones who make our life happy or unhappy, worthy or unworthy."[19] Stöcker accordingly resisted those who wanted the Federation to honor practical charity above propaganda for new ideas.

Stöcker did not, to be sure, doubt the need for such practical measures as shelters, counseling centers, and obstetrical help. She understood that mothers must be made economically independent through a general improvement in women's education and chances for employment. More specifically, she wanted extensive maternity insurance. Stöcker's insistence on economic independence made her more open than most German feminists to employment for married women and even to the idea of wages for housework. Here she felt indebted particularly to the American feminist Charlotte Perkins Gilman.[20] The plight of unmarried mothers was unquestionably important to Stöcker, and had been since she read *Faust* as a teenager. Yet the issue was symptomatic of a larger problem, "the reigning confusion of views on sexuality in general."[21] Until sexual ethics themselves were reformed, thousands of mothers would remain outcasts in a society that touted its reverence for "motherhood."

In 1922, the Federation for the Protection of Mothers consolidated its beliefs in a lengthy set of guidelines. While the rhetoric in places reflected the increasingly conservative focus on motherhood and eugenics of the Sex Reform movement during Weimar,[22] by and large this document simply codified what Stöcker had been saying for nearly two decades. Based on a "joyous, life-affirming world-view": "the conviction of the highest value, the sanctity and inalienability of human life," the movement sought "to protect life above all at its source, to let it emerge pure and strong." Hence its name. It also wished "to make human sexuality a powerful instrument not only of reproduction, but of progressive evolution [*Aufwärtsentwicklung*], and concurrently of a heightened and cultivated joy of life [*Daseinsfreude*]." Sexual reform was then "the content and ultimate goal of our efforts."[23]

Such reform required first a break with traditional values, specifically the enshrinement of the double standard in that morality which Germans call *Sittlichkeit,* with its implicit regard for what others will say. Stöcker would measure the morality of an action by whether it were "suited to making human life—social relations—richer and *more harmonious* and free of evils!" She consciously rejected the dualism which, by opposing mind and body, made sex a sin. "Next to hunger," sex was "the most elementary vital instinct [*Lebenstrieb*], which of natural necessity stirs itself in every healthy person." Women, like men, were "integral [*einheitlich*], sensual-spiritual beings, whose spiritual and physical inclinations have an equal right to healthy development, an equal claim to fostering encouragement." Thus, whatever helped transform "the individual into a personality" or led "the whole to a higher and more perfect form of existence" was "moral."[24] Unlike most German feminists who criticized the double standard, Stöcker did not simply suggest that men adopt the standard imposed on women.

The Federation further rejected the conventional equation of "virtue" with "abstinence" for men or women. Intercourse, in itself neither moral nor immoral, arose from a strong natural urge. Intent and circumstance determined the ethical nature of any given sexual act. Reproduction was, to be sure, the most important function of sex, but not its sole purpose. "Rather a sex life appropriate to one's nature and circumstance is, for the human being, a precondition for an internally and externally harmonious life." To be ethical, intercourse presupposed two similarly inclined wills. "Then, however, a love life opens a plenitude of new possibilities for life and experience, ways of deepening and refining one's knowledge of mankind and one's own view of life." It was, moreover, "the only way to the full creative unfolding of human existence and nature in *motherhood* and *fatherhood*." Such a rigorous ethics, fraught with deep responsibility for the future of humanity, precluded sex for adolescents. The 1922 guidelines suggested abstinence until "full physical and emotional maturity." Adults themselves were warned to be mindful of their responsibility for "the possible consequences" of sexual activity and of the need to respect the rights of others, which seemed to include the expectation of sexual faithfulness.[25]

Thus, despite its attacks on conventional morality and although it was anathema to conservatives, the Federation hardly endorsed sexual license. The 1922 guidelines praised *"legally recognized marriage as the highest and most desirable form of human sexual relationship,* as best suited to guarantee a lasting regulation of sexual intercourse, the healthy formation of the family, the preservation of the human community."[26] This formulation may have represented a compromise between Stöcker and more conservative elements in the Federation. Probably it reflected the search for stability after the upheaval of World War I. Nonetheless, Stöcker had always emphasized her respect for the true basis of marriage in the "trinity" of mother, father, and child. And even the 1922 statement conceded that *"life-long, strictly monogamous marriage* always and everywhere exists and has existed only as an *ideal* attainable by the few."* Most sex occurred before and outside marriage. For emotional and economic reasons, legal marriage could not encompass all the possibilities of *"justified love-relationships."*[27] The basic point Stöcker wanted to make was that legal formalities, a marriage certificate, and the state's blessing did not render an otherwise empty relationship somehow moral. Logically, the Federation lobbied to expand the grounds for divorce, especially to replace the "guilt" concept with the recognition that a marriage could simply be dead. Moreover, Stöcker's approval of legitimate marriage was conditional on the "true equality of rights of the sexes."[28] Finally, the Federation reiterated its opposition to prostitution, which "degrades love to a commercial ware, destroys woman's human dignity and creates an inextinguishable source of communicable disease and crime."[29]

Stöcker's rhetoric reveals her debt to Nietzsche. Her efforts to enlist him as a feminist are too complex and dependent on textual sources to consider in detail here. The important fact is that she found it vital to soften his misogynist reputation. Her own transvaluation of values involved liberation from the tyranny of the masculine world view, as well as from conventional ascetic morality. Women had accepted the male ideal

> without asking whether it is the right one for us. . . . Precisely that is what we must increasingly learn: to create our own personal view of the world and life, as it derives from our own nature. . . . If any view is eminently masculine, then for that reason it is impossible for us; for we are not men and do not want to be—we want to be something else altogether.[30]

Consistent with German feminist tradition, Stöcker stressed the unlikeness of the sexes, taking notable pride in women's greater sensitivity and rejecting the "masculine" tendency to abstraction. Her sex seemed also more likely to attain the ultimate synthesis of true humanity—once feminists had prevailed in their efforts.

Stöcker found in Nietzsche above all the celebrator of life and the Faustian individualist who wanted not disciples to hang on his every word but followers who would stake their own paths, create their own values. Yet she tempered heroic individualism with a more traditional liberal variety. For example, Stöcker defended abortion as simply "the right over oneself."[31] The state had no business with one's private life, so far as no second party was affected, and the fetus had no legal rights as an individual.

The one area where Stöcker made no attempt to defend Nietzsche was economics. She did, however, forgive him. "Would it not be insane," she asked, "to demand of the prophet of the Superman that he should also study economics and social science in order to identify the exact path that one must take to reach his goal?" For Stöcker, Nietzsche represented "one side of our culture, while Socialism—taken in the broadest sense—[represents] the other." The two should be related, as "social-moral efforts attempt to lay the groundwork from which a healthier, physically and mentally superior humanity can grow." Unfortunately, social reformers "easily forget to direct their glasses to the heights," while Nietzsche, from his "'perspective of eternity' . . . often seemed to overlook that an increase in strength and beauty of the human species is necessarily connected to external conditions."[32]

In her memoirs, Stöcker elaborated on the creative tension that had animated her life. The religious or ethical atmosphere of her parents' household had—after her rejection of its dogmatic elements, particularly the otherworldly heaven and its necessary hell—become transmuted into an effort to create "heaven on earth." The transformation of social and economic circumstances "was only the beginning." Beyond this was her foremost goal, the creation of a "free and intellectually highly developed personality, responsible for itself."

> This perhaps is an explanation why the two poles of human evolution, the striving for social justice and the urge for the highest personal development, for me always remained inextricably connected. This for me has for perhaps the last half-century been expressed by the words "Nietzsche *and* Socialism."[33]

Stöcker's wish to reconcile Nietzsche and socialism, the individual and society, of course reflected the complex society that such phenomena as industrialization and urbanization had produced by the late nineteenth century, and not just in Germany. In England, Havelock Ellis identified "Socialism versus Individualism" as a central quandary. A frequent contributor to *The New Generation*, Ellis shared Stöcker's belief in social and racial hygiene. "The society of the future" would be, in his words, a "house of cards" if not constructed with sound individuals, "and no individualism worth the name is possible unless a sound social organization permits the breeding of individuals who matter. On this plane," he concluded, "Socialism and Individualism move in the same circle."[34]

And so we arrive at the vexed issue of Stöcker's enthusiasm for eugenics, a notion that made particular demands on those who might be inclined to balance the demands of individual and society. Stöcker was attracted to eugenics both by its scientific pretensions and by Nietzsche's injunction not merely to reproduce but to improve the race. No doubt she also imagined a potential for ameliorating real human misery. After the atrocities of National Socialism, it is hard to discuss any German's preachings about the "improvement of the race" without cringing. Yet three points must be made at the outset. First, for Stöcker—if not for all Federation supporters—the group to be improved was the whole human race, not just Aryans or Germans. Except for her evident pride in German preeminence in the scientific study of sex, she was innocent of nationalism. Second, as is evident from the quotation by Ellis, eugenics was not solely a German fancy. Indeed, it was thought up by the Englishman Sir Francis Galton, and early carried to practical extremes in the sterilization laws that various American states began to pass before World War I, laws that German eugenics-enthusiasts looked to as models. Eugenic ideas were "in the air," to be plucked by those on the left or right. For some, eugenics promised human progress; for others, it was a way to trim the social budget. Third, few readers of this essay would probably reject such modern medical techniques as amniocentesis to detect fetal defects, although one might, of course, condemn such potential misuses as the purposeful selection of males. Such selective techniques are clearly in keeping with the eugenic impulse. Yet they make explicit the need for an answer to the question: what constitutes "defective"? And who then decides? Will it be the mother, or parents, whose life would be most profoundly touched by the birth of a severely disabled child? Or will society or the state impose their own criteria? And what, then, is the state's responsibility to those individuals as whose advocate it sees itself?

Not only could Stöcker not have foreseen the crimes against humanity committed by Nazi Germany; in the words of Walther Borgius, a leading Federation supporter and racial hygiene sympathizer: "The whole question of reproduction and heredity is today still such a dark and unexplored area; one has, in the individual instance, so extraordinarily few clues as to what the two parents and what the many ancestors are mainly responsible for contributing to the child's constitution, that it is doubtless questionable to proceed all too rigorously."[35] Attempts to be "scientific" in the absence of exact knowledge were bound to be problematic, whether through unwarranted specificity or too broad generalizations. But Stöcker sounded confident in explaining the biological basis of the "New Ethics" to *Mutterschutz* readers: "As humankind has subjected all other things to its rational insight, so must it become increasingly master over one of the most important matters for humanity: the creation of a new human. One will have to find means of preventing the incurably ill or degenerate from reproducing."[36] Hers was the same optimistic spirit with which progressives have typically turned to education to improve society.

For Stöcker, as it had been for Galton, eugenics amounted to a "new religion, a declaration of earthly existence after we had given up hope of a heavenly paradise in the hereafter."[37] Indeed one might connect her faith in eugenics with her adolescent religious turmoil, remembering that the German *Erbsünde* (literally "hereditary sin") carries a connotation missing in "original sin." Ignorant of the sometimes random nature of chromosomal changes as a basis of heredity, Stöcker's contemporaries tended to focus on environmental causes of birth defects, notably alcoholism and syphilis. For many supporters, then, the ultimate purpose of eugenics was to prevent the "sins" of the fathers—and mothers—from being visited on future generations.

Nietzsche reinforced Stöcker's attraction to eugenics. His hopes for the "Superman," his injunction to heed the quality rather than merely the quantity of offspring, and his notion that the test for a prospective spouse should be the desire to create a child together were far more ambitious than the usual Social Darwinism. Amid the hysteria over Germany's declining birthrate before World War I, Stöcker firmly resisted the coerced breeding *(Gebärzwang)* implicit in efforts to outlaw contraceptives.[38] Not only was the decline an inevitable concomitant of civilization, she explained, not only did high infant mortality effectively nullify a high birthrate, but such sanctions were an impermissible breach of women's right to self-determination, which threatened to turn them into objects. Stöcker agreed with Ellis that police measures would not produce the sense of social responsibility that must precede an effective eugenics program. She preferred to educate, although she would also use state authority to oblige would-be spouses to produce an ancestral tree.[39] She hoped that those with hereditary problems would see their responsibility to future generations and agree to vasectomies or tubal ligations.

The "socialism" that Stöcker identified as the opposite pole to Nietzsche in the forces that acted on her did not impel her into conventional politics. "I have never been a member of any political party," she reported to U.S. immigration authorities in 1942.[40] Yet this nonpartisanship should not be understood as apathy toward political issues or as self-imposed isolation from organizational activities. Throughout her life Stöcker belonged to—indeed helped found and lead—a myriad of organizations designed to influence public policy. But she identified with none of the parties from which Germans had to choose in either the Empire or the Weimar Republic. She inhabited instead the critical world of left-wing and pacifist committees.

Among the existing parties, Stöcker would seem to have identified most closely with the short-lived Independent Social Democratic Party (USPD), which arose from a wartime split within the SPD over that party's support for the war. It collapsed during the early years of the Weimar Republic, weakened by the assassination of its leader Kurt Eisner at the hands of a right-wing fanatic in 1919, and by the polarization of the left between the SPD and the German Communist Party. Stöcker admired her friend Eisner for his "idealism," his belief that "political-social renewal" demanded a "renewal of sentiments [*Gesinnung*]," "humanity and justice."[41]

The same ideas echoed in Stöcker's appreciation of Gustav Landauer, the anarchist-socialist whose desperate hope for a German revolution finally led him into the USPD and gave him sufficient prominence that, like Eisner, he was murdered. In 1917, Stöcker joined Landauer in founding the Central Office for Human Rights (Zentralstelle Völkerrecht), a human rights organization. She specifically praised Landauer's *Aufruf zum Sozialismus (Call to Socialism)*, a document that called Marxism the "plague of our age and the curse of the socialist movement."[42] Landauer criticized Marxism particularly for its inadequate attention to the autonomous will. The historical laws of capitalism would not, he asserted, bring forth socialism; rather people must desire and build it. They must also give it an ethical basis. It was, no doubt, this insistence on individual rebirth as a prerequisite for historical change that appealed to Stöcker, who noted Landauer's belief in the "inalienable value of the human soul."[43] She might also have found some appeal in Landauer's anti-urbanism and his search for a community based on such preindustrial institutions as the family. A certain anti-urbanism seems to have been involved in the purchase of a country house by Stöcker and Springer, who moved from Berlin to suburban Nikolassee in 1912.[44]

Certainly, Stöcker and Landauer shared pessimism about the SPD, which he charged with wanting just a more efficient state capitalism. By ignoring the dilemma of ends and means, Landauer predicted, the German socialists would finish as worshipers of the state. The anarchist wanted first to change society. In the voluntarist tradition of German idealism whose most notable recent example had been Nietzsche,

Landauer insisted that the state was a mere illusion, which would fade away if individuals withheld support.[45]

Stöcker's socialism was itself far removed from any rigid Marxism. She showed little concern for the precise condition of the means of production. But it was probably Stöcker who formulated the line in the 1922 guidelines according to which the Federation for the Protection of Mothers strove for a "transformation of social life in which the human being, the living personality, and no longer property, dead possessions, is *its own purpose and untouchable.*"[46] In 1929, Stöcker characterized socialism as "the striving for a higher social justice"; more than a matter of economics, it was "an ethical demand for the recognition of human dignity, a modern religion, whose demands on society must be supplemented by the demand which everyone must make on *himself.*"[47]

Stöcker did not disguise her own contempt for the SPD as a self-proclaimed proponent of socialism, particularly after it assumed the role of ruling party during the postwar revolution and as part of the Weimar coalition. She characterized the majority Socialists as opportunists *(Arrivisten),* corrupted by their newfound power. Forgetting their own past as outcasts, they were now in league with reaction to put down more radical demands with force. Throughout Weimar, Stöcker warned against the resurgence of the right and bewailed the divisions on the left. She held up as something of a model the left's unity at the time of the Kapp Putsch, when a general strike had saved the republic. Only the left's disorganization, she warned, would allow the right to triumph.[48] Yet her warnings proved futile, and she continued to condemn leftist sectarianism. Moreover, her own attacks on the SPD exemplified the divisiveness she decried.

Stöcker's disgust with mainline Socialists was not, incidentally, unrelated to her concern with sexual reform. She faulted all the large socialist parties worldwide for their indifference toward such matters as birth control.

> In the "meantime," until the abolition of capitalism and the creation of a new socialist society is completed, in the meantime in which we are living, birth control is surely able to alleviate much misery and make of women—overburdened, helpless beasts of burden—strong, free and healthy personalities, capable of taking their own necessary and active part in the struggle for a better world.

She saw birth control clinics such as those run by the Federation and by Margaret Sanger in the United States as "practical socialism."[49]

Stöcker looked east to the Soviet experiment with some interest; indeed she herself journeyed to the Soviet Union. *The New Generation* regularly reported on Soviet attempts to reform sexual life, as well as

on the progress—or lack thereof—made by women.[50] Clearly Bolshevik Russia, for all its successes, was not the most perfect society that
Stöcker might envision. Yet she was more disturbed by the intemper-
ate nature of attacks on the Soviet Union, particularly by those whose
interests were served by international tension, be they politicians or
arms dealers, the "Bloody International."[51] Human rights were often
endangered or disregarded. "But only he has the moral right to defend
human rights against Russia, who in . . . a *similar* situation has not also
sinned against the law of socialism and individual human rights."[52]

The horrors of World War I indelibly colored Stöcker's political
thought during the Weimar Republic, even as she channeled more and
more of her activism into the pacifist cause. The world conflict had
destroyed life, health, and industrial production, but still more devastating had been the "loss of faith in human reason [*Einsicht*] and culture." Anyone who might have hoped in 1914 that humankind had
made great progress beyond the cave, who had foreseen a time when
the "common man" might reach the level of "thinkers and poets," must
despair at the "regression into barbarism." The transvaluation of values
that Stöcker had optimistically envisioned had been stood on its head.
The demolition of values had spawned rampant class struggle as the
tone of domestic politics reached new heights of brutality and hatred.
The war had not discredited militarism; at most, it was momentarily
exhausted. Only generations of struggle would ever extirpate the
"spirit of violence" that was now loose. Only "serious, conscious,
understanding, unegotistical participation in the fate of the community" could heal the wounds of war. But the bloody struggles of
Weimar's birth seemed to have sabotaged "the revolution, the will to
live together in a new spirit, in truth and goodness."[53]

Stöcker characteristically sought an intellectual escape from this desperate situation. She invoked Romain Rolland, whose *Au-dessus de la
mêlée (Above the Conflict)* had been a beacon to war-weary Europeans.

> Precisely we who strive for a refinement of ethics, whose ideal of a new
> generation of purer and happier love, marriage and family life can only be
> realized on the basis of a world liberated from bloody force, have the self-
> evident duty, in these difficult days, to struggle against force, which still
> reigns on both sides, to stand "above the mêlée," to work for . . . a better
> world.[54]

In this spirit, Stöcker devoted her energies increasingly to the cause of
peace.

Stöcker's real involvement with pacifism began during World War I.
In 1915 she attended the international Women's Peace Congress at the
Hague, flouting the sentiments of most German feminists, who had
turned their energies to national defense at the home front. At the

Hague, incidentally, she argued against the congress's equal emphasis on woman suffrage, when stopping the war should be paramount. Here she was at odds with Anita Augspurg and Lida Gustava Heymann, the two German feminists most involved in planning the congress. For Stöcker, enfranchising women was only one small step in the search for peace.[55]

After the war, Stöcker filled the pages of *Die neue Generation* with reports from around the world of pacifist and war resistance activities. She herself belonged to several pacifist groups, including the Federation for a New Fatherland (Bund neues Vaterland), German Peace Cartel (Deutsches Friedenskartell), German Peace Society (Deutsche Friedensgesellschaft)—on whose central committee she served, the War-Resisters' International—which she helped found in 1921, and the Women's International League for Peace and Freedom, which ultimately grew out of the Hague meeting. Stöcker's international pacifist and feminist connections formed the network that enabled her to survive a decade of exile, which, after years in Switzerland, concluded with emigration to the United States via the far east. Terminally ill with cancer, and suffering from a variety of other physical disabilities when she arrived in California in 1941, she crossed this country and ended up on Riverside Drive, in the midst of the German emigrant culture of Manhattan's Upper West Side.

Stöcker's activities in the cause of peace were, of course, undergirded by ideas. No doubt she was primarily responsible for the "Profession of Faith in Pacifism" ("Bekenntnis zum Pazifismus"), which was the most significant innovation in the 1922 Federation guidelines. This new plank argued that the organization's goal of protecting and encouraging motherhood and *"incipient life"* would be "senseless" without further engagement for *"existing, flourishing life."* As the Federation fought against sexual violence, so it must oppose *"the principle of brute force altogether,* . . . the principle of the permissible—indeed meritorious—murder of other humans." Bitter experience had demonstrated the connection between individual happiness and general morality. "The enrichment of personal life in love, marriage and parenthood" was possible only in a society trying to liberate itself from "bloody force, from . . . the suppression of other classes, races or sexes." World War I and its aftermath had proven how hatred destroyed, while only "love, *human understanding and cooperation"* provided a basis for culture. Hence the Federation would promote "understanding and respect for the personality and human dignity" not only among Germans, but beyond the border. "The love of fatherland and one's own people does not justify injustice toward foreign peoples." Disputes between nations must be settled amicably and justly. The ultimate goal was, fittingly, the "triumph of motherliness, which expresses itself in love and cooperation, victory of a view of life and the world that overcomes hatred and barbarism through reason and love."[56]

Stöcker elaborated her views on the tactics of achieving peace in a 1922 address to yet another international peace conference at the Hague. Representing the German Peace Cartel, she proposed that in the event of mobilization, it was the duty of unions and pacifist groups to enter upon a general strike until the offending government or governments recalled their troops and submitted to international arbitration.[57] The idea of a general strike to halt war was, of course, not a new one, having been discussed in socialist circles before World War I—which, then, provided devastating commentary on the likelihood of such an event. Indeed, no one could have been more aware than Stöcker of the seductive power of national defense for existing socialist parties, particularly the SPD.

But Stöcker had witnessed the general strike that defeated the Kapp Putsch. Moreover, she linked her proposals for group action to a demand that individuals accept moral responsibility for preventing war, since a strike could not just be ordered from above by leaders. Pacifists, in particular, must awaken a sense of individual accountability, must bolster self-respect that was so attenuated that men could actually see themselves as "cannon fodder, war materiel, to be thrown against the enemy, to be deployed, misused and destroyed." The state in whose defense so many had died was, for Stöcker, "no untouchable object of moral perfection," "no God or idol." A state should be merely a "human community" that served the people living in it. A "radical pacifist"—as Stöcker identified herself—must also combat the capitalist system, because war must be fought through attacking its causes, one of which was the difference between propertied and nonpropertied classes.[58]

In 1928, Stöcker cited a study of ant behavior that seemed to show the possibility of that "psychological transformation" she thought imperative for peace. First, however, must come the understanding that wars were not—as Germans were especially fond of imagining—a matter of fate. *"Every war is a matter of will."* The question then became: why would most people—whatever their nationality—murder other humans?

Partly, Stöcker thought, people murdered out of a desire to conform, some "idiotic herd nature," bolstered by a "catastrophic inferiority complex." But at least as important as this passive trait were "dark primitive instincts," which found war actually "pleasurable [*lustvoll*]," as well as necessary. Nietzsche, of course, had explored the psychology of human cruelty, and Stöcker had herself experienced the intoxication at the outbreak of World War I, when individuals delivered themselves over to some purportedly greater whole. She speculated that an "instinct to murder" might be an artifact from primeval times, when only the strongest prevailed in the struggle for food and sexual satisfaction. Whatever the roots of violence, pacifists would not succeed unless they recognized mankind's "psychological burden of hatred and cruelty." These brutal instincts must be made conscious so that they might be suppressed. Still more effective, Stöcker argued, was their replacement by equally strong, but more benign—indeed, positive—instincts.

This exchange would require a "spiritual evolution, a total transformation," which would indeed be "the greatest and most significant of all revolutions." Instinctual hatred must be redirected from other humans to *"the inadequacy of conditions, to the senselessness of mutual destruction."* Stöcker would awaken *"the will to transform the world:* to make the world a place of joy, worth living in for all." In the ambivalent love-hate constellation, Stöcker emphasized the positive: "the pleasure in others' happiness, the empathy with another's suffering."[59]

Recent experiments with ants, designed to demonstrate Freud's instinct theory, seemed to give some basis to Stöcker's hopes for human transformation. Two groups of ants, which ordinarily would have fought to the end, were given larvae or pupae to tend. Not only had their hostilities decreased, but the two groups had finally formed an alliance, with most of the insects protecting the young. Thus, if war might prevail over the instinct for self-preservation, the urge to care for a new generation seemed supreme—"at least in ants."

These experiments suggested an obvious agenda. Peace would not come from the League of Nations or Locarno-like treaties, for these were built on the tired mentality that equated peace with defense preparedness. Nor would parliamentary votes or majority resolutions end war. Only those who educated and led the coming generations could ultimately combat the "murder instinct." They must cultivate in their charges the instincts to care for and preserve life. And the task was urgent: the tempo of technical development in warfare threatened to overwhelm the pace of psychological change.[60]

Stöcker's pacifism made her a keen observer of Gandhi's campaign for Indian independence. Defending him against Communist charges that nonviolence was counterrevolutionary, she countered that Marxism, when embodied in a party, was itself "conservative in its belief in force." Stöcker distinguished between the conservative aspects of Gandhi's world view and his methods, which recognized that it was absurd to use forces so inferior to its enemy in tanks and bombs. "Spiritual-moral weapons," in which imperialism must be the inferior force, seemed more promising. In any case, Gandhi's campaign was "an attempt of similar historic magnitude to the Bolshevik attempt to realize Socialism. Both are human feats whose grand motives we want to follow with respect—even if they cannot lead to full success, . . . with which we must reckon, given the tragic nature of the world."[61] Stöcker's relative hopefulness for Gandhi's efforts may have paid unacknowledged tribute to some perceived greater civility of British politics, even though she characterized Labour's opposition to Indian independence as perhaps ironic, but typical of normal Socialist Party behavior.[62]

If Stöcker viewed the world as a tragic stage, the drama unfolding in Germany seemed downright grim. In what turned out to have been the final years of the Weimar Republic, as worldwide depression and the rise of National Socialism signaled a resurgence of political and social conflict, Stöcker seemed increasingly haunted by the implications of her pacifist beliefs for domestic politics. Recalling Eisner, Luxemburg, Liebknecht, and the many other martyrs of the left, she wondered whether nonviolence could prevail in such a brutal political culture. Could one simply turn oneself over "with bound hands"? The ethical personality seemed helpless against the "stupidity and hardheartedness of capitalism and militarism."[63]

Like Landauer, Stöcker was compelled by what she identified as "the problem." Discussing class struggle and nonviolence in 1930, she acknowledged that means can so taint ends that we sink to the level of our enemies. The question remained how to move "as *quickly* but also as *nonviolently* as possible—in other words, in the foreseeable future—from the horrible present," dominated by hatred and the "bloody struggle" of parties, classes, and races, to a social order in which power and the means of production are accessible to all. Was not the "active revolutionary socialist, the simple Communist worker," who was courageous enough to participate in such activities as a "not completely nonviolent" general strike (which could, indeed, turn into an armed defense against reaction), at least as necessary as a "nonviolent martyr"?[64]

Stöcker explained that prophets and politicians had different tasks. Politicians were by nature impatient. And any politician who chose to struggle, even nonviolently, against oppression would almost inevitably be caught up in "destruction and killing." This "tragic" world often presented the choice between action with guilt and passivity with complicity. Stöcker borrowed a theory from Viennese feminist Rosa Mayreder to explain further the dilemma of would-be revolutionaries. The first stage of social change was presided over by a "genius" or theoretician who was not terribly concerned with reality. The organizing genius, more in touch with the world, followed. Finally came the tactician. Constraining all these figures was the law inherent in power itself: "*Whoever possesses power has only the choice between using the means appropriate to its retention,* or, on the other hand, losing power."[65] Thus was Machiavelli wed to the nineteenth century's "scientific" fondness for stages of development.

The concept of nonviolence remained in its first phase, even though its lineage reached back to primitive Christianity. Hence its leaders were martyrs like Gandhi. Class struggle, on the other hand, had generally attained the second stage, although in the Soviet Union it had already triumphed. No ideology could remain pure once in power, Stöcker explained. Nonviolence would exhibit the same contradictions should it achieve success. Meanwhile, the masses must be led to freedom and dignity. In this struggle, each individual must choose the stage most compatible with his or her talents. Above all, Stöcker counseled against arrogance: Jesus, Plato, and Tolstoy never bore political responsibility. Unfortunately, she conceded, the third stage seemed to attract harder, less scrupulous personalities.

The duty to overcome class and racial division remained paramount. If struggle seemed unavoidable, then "one must hold bravely to those who embody the higher development." Those in the first phase must constantly remind those who had gone further to remember their origins. Stöcker was herself clearly most comfortable in the first stage, upholding ideals. In 1929, for example, she had refused to sign an "otherwise excellent" declaration against war because it contained the word *Erhebung* (uprising), which she understood to imply force. "Because," she explained, "I do not want to call upon other people to engage in an action which seems to me problematic—in its effect and its motives—for which I am not sure that I myself can accept the responsibility."[66] If nothing could be kept alive of the original impulses of a movement, then idealists such as Stöcker must help create new ideas. In Weimar Germany she enjoined them "without hesitation" to "lend critical support to those struggling for the high ideals of proletarian liberation—and the stronger our moral support, the less violent means will be necessary." Finally, Stöcker warned, only someone who "grasped the whole danger and impotence of the attainment of power which promises paradise to the poor and oppressed can comprehend the deep wisdom of a statement which has not yet lost meaning: 'What profiteth it a man to gain the world, if he lose his soul?' "[67]

Helene Stöcker's biblical query in a discussion of revolutionary tactics underscores the essential integrity of her career in the service of human and social transformation. Rejecting the narrow faith of her parents, she insisted throughout her life on an ethical foundation for her ideas. It was thus fitting that she promoted her plans for Sex Reform as a "new ethics." A constant concern for individual responsibility arose naturally enough for this woman, who was first an intellectual and individualist. There is no question that this mentality created tensions for the woman who also considered herself a socialist fighting for the masses. One might argue that Stöcker's sense of the tragedy in politics was an attempt to escape from the harsh realities of power. But perhaps she knew herself, and where her own effectiveness lay. Spending her life fighting for unpopular causes, Stöcker did not lack courage.

Stöcker's life showed further continuity in her persistent feminism, though the structure of this essay might imply a transition from feminist to pacifist. Certainly World War I made peace seem a more urgent issue than ever before; moreover, the Weimar Republic and the Russian Revolution opened up new political worlds that demanded confrontation, particularly for women, who had been excluded from much political activity in Wilhelmine Germany. The decline of organized feminism in Weimar and the increasing legitimacy of the Federation for the Protection of Mothers also contributed to the impression that the field of action changed for Stöcker. Yet, as the 1922 Federation guidelines made clear, Stöcker believed that "feminine" values were a key to peace.

## Notes

1. Stöcker was one of only two women (the other, the literary figure Annette Kolb) featured in Istvan Deak, *Weimar Germany's Left-Wing Intellectuals: A Political History of the Weltbühne and its Circle* (Berkeley and Los Angeles, 1968).
2. Stöcker's unpublished "Lebensabriss," located in the Swarthmore College Peace Collection, is my primary source of biographical information. On her religious background, see especially the chapter entitled "Kindheit/Jugend."
3. Ingeborg Richarz-Simons, "Dr. phil. Helene Stöcker, 1869–1943: Sexualreformerin und Pazifistin," *Wuppertaler Biographien* 9 (Wuppertal, 1970): 81.
4. "Kindheit/Jugend," p. 31.
5. Tille, as quoted in Marielouise Janssen-Jurreit, "Sexualreform und Geburtenrückgang—Über die Zusammenhänge von Bevölkerungspolitik und Frauenbewegung um die Jahrhundertwende," in Annette Kuhn and Gerhard Schneider, eds., *Frauen in der Geschichte* (Düsseldorf, 1979), pp. 60–61.
6. Stöcker to Anna Pappritz (Glasgow, 22 February 1900). Pappritz papers, Helene Lange archives, Institut für Soziale Fragen, Berlin-Dahlem.
7. Stöcker, "Zur Reform der sexuellen Ethik," *Mutterschutz* 1 (1901): 10–11 (hereafter *MS*).
8. *Zur Kunstanschauung des XVIII. Jahrhunderts: Von Winckelmann bis zu Wackenroder* (Berlin, 1904).
9. Karoline Michaelis, *Eine Auswahl ihrer Briefe*, ed. and with an Introduction by Stöcker (Berlin, 1912).
10. Ibid., p. XVI.
11. Ibid., p. IX.
12. Ibid., p. XIII.
13. Ibid., pp. XVII–XVIII.
14. Ibid., pp. XXI.
15. The most complete and accessible account in English of the Federation for the Protection of Mothers is in Richard J. Evans, *The Feminist Movement in Germany 1894–1933* (London and Beverly Hills, 1976), pp. 115–43. See also Katherine Anthony, *Feminism in Germany and Scandinavia* (New York, 1915).

16. The Federation's first proclamation reflected Bré's concern for the *Volkskraft.* "Aufruf," *MS* 1 (1905): 254–58. See Bré [Elisabeth Bouness], *Das Recht auf Mutterschaft: Eine Forderung zur Bekämpfung der Prostitution, der Frauen- und Geschlechtskrankheiten* (Leipzig, 1903).
17. "An unsere Leser!" and "Geleitwort zum IV. Jahrgang," *MS* 3 (1907): 500–04.
18. "Lebensabriss," chap. "Vortrags- und Erholungsreisen 1905–1912," p. 65.
19. "Zur Reform der sexuellen Ethik," *MS* 1 (1905): 3.
20. Stöcker, "Die Hauswirtschaft als Beruf," *Die Liebe und die Frauen,* 2d ed. (Minden in Westf., 1908), pp. 65–70.
21. "Zur Reform," p. 1.
22. Atina Grossmann discusses this trend in "The New Woman and the Rationalization of Sexuality in Weimar Germany," in Ann Snitow, et al., eds, *Powers of Desire: The Politics of Sexuality* (New York: Monthly Review Press, 1983), pp. 153–71.
23. "Richtlinien des Deutschen Bundes für Mutterschutz," *Die neue Generation* 18 (1922): 383 (hereafter *NG*).
24. Ibid., pp. 383–84.
25. Ibid., p. 384.
26. Ibid., p. 385.
27. Ibid.
28. Ibid., p. 386.
29. Ibid., p. 385.
30. "Unsere Umwertung der Werte," *Das Magazin für Literatur* 67 (1898): 1016–17 (hereafter *NfL*).
31. "Das Recht über sich selbst," *NG* 4 (1908): 270–73. In this essay, Stöcker harked back to a German source, Wilhelm von Humboldt, for a defense of the individual against the state. Humboldt was also an inspiration for John Stuart Mill, *On Liberty,* ed. and with an Introduction by Currin V. Shields (Indianapolis, 1956), pp. 69–70. Havelock Ellis was another Englishman who cited Humboldt. See *The Task of Social Hygiene,* 2d ed. (Boston and New York, 1927), p. 61, on the impermissibility of state interference in marital relationships.
32. "Friedrich Nietzsche und die Frauen," *MfL* 67 (1898): 156–57.
33. "Lebensabriss," chap. "Lebensgemeinschaft," p. 20.
34. Havelock, Ellis, "The Care of the Unborn" (1908) in *Views and Reviews: A Selection of Uncollected Articles, 1884–1932* 1 (London, 1932): 245–46.
35. Walther Borgius, "Mutterschutz und Rassenhygiene," *MS* 1 (1905): 211.
36. "Zur Reform," p. 9.
37. "Lebensabriss," chap. "Arbeit im Bund für Mutterschutz," p. 42.
38. "Staatlicher Gebärzwang oder Rassenhygiene?," *NG* 10 (1914): 134–49.
39. For a discussion of such ideas, which emphasizes the appeal of their seemingly scientific and progressive underpinnings, see Janssen-Jurreit, "Sexualreform und Geburtenrückgang," esp. pp. 62–64, which mentions the popularity of the "genetic biography" notion.
40. Stöcker to Donald Parry, Dept. of Justice, Alien Registration Bureau (New York City, 29 January 1942). Copy in Stöcker papers, Box 7.
41. "Kurt Eisner: Zum zehnjährigen Todestag. 21. Februar 1919," *NG* 25 (1929): 113.
42. Cited in Eugene Lunn, *Prophet of Community: The Romantic Socialism of Gustav Landauer* (Berkeley, 1973), p. 190. For a lengthy discussion of Landauer's relevant ideas, see pp. 190–231. For Stöcker's praise, see "Zu Gustav Landauers Gedächtnis," *NG* 25 (1929): 152.
43. Ibid.
44. "Lebensabriss," chap. "Vortrags- und Erholungsreisen, 1905–12," pp. 50–51.
45. Lunn, *Prophet,* pp. 210–12, 224–25.
46. "Richtlinien," pp. 286–287.
47. Review of the proceedings of the 1928 Dutch Socialist congress in *NG* 25 (1929): 241–42.

48. "Entmilitarisierung," *NG* 16 (1920): 113–24.
49. Report on 1925 birth control congress in New York City, which Stöcker attended, in *NG* 21 (1925): 183–84.
50. See, e.g., *NG* 25 (1929): 174, which reported that Russian women's participation in elections was low, despite agitation directed at them; and 225–31, for a favorable discussion of marriage and divorce in the Soviet Union. *NG* 26 (1930): 101 cited a Russian proverb, "A hen is no bird—a woman is no person," and commented that "new attitudes" had not yet totally replaced such views, but that women were making strides; a later issue that year (pp. 204–06) published a positive report on Soviet abortion clinics by two German physicians.
51. See, e.g., "Der Zug nach rechts," *NG* 26 (1930): 84–86; *NG* 25 (1929): 27–28.
52. Ibid., p. 129.
53. "Über dem Handgemenge," *NG* 16 (1920): 1–4.
54. Ibid., p. 4.
55. *Bericht-Rapport-Report: International Congress of Women, The Hague—28th April–May 1st 1915* (Amsterdam, [1915]), pp. 126–27.
56. "Richtlinien," pp. 287–88.
57. "Generalstreik und Kriegsdienstverweigerung (Radikalpazifismus)" (speech at 1922 International Peace Conf., the Hague) in Gisela Brinker-Gabler, ed., *Frauen gegen den Krieg* (Frankfurt/M., 1980), pp. 100–02.
58. Ibid.
59. "Psychologische Umwandlung" (1928), ibid., pp. 103–09.
60. Ibid., pp. 109–11. The study cited was R. Brun, *Biologische Parallelen zu Freuds Trieblehre* (Vienna, 1926).
61. *NG* 26 (1930): 131.
62. Ibid., pp. 127–30. Yet Stöcker also criticized the exclusion of an English Laborite from an anti-imperialist congress for not supporting Gandhi; she noted that there was no easy solution to all of India's problems, certainly not independence alone (ibid., pp. 130–31).
63. "Kurt Eisner," pp. 115–16.
64. "Klassenkampf und Gewaltlosigkeit," *NG* 26 (1930): 220–21.
65. "Ibid., p. 224.
66. *NG* 25 (1929): 26–28. In the case of the Soviet Union, she elaborated: "It is one thing to *defend* . . . the grandiose, if also tragically incomplete attempt at social change, . . . against hateful attacks by a hostile band of capitalist regimes—another, *oneself* to assume the responsibility for such a tremendous transformation."
67. "Klassenkampf," pp. 224–25.

# Mother's Day
# in the Weimar Republic

## Karin Hausen

*Unlike Helene Stöcker, who fought for the welfare of mothers, the proponents of Mother's Day encouraged women's self-sacrifice. This essay examines the introduction, propagation, and institutionalization of Mother's Day in the midst of socioeconomic and political crises. Against the backdrop of the recently acquired vote for women, a vocal (if relatively powerless) women's movement, and leftist challenges to the antiabortion laws, business and conservative political groups converged around the issue of Mother's Day. Florist associations in search of a new market combined with a "moral majority" of antiabortion, pro-population, and pro-family groups and used modern forms of advertising to bring about the swift adoption of this holiday. Karin Hausen shows how the Mother's Day ideology glorified the idea of motherhood in order to promote population increases and to obscure the cutbacks in social welfare and other services.*

Mother's Day made its appearance shortly after Germany's defeat in World War I. The day that we know as the time to "give mom a gift," "send her flowers," or "make her breakfast" was propagated in the Weimar Republic during a period of runaway inflation, political turmoil, and social dislocation. It achieved popularity at a time when government cutbacks hurt mothers and children and the real economic and physical situation for mothers became desperate. In an era of depression and mass unemployment, of leftist ferment and right-wing backlash, Mother's Day was promoted by people who hoped to cover up disorder and reinforce tradition: it was a whitewash decorated with roses.

Mother's Day was promoted by florists, other business interests, and public nonprofit organizations used by these same interests. Conservative and church groups eagerly joined in. It served not only to camouflage the real social and economic conditions burdening women but also to promote the idea of a racially pure and healthy *Volk*. It was used by conservative and right-wing forces to spearhead their campaign for a "better" society. On the one hand, they used the symbol of "mother" as one that was supposed to "unify" the nation—an explicit critique of what they saw as the divisiveness of democratic party politics as it was being practiced. On the other hand, in the guise of glorifying motherhood, they worried loudly about the loss of "morality," a code word for what they perceived as women's increased economic and sexual agency. They defined women in terms of their capacity to raise the "right kind" of large families which were to be the building blocks of a racially "healthy" nation.

As we look behind the meaning of Mother's Day, we begin to notice many phrases, mind sets, and groups that helped to pave the way for, and later found a comfortable home in, Nazi Germany. Thus this essay reflects on some of the social and political attitudes and describes some of the "neutral" and right-wing groups that influenced public discourse in Weimar Germany. By the time of the Nazi seizure of power, German society had already become used to racial, *völkisch* ideas and language, to moral and clerical conservatism, and to the beginnings of modern propaganda politics, all of which had been promoted by—among others—the Mother's Day advocates.

### The "German Mother's Day"

In a major ethnographic survey in 1932, respondents in 23,000 localities were asked, among other questions, about the prevalence of Mother's Day. The responses, collected mostly by teachers, give the impression that not only had Mother's Day become known within less than ten years, but that it was also celebrated throughout Germany.[1] How was that possible? Apparently, Dr. Rudolf Knauer was the first public advocate of Mother's Day. In 1922, he started writing and lecturing to promote this idea. The "Founder of German Mother's Day," as he dubbed himself in the Nazi newspaper *Völkischer Beobachter*, got a warm reception from the "town councils, the clergy, schools, women's organizations, etc."[2] He was responsible for the establishment of local Mother's Day committees, which came under the administration of a national committee in 1925. In 1926 this central committee joined the Task Force for the Recovery of the *Volk* (Arbeitsgemeinschaft für Volksgesundung), whose efficient director, Hans Harmsen, henceforth headed and promoted the campaign for Mother's Day, which continued until it was declared an official *Volk* holiday under the Nazis.

*Invention—The Association of German Florists*

Rudolf Knauer was by no means acting in a private capacity in his advocacy of Mother's Day. Rather, he developed his enterprise as a project of the Association of German Florists (Verband deutscher Blumengeschäftsinhaber), whose business director he had been since early 1923.[3] Following the example of America and Sweden, the association had, in 1922, already decided to introduce Mother's Day into Germany.[4] In spite of the Ruhr battles and galloping inflation, Knauer began his first promotional campaign for Mother's Day in 1923. His advertising strategy was to have Mother's Day promoted by "some sort of nonprofit organization" coming from a "neutral position," because "having the florists show too much leadership would not be to the advantage of a quick introduction."[5]

Consequently, the first of Knauer's press releases dealt with the "quiet heroines of the people" and the "German wife and mother" in terms of their irreplaceable importance for family and state.[6] Through women in the family, the "true spirit of joy in work, responsibility and selfless devotion to the fatherland" were cultivated. The "revolutionary and post-revolutionary period" had brought forth "disastrous forget-fulness."[7] Thus it was time to celebrate a day of honor for German mothers. Florists were to advertise their selflessness by donating flowers to mothers in hospitals and old-age homes.

The success of this advertising strategy depended on the cooperation of nonprofit organizations. In 1925, when Knauer succeeded in bringing the central Preparatory Committee for German Mother's Day (Vorbereitender Ausschuss für den Deutschen Muttertag) into the Task Force for the Recovery of the *Volk*, the association paper made sweeping predictions: "We hope that this task force will succeed in getting broad circles involved in winning government, church, and school support for the establishment of Mother's Day, the second Sunday in May, as an official holiday."[8] Florists were asked to retreat from public view, but to continue participating in Mother's Day advertising by donating flowers, decorating display windows, distributing prepared Mother's Day materials in conjunction with the task force, and discussing the topic with customers and other acquaintances. However, they had to be careful not to "besmirch the purity and dignity of the idea" with their business interests.[9]

In 1927 the journal of the Association of German Florists published a major Mother's Day issue. Its theme was not business interests, but rather the "high ethical idea" of Mother's Day.[10] The high point for advertising campaigns stressing the idealistic meaning of Mother's Day occurred in 1927. One could still find an appeasing remark about there being no cause for alarm if other types of businesses also got involved in the burgeoning Mother's Day market. In the following years, articles about the spirit of this day yielded to articles about Mother's Day as a business. In 1928, for example, "Advertise for Mother's Day" was the heading for the first Mother's Day article. Now there was a full-fledged competitive battle to be won, fought by all sorts of business groups.[11] To make Mother's Day into a "flower day," florists would have to compete against sellers of candy and confectionery, perfume, lingerie, clothing, and porcelain. Therefore, flower shops were told to begin their advertising early; only in that way would the idea that Mother's Day and flower-giving were synonymous take root.

The Association of German Florists developed, tested, and distributed new advertising materials for German Mother's Day. By 1927, individual local organizations had a full arsenal of advertising materials.[12] There were group ads for local associations, group notices of "entirely neutral content" ("Honor your Mother" or "Give Flowers on Mother's Day"), advertising posters, and even advertising films. Mother's Day postcards were distributed to schoolchildren, as were bookmarks, tags, and calendars. The association's leadership used its journal to direct brief Mother's Day articles toward the local press, boosting the lofty ideal of Mother's Day and the flower as a symbolic present; it also suggested psychologically effective window displays. For example, during the four-hundredth anniversary of the artist Albrecht Dürer's death (1928), it suggested that his portrait of his mother would be an especially suitable Mother's Day decoration "in order to appeal to public sentiment."[13] The journal recommended, in particular, that Mother's Day materials prepared by the task force be purchased so that they could be distributed to customers as "elegant and effective advertising."[14] In 1927, a Mother's Day edition of a customers' newspaper first appeared; in 1929, 280,000 copies were said to have been distributed.[15] In Cologne, the local group added an innovation to Mother's Day publicity: together with the landscaping industry it sent ten flower-covered delivery trucks through the city—a flower convoy bearing the slogan "Say it with flowers on Mother's Day—Second Sunday in May."[16]

Yet in all its promotion efforts the Association of German Florists took great pains to hide its business interests. It kept to the maxim "We must be quiet, selfless helpers and comrades-in-arms for the German Mother's Day."[17] Warning against blatant commercialism, an article in its journal entitled "Mother's Day and Us" noted that some business colleagues

> thought that Mother's Day was created exclusively for business interests. They interpret any commercial restraint as a lack of good business instincts . . . , as professional laziness. Yet, there is more at stake here than mere profit-hunting. Mother's Day was one of the first signs of a re-

awakening self-consciousness of the *Volk* after years of the spiritual decline of our national strength *(Volkskräfte)*. This day which is dedicated to honoring Mother, embodies powers which will reconstruct our national life [*Volksleben*]. Seen in this way, we too must take up Mother's Day as it was originally intended, contrary to the distorted effects of those who think otherwise. The day is disgraced by any shrill advertisement.[18]

Luckily for the florists, they merchandised a very special item: "Only the language of flowers is so attuned to the idea of Mother-honoring that the end justifies the means."[19] How, then, did business interests profit from Mother's Day? And, conversely how was Mother's Day affected by business interests? To answer the first question: in 1927, for the first time, the florists' association journal reported a "growth in sales" almost everywhere. "In most cities, we heard of a big boom."[20] This upward trend seems to have lasted until 1929 when Mother's Day profits began to decline in the general panic of the Great Depression. Increased advertising efforts could not adjust to empty pocketbooks. By the time Mother's Day came around in 1933, the florists' association had already been incorporated into a Nazi organization. To answer the second question: whether a commercial success or not, Mother's Day was markedly shaped by florists' business intentions. For example, "Fleurop" (a flower-dispatching service founded in 1927) furnished Mother's Day contact for those who no longer lived with their mothers. It was even more promising to target advertising at school-aged and younger children, since no one would deny them their flower money. For any honoring of mother, the mother-child relationship was especially important. The image of a mother with small children was seen as an effective appeal to adults, because it supposedly reminded them of their own relationship to their mothers. Advertising left no doubt as to the "rules" of this relationship: "Gratitude" and "admiration" were the feelings and attitudes a child had to exhibit toward its mother, and gifts were established as the best way of expressing those feelings.

### Propaganda—The Taskforce for the Recovery of the Volk

Business interests were not alone in introducing Mother's Day nor in deciding how it would be developed in Germany. Public nonprofit organizations, used as vehicles by business people, also pursued their own ideas and interests. In order to gain some insight into these connections we must investigate the task force. It was through this task force that Knauer directed his central Mother's Day committee.

The task force was founded in November 1924 and grew by incorporating the German Society for Population Policy (Deutsche Gesellschaft für Bevölkerungspolitik) in 1926.[21] The task force originated in the postwar concern for public morality. In 1919, sixty-three associations formed the Committee of Berlin Associations for Questions of *Volk* Morality in order to pursue the "demand for moral renewal beyond party and confessional controversies." That same year, the National Organization for the Protection of Decency and Proper Morals was founded. This "moral front" stood up against "filth and trash" on stage and in films and print. Also, it purported to fight the "demoralization" of sexual life through the double standard of morality, prostitution, abortion, and the abuse of minors. The task force took over this program.

The purpose of the organization was

> to make the public recognize German dignity and good morals by means of an organization of Germans imbued with an awareness of their moral obligations and responsibilities, [to] educate the *Volk* to a sense of spiritual renewal and physical improvement with special consideration for the aims of population politics, and [to] keep an eye on the legislative and administrative branches in order to achieve the internal and external recovery of the *Volk.*[22]

The task force seems to have had a wide influence. It established itself as a liaison for several major welfare organizations in order to represent "special issues in social ethical spheres . . . on neutral territory" and to represent effectively the goals common to all organizations. It understood itself to be a general lobbyist of the "public conscience" and acted as a professional expert engaging in discussions with government boards and elected representatives. A report of activities for 1932, published in the summer of 1933, expressed a clear dissatisfaction with the now defunct Weimar Republic:

> The year 1932 witnessed a decisive moment in the battle for the internal recovery of our *Volk.* Up to now, the battle against cultural and moral emergencies was led mostly by organized religion: now it has received general and official recognition from leading governmental offices under Adolf Hitler's chancellorship. Furthermore, ways have been found allowing this "will to transform" [*Willen zur Neugestaltung*] to take legal and practical effect.[23]

At the end of 1927, two years after its founding, the task force listed 171 individuals and 349 corporate members (organizations that brought together individuals or clubs), among them twenty-six local administrative authorities. The task force worked most closely with the leagues of the three religious welfare organizations. Among the twenty people on the broader governing board were representatives from the German League for Welfare Care (Deutsche Liga der Freien Wohlfahrtspflege), an alliance of all the religious and secular welfare groups, except for the newly founded Social Democratic Workers' Welfare (*Arbeiterwohlfahrt*). The broader board encompassed representatives of Protestant, Catholic, and Jewish women's organizations, various morality and temperance associations, the National League of Large Families (Reichsbund der Kinderreichen), and the Society against Venereal Diseases (Gesellschaft zur Bekämpfung der Geschlechtskrankheiten). These were the "educational circles of the German *Volk.*"

The task force developed commissions on (1) population policy; (2) health care, body culture,* and the temperance question; (3) sexual ethics and sex education; (4) motion pictures, plays, and reviews; (5) the fight against indecency, or filth and trash, the protection of juveniles at places of entertainment; and (6) preparation for Mother's Day. This, in general, comprised the program delineated by the term *Volksgesundung* (recovery of the *Volk*).[24] The newsletters of the Task Force for the Recovery of the *Volk* kept members and other interested parties informed about matters of "social hygiene and daily social-ethical questions." Until 1929, about forty issues appeared each year. After that, around twenty-five bulletins were published, at first in editions of about 700 to 800, sometimes 1,200. Their most frequent topic, the "fight against filth and trash," was accompanied to a lesser extent by the "alcohol question," "social and sexual ethics," and "population policies." Besides the newsletters, pamphlets entitled *Writings on the Recovery of the Volk* and *Short Texts on Population Politics* rounded out the publication program.

Constituents of the task force were ideologically at home on a spectrum from religious-conservative to racial ideologies. Beyond this, their writings show that they saw the family as crucial to the recovery of the *Volk:* "Until now, the family has been the basis of what our entire social system has meant: family, kin, clan, *Volk*, nation. The life of our *Volk*, as well as a spiritual internationalism, was built upon these foundations."[25] However, they saw this family threatened from all sides, if not already in crisis. Germany had just experienced "the deep and destructive influence that war and revolution have exerted on family life." They prophesied an even more dismal future if "modern industrialism and materialism" from the United States or the "liberalistic, atomizing ideology of the Soviet Union were to gain ground. Already "marriages gone astray" and divorces were cause for concern, as was "the way sexual life had gone wild."

The task force took note of the declining birth rate as an alarming symptom and painted a picture of the certain "death of the *Volk.*" Harmsen, the executive director, identified the causes of the trend toward one- and two-children families, birth control, and abortion as "economic need," "lack of living space," "marital and family discord,"

---

*"Body culture" was a celebration of the body, emphasizing physical fitness, hygiene, strength, and beauty.—Eds.

and the "general national crisis," which included every acute exigency from the Versailles Treaty to "spiritual rootlessness."[26] According to Harmsen, birth control had, unfortunately, been most widely practiced by the "most valuable sections of the population," and thus harmed the production of new generations not only quantitatively, but also qualitatively. These self-appointed "educators of the *Volk*" especially noted the "crisis of the family," which they saw as a collective moral problem threatening the *Volk*. Mother's Day seemed to be a newly discovered medicine prescribed for the ailing "body politic." The task force placed its endeavors for Mother's Day within the "framework of our efforts to enhance and preserve healthy family life."[27]

Propaganda efforts were centrally organized in Berlin by the nine-member Preparatory Committee for German Mother's Day, which in 1931 renamed itself the National Committee for German Mother's Day (Reichsausschuss für den Deutschen Muttertag). Besides Harmsen and Knauer, the preparatory committee included the director of the National League of Large Families and one representative each from the Catholic charities (Deutscher Caritasverband), the main Protestant welfare office (Evangelisches Hauptwohlfahrtsamt), the Association for Fighting Public Immorality (Verband zur Bekämpfung der öffentlichen Unsittlichkeit), and the Protestant Women's Aid (Evangelische Frauenhilfe). Contributions and proceeds from sales of Mother's Day literature covered the costs of advertising. The business offices of the task force handled correspondence. Mother's Day literature, as well as press and radio material, was produced and distributed. In 1928, this involved 4,800 advertising letters, 18,450 leaflets, 8,500 prospectuses about advertising materials, 3,800 postcards, 40 slide shows, and 550 other writings.[28]

What messages did these promotional tracts carry? In the Mother's Day issues of the *Writings on the Recovery of the Volk* one can find guidelines for the implementation of Mother's Day celebrations in various locations, diversified materials as aids in setting up Mother's Day, and a summary of the quick and inexorable progress of the movement, both at home and abroad.[29] The preparatory committee wanted Mother's Day to become a uniform "custom."

The committee was to work under a "leading personality." It was to win over schoolteachers, the clergy, local youth groups, the press, and radio and make sure that all public activities on the second Sunday in May fell under the guise of Mother's Day. The primary goal of Mother's Day, however, was to introduce it as a "peaceful and quiet celebration of home and family." Children were to carry the responsibility of these intimate and individual Mother's Day affairs. "The Ten Commandments of Mother's Day" would lend the holiday proper structure and a sacred aura:

1. Take over mother's work on Sunday so that she has a holiday.
2. Place flowers at the bed or on the table early in the morning.
3. If, for the time being, you are away from your mother, send her a letter or a card and include a little gift as a token of the occasion.
4. Go to the cemetery if your mother or another mother from your family is buried there and decorate the grave with blossoms of springtime.
5. Listen around in the neighborhood, and if there is a mother suffering from need and worry, say comforting words to her, take her hand and be attentive to her.
6. If you know a mother in a hospital, in a convalescent home, or in an old-age home, think of her. Don't even ask if there are others responsible for her.
7. If you see a little old lady on the street, go to her, be friendly, or if you think it is necessary, give her a little gift.
8. Ease a mother's burden, be she young or old. Carry things for her, escort her, support her, if it is necessary.
9. Campaign now and on Mother's Day for the idea of Mother's Day. Do something about it and urge others to do so.
10. Always pledge to respect your mother and all German mothers, now and in the future, to honor them and to support them, now and forever, as on Mother's Day. Urge others to do so. Thus, German Mother's Day will become a blessing for the German people!

To help prepare and set up private and public Mother's Day celebration, interested parties could receive even more elaborate explanatory materials. Besides postcards and slide shows, prose literature, poetry, songs, proverbs, and dramatic readings were offered.

Reports in issues of the newsletter about activities specifically designated for Mother's Day show that clubs, churches, schools, and other official bodies increasingly took their own initiatives. In order to establish Mother's Day as a family holiday, children and youth were mobilized. Teachers and clergy distributed materials for Mother's Day in confirmation classes, nurseries, and youth clubs. They sometimes took up the initiative as individuals and sometimes were required to do so by their superiors.[30] No doubt, all promotion directed at children benefited from the fact that teachers and clergy formed a part of every local "neutral" Mother's Day committee.[31]

The local Mother's Day committee was not only in charge of getting churches, schools, and the media to involve the public in Mother's Day. The committee also supported, set up, or coordinated public festivals in order to make Mother's Day a worthy folk festival. Local youth and women's groups found a rich field of activity here. Branches of the National League of Large Families, for example, constantly tried to prove themselves to be in the vanguard of the Mother's Day idea. Citing numerous reports of Mother's Day celebrations in towns of all sizes and rural communities, the central Mother's Day committee in Berlin described the course of public Mother's Day proceedings in 1928 in the following terms:

> Mother's Day events generally started out with an early morning concert—usually a hymn from the church tower. Services concentrated on honoring mother. The afternoon was usually devoted to celebrations within the family or in clubs. During the course of the day young girls and children often visited hospitals, convalescent and old-age homes. The little gifts, songs and performances which the young people gave to sick and lonely women brought great . . . joy. In the evening mothers were entertained in public and club celebrations. The obligatory speech was framed by tableaux, poetry recitals and musical performances. Our slide show usually brought the evening to a close. Sometimes a small entry fee was collected to defray costs or to benefit the mothers.[32]

Two important details were left out of this description. First, the public honoring of mothers always included bouquets of flowers.[33] Second, mothers of four or more were often honored at solemn public ceremonies.

The true intention of Mother's Day was established by the preparatory committee in its interpretation of the day as a popular custom with profound meaning.[34] This was declared more necessary than ever. The "ethical idea of motherhood seemed to be on the verge of disintegration," because "rationalization and industrialization" from America and the "boundless individualism" of Soviet Russia were plotting the "destruction of the family and all sexual morality." Therefore, Mother's Day would have to awaken "the deep powers of the German soul which still lie dormant in the people." These self-appointed "educators of the *Volk*" were not interested in mothers as persons in distinct social and economic relationships, but rather in *the* mother as the embodiment of ideal virtue and behavior. They stylized the "good" or "true" mother as one who exhibited "loving care," "devotion," "self-renunciation," "the epitome of patience and forgiveness, the quintessence of love."[35] With this ideal image in mind, the Mother's Day propagandists saw the "decline of femininity and maternal qualities in our people" and blamed it on the slackening of domestic education by mothers and on the "denigration of the housewife and mother." In general, they lamented the "dwindling respect towards elders, the helpless, the poor and especially women and mothers." Things had gotten so far out of hand "that our young women and mothers, because of vanity, egotism, or laziness, no longer feel joy in having children." Therefore, Mother's

Day should work first of all as a "strong constructive force" to help "strengthen the will to motherhood."[36] Mother's Day should by no means only "bring honor and happiness to mothers," but, above all, should "raise the consciousness of all women to their maternal responsibilities and duties."[37]

Furthermore, Mother's Day should also spread consciousness of the "major questions about the existence of our *Volk*," the meaning of "motherhood," "racial hygiene," and "sex education." The long-term "popular-educational" goal, via Mother's Day, was to renew family bonds with "large families seen as the wellspring of the people's strength and virtue."[38] A desirable precondition would be to "limit women's employment accordingly."[39] In 1929, the preparatory committee formulated these ideas as concrete political demands for the first and only time: "Protect mothers of large families! Reorganize women's work! Better housing conditions!"[40] This allegedly unpolitical Mother's Day concept was, in fact, intended to have a political effect. Mother's Day was introduced as a "powerful neutral thought" when the "fratricidal battle" of political parties [a veiled slap at the Weimar democratic system] revealed the "decay of our *Volk* community [*Volksgemeinschaft*]."[41] Through the power of a "nonpartisan and ecumenical bond," Mother's Day might succeed in reuniting the community once again and might "reawaken and liberate values which were totally lost during the period of inner collapse between 1917 and 1923."[42]

Thus all troubles were seen to have begun at the time of the military collapse, of the revolution of 1918, and of the immediate postrevolutionary period when it was not yet at all clear which political forces would prevail. It was hoped that Mother's Day would revive the national solidarity that Germans had experienced during World War I.[43] The initiators of Mother's Day approached this much-desired idea of national integration in its broadest sense. They recommended to Germans in bordering countries and overseas that they build a bridge from Mother's Day to the "mother country" and fight for the "maternal soil."[44]

Were these irritating Mother's Day activities and ideologies limited to a small circle of people they would not really be worth further research. One might well ask if the annual 280,000 copies of the customers' Mother's Day newspaper were even read and if the Task Force for the Recovery of the *Volk* successfully conveyed its message. I do suspect that Mother's Day, with its carefully and cultishly stylized figure of Mother-as-Savior, gave broad strata of the bourgeoisie a much-desired alternative to the anxiety and confusion generated by the transitional interwar society. However, before trying to interpret the striking position foisted on "the Mother," I would like to give examples that show how and why Mother's Day was, indeed, accepted as a holiday by broad sections of the public.

## Dissemination

The National League of Large Families of Germany to Safeguard the Family (Reichsbund der Kinderreichen Deutschlands zum Schutze der Familie) was founded in 1919.[45] Parents with four or more children could become members. The organization was to lobby for special rights among legislators and administrators and to campaign for the interests of large families (the "child-rich," *kinderreich*). With the perceived social danger posed by a declining birthrate as its main theme, it succeeded in signing up the best-known population experts of the Weimar era for its newsletter and its rallies. It considered only mothers with many children as exemplary; by contrast, employed or politically active women were "masculinized." It considered abortion murder and birth control a national threat. In one of its regular articles for Mother's Day, a minister described his image of the ideal woman: "Mothers full of spirituality and piety, mothers full of modest womanly dignity, mothers full of conscientiousness, feelings of responsibility, sense of sacrifice, and selfless love."[46]

The over 700 chapters of the National League of Large Families supported public Mother's Day events. There they placed great value on public appreciation of mothers with many children.[47] In 1926 in Münster, for example, they presented coffee and cake dishes with the inscription: "To the German Mother—the City of Münster, German Mother's Day, 1926."

In Kiel, needy mothers of large families received a savings account of over 20 marks, and their counterparts from "other social circles" were invited as "honorary mothers." Such mother-honoring was not a mere byproduct of Mother's Day. The president of the Weimar Republic was designated the "honorary godfather" of every child after the eleventh in any family. In Prussia, as of 1927, a mother with twelve or more living children was entitled to apply for special honors. If she had a good reputation and the children were well brought up, she received an honorary present, a porcelain cup or the equivalent of 100 Reichsmark supplementing her state aid for childrearing.[48] Later, the "Cross of Honor of the German Mother," established by the Nazis on Mother's Day 1939, became better known than these precursors. It was awarded according to the number of offspring, in gold, silver, or iron.[49]

Another organization that took up Mother's Day and used it for its own purposes was the Protestant Women's Aid (Evangelische Frauenhilfe).[50] It was one of the many large organizations for housewives and religious and nationalistic women that viewed women's emancipation as a threat because it was seen to challenge the stability of the family. Founded in 1897, the Women's Aid, in close cooperation with the clergy, organized women's service in the church community. It helped train women as deaconesses, congregational helpers, or volunteers for sick care, social work, and Christian community work. From a mere 14,000 members in 1900 it grew to a mass organization of 600,000 members in 1929 and 900,000 members in 1936. During a time of "excessive demands on women and mothers," it tried to support women in their daily lives. From the mid 1920s, it devoted itself with increasing intensity to the school, welfare, and recuperation of overtaxed mothers. In 1930, it established an independent department for "mother service" (Mütterdienst). The founding of the Mother's Service Organization of the Protestant Church (Mütterdienstwerkes der evangelischen Kirche) was announced on Mother's Day 1933. By then the Protestant Women's Aid administered over forty-two convalescent homes and fifty-four schools for mothers. Funds came, for the most part, from door-to-door and street collections on Mother's Days from 1930 to 1933. In spite of the severe economic crises of 1931 and 1932, they brought in 2 million marks. In 1933 the Protestant Women's Aid was joined to the Nazi's German Women's Bureau (Deutsches Frauen-werk.)[51]

The readiness of the Protestant Women's Aid to get involved in the Mother's Day movement developed haltingly and apparently parallel to its increasingly strong concentration on the tasks of mothering. In 1927, the first allusion to Mother's Day material from the Task Force for the Recovery of the *Volk* appeared in its monthly newsletter along with recommendations to participate in Mother's Day celebrations.[52] In April 1928, the newsletter stated: "As things now stand, we have no choice but to recognize the facts; Mother's Day is here and as far as we know, it is not going to go away. So, it is appropriate to make the best of it." According to the newsletter, Mother's Day should be both an "educational and a beautiful thought." It argued that this would occur if instead of "glorifying mothers" the day would be used to help mothers understand the "joy and lofty feeling of duty in their office as mother." Above all, on Mother's Day women were to be offered special help.[53]

In order to separate itself from the "godless" Mother's Day movement and to spread the "Christian idea of motherhood and mother-liness," the Protestant Women's Aid published its own Mother's Day materials.[54] From 1930 to 1935 it published a yearly brochure with texts and suggestions for religious services, congregational evenings, and Mother's Day celebrations.[55] In these events, the mother was to be presented in the "ancient Germanic style," as the "protector of the hearth and home, of the old patriarchal beliefs of good breeding and morality."[56] For example, in 1931 one of its suggestions for an amateur play was: "Today when the destruction of the family has caused so much damage to our people, we must infuse the soul of the people with the notion of a vital and attractive German-Christian family that has the mother as its center." This was to be done in tableaux with actors all wearing "the same national costumes" and always with three to five children shown gathered around the mother, or both parents.[57] In its "General Thoughts for Mother's Day" brochures, it did not forgo mention of the "death of the *Volk*," "partisan feuding, greed and lazy pleasure" as the destroyers of "motherly joy," and of the "desire for motherhood, the joy of motherhood and the pride of motherhood" as healing counterforces.[58] The only thing criticized as a danger to the whole Mother's Day movement was the overglorification of mothers. They contrasted this on the one hand with the need to train women to be good mothers and on the other hand with the need for more help from men and children.[59] To be sure, this in no way eliminated the propensity toward a mother cult. In 1934, they put in a good word for the mother cult: "Everyone today recognizes the great creation that motherhood represents," and, "Mother's Day, 1934, already finds us women and mothers of the *Volk* standing before a common task, to renew motherhood as a service to the nation."[60]

In 1935, by contrast, there is a renewed warning: "Motherhood in itself is neither grand nor holy. It only becomes that way when God's grace shines upon it. . . . In past years the danger was contempt for mother—today she is easily overvalued."[61] Even though the Protestant Women's Aid professed not to glorify mothers, every one of its Mother's Day brochures elevated mothers in a religious manner. These recommended that people "believe in the victory of life in mothers" and thus defy the anti-Christ embodied in Bolshevism, which had come to destroy the heavenly order of the family and motherhood.[62]

Further, these writings conjured up a "halo around the mother's head." The borderline between godless mother glorification and the "Christian idea of motherhood" had become a bit fuzzy. "For us Protestants a picture of the Madonna is something incredibly grand. Not in the sense of saint worship and the cult of Mary. But . . . the mother with her child in her arms . . . is correctly understood as a Protestant holy image."[63] And so, the Protestant Women's Aid swam along with the tide of the Mother's Day movement. What differentiated it from other Mother's Day organizers was not its ideological position, but only the practical manner with which it raised funds to finance its Mother's Service Organization.

Daily newspapers present an even clearer image of Mother's Day promotions than do the two preceding organizations because of their interest in advertising. Local newspapers were the main organs for

Mother's Day publicity. By 1927 the respectable regional paper, the *Lippische Landeszeitung,* dignified Mother's Day as a "day to reflect upon our duty toward our racial origins." In 1929, it used Mother's Day to crusade against the "false idea of womanhood," claiming that "woman's true work is motherliness, and thus sacrifice."[64]

By contrast, national dailies held out longer against Mother's Day. The venerable *Vossische Zeitung* of Berlin, which inserted its first Mother's Day poem in 1929, did not get involved in a full-scale promotion until 1931. Then, there were probably connections between a column about the "domestic power of women" and a nearby notice of a meeting of the Task Force for the Recovery of the *Volk,* which had opposed amending Paragraph 218 of the penal code and had underscored the dangers of abortion.[65] In 1933, the Protestant Women's Aid provided Mother's Day copy for the paper with the founding of its Mothers' Service subsidiary.

The *Berliner Tageblatt* actually waited until 1931 before it honored "today's fifth Mother's Day" as a new "folk custom." In 1933 it concerned itself with the Mothers' Service Organization and the task of "resurrecting the figure of Mother through a spiritual experiencing of blood and soil." There was no reference to Mother's Day in 1934.[66] The *Deutsche Allgemeine Zeitung* only found its way to Mother's Day in 1933, but then all the more excessively. It featured the "daily lives of mothers of large families" who felt it their duty "as German mothers to give the German people healthy children, thus caring for the future of the nation." In 1934, to be sure, it reported the official Nazi radio address for Mother's Day without the pathos of the previous year.[67]

At the right-wing extreme of the newspaper world, the Nazi *Völkischer Beobachter* used Mother's Day as early as 1929 to polemicize against abortion, contraception, and the "psychic and spiritual dematernalization of women" and to advance women's compulsory service in the future Nazi state as the "systematic preparation of female youth for their maternal responsibilities." In 1930, the Nazis commemorated the self-sacrificing mothers of SA men and the "mysteries" of the mother-to-be. By 1931, Mother's Day had grown into a "solemn holiday for our *Volk.*" Surprisingly, this torrent of mystification subsided during 1932 and 1933, to be replaced by spare and guarded Mother's Day reports.[68] It was precisely during these years that the Nazis changed their position on women and family policy, integrating and subordinating the previously largely autonomous Nazi women's groups into the party organization.[69] This new tendency seems to have hardened by 1934, when the *Völkischer Beobachter* published the "Mother's Day Address" given over the radio by the minister of the interior. This explained that the Nazi Mother's Day should no longer be celebrated as an intimate family holiday, but rather as a day that dignified the "mother as the refuge of the *Volk*, the protector of our racial heritage."

## Linkages

I have tried to show the many sources and forms of the Mother's Day movement and to outline the results of my preliminary research. New areas should be used to round out the picture of the movement. For example, why did *Die Frau (The Woman)*—the newspaper of the Federation of German Women's Associations, the umbrella organization of the moderate bourgeois women's movement—remain silent about Mother's Day? Was Mother's Day, whose propagandists recruited primarily from bourgeois circles, so uncompromisingly committed against women's emancipation that even the moderates had to reject it? Even the opponents of Mother's Day—Communists, Socialists, and progressives in general—could round out the picture we have drawn so far. The following poem, published in the Social Democratic paper *Vorwärts (Forward)*, in 1931, emphasizes the contradictions it saw in Mother's Day:

> The signs are seen in every store
> Decorations, pictures and much much more
> Saying, "Think of mother on Mother's Day
> Give her in excess of what she can pay
> Give her flowers and give her candy,
> Stockings, lounge chairs, champagne are dandy—
> If 'mother' is a loving thought,
> Then give you ought!"

> Some women stare at the window displays
> Their husbands are unemployed these days.
> They look at the riches, the special stuff,
> They're mothers too, but that's not enough—
> "We have children but have no bread,
> We've got troubles like no housing instead,
> If you haven't got food
> Honor's no good."

> "Mother's Day? A salvation you said?
> When we haven't got diapers, not to mention a bed?"
> Neither mother nor child can celebrate
> When motherhood is a helpless fate
> Mothers are deserted, left high and dry
> While society shuts its purse and its eye,
> And pregnant women must be afraid
> Because there's no financial aid.

"So, once a year, we're honored right,
Once a year, we're a moving sight,
And otherwise it's pretty sad
We're forgotten because it's just an ad—
People make a wonderful fuss
And then collect high profits from us
They set up a day when mothers' value is high—
And then buy and buy and buy and buy!"[70]

This poem expressed what Mother's Day left out. During the world economic crisis of 1929–1933, concrete economic needs above all burdened working women and their children. Even in middle-class families, it seems that the situation greatly deteriorated for innumerable housewives as a result of the war, inflation, and the Great Depression. When domestic help became too expensive for the households of small businessmen and civil service employees, the housewife had to do the job herself. Her labor became ever more necessary as the standard for well-run households rose. The wave of new consumer goods had made it possible to fill the home with decorations and gadgets that needed to be maintained. Nineteenth-century hygiene campaigns set new expectations for household cleanliness. Since the turn of the twentieth century the campaign against infant mortality had raised the norms for nursing infants. Also, proper schooling and the career-oriented education of children came to be seen as more of a problem than ever before. Such progress particularly burdened mothers and housewives, who were supposed to effect the improvements.

One answer to the dilemma faced by women, who constantly had to achieve ever more with limited resources, was birth control, already practiced by all classes of the population before World War I. But family planning brought out the population and race politicians for whom the issue was not the survival and happiness of individual families and women, but rather the hazy concept of "the whole *Volk*," "the *Volk*-body."[71] Women's paid labor (which could no longer be ignored), their admission to higher education (since shortly after the turn of the century), and their political equality (assured for the first time in the Weimar constitution) raised fears not only among conservatives.[72] There were also general fears about a future in which even women of the upper and middle classes might no longer be willing or able to take on the roles and burdens traditionally assigned to them. These and other fears, experiences, and expectations consolidated around the end of World War I. By the late 1920s, the hubbub about the "crisis of the family" grew even louder.

Precisely because the Weimar Republic raised hope for more democracy and freedom, its opponents mobilized in the name of the "community of the *Volk*" and the "recovery of the *Volk*." The struggle between these two sides not only marked different social and political views, but also acutely expressed the blatant contradictions in the existing social and economic system. The interests of political economy opposed those of home economy; principles of wages based on individual merit contradicted those of family needs; the demands for individual development and freedom opposed the patriarchal family; and societal demands ran up against the limited abilities of private families. More than ever, the developments of the twentieth century indicated that women were required to mediate the severity of public contradictions through their double role. Yet neither women nor their husbands could choose which burdens to bear. The vehement debates over the availability of contraception and the relaxing of the draconian penalties for abortion revealed the sociopolitical constraints. Although it was possible to weaken Paragraph 218 in 1926, the 1931 and 1932 campaigns for abortion without punishment were unsuccessful. In 1933 the Nazis, with the approval of church conservatives, once again increased the penalties for abortions. They also forbade distribution of contraceptives and dissolved the numerous birth control counseling centers that had been set up during the Weimar Republic.[73]

In the 1920s there had already been a lively discussion about how unjust and damaging it was to punish families materially just because they were raising children under the existing rules of commodity distribution. It was not until the arrival of the Nazis that some of the numerous propositions for "equalizing the family burden" were realized. The Nazis implemented marital loans, punitive taxes on unmarried people, and financial aid and benefits for large families. The marriage loans were also considered a way of removing the female workforce from an overcrowded labor market in 1933.[74]

Finally, during the Weimar Republic, training women to become housewives and mothers was done more intensively than ever before. At the same time, the network of welfare arrangements expanded to assist mothers with support, care, and control. If, in spite of all these supportive measures, a mother's strength began to wear down—and this happened often—the preventive Mother's Recovery Care took over. Here too the Nazis made use of solid, existing foundations, while ceremoniously introducing the "Reich's Mother Service" as a new institution in 1934.

Now women had to learn to see themselves not privately, as housewives and mothers, but as "mothers of the nation."[75] They were addressed as individuals even less than before. Considered indispensable embodiments of "motherhood," they were expected to observe "racial and eugenic standards."[76]

The magic formula offered by the Mother's Day movement to bridge almost unbearable contradictions was "readiness to sacrifice" and "devotion." It seems plausible to take these mottos literally, for the movement asserted that every woman had to be a selfless, self-sacrificing mother. Mother's Day celebrated this sacrifice both publicly and privately in an attempt to implant the seeds of self-sacrifice in future generations of young women. This maternal self-sacrifice, however, was always ambiguous. On the one hand, mothers were expected to be ready to work without return, unmindful of their own needs, in a properly functioning household with children. But this socially expected commitment was so far removed from all other forms of behavior where performance and rewards are linked, that, on the other hand, mothers' efforts were perceived as sacrifice in a religious sense. The mother sacrifices herself and she is sacrificed and the result is supposed to be social salvation.

Motherliness and motherhood were common words in the Weimar period. These words abstracted qualities from real mothers in order to avoid the actual situation confronting mothers.[77] In fact, mother glorification grew most rampantly exactly where the actual social conditions made it increasingly difficult for housewives and mothers to fulfill the obligations expected of them. Life as self-sacrifice is self-destruction; women were expected to sacrifice themselves and society covered up this self-sacrifice by deeming it their strength and power.

—Trans. Miriam Frank with Erika Busse Grossmann;
ed. Marion Kaplan with Ellen Weinstock

## Notes

This is a translated and revised version of an article which appeared as "Mütter zwischen Geschäftsinterressen und kultischer Verehrung: der "Deutsche Muttertag" in der Weimarer Republik," in *Sozialgeschichte der Freizeit: Untersuchungen zum Wandel der Alltagskultur in Deutschland*, ed. Gerhard Huck (Wuppertal, 1980).

1. Cf. H. Harmjanz and E. Röhr, eds., *Atlas der deutschen Volkskunde*, Vol. 1, (Leipzig, 1937–1939), pp. 1–120; "Vorkommen des Muttertages 1932" and charts 33 and 34.
2. R. Knauer; "Entwicklung des Muttertages," in *Völkischer Beobachter*, Norddeutsche Ausgabe 13/14, 5, 1934, # 133/134, discussion edition. The religious organizations mentioned here were primarily religious ones and housewives' groups.
3. *Verbandszeitung Deutscher Blumengeschäftsinhaber*, April 4, 1923, p. 88 (hereafter *VDB*). The people who joined this organization were shop owners.
4. *VDB*, September 23, 1932, p. 9.
5. *VDB*, March 20, 1923, p. 68.
6. *VDB*, April 3, 1923, pp. 88f.
7. *VDB*, January 25, 1924, pp. 29f.

8. *VDB*, March 26, 1926, p. 262; also for the following quotes.
9. *VDB*, April 16, 1926, p. 317.
10. See, for examples: *VDB*, April 29, 1927, p. 344 and p. 310; July 15, 1927, p. 537.
11. *VDB*, April 13, 1928, pp. 349f. Cf. the headline in *VDB* April 27, 1928, p. 384.
12. On advertising, cf. *VDB* July 15, 1927, p. 537; April 27, 1928, p. 384; April 15, 1932, p. 10.
13. *VDB*, April 27, 1928, p. 380.
14. *VDB*, April 27, 1928, p. 384, and April 16, 1926, p. 317; April 22, 1927; p. 326; May 4, 1929, p. 401.
15. *VDB*, April 18, 1930, p. 142.
16. *VDB*, May 27, 1932, p. 2.
17. *VDB*, May 4, 1928, p. 401.
18. *VDB*, May 3, 1929, p. 343, and April 18, 1930, p. 142, April 3 and 10, 1931, pp. 108 and 114f., and April 1, 1932, p. 1.
19. *VDB*, April 1, 1932, p. 1; May 5, 1928, p. 415.
20. *VDB*, July 15, 1928, p. 537. Later reports July 7 and August 8, 1930, pp. 240f and 275f.
21. See the article by H. Harmsen in J. Dümer, ed., *Handwörterbuch der Wohlfahrtspflege*, 2. Aufl. Berlin 1929, pp. 59f. Cf. also the *Tätigkeitsberichte* (activity reports) of the "Task Force" 1926–1932, such as numbers 4, 6, 10, 14, 16, 18, 20 in *Schriften zur Volksgesundung* (hereinafter cited by their *Heft*, or issue, numbers). The German Society for Population Policy was founded in 1915.
22. *Tätigkeitsbericht* 1926, p. 4.
23. *Tätigkeitsbericht* 1932, p. 3.
24. *Tätigkeitsbericht* 1926, p. 21–27, presents a list of member organizations. In all these activity reports there is information on the personnel of the administrative committee and the broader board; overview of special committees in *Tätigkeitsbericht* 1928, p. 4.
25. *Heft* 12 (1929): 6f. See also *Heft* 1, May 2, 1926. In 1935, the postwar years were portrayed by these "peoples' educators" as a nightmare with "beliefs in progress, free trade, female emancipation, pacifism, co-education, equality for all people, enlightenment, nudism," and above all "freedom"—most obviously in the area of "love." (*Heft* 20 [1935]: 2).
26. *Heft* 7 (1927), pp. 7 and 13.
27. *Tätigkeitsbericht* 1930, p. 6, and 1926, p. 11; 1932, p. 5.
28. *Tätigkeitsbericht* 1928, p. 18, and 1929, p. 21.
29. *Heft* 3 (1927), Der Deutsche Muttertag; *Heft* 5 (1928), Der Deutsche Muttertag, Grundlegendes und Erfahrungen 1927; *Heft* 9 (1929), Der Tag der Mutter—Muttertag. Rückschau auf 1928, Ausblick 1929; *Heft* 13 (1930), Wie feiern wir den Muttertag? These booklets, each about 40 pages long, were published in editions of about 3,000. They always included the "Ten Commandments of Mother's Day."
30. By 1926, the archbishop of Breslau and the chairman of the Fulda Bishops' conference were advising their priests to actively support Mother's Day, cf. *Heft* 3 (1927), p. 19. For presidents who delegated Mother's Day work to school councils, see *Heft* 5 (1928) pp. 10f.
31. For the efforts of the city of Mannheim, see *Heft* 5 (1928), pp. 15f.
32. *Heft* 5 (1928), p. 14.
33. *Heft* 5 (1928), p. 18.
34. *Heft* 9 (1929), p. 9; *Heft* 3 (1927), p. 4; following quotations in ibid., pp. 3f. and 7.
35. *Heft* 9 (1929), pp. 3 and 22, *Heft* 5 (1928), pp. 5 and 15.
36. *Heft* 9 (1929), pp. 16–19.
37. *Heft* 5 (1928), p. 4.
38. The above quotations are from *Heft* 3 (1927), pp. 7f. and 11f.
39. *Heft* 5 (1928), p. 4.

40. Heft 9 (1929), p. 18.
41. Heft 9 (1929), p. 16.
42. Heft 3 (1927), p. 3.
43. Heft 3 (1927), p. 8.
44. Heft 3 (1927), pp. 8f, and Heft 5 (1928), p. 5.
45. *Bundesblatt für den Reichsbund der Kinderreichen Deutschlands zum Schutze der Familie e.V.* for the following statements.
46. *Bundesblatt,* 1928, p. 50.
47. Examples can be found in *Schriften zur Volksgesundung,* Heft 3 (1927), p. 22; Heft 5 (1928), pp. 25 and 18; more in Heft 13 (1930), p. 5.
48. Cf. *Bundesblatt,* 1929, p. 132. (100 Reichsmark would be about half of an average male worker's monthly income in 1927.—Ed.)
49. Cf. George L. Mosse, *Der Nationalsozialistische Alltag* (Königstein, 1978), pp. 69f.; and J. Stephenson, *Women in Nazi Society* (London, 1975), pp. 49f.
50. Cf. J. Dümer, ed., *Handwörterbuch,* pp. 213f.; A. Brandmeyer: *Evangelische Frauenhilfe, Auftrag—Weg—Werk: Ein Wort zur 40 jährigen Geschichte Potsdams* (1937); membership figures according to A. Branmeyer; "Das Werk der Frauenhilfe in vier Jahrzehnten" in *Frauenhilfe, Monatsblatt für kirchliche Frauen-Gemeindearbeit* (1939), pp. 121–126, figures p. 123 (quotation from *Monatsblatt*). On Mother's Day collections, cf. *Vossische Zeitung,* May 14, 1933, #229, first supplement.
51. *Monatsblatt* has a significant call to arms, "An die Frauen und Mütter unserer evangelischen Kirche," in which women's much-praised maternal qualities are called on to enlist in the home-front battle "against the inner enemy." "Loyalty, readiness for sacrifice, goodness, willingness to help, honesty and respectability must be our rules."
52. *Monatsblatt* 1927, p. 62.
53. *Monatsblatt* 1928, p. 149.
54. *Monatsblatt* 1929, p. 80, in the article "Der Muttertag wie wir ihn sehen und ausgestalten wollen."
55. The brochures appear as issues of the "Arbeitsbücherei der Frauenhilfe," Heft 17 (1930); Heft 22 (1931); Heft 25 (1932); Heft 27 (1933); Heft 31 (1934); Heft 34 (1935).
56. Heft 17 (1930), p. 18.
57. Amateur play in Heft 22 (1931), pp. 22–29, quotes on p. 22 and 29.
58. Heft 17 (1930), pp. 3f.
59. Quotation in Heft 22 (1931), p. 3. Remarks in *Monatsblatt* 1929, p. 80, and Heft 22 (1931), pp. 3–5.
60. Heft 31 (1934), pp. 11 and 10.
61. Heft 34 (1935), pp. 7 and 11.
62. Heft 27 (1933), pp. 4f.
63. Heft 27 (1933), p. 6.
64. *Lippische Landeszeitung,* Detmold—May 8, 1927, May 12, 1929, and May 11, 1930.
65. *Vossische Zeitung* of May 12, 1929, #109; May 10, 1931, #111; May 8, 1932, #221; May 14, 1933, #229, first supplement of each issue. For Paragraph 218 and the abortion issue, see Atina Grossmann's article in this volume.
66. *Berliner Tageblatt,* May 10, 1931, #218; May 9, 1933, #213; May 14, 1933, #223; first supplements.
67. *Deutsche Allegemeine Zeitung,* May 11, 1933, #218; May 13, 1933, #222; May 14, 1933, #224; May 13, 1934, #219; as well as *Berliner Rundschau* and *Frau und Welt.*
68. *Völkischer Beobachter* (Munich edition), May 12 and 13, 1929, #109; Daily supplement, May 10, 1930, #110; weekly edition, May 11 and 12, 1930, #111; daily supplement May 10 and 11, 1931, #130/131; May 7, 1933, #132; weekly edition May 15, 1933, #135; May 9, 1934, #129, weekly edition; May 13 and 14, #133/134, discussion edition.
69. Claudia Koonz: "Mothers in the Fatherland: Women in the Third Reich," in Renate

Bridenthal and Claudia Koonz, eds., *Becoming Visible: Women in European History* (Boston 1977), p. 445–73. Also see Koonz article in this volume.

70. *Vorwärts,* May 10, 1934, supplement.

71. The Reich's Ministry of the Interior considered these problems urgent enough to establish the Commission for Population Politics and Measures.

72. On women's wage labor see Stefan Bajohr; *Die Hälfte der Fabrik, Geschichte der Frauenarbeit in Deutschland, 1914–1945* (Marburg, 1979); T. Mason, "Zur Lage der Frauen in Deutschland 1930–1940," *Wohlfahrt, Arbeit und Familie in Gesellschaft: Beiträge zur Marxistischen Theorie* 6 (Frankfurt, 1976): 118–93; Dorte Winkler; *Frauenarbeit im, "Dritten Reich"* (Hamburg, 1977).

73. See Grossmann's article in this volume; and J. Stephenson, *Women in Nazi Society,* pp. 56f.

74. Cf. K. Jurczyk, *Frauenarbeit und Frauenrolle, Zusammenhang von Familienpolitik und Frauenerwerbstätigkeit in Deutschland 1918–1975* (Frankfurt, 1978).

75. According to the (Nazi) National Women's Leader, G. Scholtz-Klink, in *Frauenkultur im Deutschen Frauenwerk,* 1937, Heft 1, p. 1.

76. On the organization of women cf. Gisela Bock, "Frauen und ihre Arbeit im Nationalsozialismus," in Annette Kuhn and G. Schneider, eds., *Frauen in der Geschichte* (Düsseldorf, 1979), pp. 113–49. Informative reading also in E. Zuberbier, *Die nationalsozialistische Auffassung vom häuslichen Dienst der deutschen Frau und ihre praktische Verwirklichung* (Diss. jur. Leipzig, 1939).

77. As examples of the mystification of woman in Weimar, see E. Bermann, *Erkenntnisgeist und Muttergeist, eine Soziosophie der Geschlechter* (Breslau, 1932); M. Weber, *Aufstieg durch die Frau* (Freiburg, 1933); further connections are given by Klaus Theweleit, *Männerphantasien,* vol. 1. (Reinbeck, 1980), esp. pp. 107–14 and 378–87.

# "Professional" Housewives: Stepsisters of the Women's Movement

## Renate Bridenthal

*Motherhood and housewifery were idealized and commercialized by business interests, but some women themselves used this idealization to further their economic interests. Renate Bridenthal shows how some middle-class housewives organized themselves professionally, as a housewives' association, in order to protect their economic interests. These interests included working together as employers to counter domestic servants' unions, representing bourgeois consumer interests, and mutual aid during economic crises. While the association professed religious and political neutrality, it was nevertheless predominantly Protestant and conservative. Its members were divided in their loyalty to the organized women's movement, which helped to establish it and with which it was formally associated. Ultimately, the antifeminist wing won control and brought the association into the service of the Nazi state, which propagated its image of woman as primarily housewife more widely.*

The first German women's movement has perplexed and angered its historians.[1] Split from the start into often hostile bourgeois and socialist wings, it confronted with anxious ambiguity the new challenges to women provoked by the transformations of rapid industrialization, war, and revolution.

The socialist women's movement, for a time separated from the bourgeois movement by state repression, as well as by its focus on working-class women and its struggle for an end to class as well as gender inequalities, remained close to the Socialist and Communist parties and also mirrored their split from one another.

The bourgeois women's movement, by contrast, had a vision of women's moral superiority and its potential to reform—but not revolutionize—society. While its Anglo-American counterpart had rejected the Victorian "pedestal" image and made increasing demands for sex equality, (though still not challenging class inequalities among women), German bourgeois feminism meandered through the early twentieth century with an ideological profile so low as to bring its feminist credentials into question. Far more modest in its demands for individual rights and for equality, it was constrained by historical limitations, like the German idea of freedom from which it had emerged.[2] Important among these limitations were the circumstances of national unification in 1870, which involved the authoritarian tactics of Chancellor Bismarck in overriding a supine Parliament to conduct a series of wars that brought the several German states together under Prussian leadership. Unity brought protective and supportive measures to capitalist entrepreneurs at the price of their continuing political docility. This mixture of patronage and repression affected women of that class as well. They tempered their aspirations for economic, educational, and political participation by abjuring "selfish" individualism. As a subgroup of the national family, they primarily asked to develop their unique womanly qualities in the service of the whole and petitioned for more autonomy within a more or less separate sphere.

These broad generalizations do not account for the several tendencies within German bourgeois feminism, some of which aimed at more social integration than others—for example, in education and employment. However, it does represent the views of the Federation of German Women's Associations (Bund Deutscher Frauenvereine; BDF), the umbrella organization for most groups identified with the women's movement, founded in 1894. This organization, which boasted about 1 million members at its peak in 1931, was one of the largest and most active in Europe in the 1920s and 1930s. Yet when the Nazi Party, with its reactionary program for women, came to power in 1933, the BDF quietly folded its tents.

One way to understand its odyssey is to take a closer look at its member organizations. The BDF's relative conservatism was intensified by its inclusion of previously non- or even antifeminist groups, in an attempt to broaden the base of the women's movement. Two of the largest, together comprising one-fifth of the BDF's total membership, were the urban and agricultural housewives' associations, the National Federation of German Housewives' Associations (Reichsverband Deutscher Hausfrauenvereine; RDH) and the National Federation of Agricultural Housewives' Associations (Reichsverband Landwirtschaftlicher Hausfrauenvereine; RLHV), respectively. Both represented women in their "place," at home, in traditional functions and relationships.

In this essay, I will show how organized housewives, as auxiliaries to a male-run state and social structure, contributed to the demise of the

German bourgeois women's movement and even to the success of Hitler's programs for women. In trying to explain some bourgeois women's *gender-specific* attraction to fascism, it is important to recognize that it was not based on simple adulation, as Hitler's own propaganda machine tried to convey and as has too often been accepted as truth by gender-biased historians who could not imagine women acting (however mistakenly) in their calculated self-interest. Rather, it was the logical outcome of a long development of middle-class housewives organizing to gain some control over their own lives. I will trace the movement from conservatism to fascism by looking at the national organization in general and one of its more important locals in particular.

### The National Federation
### of German Housewives' Associations (RDH)

The RDH was a national organization formed within a year of the outbreak of World War I. It had been preceded by a number of local and regional associations, primarily concerned with the "servant problem," or shortage of qualified household help. These associations were mobilized, multiplied, and centralized in 1915 by leaders of the Federation of German Women's Associations, organizers of the National Women's Service (Nationaler Frauendienst), to assist in the war effort. One of Germany's most radical feminists and suffragists, Martha Voss-Zietz, was present to inaugurate and head the new group. Also present were Dr. Agnes von Zahn-Harnack, one of the first historians of the German women's movement and last president of the BDF; Anna Blos, future Reichstag delegate for the Social Democratic Party; and disparate feminists from all parts of the political spectrum. They came with the hope of bringing housewives into the women's movement;[3] of improving housewives' rights; of gaining recognition of housewifery as a profession *(Beruf)*; some even considered demanding a stable income independent of husbands.[4]

At its founding, the RDH, like the entire BDF, was buoyed by nationalism and a spirit of service. It facilitated food distribution and performed a public relations function for the state, by mediating information on price control and explaining the economy in "pacifying lectures" whose purpose was to make the increasingly unpopular war acceptable. In the process, housewives formed contacts with each other and with bureaucrats, which would be valuable in the postwar years. Housewives proved they could organize efficiently and had grass-roots influence. The question that arose was, for what?

In Germany, the war shaded over into a revolution that polarized German society sharply for the next six years. Social revolution petered out into protracted class conflict, which ultimately left the powers that be in control. Women were not exempt from this civil war. They had to take sides, and they did.

The RDH felt it immediately around the troubled old servant problem. Suddenly, servants became more "uppity," and insisted on their rights. Unions of domestic workers, dating back to 1906, mushroomed and expanded. The revolution, such as it was, had abolished the semi-feudal regulation of private servants, which had kept them in virtual serfdom. Now, they entered the "free" labor market and, predictably, organized to win gains similar to those won by other organized workers: regulation of hours and wages, fringe benefits, dignity as equal contracting partners in collective bargaining. Their immediate employers were housewives. The scene was set for a struggle that continued, unabated and unresolved, throughout the Weimar Republic. The RDH unequivocally entered the lists on the side of the counter-revolution, a process that did not bode well for its feminist components.[5]

The same period saw a vast increase in local housewives' associations, with membership peaking in 1924 at 280,000 in 228 locals organized into 22 regionals.[6] What attracted recruits? Stepped-up activities and services. After considering a variety of legal identities—such as employer group, consumer group, professional group—to represent their constituency on the new political scene, the RDH finally settled on the latter, which allowed it to negotiate publicly on all three issues.

As a registered association of professionals in housework, the RDH drafted a guildlike plan for domestic labor, which permitted some upward mobility through a series of steps from apprentice to master, all supervised by housewives in the RDH, with cooperation from home economics school instructors. The purpose of this plan was to circumvent normal adversary labor relations with an independent domestics' union, by asserting hierarchical professional control instead.

Weakly implemented and lacking the force of law, the plan nevertheless provided an alternative model to labor contracts and to the draft legislation regulating domestic labor that remained stalled throughout the Weimar Republic. As professionals, organized urban housewives also claimed technical expertise, which opened the door to representation on government agencies and industrial boards. Drawing on the experience and personal contacts of the war years, the RDH was present on national committees regulating the export of such disparate items as films, wood, distilled tar products, coffee, cosmetics, chemicals, flax, and linoleum. It served on soap inspection committees and advised on the meat trade. It had representatives on the price control commission of the Prussian Ministry of the Interior, in the national coal council of the Labor Ministry, and on advisory commissions to combat the black market in the Prussian Health Council. Many locals of the RDH were represented on their city's price control commissions, labor bureaus, and consumer chambers, and on agricultural chambers of the region.[7]

The RDH's ambition for recognition also got a response from some industries, which saw it as a potential advertiser. Every other page of its journal, *Die Deutsche Hausfrau (The German Housewife)*, was given over to advertising, and the locals were channels to potential customers, courted by free or cut-rate sample products. Some new recruits came to the RDH attracted by cheap commodities and representation in economic bodies for their employer and consumer interests. Nor was this all. With the runaway inflation of 1923, the RDH assumed new responsibilities for its feebler members. Along with other middle-class organizations, it moved energetically into emergency aid for the suddenly impoverished members of its own class. Thus, it collected and redistributed food and clothing for pensioners; it set up middle-class soup kitchens, children's homes, vacation homes for housewives, home care for the sick; it organized auctions; it gave courses in cooking, shoe repair, clothes mending and alteration, home repairs, and so on. RDH offices advised on rent and tax matters, and individuals lectured on the legal rights of women, their participation in communal affairs, and health. Throughout, the RDH never forgot what side it was on. While petitioning the Ministry of Economics to include widows and divorced and abandoned single women in sickness insurance, it also asked the Ministry of Finance to free employers from withholding and remitting taxes for social insurance from their domestics' paychecks.

Nationalist and middle class it was. But could one call it feminist? At its founding, it seemed to have a strong feminist voice. An early press notice explained: "No man can, in the final analysis, grasp the professional needs of the housewife to the extent that he will intercede for them unequivocally. Housewives themselves must find their voices."[8] By 1924, its leadership boasted some success: its members had been received in the above-named offices of administration and in courts as witnesses and jurors.[9] If nothing else, the boast expressed pride of gender and some aspirations to power.

### The Hanover Housewives' Association

The mid-1920s brought the RDH some interesting new leadership, which pulled it, reluctantly at times, further to the right and further from the feminist orbit. A determined figure stepped out of the wings, from the Hanover local onto center stage, where she hovered on and off up to the RDH's dissolution in 1934 and beyond, to help implement its program under Hitler. Her name was Berta Hindenberg-Delbrück.

Up to 1924, when Hindenberg-Delbrück entered it, the Hanover local had been a genteel, almost sleepy little group, made up of old aristocrats, middle-class housewives, and some feminists anchored in the City Federation of Women, a local of the BDF. It too had been founded by the National Women's Service in 1915. About 700 women attended the first two meetings and membership rose to over 1,900 by 1917.[10] With the revolution membership halved, but the association did not disband. Instead, it redefined housewives' peacetime interests.

New tasks appeared: hardships suffered by the middle class during the runaway inflation were met by self-help organization, in which the Housewives' Association took a leading part. With the help of Hanover's legislature, it set up emergency kitchens that fed up to 250 pensioners a day; it helped to distribute aid from the United States; and it arranged exhibits and private sales of the products of middle-class home industry.[11]

But the most lasting problems were the servant question—which meant a shortage of cheap, qualified, and docile personnel—and the new consumer environment. These preoccupied the Hanover local, as they did the national RDH, throughout the Weimar Republic. To deal with them, the organization had to acquire a credible public identity with official recognition. The RDH had defined itself as a professional organization. On the local level in Hanover, this meant getting representatives on the city and provincial labor bureaus to work out contracts with domestic servants, which were increasingly merely low-paid apprentice contracts, for the acquisition of the "skill" of housework, to be taught by the "professional" organization of housewives. It meant getting into career counseling offices to channel girls and demobilized women workers into domestic service. It meant working on mediation committees and in the sickness insurance office on employer-servant issues. It meant serving on higher education committees to establish home economics training, mainly for potential servants. And up to 1928, the Hanover local maintained its ties with the women's movement through its membership in the City Federation of Women.[12]

On consumer matters, the local was less well-defined. Nevertheless, it supported "Buy German" campaigns; got on provincial committees for price control of coal, sugar, and potatoes; and opened its gathering to some industries for demonstrations of their new commodities. In hard times, however, specifically the runaway inflation of 1923, membership continued to drop, reaching a low of 412 in 1924.[13] Its outgoing chairperson, Adele Hornkohl, admitted in 1925 that the Hanover

Housewives' Association could not have survived as an organization without the support of the upper house of the city legislature, a heritage of wartime contacts.[14]

In 1925, the flagging fortunes of the Hanover Housewives' Association were suddenly revived, and the organization snatched from obscurity, by the entry of Berta Hindenberg-Delbrück. She joined in May 1924, at the age of thirty-nine, with a three-year-old daughter and an invalid husband, having moved to Hanover four years earlier. She showed herself to be a doer, soon volunteering to develop a plan for home economics training in households. This embroiled her almost immediately in a conflict with the City Women's Federation, which had a different plan based on training through the school system.[15] It was the beginning of a long struggle, which became a campaign by Hindenberg-Delbrück to pull the Housewives' Association out of the organized women's movement. Her motives appear to have been general politics, rather than single-minded antifeminism. In a confidential letter of 1925 on stationery of the German National People's Party, she wrote:

> Every day in my practical work, I see how important it is that we German National women systematically gain influence outside of the party organization in the neutral women's federations, through collective action and high achievement. This is the only way successfully to oppose pacifist-democratic influence.[16]

Hindenberg-Delbrück brought a welcome energy to the faltering Hanover Housewives' Association. Her organizational talent showed itself in several ways. She recruited among the wives of city senators and sent leaflets for distribution to the counseling offices of the city's utility works and to the employment offices. She made connections with industry to induce advertising through the association. She followed up a personal interest in architecture by heading the new Housing Commission in the association, which tried to influence planning commissions of the city, arguing that housewives should advise on the space that is their workplace. In fact, she won a seat on the city's prize committee for best design.[17] And she worked steadily on the home economics plan.

However, her political passion was at odds with the official political neutrality of the association and with its politically diverse membership, and so was her political style. For example, the process by which she assumed power was jarring. She requested that the executive committee complete its full complement of members without the general elections called for by the by-laws. Her motion failed, but the episode presaged undemocratic procedure and led to a flurry of resignations, especially of women connected with the City Women's Federation, including not a few founding members of the Housewives' Association.[18]

However, thanks largely to Hindenberg-Delbrück's efforts, the Hanover local grew by leaps and bounds. By 1928, membership, about 500 in 1925, had risen to 1,050. The newspaper reached even more people: the local distributed 1,650 copies. By 1928, the office had to move to larger quarters, including a hall accommodating about 200 or a large exhibit. Under its new leadership, the Hanover Housewives' Association seemed to have found a stable and respected place in postwar society.[19]

From this strengthened power base, Hindenberg-Delbrück took on her two major enemies: political liberals inside the Housewives' Association, nationally as well as locally, and the organized women's movement. This she did through a combination of overt attack, astute maneuvering, and sheer hard work.

In February 1928, the Hanover Housewives' Association pulled out of the City Women's Federation. It was a carefully staged exit. It began with polite refusals, on flimsy grounds, to cooperate in various endeavors. It came to a head over the alleged misuse of the association's membership list. The General German Women's Association (Allgemeiner Deutscher Frauenverein), a leading member of the City Women's Federation, had solicited other members' lists for the purpose of nominating female jurors, a new right accorded in the Weimar Republic. These lists then had also been used to invite people to hear Gertrud Bäumer speak. Hindenberg-Delbrück made much of the propriety of how the membership list had been used, but the real issue was political, and on February 1, the Housewives' Association withdrew from the Federation.[20]

The matter did not, however, end there. Outraged members of the association objected to the action. Word leaked out that the Executive Committee of the Housewives' Association was not united behind its head. The Jewish business manager was blamed for the leak and finally resigned. Not understanding the hidden agenda, she registered a moral complaint, and with it gave us an insight into the new political atmosphere: "None of this would have gotten so sharp, if you had not insisted on a clear for or against position. The idea that all Executive Committee members must agree on everything or else repress their opinions is neither desirable nor fruitful."[21]

In June, the opposition rallied to try and rescind the association's withdrawal from the federation, but Hindenberg-Delbrück did not let the motion come to a vote, on technical grounds.[22] Still undaunted, the dissidents next appealed to the national level. It did no good. The national executive committee stayed aloof from the local quarrel.[23]

The core of the opposition, approximately thirty people, made one last attempt to bring the matter to the membership at large. It sent around a circular explaining its position. Now the executive committee could righteously object to a breach of the by-laws. The leaders of the revolt were forced to resign,[24] and the Hanover Housewives' Association came firmly into the grip of its right wing. Both the result and the procedure previewed things to come.

### Housewives Against the Women's Movement

Meanwhile, at the national level of the RDH, ambivalence toward the organized women's movement remained pronounced. A number of pressures to leave it came from the right. One of these was the existence of a competing housewives association, formed by a breakaway right wing of the RDH. It was headed by Martha Voss-Zietz, an early founder of the RDH, whose nationalism increasingly eclipsed her early radical feminism. The new association made no pretense of neutrality like the others, but was avowedly anti-Marxist and Christian-national. Both groups actively recruited from a middle class increasingly reactionary in the spreading economic depression, and both groups strove for industry support and public representation.

In fact, the RDH had little to fear, since it was way ahead in numbers, organization, and recognition. It belonged to local and national building commissions representing housewives' needs for space allocation and design.[25] It worked with the milk industry on laws regulating pasteurization, fat content, butter products, inspection, prices, and, not least, the distribution of milk and milk products; a good deal of propaganda selling milk appeared in the publications of the RDH and its locals. It worked with the sugar industry, whose interest was great enough to pay travel expenses for the RDH representative to its meetings. The National Ministry for Nutrition Education gave the RDH 8,000 marks in 1928 for its "Buy German" campaigns. On an understanding with the Ministry for Nutrition and Agriculture, the RDH pushed rye bread over other grains, reflecting the interest of East Elbian Junker growers. On most of these issues, the RDH, true to its nationalist principles and to its coalition with the Agricultural Housewives Association, tended to support protectionism, an odd position for an official consumer group.[26]

RDH connections with industry were also well established. Its consumer-products testing laboratory in Leipzig dispensed the RDH logo, a sunburst, to acceptable products. This was a desirable form of advertising, though even untested products might still be advertised in paid space in *Die Deutsche Hausfrau* and in the newsletters of locals. The "Buy German" campaign gave the Singer Sewing Machine Company such a fright (it was capitalized by American investors) that it invited

RDH representatives to visit its plants to assure themselves that the products were German-made.[27] In sum, more than any other house-wives' organization, including the large religiously organized ones, the RDH had achieved a degree of legitimacy and official recognition that made it a force to be reckoned with. Dispensing with sentimental appeals to motherhood (divided opinions on the executive committee prevented its endorsement of Mother's Day in 1931),[28] it presented instead the sober, rational face of professionalism to the powers that be and to the general public.

Then came the Depression. The domestic-servant issue became central again, for two main reasons. One was the further impoverishment of the lower strata of the middle class, which put more of its members in danger of not affording even one servant and thus of losing middle-class status. This led to an escalating demand for domestics to be dropped from compulsory social insurance, partly paid by employers. The other reason was the demand for a cheap form of service, not liable to union regulation, such as apprenticeship under guildlike conditions might provide. The RDH officially represented the employer side in matters pertaining to organized domestics, such as the question of their social insurance and legislation regulating service (hours, wages, residence conditions, vacations, dismissal, recommendations) still pending in the National Economic Council (Reichswirtschaftsrat) and Reichstag. It supervised an interim voluntary nationwide model con-tract between housewife and servant, which mimicked industrial con-tracts between nationally organized employer and worker groups, and voluntary apprentice contracts.

The last provided for a year of home economics in the required vocational schools, then a year of apprenticeship in a household, fol-lowed by qualifying examinations for certification as an approved "household assistant." A ladder of professional mobility was built on that foundation, with advanced degrees for "household caretaker," "licensed housekeeper," "Master," and "Home Manager," the last two requiring some secondary education, an additional year and a half of school, and a minimum age of twenty-four on taking the examination.[29] While it put occupational mobility beyond the reach of most proletar-ian families, the Central Union of Domestic Employees finally en-dorsed it, knowing that the labor legislation regulating domestic service was stalled and that apprentice wages and conditions had be-come widespread and inevitable. They hoped that professionalization would allow some upward mobility and control, through contracts, over conditions of work.[30]

However, some housewives' associations, including that in Hanover, disassociated themselves from the national model, like Hindenberg-Delbrück, who came into direct conflict with it from 1927 to 1934. She had her own plan, for a nonschool, totally household-based home economics training for all female elementary school graduates, except for those headed for higher education, under supervision of qualified housewives selected by the RDH. Her plan, she pointed out, had the advantage of being cheap, as it cost the state nothing, and left control totally in the hands of organized housewives, while ignoring unions of domestic employees.[31]

The deeper issues of both plans were twofold: the acknowledgement of unions and of state mediation between employers and organized workers; and the possibility of upward mobility for domestics. The original plan incorporated both, thus mirroring modern capitalist labor relations in industrial production. That is why the Central Union of Domestic Employees accepted it, though critical of many exploitative sections. The Hindenberg-Delbrück plan, by contrast, harked back to precapitalist service relations and guild regulation, in which masters retained private corporate control over work conditions and carefully limited access to privileges.

The Depression tilted the scales against the school plan with its optimistic assumptions. It cleared the way for the cheaper, antischool and antiunion apprenticeship plan developed by Hindenberg-Delbrück. Her argument—that the household was not a factory and could not be regulated as such with set work times, contracts, inspectors, and so on—seemed increasingly plausible, especially as the infrastructure for such an approach could not be financed by a bankrupt state. The same economic pressures also led to a shift of emphasis in the ideology of organized housewives from viewing housewifery as *one* honorable profession among several to claiming it as *the* profession for women. The tight labor market contributed to illusions about returning women to their place in the home, so the message fell on willing ears, though not all in the RDH were yet ready to give up the more feminist vision.

The issues sharpened in 1932, as the Depression deepened. In June, at a general meeting of the RDH in Weimar, about thirty co-signed locals moved to leave the BDF and to establish, instead, a work committee that would be an equal partner of the BDF and RDH, rather than subordinate membership of the latter to the former. That was a bombshell. It divided the RDH nearly in half.

A number of reasons for leaving the BDF surfaced in the discussion. One was pressure from the right outside the RDH. The right-wing competitor housewives' organization and the League of Catholic German Women (Katholischer Deutscher Frauenbund) had reproached the RDH with implicitly supporting the abolition of Paragraph 218 of the penal code prohibiting abortion, simply by belonging to the BDF, which did not go on record as opposing abortion.[32] Another reason was recruitment among the young, many of whom did not identify with the aging women's movement. Hindenberg-Delbrück noted that new currents were

> away from liberalism, toward obligations; away from the career woman, toward the housewife and mother. Everything we have emphasized now comes into the foreground. This is the hour for us to leave traditional ties like the BDF; for our work we need freedom; if we miss this hour, we miss a strong means of recruitment, and especially youth will remain alien to us. . . . We are not against women, but for the family and the state.[33]

Some feared that the BDF concentrated too much on the needs of employed women, who were directly endangered by unemployment. Other political issues also divided the RDH from the BDF, not the least of which, in 1932, was National Socialism.

The BDF had warned repeatedly against the Nazi Party and its antifeminism. But not all its members were convinced; among them were the members and sympathizers of the conservative German National People's Party, some of whom leaned toward the new persuasion. In this struggle around BDF membership, the matter came up in the form of denial. Thus, the leadership of the National Federation of Agricultural Housewives' Associations, coalition partner of the RDH, had decided to leave the BDF in October 1931. Its head, denying any ties with National Socialism, declared simply that they had wanted to leave for several years;[34] but in fact its retired founder, Elisabeth Böhm, still a revered leader *emeritus,* had been wearing a swastika for some time, saying it appealed to her as an ancient Germanic symbol.[35]

For the RDH, it meant losing a coalition partner and appearing pointedly pro-BDF at a time of growing political polarization. For its right wing, this was unacceptable. Moderates and liberals of the RDH, including its head, fought hard to keep ties with the already severely diluted women's movement. Others pointed to good relations with associations of career women in their locals, which held true especially in the more liberal south.[36] But when the ballots were counted, 587 had voted for the motion, 478 against, and 5 ballots were declared invalid.[37] By the slim margin of six to five, the RDH had chosen to leave the BDF.

Echoes of the fight reverberated for months and the split widened after Bäumer attacked the decision. In an article entitled "The Women's Front," in the BDF organ *Die Frau* of July 1932, she deplored the fragmentation of the women's movement during the ongoing economic crisis and the threat of National Socialism, which, she thought, aimed to push women out of the parliamentary system. Nazis, too, were mobilizing women. In this context, the RDH's step was reactionary in the original and sterile meaning of the word, she wrote. But Hindenberg-Delbrück retorted: "We'll see who looks further into

the future. From the start, the housewives' movement saw the housewife as performing, achieving, creating, serving for the family, the
people, the nation, and not challenging them."[38] She rejected the
undercurrent of the women's movement, which women organize for
women's own sakes. Housewives were the true vanguard, having supported motherliness long before it was popular, she said. "We housewives feel we are on the brink of a new morrow and that we contribute
to it. We wish the sisters in this great hour would 'die and be reborn
and strive toward the same goal: the rebirth of the nation through the
family.'"[39]

In fact, the pull-out posed a major challenge. Feeling the winds of
change in the national political climate, conservatives in the RDH felt
the time had come for them to present themselves not merely as
opponents within the BDF, but as a housewives' movement presenting
a major alternative to the "old" women's movement. Opposing the
integrationist impulse of the career women who directed the BDF,
they resurrected the vision of complementary spheres, dressed in the
new clothes of rationalized home economics. The modern housewife,
with the aid of new technology and work practices, would serve the
people directly by serving her family and indirectly by training all
young girls in the skills of home economics: some, like themselves, to
be managers; others, like the working class, to be domestics. A victory
would have put the RDH at the top of the female hierarchy in a sex-
divided system for a politics of the harem in contemporary garb.

## The "New Order"

A few months later, both challenger and challenged were in disarray.
Hitler had become Chancellor, and the Nazi Party organization had
begun its takeover of the myriad associations in Germany, through a
process of purges and political synchronization called *Gleichschaltung.*
This, according to the new government, meant, among other things,
that the composition of executive committees be one-third Nazi, one-
third German National People's Party, and one-third "reliable nationalists." Jewish members could remain, but not in leading positions, and
no more were to be admitted.[40] For women's groups, it involved control by the Nazi Women's Group and absorption into a state corporate
body, either the Women's Front or else a mixed-gender group such as
the Labor Front, which absorbed wage workers, or the Peasant Estate,
into which the National Federation of Agricultural Housewives' Associations was dissolved.

The BDF dissolved itself, but the RDH submitted to the new rules.
Its right wing felt close enough to the Nazi Party to join, and even its
moderates accommodated in hope of rescuing some autonomy for the

organization and its work. Jewish members of the national's executive committee resigned early, but the locals had varying experiences. In some cases, Jewish members were pressured out quickly, allowing their associations to report "no further problem" in cooperating with local Nazi authorities. Elsewhere, locals defended the presence of Jews on their executive committees and correspondingly had to report trouble in their areas. Finally, there were those locals who had kept out or removed Jewish members even before the decree.

The East Prussian regional Housewives' Association reported that it "had already functioned in the spirit of the National Socialist movement and retrospectively must almost be seen as a female accompaniment to the male idea embodied in National Socialism."[41] Hindenberg-Delbrück, who joined the Nazi Party in 1933, took a pragmatic position: its Women's Group had youth behind it and should therefore be a welcome partner. Privately, she went somewhat further. She claimed to have purged her local of Jews during the campaign against the City Women's Federation in 1928.

> Here in Hanover, I had the good luck, that the betrayal of a Jewish Executive Committee member, which I discovered on taking office, provided the opportunity to boot her out. To our joy, almost all Jews left our association during that struggle and I have arranged since then to stress Christianity in our work and newspaper, for example on the occasion of Christian holidays, so that Jews could not feel comfortable and therefore not strive for membership. . . . The whole RDH should have done similarly.[42]

Thus, with varying degrees of commitment, the locals of the RDH voted to join the newly formed Women's Front of the state—it was the first "professional" women's group to do so—and to cooperate with the Nazi Women's Group.[43] But anti-Semitism alone did not ensure success in the new regime, for it demanded surrender of autonomy as well. Here, the RDH fought hard. Its head was empowered to negotiate jurisdictional questions. Internal party struggles created confusion in Berlin during the first two years after Hitler's takeover.

Different blueprints existed for the corporate state. Women's place in it and their leadership were also in flux, leaving local fanatics considerable room for maneuver. Complaints began pouring in. Still, many hearts were won when the new regime lifted the onerous social insurance taxes from domestics' salaries, so long a desired goal of the RDH. "Nothing is impossible in the new Germany!" gloated *Die Deutsche Hausfrau.*[44] Hindenberg-Delbrück, invited to the Nuremberg rally of the Nazi Party in the fall of 1933, returned grateful "for the overwhelmingly beautiful experience."[45] She claimed to understand that, during the time of struggle, the masculine element had had to predominate, but hoped that in the new state, the feminine would again come into its own. Quiet patience would lead to harmony.[46] She wrote to the resigning legal counsel of the Hanover Housewives' Association:

> We are working for a state and a social order that will allow women to return to the family through economic improvement. It is our greatest joy, that the government is clearly going this route. . . . We hope that you, too, will some day return to our circle as a full-time housewife and as only a housewife.[47]

How many other housewives shared this deadly welcome of their professional "sisters"? Certainly others also shared the new euphoria. One, who had just read *Mein Kampf,* found herself "deeply moved by the simplicity and greatness of this man. . . . One can only say, God protect this man until he has completed his work."[48] Even the patient head of the RDH, Maria Jecker, who had come out of the League of Catholic German Women and had tried to stay loyal to the BDF, now also joined the party, for the sake of the RDH, she said.[49] Her goal was to establish an "Estate [*Stand*] of Housewives" in the corporate state, arguing that it would encompass 15 million housewives and over 1.5 million domestic servants, to be administered, of course, by the RDH.

But good faith did not suffice. Young female Nazis, heady with victory, pushed past "outdated" forms, individuals, and ideas. Arrogantly, they demanded membership lists, minutes, and account books of local housewives' associations.[50] There were other jurisdictional problems too. In the late fall and winter of 1933, the new House and Home Assistants' Union aggressively began to organize domestic servants. It replaced the dissolved unions of domestics, and was slotted into the Labor Front. This had two major effects on the housewives' associations. In the first place, for those who opposed unionization of domestics, it smelled of class struggle and Marxism. In the second place, the official goal of the RDH had been to incorporate servants into a female hierarchy, not a labor hierarchy. Labor Front organizing threatened their ambitions, which they had hoped were on the threshold of fulfillment.

Finally, women's groups dedicated to the ideology of wife and mother were split into different divisions, thanks in part to the prior competition between them. Thus, the Catholic and Protestant women's groups, the Patriotic Women's Association, the National League of Large Families and others with whom the RDH had cultivated good relations now jostled one another and the new Nazi women's groups for the privilege of "administering" housewifery and motherhood in a state that aimed to replace these myriad voluntary groups with monolithic control. The National Socialist Welfare took over relief for the unemployed poor, the Labor Front assumed regulation of domestic servants, the consumer testing lab in Leipzig was dismantled on charges of corruption, and child care was relegated to a new "Mothers' Service" under the minister of the interior and jointly run by Protestant and Catholic "mothers' services" and the Association for Infant and Toddler Care. Alarmed, the RDH saw all its turf cut up. That left only one thing: home economics. And they had better claim it fast, for even here they weren't safe.[51]

The specialization in home economics gave Hindenberg-Dëlbruck her big chance to bring her plan for a compulsory year of service in private households to fruition. In the fiscal crisis of the state, cheapness was its main appeal. Presenting it to the RDH Executive Committee in May 1933, she argued that since the Chancellor had set a goal of compulsory labor service for girls, the possibility now existed for the success of such a plan coming from the RDH. The plan recommended that girls not be allowed to marry, work for wages, or do vocational training until they had completed a year of service in a private household. The site could be their own family or friends, though the housewives' associations might act as clearinghouses, preferentially allocating assistance to large families. They were to be paid with room and board alone, tested at the end of the year, and, if they passed, given a certificate as proof of completion of the service year. They were to supplement, not replace, domestic servants as such. The political value of the plan, Hindenberg-Delbrück concluded, would be that "the German household would once more become a site of national education in which the various social strata get to know one another and cooperate."[52]

In April 1934, the RDH and its competitor were merged and incorporated into the state's Women's Bureau. Calls to implement the household service year came from the national women's leader, Gertrud Scholtz-Klink, the National Labor Registry, and the National Youth Leader.[53] Hindenberg-Delbrück's plan was adopted, with revisions, and she was promoted to the top of the now hierarchically organized housewives' group—to its "small ring of leaders," which also included its former head and four others.[54] The new RDH saw itself as the "picked troops" of the new Department for Economics and Home Economics in the Women's Bureau established in September 1934, and there Hindenberg-Delbrück became chief adviser for implementation of the plan. Together with locals of the Nazi Women's Group, RDH locals swung into action on a national scale early in 1935. Not that enthusiasm was uniformly high among the plan's target population. Even the official report conceded that some girls resisted going to work on the land, despite high unemployment. But social and political pressure could be used to overcome recalcitrance.

The RDH appeared to have won in its challenge to the organized women's movement. But the victory, under the conditions of National

Socialism, entailed suicide. Bit by bit and ever faster, the RDH did, after all, lose its identity in the state organization and its autonomy to the party organization, both of which were subordinate to the male-dominated party and state.[55] Finally, the hollowed-out organization itself was dissolved. In September 1935, the national women's leader, Scholtz-Klink,

> considered the time ripe to drop the Association's boundaries inside the Department of Economics and Home Economics and to make individual membership in the Department accessible to every German woman without going through an Association.[56]

This "inclusion of all women serving the Fatherland from the household was greeted by our Association as the fulfillment of a goal held since 1915."[57] Accordingly, the RDH resolved at its last general meeting, September 4, 1935, to disband at the end of the year and to ask its members to enter the Department of Economics and Home Economics as individuals, in order to continue the work.[58] Some of those who did kept up a network.[59] Others were purged. Even so accommodating a person as Hindenberg-Delbrück could be removed, as "representative of naked bourgeois interests," and she fell into private obscurity thereafter.[60] The RDH had "died and been reborn" in the new mass housewife of the sex-segregated Nazi state.

## Conclusion

What can we conclude from this story? The housewives' associations, formed spontaneously before World War I to protect the class interests of women as employers of servants, were re-formed by feminists during the war, who hoped to raise their consciousness as women. And, indeed, they acquired the precious feeling of entitlement and the invaluable skills of political organizing that were among the main achievements of the first women's movement. But they were step-sisters to it, alien from the start, poorly integrated, and ultimately hostile to their adoptive family. Envious, perhaps, of the rare success that some career women enjoyed, and threatened in their identity by new, if limited, opportunities, they clung all the more steadfastly to the notion of female domesticity. Riding on the coattails of the women's movement in elevating housewifery to a profession, they eventually cut loose to make a fateful bid for supremacy when the time seemed opportune; they reverted to insistence that housewifery was *the* profession for all women. It must have felt like a comfortable retreat for many, when the Depression limited other options even more severely.

Class interests played an even more important part. The RDH was not alone in seeing its main enemy on the left, from the beginning of the Weimar Republic, but it had distinct interests of its own. Having servants remained a mark of status as well as the means to avoid the worst housework, which no amount of glorification could make palatable. The Weimar Republic threatened to make those harder to keep through its labor legislation. The RDH's program of a household service year for "common" girls—that is, those not moving into higher education, a preserve of the elite—prepared the public for an acceptance, under the Nazis, of this return to partial serfdom, dressed in the modern garb of national interest.

Furthermore, the Socialist and Liberal parties were unjustly blamed for economic disasters and structural changes that impoverished the lower strata of the middle class. To the right, they saw liberalism as shading easily into Marxism. Both implied expropriation, and a leveling of class, gender, and race that seemed to entail the political and social derogation of these already precarious strata. To the middle-class organized housewives, liberal feminism appeared dangerously close to socialism, whatever the protestations of the BDF to the contrary and despite its historical antagonism to the socialist women's movement. Middle-class housewives preferred to serve the masters they knew, rather than the masters or mistresses of an upstart class. The former, at least, they might manipulate, in the tried-and-true tradition of womanhood, and indeed the men of their class gave them some reason to hope for success.

Finally, one could speculate on the feasibility of feminists organizing housewives as such. Households, after all, are the carriers of class property, and identification with the household is likely to reinforce class consciousness, rather than to break it down along feminist lines. Certainly this was so in this historical case. One household is not like another, and one housewife is not like another. As long as men are "heads of households," and class-divided among themselves, one man's wife may be another man's servant. Neither mistress nor maid is free in that situation. Nor are they likely to unite in common cause. The mistress has too much to lose.[61]

If one cannot move forward to equality, one may embrace inequality and call it good. Capitalism is based on inequalities and continually recreates them: among classes, among races, between women and men. For those women whose stake in capitalism is high, such as those whose income derives from ownership of profitable property, usually held by the men of their family, these inequalities must be accepted (except for renegades of the class) and either justified or ameliorated. Bourgeois *feminists* leaned toward amelioration, sometimes seeking alliance with working-class feminists. They sought to lower the ladder of meritocratic social mobility to women as well as to men, demanding "equal opportunity" along liberal lines, though many understood the limiting nature of class inequality from birth. But bourgeois *antifemin-*

*ists* resisted even these barely equalizing tendencies. They mobilized, with tactics and weapons learned from feminists, to defend and exalt women's "natural" place as a family-circumscribed being, perpetually on call by men and children. And they also accepted relatively static class differences as natural and tried to use them to their own advantage. As servants to their families, they wanted servants of their own— for status, for work relief, for a sense of power in their own "sphere," failing having it in other spheres.

The organized women's movement collapsed, after a slow demise during which it nurtured and conflicted with antifeminists, who absorbed, while distorting, much of its message. Women who voluntarily cooperated with the Nazi state hoped to share power in a complementary sphere, now organized along trim, modern, rational lines. It was old wine in new bottles, but they had to taste it before they knew.

## Notes

This article owes much to the critical readings of Bonnie Anderson, Barbara Engel, Amy Hackett, Deborah Hertz, Claudia Koonz, Mary Nolan, and Hobart A. Spalding, Jr., as well as to my co-editors of this volume and to the board of the New Feminist Library. I am especially grateful to Claudia Koonz for calling to my attention the value of the holdings in the Niedersächsisches Hauptstaatsarchiv. The research was made possible by a grant from the American Philosophical Society in 1981 and by a Professional Staff Congress–Board of Higher Education Award in 1982.

1. Richard Evans, *The Feminist Movement in Germany, 1894–1933* (London and Beverly Hills: Sage Publications, 1976). Amy Hackett, "The German Women's Movement and Suffrage, 1890–1914: A Study in National Feminism," in Robert J. Bezucha, ed., *Modern European Social History* (Lexington, Mass., 1972), pp. 354–86. For greater detail, see her Ph.D. dissertation, "The Politics of Feminism in Wilhelmine Germany, 1890–1918," at Columbia University; Barbara Greven-Aschoff, *Die bürgerliche Frauenbewegung in Deutschland 1894–1933* (Göttingen: Vandenhoeck & Ruprecht, 1981).
2. Leonard Krieger, *The German Idea of Freedom* (Boston, 1957).
3. *Zentrales Staatsarchiv Potsdam* (hereafter ZSAP), 70 Re 2, Akte 5, RDH general assembly in Hamburg, June 8–9, 1916.
4. Ibid., Akte 1. RDH general assembly in Munich, June 28–29, 1917.
5. Renate Bridenthal, "Class Struggle around the Hearth: Women and Domestic Service in the Weimar Republic," in Michael Dobkowski and Isidor Walliman, eds., *Towards the Holocaust: Anti-Semitism and Fascism in Weimar Germany* (Westport, Conn.: Greenwood Press, 1983), pp. 243–64.
6. *Niedersächsisches Hauptstaatsarchiv* (hereafter NH) HANN 320 I, Akte 1. Seventh Annual Report of RDH, June 1, 1922, to May 15, 1924.
7. Ibid.
8. Ibid., Akte 74. Undated press notice announcing the founding of the RDH.
9. Ibid., Akte 1. Seventh Annual Report of RDH.
10. Ibid., Akte 2. Second Annual Report of Hannover local, May 1, 1916, to April 30, 1917.

11. Ibid., Akte 4. Ninth and Tenth Annual Reports of Hannover local, 1924 and 1925.
12. Ibid., Tenth Annual Report, 1925.
13. Ibid., Akte 5. Undated letter to Hornkohl from the RDH central treasury.
14. Ibid., Akte 4. Tenth Annual Report.
15. Ibid., Akte 21. Correspondence of March 1925 between Hornkohl and Hindenberg-Delbrück.
16. Ibid., November 20, 1925, letter from Hindenberg-Delbrück to Freifrau von Bülow of the local Agricultural Housewives Association. More research is in order on associational life in Weimar Germany and the degree to which it mediated political currents, including the onset of Nazism.
17. Ibid., Akte 4. Tenth Annual Report, 1925, and Akte 9, Eleventh Annual Report, 1926.
18. Ibid., Akte 22. Executive Committee meeting of January 13, 1926, and correspondence of March through June.
19. Ibid., Akte 9. Annual Reports, 1926–1928.
20. Ibid. Executive Committee meeting of January 23, 1928.
21. Ibid., Akte 10, II. April 8, 1928, letter from Tilla Meyer to Hindenberg-Delbrück.
22. Ibid., Akte 10, I. July 11, 1928, letter from Mathilde Drees to Hindenberg-Delbrück, summarizing events to date.
23. ZSAP, 70 Re 2, Akte 3. Steering Committee of RDH, meeting of January 17, 1929.
24. NH, HANN 320 I, Akte 10, I. January 9, 1929, letter of resignation from Drees, Brauns, Graefenhain, and Drechsler.
25. ZSAP, 70 Re 2, Akte 7. February 19, 1931, letter from RDH business office to Housing Commission.
26. Ibid., Akte 20. Matters pertaining to the National Ministry for Nutrition and Agriculture, 1923–1929.
27. Ibid., Akte 3. Steering Committee of RDH, meeting of January 17, 1929.
28. Ibid., Steering Committee of RDH, meeting of June 7, 1931.
29. Ibid., Akte 3. Steering Committee of RDH, meeting of February 26, 1931.
30. *Zentralbibliothek der Gewerkschaften, Freier Deutscher Gewerkschaftsbund,* Berlin, Protocol of First National Conference of *Zentralverband der Hausangestellten Deutschlands, Reichsfachgruppe im Deutschen Verkehrsbund,* June 28–29, 1925, pp. 31–35; Protocol of Third National Conference of *Reichsfachgruppe Haus und Wachangestellte im Gesamtverband der Arbeitnehmer der Öffentlichen Betriebe und des Personen- und Warenverkehrs,* March 22–24, 1931, pp. 59–71.
31. NH, HANN 320 I, Akte 66. Meeting of Hanover Provincial Housewives' Association, May 3–4, 1927.
32. Atina Grossmann, "Abortion and Economic Crisis: The 1931 Campaign against Paragraph 218 in Germany," in this volume.
33. NH, HANN 320 I, Akte 83. General assembly of RDH, June 8–10, 1932.
34. Ibid. Executive Committee meeting of RDH, June 9, 1932.
35. *Land und Frau,* September 19, 1931, p. 694. Böhm joined the Nazi Party in 1935, according to her file in the Berlin Document Center. In that year, she came out of retirement to dissolve the National Federation of Agricultural Housewives' Associations into the Peasant Front.
36. NH, HANN 320 I, Akte 83. Executive Committee meeting of RDH, June 9, 1932.
37. Each local was entitled to one vote per one hundred members, with any excess going to its federation at the province level. The vote at this meeting represented 107,000 members, half of the RDH's peak in 1928.
38. *Mitteilungen des Hannoverschen Hausfrauenvereins,* August 1932.
39. Ibid.
40. NH, HANN 320 I, Akte 85, I. Minister of Finance answering Jecker's query on the matter, reported at Executive Committee of RDH, meeting of May 11–12, 1933. The regulation became moot with the dissolution of the RDH in 1935.

41. Ibid.
42. Ibid., Akte 72, I. March 30, 1933, letter from Hindenberg-Delbrück to Dralle. She may not have been exceptional in this; the preservation of her records simply makes her more easily identifiable.
43. Ibid., Akte 85, I. Circular to Executive Committee of RDH, May 14, 1933.
44. *Die Deutsche Hausfrau*, August 1933, pp. 113–15.
45. NH, HANN 320 I, Akte 15. Executive Committee of Hanover local, meeting of September 8, 1933.
46. Ibid., Akte 71. Hindenberg-Delbrück's report to Hanover Provincial Housewives' Association, September 21, 1933.
47. Ibid., Akte 14. June 3, 1933, letter from Hindenberg-Delbrück to Dr. jur. Gertrud Rahmsdorf.
48. Ibid., Akte 72, II. June 20, 1933, letter from Franziska Wieman, head of the Hanover Provincial Housewives' Association, to Hindenberg-Delbrück.
49. Ibid. Also, Maria Jecker's file in the Berlin Document Center.
50. NH, HANN 320 I, Akte 85, II. June 24, 1933, letter from Hindenberg-Delbrück to Wissdorff on the RDH Executive Committee.
51. Ibid., December 13, 1933, letter from Emma Kromer to Jecker.
52. Ibid., Akte 85, I. Steering Committee and Executive Committee of RDH, meetings in May 1933.
53. Ibid., Akte 7. *Zwanzig Jahre Hausfrauenarbeit in Hannover, 1915–1935*, p. 27.
54. ZSAP, 70 Re 2, Akte 3. Meeting of *Kleiner Führerring* of RDH, July 6, 1934.
55. Claudia Koonz, "The Competition for a Women's *Lebensraum*," in this volume.
56. NH, HANN 320 I, Akte 7. *Zwanzig Jahre. . .* , p. 32.
57. Ibid., p. 33.
58. Ibid.
59. Personal interview, August 21–22, 1981, with Regina Frankenfeld in Stuttgart, formerly of the Pomeranian Agricultural Housewives' Association and later employed in the Department for Economics and Home Economics in the Women's Bureau of the Nazi state.
60. Hindenburg-Delbrück's autobiographical sketch of 1967, contributed by her daughter, Gisela Baumhauer, who in many other ways has been extremely supportive in the reconstruction of this history.
61. Rayna Rapp, Ellen Ross, and Renate Bridenthal, "Examining Family History," *Feminist Studies* 5, no. 1 (Spring 1979), reprinted in *The Doubled Vision*, J. Walkowitz et al., eds., (London: Routledge & Kegan Paul, 1983). Also, Renate Bridenthal, "The Family Tree," in Amy Swerdlow, ed., *Household and Kin: Families in Flux* (New York: The Feminist Press and McGraw Hill, 1980).

# Sisterhood under Siege: Feminism and Anti-Semitism in Germany, 1904–1938

## Marion Kaplan

*Jewish women in the Weimar Republic faced the double burden of sexism and racism. Marion Kaplan's essay focuses on the League of Jewish Women (Jüdischer Frauenbund; JFB), which struggled to promote feminist goals within the Jewish community and which belonged to the organized bourgeois German women's movement until the Nazis seized power. It suggests that within a broad, middle-class context women shared common gender-specific experiences across ethnic/religious lines and yet suffered divisions created by these same identities. The relationship between the German and German-Jewish women's organizations points to the strengths as well as the limits of sisterhood in an increasingly racist (in this case, anti-Semitic) society. Parallels with modern minority feminist politics are often apparent. Jewish women identified positively with their Jewish community and heritage and were so identified—negatively—by anti-Semites. At the same time, they had to fight for civic equality within their own Jewish community. During the Nazi era, however, they were increasingly ostracized and persecuted as Jews. Previous feminist solidarity vanished into thin air, and strategies of sheer survival replaced the earlier gender-specific concerns of Jewish feminists.*

This essay explores the relationship of the Jewish feminist movement in Germany to its German counterpart and to the surrounding society. German-Jewish women suffered a dual stigmatization of gender and "race" in a society that became increasingly misogynist and anti-Semitic. In times of relative social peace and harmony, Jewish women fought the sexism of their own German-Jewish community. Often, they combined with their German sisters in feminist solidarity, focussing on common concerns. But as radical, racist anti-Semitism grew, Jewish women were forcibly divided from other feminists. They fought for Jewish survival, as feminist loyalties dissolved in the face of increasingly hideous anti-Semitic persecutions.

This history is divided into three parts. The first will delineate the programs of the League of Jewish Women (Jüdischer Frauenbund; JFB) within the Jewish community. The second will describe the League's cooperation with the German feminist movement during the Weimar Republic. The third part will discuss the survival strategies of Jewish women under the Nazi dictatorship. The story of the successes and defeat of the League of Jewish Women reveals a good deal about the roles of all women (regardless of race), the discrimination against all Jews (regardless of gender), and the political and social strengths and weaknesses of the German middle classes.

### Loyalty and Community

German-Jewish women lived in a position of double jeopardy as a result of their ethnic/religious heritage (which the Nazis would later label "race") and their sex: as Jews and as women they endured discrimination in Germany, and as women they suffered from second-class citizenship in their own Jewish community. They were, for example, disenfranchised in the German states as Jews; and when the vote was extended to Jewish males in the German Empire, Jewish women had to await the enfranchisement of German women. Even when female suffrage was granted in 1918, the victory of Jewish women was only a secular one; as women, they were still denied the vote in elections for Jewish communal office. Similarly, when German women began to achieve modest advances as teachers (1860s and 1870s) and civil servants (1880s), anti-Semitism blocked Jewish women from a share in this progress. Nevertheless, in Imperial Germany, German-Jewish women benefited from the political and economic successes of Jewish men and from the inroads carved by German feminists into the male sanctuaries of higher education and the professions (circa 1900), and, finally, politics (after 1918). By the turn of the century, Jewish middle-class women were increasingly able to turn their energies beyond home and family, to volunteer in Jewish charities, obtain higher education and career entrance, and become active in the German women's movement. In 1904, on the occasion of the meeting of the International Council of Women,[1] the more progressive members of the traditional Jewish women's religious societies as well as Jewish women who were involved in the German feminist movement formed the nucleus of the JFB. Its founder and president was Bertha Pappenheim,[2] a dedicated feminist and a devout Jew. Her organization attracted a large following—50,000 women, or approximately 20 percent of all Jewish women over the age of 30. It played a vital role within the Jewish community until 1938 while maintaining a cooperative and supportive role within the German women's movement until 1933. The League combined feminist goals—"for women's work and the women's movement"—with a strong sense of Jewish identity. Its efforts were directed toward: (1) strengthening community consciousness among Jews; (2) furthering the ideals of the bourgeois women's movement; (3) expanding the participation of women in the Jewish community on the basis of equality with men; (4) providing Jewish women with career training; and (5) combating all forms of immorality, specifically white slavery. Its support of the goals of the German bourgeois women's movement distinguished the JFB from other Jewish women's organizations that preceded or paralleled it.[3] Its endorsement of the bourgeois movement separated it, as well, from the major Protestant and Catholic women's organizations.

The JFB belonged to the mainstream of the nineteenth- and twentieth-century bourgeois women's movements, which tried to enlarge woman's sphere by increasing her opportunities and broadening her outlook. Its demands were essentially reformist, shaped not only by the position of women in Judaism, but also by the situation of Jews and women in Germany, the omnipresence of anti-Semitism, and the intransigence of antifeminism. The JFB engaged in traditional, liberal strategies to acquire political power. Simultaneously, it developed its own alternative to "male power" by building an organization "of women, for women."

Allegiance to the JFB was a product of class and age. Its members reflected the overwhelmingly middle-class socioeconomic position of German Jews.[4] JFB members were middle-class housewives who did not work for pay. They had neither the professional careers nor working-class allegiances that could have facilitated their entrance into professional women's organizations or working-class women's associations. The JFB offered such housewives the opportunity to associate with women who shared their primary religious and class identities. The Jewish working class was not represented in the JFB. It consisted of successive waves of Eastern European immigrants who engaged in petty trade and were employed in light industries in Germany's urban centers. These Eastern European Jews remained the objects of JFB concern and the recipients of its ministrations. Not only did the JFB fail to enroll working-class women; younger women, too, remained aloof. Organizations such as the JFB were best suited to an era of middle-class prosperity such as had existed in the decade before World War I. With the war and postwar economic crises, the JFB was unable to recruit young volunteers, since few had the option of becoming leisured ladies. By the 1930s only a few young faces could be found amid the widowed and aging membership.[5]

Jewish feminists acknowledged the positive attachments of faith, culture, and destiny that they shared with Jewish men. Despite the obvious and considerable tensions involved in being both feminists and observant Jews,[6] League members were unwilling to focus on secular feminism in Germany to the neglect of their Jewish roots. Their position reflects in microcosm a more general dilemma of modern minorities: the desire to be accepted by the majority while guarding their own distinctiveness. While the women of the JFB strongly supported German middle-class feminism, they did not desire complete absorption at the expense of their religious/ethnic identity. The loss of a strong Jewish identity was too high a price to pay for social acceptance. They sought acculturation, not total assimilation. This stance was not unusual among Jews in Germany. Many Jews had seen emancipation as an opportunity for the entry of "Jews as Jews to the ranks of humanity," not as a signal solely to imitate Gentile society.[7] In fact, the extent of Jewish organizational and communal activity indicates a strong, positive bonding that was often heightened—but not always caused—by periods of anti-Semitism. The very vitality of Jewish communal life, not simply the degree to which Jews were absorbed into the German milieu, provided the successes and hopes that ultimately blinded many Jews to the realities of Nazi Germany.

Jewish women also recognized the more negative bonds that they shared with Jewish men. Like their male counterparts, they were outsiders: both sexes were the objects of a lingering and persistent anti-Semitism that spurred them to join forces in self-defense. Thus, organizing a women's movement along religious lines was the result of legal and traditional circumstances beyond Jewish feminists' control: the result not only of positive feelings, but of a lack of social integration. Despite their seeming political and economic success, Jews remained segregated in a religious and organizational subculture. Social acceptance was impeded by German attitudes ranging from a lingering phobia against Jews with roots in ancient and medieval religious prejudices to a virulent, racist, political anti-Semitism originating in the 1870s and 1880s. Sporadic outbursts of hostility poisoned the atmosphere and wounded and confused Jews. Still, Jewish feminists were as unwilling to sacrifice women's issues for Jewish solidarity as they were to forfeit Jewishness for feminist solidarity. They persisted in demanding both, while their campaigns reflected the larger political and social forces that fettered Jews and women in Germany.

Although the importance of the German women's movement to the ideas and activities of the Jewish organization must be underscored, the JFB's primary efforts were directed toward the Jewish community. Thus, we turn first to the Jewish aspects of Jewish feminism and next to the broader feminist interests. The JFB's campaigns within the Jewish community included the attempt to provide career training for women, the fight against white slavery, and the pursuit of equality in Jewish communal affairs. Each of these efforts reflected feminist aspirations as well as the insecurities of Jews in Germany. In support of the first, career training, the JFB set up employment offices, vocational guidance centers, night courses to improve job skills, and several schools (offering courses in the traditional female fields of home economics, child care, basic health care, and social work). While Jewish feminists insisted that housework be treated with the same respect as other employment, they challenged the attitude that a woman's place was *only* in the home. Jobs were seen as a means of economic, psychological, and emotional independence and the JFB looked toward the growing collective importance of all working women. As a Jewish organization, the JFB was concerned that the job profile of German Jews was conspicuously different from that of all other Germans; as a result of historical discrimination as well as of new opportunities open to them after their emancipation, Jews were heavily concentrated in commerce. For Jewish women, this meant, for example, that in 1925, 53 percent of those who were employed were engaged in commerce and 3 percent in agriculture, compared with 14 percent and 43 percent, respectively, for non-Jewish women.[8] In the face of extreme anti-Semitism during and after World War I, Jewish organizations, including the JFB, committed themselves to a policy of vocational retraining: shifting Jewish youth away from commerce and toward vocations more typical of the general population. For boys this meant industry, crafts, and agriculture; for girls it meant home economics careers.

Despite years of propaganda in favor of training women for domestic careers, in the midst of the Weimar era only 9.3 percent of employed Jewish women—up from 8.8 percent in 1907—worked as domestics. These women, to be sure, were not the daughters of bourgeois Jews. Class position determined that young middle-class women would remain immune to the lure of the "domestic service professions," using the skills they acquired in household management courses to become better housewives. In fact, while serving their own middle-class interests in a period in which a servant shortage preoccupied most bourgeois housewives, JFB members could congratulate themselves for helping immigrant and German-Jewish working-class girls find jobs.

Through prevention and rescue efforts the JFB fought commercial prostitution, or white slavery, particularly among Jewish women from Eastern Europe lured abroad and sold or forced into prostitution by traffickers.[9] To thwart procurers, the JFB established railroad and harbor outposts for women traveling alone; offered food, hostels, financial aid, and information to needy young women or female travelers; and organized evening recreation for young women in Germany (to "keep them off the streets" and to inculcate a sense of Jewish community). As part of a "prevention program," it supported vocational and educational institutions for Jewish girls in Eastern Europe; sent teachers and nurses to Eastern Europe; and published leaflets and warnings on the dangers of white slavery. It cooperated with national and international volunteer organizations to suppress the traffic and founded the first Jewish home for delinquent girls, unwed mothers, and illegitimate children in Germany. Its defense of unwed mothers and its concern for Jewish prostitutes (its "erring young sisters") were its most radical challenges to the norms of its community. These met with the indifference or hostility of much of the Jewish community, which preferred to shun such issues or voice moral condemnation of "fallen women." Also, its determined campaign against white slavery met with resistance by Jewish leaders who feared that, by recognizing that Jews took part in this vice, the JFB was adding to the arsenal of the anti-Semites.

Bertha Pappenheim responded that the Jewish community would be guilty of complicity if it did not act against these crimes. Moreover, she was aware that the energetic participation of Jews in the campaigns against white slavery put a damper on that anti-Semitism which could have arisen among reformers as a result of substantial Jewish involvement in this traffic in women. She felt the need to explain that the extreme poverty and discrimination suffered by East European Jewry were the prime causes of this crime. As Jews, League members attempted to rescue Jewish girls and protect the Jewish community. The JFB members were not, however, simply on a rescue mission or an anti-vice crusade: as feminists, they sought at all times to call attention to the sexual discrimination that lay at the root of sexual vice, to challenge traditional roles, to construct new institutions for women, and to improve the status of women within Judaism.

Of all the JFB's efforts, the fight for political power in the Jewish community was its longest and most arduous, ending well after women had attained suffrage in Germany. The Jewish community in Germany, like other religious entities, was a publicly constituted corporation embracing all Jews in any one place of residence.[10] It was vested with the power to levy taxes on its members and its representative assembly appointed communal leadership. Only men could vote in assembly elections. Participation and equitable representation were serious issues to feminists, who hoped to gain the power to redirect more community revenues toward the needs of women. The JFB campaigned vigorously in individual Jewish communities (there were 1,611 in 1932). It lobbied and petitioned rabbis and community leaders and offered its cooperation to the major national and international Jewish welfare organizations in return for representation on their boards of directors. It insisted on women's participation in every aspect of community life, not just as "honorary ladies" or on "entertainment commissions." When, after World War I, the German government granted German women the vote, Jewish women expected the Jewish communities to follow suit. They were sorely disappointed and had to continue their campaign—stepping it up to include public meetings, a national suffrage week, advertisements in Jewish newspapers, and legal battles—well into the 1920s.[11] By the end of the 1920s, women had wrested the vote in six of the seven major German cities (containing over half of all German Jews) and in various areas of southern and western Germany.[12] Thus, the majority of Jewish women were enfranchised. While lacking the power of dominance or control, they had achieved formal, visible participation.

In this campaign, too, the JFB was motivated by feminist and Jewish concerns. The former included the equal participation in politics that had been the demand of women's organizations since the first decade of the twentieth century. Jewish concerns were expressed in reminders to Jewish leaders that by modernizing women's status they would be revitalizing Judaism, bringing women, "the culture bearers," back into the fold and, through them, their offspring.[13] Further, feminists played on the desire of Jews to acculturate to German norms by shaming their opponents for holding onto non-Western customs evident in the unequal treatment of Jewish women. They pressed, instead, for a form of male/female participation in Jewish communal affairs similar to that of their Gentile counterparts to diminish social antagonisms between Jews and other Germans.

As important as its campaigns to improve the status and conditions of women were, the League itself provided an essential focal point for its members. It enabled them to derive a sense of solidarity and strength, to achieve self-expression, self-help, and self-respect. Through this association women were able to influence each other and to transform aspects of their own lives. Not only did they achieve a modicum of social reform for their more needy sisters; they, themselves, matured as they organized, agitated, and created in the public sphere. The boundless enthusiasm of League members, interviewed almost forty years after its demise, speaks to the personal growth, the self-actualization and enhancement of self-confidence experienced by women aware of and acting for themselves and other women. The League of Jewish Women, with over 485 locals and 20 provincial associations, allowed Jewish women to take initiatives beyond those envisioned by the male Jewish establishment and outside areas defined by the German women's movement.

## The Limits of Sisterhood

The League of Jewish Women joined with other women's organizations that pursued feminist or social welfare goals. Its leaders and individual JFB members attended conferences of the German League of Women Voters *(Deutsche Staatsbürgerinnen Verband)*, the international suffrage movement, the international organizations against white slavery, and the German and international abolitionist associations.[14] The JFB also worked in conjunction with other women's organizations, both religious and nonsectarian.[15] Its locals joined with women's groups in towns and provinces to effect cooperative projects: the Breslau local, for example, was also a member of the Silesian Women's Association (Verband schlesischer Frauenvereine), participating in general events and helping out in special emergencies.[16] Further, the JFB showed strong interest in joining international Jewish women's organizations. In all, the Jewish feminist movement attempted to implement its (revised) goals of 1914, to promote sisterhood on three levels: between German and Jewish women's organizations; among Jewish women of all lands; and within a nondenominational, international framework. This section focuses on the first of these, the JFB's sense of female solidarity with German women.

Seeing itself—as others may not have—as an "important factor" in the German women's movement, the JFB accepted the Federation of German Women's Associations (Bund Deutscher Frauenvereine; BDF) as a model. Bertha Pappenheim wrote: "The German's women's movement gave the shy, uncertain advances of Jewish women direction and confidence."[17] The BDF, founded in 1894, was Germany's largest bourgeois feminist organization,[18] attracting a membership of approximately 300,000 in 1912 and 900,000 in the 1920s. Its "feminism" evolved from the widening of women's narrow sphere within a framework of traditional social values. The conservatism of its credo— one that bowed to separate spheres, emphasized maternal clichés, and adhered to bourgeois respectability—was a legacy not only of the failure of German liberalism and the concomitant political and social timidity of the middle class, but also of the specific constraints women faced. The BDF accepted the conventional notion that there were fundamental differences between the sexes, which destined them to serve important but different functions. The League, too, believed woman's instinctual maternal nature, her self-sacrificing personality, mildness, and patience, would complement man's energy and initiative in the public sphere. The JFB followed the BDF in stressing duty and service and avoiding the equal-rights issues so central to Anglo-American feminism. They both challenged the status quo indirectly, in the name of traditionally accepted values and roles. The tactics of the JFB were also similar to those of the BDF. Both renounced political agitation, opting for unobtrusive methods. They petitioned, published information, and educated women who did not belong to their respective organizations about the goals of feminism. With few exceptions, they were proper bourgeois ladies who eschewed all radicalism in order to court public opinion and allay hostility.

The JFB belonged to and maintained friendly relations with the BDF from 1907 until 1933. In contrast, the Catholic women's organization (of about 220,000 members in 1921) never joined the BDF, and the Protestant women's association (of about 200,000 members in 1928) joined in 1908 and withdrew in 1918. Pappenheim served on the board of directors of the BDF from 1914 until 1924. Her participation in the BDF reflected the symbiosis of her feminist and Jewish loyalties. Her feminist attitudes derived from those of German feminists. Yet, she hoped to preserve the communal and religious distinctiveness of her people. Also, she was sensitive to anti-Semitism. She believed that if Jewish women as Jews worked within the German movement, they could fight anti-Semitism through personal interaction. Her collaboration with German feminists was, thus, a means of combating prejudice, but it was also proof to Pappenheim that there was a possibility for friendship among Jews and other Germans. This possibility for friendship, that is, for solidarity and cooperation as well as for disagreement regarding issues affecting all German women, will be explored first. Then, we will turn to the relationship of JFB members as Jews to their non-Jewish feminist colleagues.

The JFB sent delegates to the general and executive meetings of the BDF and participated in many of its undertakings.[19] It discussed these meetings and the resolutions taken there at its own executive and general conventions and in its newsletter. Often, JFB leaders were asked to participate as lecturers[20] or workshop leaders at the general assemblies of the BDF, and one of its most active members also ran for president of the BDF.[21] Generally, the JFB supported the BDF stance on issues relating to women: "Above all separations of world view (*Weltanschauung*) and religion, we women are on a mutual path, heading toward mutual goals."[22]

The JFB newsletter reported approvingly on the BDF's attitudes toward women's work as a means of self-development. During the Depression, "double-earners" (*Doppelverdiener*) came under attack by those who claimed that women who brought "second incomes" into the family should give up their jobs for unemployed men. The BDF discouraged feminists from making "further difficulties for those who choose a double path," but hesitated to encourage wives and mothers to work. The JFB concurred, unlike the other confessional women's organizations, which argued that marriage and career could never be combined. It continued to support married women who chose to pursue careers, but suggested that mothers of infants stay home. It reminded all women of the "double burden" *(Doppelbelastung)* of housework and careers.[23] The JFB understood the double-earner issue to be a particularly threatening one for Jewish women, since a large percentage of Jewish professional women worked in declining sectors (such as academia, which was referred to as "the waiting room of the unemployed") where women's participation was under special attack.[24] Also, many Jewish professional women were among those women bearing the brunt of a vigorous campaign against the "big" double-earner, a professional woman married to a professional man.

The League of Jewish Women also shared many of the prevailing social attitudes toward the reproductive sphere, though with some significant differences. Most Germans before World War I praised marriage, extolled motherhood, and held sexuality to be inextricably linked with reproduction. Even the more progressive socialists refused to accept birth control or abortion. Clara Zetkin, for example, had argued that the solution to working-class women's oppression was a redistribution of wealth, not family limitation. The latter was an "easy answer for egotists."[25] After the war, socialists, more radical feminists, and communists openly supported birth control and abortion, the latter insisting that "your body belongs to you."[26] The mainstream of German feminism, however, as well as some leading socialist feminists, remained aloof from or hostile to the pro-abortion forces. Many bourgeois feminists, in fact, considered birth control the lesser of two evils. As late as 1928, the answer to unwanted pregnancies was still, according to Agnes von Zahn-Harnack, president of the BDF, "the education of our people to a restrained sexuality."[27]

From its founding, the League exhorted Jewish women to raise larger families. The JFB objected to birth control as further hastening an already drastic decline in the Jewish birthrate as well as on religious grounds. However, it clearly recognized its widespread use among Jews both before and after World War I. Describing such family limitation as "a sickness of the *Volk* soul *(Volksseele)* caused by economic and emotional needs," the League still preferred it to abortion. On abortion, a major social issue of the Weimar Republic, the JFB held a complex position. Its spokespersons viewed the law in general as having "educational meaning for the German people," and insisted on seeing "respect for life" firmly anchored in the German legal code.[28] Thus, in 1920, the JFB initiated and led the attack of religious women's organizations against bills introduced by Independent Socialists (USPD) and Social Democrats (SPD) that would have respectively abolished and modified the antiabortion law, Paragraph 218 of the

Criminal Code. However, its leaders were acutely aware of the "irreconcilable contradiction between moral principles and reality, between what should be and what is."[29]

By 1925, the JFB accepted abortion for "valid" reasons, medical and social, even though it warned that abortion had "serious physical dangers for women."[30] In that year it supported the BDF demand to modify Paragraph 218, urging that punishment for women who aborted be reduced, that they not be sent to prison (*Zuchthaus*), and that the law specifically state that doctors were empowered to end pregnancies in the event of danger to the mother's health, social conditions being taken into consideration in any medical assessment.[31] Even as it firmly maintained a moral and religious stance against abortion—the JFB argued that the problem could not be solved by "living an unbridled life and then unscrupulously eliminating the undesired consequences," and that abortion was a "cheap manner of self-determination of women over their bodies, an unethical resolution of a social problem"[32]—the JFB's acceptance of social conditions as justification for abortion was a major modification, a major liberalizing stance. Acknowledging the reality of social conditions also led to demands for social reform. JFB leaders called for better care for pregnant women, infants, and children; housing reforms; tax incentives for large families; care for unwed mothers and illegitimate children; and job security for unmarried, pregnant women (a more progressive stand than that of the BDF, which was more punitive toward the unmarried mother).[33]

The JFB did not, however, agree with the BDF on the acceptance of eugenic indications as a valid reason for abortion. This was an important break not only with German feminism, but with a general consensus on the issue. Arguing that there was "no scientific proof with which one could with certainty analyze the value [*Wertigkeit*] of the newborn,"[34] the JFB rejection grew out of its grudging acceptance of valid causes rather than out of an absolute position against abortion. The mistrust of eugenic indications for abortion seems prescient, given the uses that the Nazis later made of control over reproduction.[35] Yet its argument, based on scientific proof, obscured other issues that would become piercingly relevant after 1933. Issues of power and control, of who would define what was eugenically "positive" or "negative," and who would have decision-making power over abortions were left unexamined. But here the JFB's myopia was fully shared by the BDF.

Over the issues of peace and pacifism, major issues of international feminism, there was early cooperation and later disagreement with the BDF. During World War I, the JFB, like the German women's movement, supported the "Fatherland." It joined the National Women's Service (Nationaler Frauendienst), an organization set up by the BDF to aid in the war effort.[36] This national association looked after the families of men at the front and helped women find work and set up soup kitchens, hospital wards, knitting circles, and the like. After the war, the Jewish organization quickly supported the peace movement, whereas the BDF maintained a more nationalistic stance. Leading members of the JFB were pacifists, and the JFB newsletter regularly printed reports and announcements of peace conferences or of the Women's International League for Peace and Freedom (WILPF), a pacifist organization founded (1915) and led by Jane Addams.[37] In 1927, the JFB formally urged its members to join WILPF, a radical step given the internationalism of the latter and the atmosphere of wounded German nationalism that surrounded the JFB and that was found to no small extent in the BDF.[38] The League also sent unofficial observers to disarmament conferences and circulated petitions in favor of disarmament. It argued that a women's movement *(Frauenbewegung)* had to be a peace movement *(Friedensbewegung)* or it was useless; there was a "natural connection between motherhood and peace."[39]

The JFB also maintained ties with the peace movement from a sense of Jewish consciousness. It sustained ties with the section of WILPF that combated "anti-Semitism as an enemy of world peace."[40] In 1920, the German branch of WILPF wrote an open protest against German anti-Semitism to the International League. They saw a "symptom of sickness" in the anti-Semitism resulting from the war. As pacifists they condemned it from a religious, patriotic, and women's standpoint.[41] In 1926, WILPF adopted a resolution against anti-Semitism. Thus, the JFB felt justified not only in its "women's" position, but also as Jews, in supporting WILPF and the peace movement.

Beyond the various issues on which the JFB and the BDF agreed or disagreed, it is clear that the BDF played a fundamental role in the education of JFB leaders. Some of its most important activists had their earliest education in the ranks of the BDF.[42] This was the case for all its presidents as well as for many of its prominent figures. In fact, its last president, Ottilie Schönewald, recognized that "for political or, perhaps, psychological reasons the German element [in the history of the JFB] has been played down . . . the JFB was a part of the German women's movement and has to be understood in that context."[43]

Importantly, the JFB considered the BDF an ally in its fight against anti-Semitism. When, for example, it noticed an initiative to form an anti-Semitic women's organization in Leipzig, it turned to the BDF for assistance.[44] As the amount of anti-Semitism in Germany dramatically increased during the Depression, the newly elected leader of the BDF, Agnes von Zahn-Harnack, immediately visited the JFB and declared that neither she nor the BDF would tolerate attacks on Jews or Judaism.[45] By 1930, the BDF became an integral part of the "enlightenment work" *(Aufklärungsarbeit)* that the JFB, like other German-

Jewish organizations, pursued in order to stem bigotry. The JFB invited non-Jewish women's and youth organizations to their lectures, social evenings, and tours of synagogues. Agnes von Zahn-Harnack led one of these meetings. Representatives of the Catholic women's organization, women theologians, and feminist leaders attended. Zahn-Harnack asked the JFB to invite Christian women to holiday festivals, synagogue services, and discussions, noting "the fight against anti-Semitism must originate with Christian women."[46] The JFB prepared and distributed literature explaining Jewish history, ethics, and customs to its Gentile guests.[47] It often compared the emancipation of Jews with that of women, asserting that while each group hoped to fit into the dominant society, each had acquired a consciousness of its unique qualities, which it deserved to retain. Recognizing that race and gender discrimination were mutually reinforcing and equally oppressive, the JFB argued that German and Jewish women should fight anti-Semitism because Jews and feminists shared the same struggle for emancipation. Both groups required an open, liberal, pluralistic society. It appealed to the women's movement to fight anti-Semitism, "not *for us*, but for the idea of a German spirit in which we all believed."[48] With the growth of the Nazi Party, the BDF published *Gelbe Blätter, (Yellow Leaves)* pamphlets aimed mainly against the Nazis. The BDF was seeking to protect women's rights, rather than Jewish ones, and too often believed its own interests to be more important than those of Jews, not recognizing a mutual danger.[49] Nevertheless, the JFB could take satisfaction from the German organization's official hostility to the Nazis. The BDF's final appeal of March 1933 to German women to vote only for parties that accepted the rights of women and the state of law was printed in large headlines across the front page of the JFB newsletter.[50]

Yet, JFB leaders were also sensitive to what they felt to be slights of the German organization to Jewish needs, as well as to a lack of respect for Jewish particularism and a certain amount of anti-Semitism. While the JFB and BDF shared similar gender and class concerns, the latter organization's large membership reflected some of the more negative attitudes toward Jews of the surrounding society. These ranged from liberal impatience with Jewish distinctiveness[51] to covert or overt anti-Semitism. As a historian of Weimar Germany has recently stated, "More common and widespread than outright hatred or sympathy for the Jews was what we have called moderate anti-Semitism, that vague sense of unease about Jews that stopped far short of wanting to harm them but that may have helped to neutralize whatever aversion Germans might otherwise have felt for the Nazis."[52] Whereas few Jews had been the targets of personal attacks, virtually all knew anti-Semites and viewed anti-Semitism as a fact of life.[53] This was certainly the case to varying degrees in the universities, among rightist political parties, in the churches, and in certain echelons of the civil service and army.[54] Nevertheless, even with manifestations of social and governmentally tolerated anti-Semitism as well as the growth of right-wing anti-Semitic organizations (numbering over 200,000 people by 1922), most German Jews believed that Jews had a place in Germany and that a German-Jewish symbiosis was possible.

League members, too, were convinced of this. Yet they were aware of the distance that separated them and their BDF sisters. Even those non-Jewish women who volunteered to assist the JFB to fight racism remained remote. As one JFB member noted:

> We lived among each other, sat together in the same school room, attended university together, met each other at social events—and were complete strangers. Was it their fault? Ours? Hard to say but also meaningless. It was a fact, of portentous consequence for the time, that those who wanted to stand up for us knew nothing about us.[55]

Members of the JFB felt that they were accepted by their liberal feminist sisters only when they "closeted" their Jewishness. As one JFB leader stated, "Those who do not call attention to their Jewishness are valued."[56] Their perceptions were correct: the BDF avoided what it considered "sectarianism." Mirroring German liberalism, it invited Jewish integration at the price of Jewish identity and was decidedly uncomfortable in the face of Jews who resisted homogenization. Pappenheim referred to those Jewish women who joined the BDF directly (thus subsuming their Jewish identity) as "half-Jews" *(Halbe)*.

On occasion, the BDF also reflected the insensitivity or anti-Semitism of some of its members.[57] In 1908, leaders of the JFB attended the BDF general assembly. The JFB was already a BDF member and the Protestant women's organization had just joined. In an attempt to win the adherence of the Catholic women's association, the BDF leadership invited, consulted with, and encouraged leaders of the Catholic women to participate in the general debates. Feeling slighted—the JFB had brought 120 affiliated clubs into the BDF to the Protestants' 43—Pappenheim took the floor during one debate "not because she had been asked to respond, like the representative of the Catholic women's groups, but because she had not been asked to speak at all."[58] A similar slight, which provoked a public outcry, occurred in 1915. Pappenheim was furious with Helene Lange (one of the founders of German feminism) when the latter in a speech omitted the JFB while naming several Catholic and Protestant women's associations that belonged to the BDF. Gertrud Bäumer, the president of the BDF, told Pappenheim that she, Bäumer, could not censure a private member of the BDF. (Of course, Lange was well known and therefore not simply a private member.) Pappenheim angrily withdrew from the National Women's Service, accusing Lange and Bäumer of "*hatefulness* towards Jewish women and Judaism." Lange responded to a Jewish(!) colleague: "It is a terrible pity that just now, suddenly, Jewish women too stress their religion, something from which they judiciously restrained themselves in the past."[59] The problem was not solved, but the disagreement ended when Bäumer sent a letter of apology to Pappenheim. Insensitivity could turn to a more overt manifestation of hostility, as in the case of the Bavarian Provincial Union for Women's Suffrage. In 1913 this organization agreed to condemn kosher butchering, a rather well-known anti-Semitic stance. The JFB protested and was assured by the German and Prussian Unions for Women's Suffrage that they rejected the position of the Bavarian group.[60] In the postwar era, anti-Semitism seemed to play a role in the denial of the BDF's top position to Alice Salomon. Despite her conversion to Protestantism, the leadership decided that in order to preserve the movement, a woman with a Jewish last name could not be president.[61]

The exaggerated "neutrality" of the BDF's political endorsements also hurt its Jewish supporters. In general, the political leanings of the majority of JFB members reflected those of the Jewish community. Most Jews supported the middle-class German Democratic Party. Founded in 1918, it was a liberal party of business and professional people that supported the Weimar constitution and opposed anti-Semitism as incompatible with reason, tolerance, and individual freedom. After 1930, with the increasing polarization of politics, most of the Jewish vote split between the Social Democratic Party and the Catholic Center Party (the latter as a defender of minority religious rights and an opponent of racism). In the early Weimar years, the JFB was comfortable with the pro–Democratic Party leanings of the BDF leadership, but found itself more isolated by the mid-1920s as the right began to enter leadership positions. Claiming the need to remain "above parties" in order to hold on to its rank and file, many of whom were to the right even of the leaders, the BDF invited conservative and right-wing representatives, whose parties were often officially anti-Semitic, to its political debates. In fact, this alleged need to be "fair"— and possible anti-Semitic intentions—caused the German League of Women Voters, an affiliate of the BDF, to invite Nazis, along with speakers from other parties, to present a lecture on what women should expect from the Nazis. The German women sent a note of apology to the JFB hoping that "you will understand we came to this decision after serious discussion."[62] By the early 1930s even the staunchest supporters of Jewish involvement in the German feminist movement had to admit that "quiet, subterranean currents" could be felt in affiliates of the BDF. While these were purportedly not anti-

Semitic tones, they were "mystical, irrational currents," which also began to dismiss the feminist movement as too rational. Jewish feminist observers experienced these currents as directed against Jews and the women's movement. They feared not only for their own collaboration in the "unbiased" feminist movement, but for feminism itself.[63]

The JFB seemed to recognize—and in some ways epitomize—the ambivalent position of Jews in German society. On the one hand, it attempted to achieve a working relationship with the BDF in order to support the goals of feminism, be accepted as part of a German movement, and stem the growth of anti-Semitism. On the other hand, the JFB provided a congenial atmosphere for Jewish women who, while making the proper obeisances to their German heritage and to German feminism, enjoyed a feeling of ethnic community and a consciousness of kind, and reacted to a feeling of exclusion. Thus, the League provided a separatist alternative for Jewish women: independent of male Jewish leadership and independent of the German women's movement. Allied with both, they felt truly comfortable with neither.

## The Jewish Feminist Struggle for Survival

The choices of whether to work within the German women's movement or in the Jewish community were vitiated by the maelstrom following the Nazi seizure of power. Strategies of sheer survival were forced on Jewish women. In June 1933, the Federation of German Women's Associations disbanded itself rather than face *Gleichschaltung*—the process by which all leaders were replaced by Nazi activists and all organizations were forced to participate in Nazi programs. The JFB had resigned from the German feminist organization a few days earlier, and the BDF had accepted the withdrawal with "deepest regret."[64]

If Jewish feminists expected their German counterparts to maintain a sense of sisterhood and loyalty, they were to be sorely disappointed. Paula Ollendorf, a JFB leader, became very depressed at the behavior of former friends in the German movement. Right after Hitler's accession to power, colleagues with whom she had worked for many years had "stupid excuses" so that they "would not be caught with Jews." One feminist, a well-known member of the Democratic Party, asked her and another Jewish colleague, Martha Parker, to help her prove that she had always been "nationalistic" *(national)*. Amused by the absurdity of two Jews testifying to a German colleague's anti-Semitism, Parker reported: "I laughed and said sure, I can get signatures for you but they won't help. Paula could not laugh—she said 'everything is completely bankrupt.' I said it was Germany's bankruptcy and she responded it was also hers."[65] Of course, there were exceptions, but

Ottilie Schönewald, the last president of the JFB, also suffered from the absence of female solidarity among her bourgeois sisters:

> Where were German women then? If shortly after the 9th of November 1938 they had found the same words for me that are in their letters today [1955] they would have meant so much to me. Hardly one of our German, so-called friends , . . found their way to us. This was, unfortunately, not a personal, isolated phenomenon. Yes, employees, . . . workmen, the people who received poor relief in my constituency were not too shy to show their affection . . . they knew where to find us in broad daylight. And, as far as I know, it caused no harm to any of them.[66]

This lack of solidarity did not stop Schönewald from writing a letter of protest in 1935 to the head of the new Nazi women's organization, Gertrud Scholtz-Klink, against a speech of the local Nazi leader of Cologne to thousands of children in which he stated that "if humanity wants to live in peace, Jews must die." Needless to say, Schönewald did not receive a response. Her effort was a courageous, if futile, attempt at female solidarity among mothers.[67]

Between 1933 and 1938 the League of Jewish Women joined other Jewish organizations in a struggle for survival. This endeavor took several forms: fighting anti-Semitism, preventing the disintegration of communal organizations, ensuring the continuation of Jewish practices, helping needy Jews, and preparing people for emigration. During the Hitler years the feminism of the JFB became less pronounced, and the organization concentrated instead on social work. While the JFB continued to demand equality for women within the Jewish community, maintained its services and institutions for women, and represented the needs and views of women to the newly established Jewish central organization, the Central Association of German Jews, (Reichsvertretung der Deutschen Juden) the needs of German Jews took precedence over purely feminist goals. Furthermore, anti-Semitism aside, the impossibly misogynist nature of the Third Reich made feminism both futile and dangerous.

The JFB's "enlightenment efforts," like those of the rest of German Jewry, had been less than successful, since those who heard JFB pleas for a liberal, pluralistic society were not the same people who promoted racial hatred. After 1933, Jews were unable to meet with Christian groups; their social, legal, political, and, ultimately, physical ostracism commenced. In a defensive gesture, the JFB concentrated its attempt to lessen anti-Semitism on a "self-discipline" (*Selbstzucht*) campaign. Begun in 1915 and continued throughout the 1930s, this attempt to encourage "simplicity in the appearance of women and girls" was the JFB's second answer to the hostility of other Germans. As in previous JFB campaigns against white slavery or an "unrepresentative" job profile, it reflected the defensive posture of those who saw self-discipline as a key to acceptance and self-defense: an attitude that "stepchildren had to be doubly good."[68] It also mirrored a century-old reflex of Jews who had learned to be inconspicuous for fear of reprisals from their enemies. All Jews, particularly women, were cautioned to avoid the envy and resentment of anti-Semites by maintaining a simple standard of living. Jewish newspapers and organizations urged Jewish women to avoid any dress or action that could lead to embarrassment and warned "women who drape themselves in glittering jewelry" that they were abetting the enemy.[69] By accepting the negative images of Jewish women that were shared by Jewish men and anti-Semites alike as reality, the JFB inadvertently propagated them. In doing so, it conveyed several false impressions: an exaggeration of the number of Jewish women who dressed ostentatiously (particularly in a period of increasing unemployment and a boycott of Jewish businesses) and a delusion about modesty mitigating or dress causing anti-Semitism. Under double jeopardy as Jews and as women, members of the League demonstrated a common characteristic of oppressed minorities: blaming themselves for their victimization.

The League was modestly successful in helping to sustain the Jewish community. It cooperated with Jewish central welfare organizations, providing volunteers for some of the social welfare offices and sharing responsibility for the divisions in charge of Jewish schools and institutions.[70] It also added its own new local chapters, attracted new members (many of whom came from the dissolved German women's movement and professional women's organizations), and initiated closer ties with other national and international Jewish women's associations. Its newsletter and cultural activities concentrated on teaching Jewish customs, history, and religion. The JFB had always promoted Jewishness, but its efforts took on a new, psychological dimension in these years. In Nazi Germany, Jews were depicted as evil and inferior. Cultural and religious activities gave a sense of perspective and an *élan vital* to a group facing rejection and hopelessness.

The JFB was as conscious of the need to provide material assistance to people whose social and economic conditions were deteriorating as it was of the need for psychological encouragement. It aided other Jewish groups in the collection of money, clothing, and fuel. As Jews continued to lose their livelihoods, the JFB was active in helping Jewish middle-class women and their families adjust to a lower standard of living. It increased its housewife assistance programs; set up cooking, darning, sewing, nursing, and home-repair courses; and wrote its own cookbook for Jews, who had difficulty buying kosher meat after Hitler forbade ritual slaughtering. Mutual aid was encouraged, and in various cities the JFB organized communal kitchens, children's "play circles," communal maid services, and dialogue afternoons, where women could discuss their problems and receive advice as well as moral support. The League repeatedly emphasized the pivotal role of women in maintaining the equilibrium of the home. In turn, it attempted to offer women practical, intellectual, and spiritual support.

The final major area of JFB concern was the preparation of women for emigration. In 1935, the Nuremberg Laws deprived Jews of the rights of citizens and forbade marriages as well as extramarital intercourse between Jews and Aryans. Convinced by this Law for the Protection of German Blood and Honor that emigration was necessary, the JFB increased its efforts to retrain girls for vocations suited to places of refuge. The JFB newsletter devoted issues to the process and problems of female emigration and members also accompanied children to safety in foreign lands, returning to Germany to continue their work.

After the Nazi-led pogrom of November 1938, known as "Crystal Night" *(Kristallnacht),* the league was ordered dissolved. Its treasury and institutions were absorbed by an umbrella organization representing the collective interests of German Jewry. Its leaders joined the staff of that organization. Although these women had many opportunities to emigrate, they continued to work for the Jewish community. Those women who were not in the national leadership continued to perform social work along with other Jews from their community. Most of the JFB leaders were deported in 1942 and became victims of Hitler's "final solution to the Jewish problem." Hannah Karminski (the former executive secretary of the JFB) wrote a friend of her last visit with Cora Berliner (the former vice-president of the JFB) on the day of the latter's deportation:

> C. and our other friends took books along. They agreed on the selection. To my knowledge C. took *Faust I* and an anthology. When I went to visit them on the last day, shortly before their departure, they were sitting in the courtyard in the sun reading Goethe.[71]

## Conclusion

The chronicle of the League of Jewish Women presents us with the complexities of the gender and ethnic (or as the Nazis would have it, "racial") determinants of women's history. Within a specific middle-class context, it allows us to identify a particular case in which both gender and race struggles occurred and the way in which they related to each other. Jewish feminists suffered from the double burden of being women in a sexist society and Jews in a racist one. They shared common experiences as women across ethnic/religious lines and yet suffered divisions created by these same identities. In the liberal, pluralistic framework of the Weimar Republic, Jewish feminists attempted to combine ethnic pride with feminist aspirations by working for women's interests within their own Jewish community and allying with German feminism. Often, however, their fears of or reactions to anti-Semitism forced them into an alignment with their male co-religionists, where they faced the need to subsume feminist demands to the good of the whole. Ultimately, in a period of crisis, racial identity prevailed over female solidarity not only among Jews, where the identity was imposed, but also among German Gentile women, who accepted and sometimes embraced racist divisions. Thus, the history of German-Jewish women forces us to acknowledge the salience of race in the current struggles for women's equality.

## Notes

1. The International Council of Women was founded in 1888 and fought for legal, educational, and career reforms for women, linking feminist reform to the peace movement. See Edith Hurwitz, "The International Sisterhood," in Renate Bridenthal and Claudia Koonz, eds., *Becoming Visible: Women in European History* (New York 1977).

2. Bertha Pappenheim was the first person to be treated by cathartic psychotherapy and her case became well known as the case of "Anna O." Treated by Josef Breuer in Vienna from December 1880 until June 1882, her case was included in Freud and Breuer's book *Studies in Hysteria*. See Ellen Jensen, "Anna O—A Study of Her Later Life," *The Psychoanalytic Quarterly* 39 (1970): 269–93. This article includes a bibliography of psychoanalytic commentary on Anna O and on Pappenheim. Before founding the JFB, Pappenheim wrote several plays and pamphlets with feminist themes and translated Mary Wollstonecraft's *A Vindication of the Rights of Women*. For further information, see my chapter on Pappenheim in *The Jewish Feminist Movement in Germany: The Campaigns of the Jüdischer Frauenbund, 1904–1938* (Connecticut, 1979) and my article "Anna O and Bertha Pappenheim: An Historical Perspective," in Max Rosenbaum and Melvin Moff, eds., *Anna O: Fourteen Contemporary Reinterpretations* (New York, 1984).

3. "For Women's Work and the Women's Movement" was the subtitle of the JFB newsletter: *Blätter des Jüdischen Frauenbunds: Für Frauenarbeit und Frauenbewegung* (hereafter *BJFB*). The goals can be found in *BJFB*, January 1928, p. 1. In 1905 their goals were similar, but the emphasis was on the "need to work for women in any aspect that affects them, to educate them about the world around them, to help them find jobs and to offer them diversions from the difficulties of earning a living (*Jahrbuch der Frauenbewegung* [1912]). Organizations that preceded the JFB are described by Jacob Segall in "Die Jüdischen Frauenvereine in Deutschland," *Zeitschrift für Demographie und Statistik der Juden* (hereafter ZDSJ 10 (January 1914): 2–5 and 10 (February 1914): 7–23). The JFB had a far more extensive program than earlier women's auxiliaries or the B'nai B'rith Sisterhoods (in Germany), which grew to 80 women's auxiliaries in the 1930s. The latter were adjuncts to the male lodges and did not engage in the struggle for women's rights.

4. By 1870, about 60 percent of German Jews were in the upper and middle classes and another 25 percent could be described as lower middle class (Monika Richarz, ed., *Jüdisches Leben In Deutschland. Selbstzeugnisse zur Sozialgeschichte im Kaiserreich* [Stuttgart, 1979], p. 24). By 1933 only 8.7 percent of German Jews classified themselves as "workers" compared with 46.4 percent of non–Jewish Germans.

About 46 percent of Jews were "independent," i.e., owners of small or medium-sized shops, individuals engaged in trade or commerce, or members of the free professions (doctors, lawyers, journalists, etc.) (*Volkszählung, Die Bevölkerung des Deutschen Reichs nach dem Volkszählung 1933*, Heft 5, Verlag für Sozialpolitik, Wirtschaft, und Statistik [Berlin, 1936], pp. 25, 27).

5. This reflected Jewish demographic trends as well, a result of an earlier decline in Jewish fertility. By the 1930s more than 50 percent of German Jews were above the age of 40 (Erich Rosenthal, "Jewish Population in Germany, 1910–1939," *Jewish Social Studies* 6 [1944]: 243–47).

6. Today, too, women who consider themselves feminists and observant Jews are demanding greater equality within the Jewish community and—unlike the JFB—a greater role in performing Jewish rituals. See, for examples, Susan Dworkin, "A Song for Women in Five Questions," *Moment*, May/June 1975, p. 44; Sally Priesand, *Judaism and the New Woman* (New York, 1975); Blu Greenberg, *On Women and Judaism: A View from Tradition* (Philadelphia, 1982); and current issues of *Lilith* magazine.

7. Donald L. Niewyk, *The Jews in Weimar Germany* (Baton Rouge and London, 1980), pp. 99–100; quotation from Hannah Arendt, *The Jew as Pariah* (New York, 1978), p. 68.

8. Heinrich Silbergleit, *Die Bevölkerungs- und Berufsverhältnisse der Juden im Deutschen Reich* (Berlin, 1930), p. 109.

9. For details on the white slave traffic and the campaign to end it, see Edward Bristow, *Prostitution and Prejudice: The Jewish Campaign against White Slavery, 1870–1939* (Oxford, 1982); see also chap. 4 of my book *The Jewish Feminist Movement*.

10. Kurt Wilhelm, "The Jewish Community in the Post-Emancipation Period," *Leo Baeck Institute Yearbook* (hereafter LBIYB) 1957, pp. 47–75.

11. *BJFB*, August 1927, pp. 6–7; February 1928, pp. 1–2.

12. *BJFB*, February 1928, p. 1.

13. Siddy Wronsky, "Zur Soziologie der Jüdischen Frauenbewegung in Deutschland," *Jahrbuch für Jüdische Geschichte und Literatur*, 1927, pp. 84–92.

14. Abolitionists fought to abolish police registration of prostitutes: *BJFB*, July 1929, p. 13, August 1926, pp. 3–4; Deutsches Nationalkomitee, *Bericht über die 9. Deutsche Nationalkonferenz zu internationaler Bekämpfung des Mädchenhandels zu Stettin, 13–14 November, 1912; Bericht über die 6. Deutsche Nationalkonferenz zu internationaler Bekämpfung des Mädchenhandels zu Breslau am 8–9 Oktober, 1908; Bericht über die 8. Deutsche Nationalkonferenz zu internationaler Bekämpfung des Mädchenhandels zu Karlsruhe am 10–11 Oktober, 1911.*

15. For example, it cooperated with Catholic and Protestant railroad station missions (*Bahnhofsmissionen*) in helping traveling girls and women. See also *Allgemeine Zeitung des Judentums* (hereafter AZDJ), April 4, 1919, supp., p. 4; *BJFB*, April 1933, p. 11.

16. *Israelitisches Familienblatt*, August 7, 1930, p. 11; *AZDJ*, June 27, 1913, supp., p. 2.

17. *BJFB*, July 1936, p. 8.

18. See Amy Hackett, "The Politics of Feminism in Wilhelmine Germany, 1890–1918" (Ph.D. diss., Columbia University, 1976); and Richard Evans, *The Feminist Movement in Germany, 1894–1933* (Beverly Hills, 1976).

19. See, for examples, *BJFB*, November 1927, p. 4; November 1929, pp. 7–9; November 1930, p. 12; November 1932, pp. 8–9. Also see Ottilie Schönewald, memoir collection, Archives of the Leo Baeck Institute (hereafter ALBI).

20. See, for examples, *BJFB*, June 1928, p. 7; August 1928, pp. 4–5. Also, Schönewald memoir.

21. In 1931, Margarete Berent, a lawyer, ran for president of the BDF, but lost.

22. *BJFB*, November 1929, pp. 7–9.

23. *BJFB*, June 1931, pp. 9–10.

24. *BJFB*, November 1931, pp. 4–6.
25. Karen Honeycutt, "Clara Zetkin: A Socialist Approach to the Problem of Women's Oppression," *Feminist Studies*, Spring-Summer 1976, pp. 131–44. See also Robert Neuman, "The Sexual Question and Social Democracy in Imperial Germany," *Journal of Social History* 7 (1974).
26. See Atina Grossmann, "Abortion and Economic Crisis: The 1931 Campaign against Paragraph 218" in this volume.
27. Agnes von Zahn-Harnack, *Die Frauenbewegung: Geschichte, Probleme, Ziele* (Berlin, 1928), p. 105.
28. *BJFB*, January 1926, p. 4.
29. *BJFB*, January 1926, p. 2.
30. *BJFB*, January 1926, p. 3. In this respect the JFB was not so far from the SPD position. For many in the SPD, opposition to Paragraph 218 meant the acceptance of valid indications, not abolition of the law. See Grossmann, "Abortion."
31. *BJFB*, January 1926, p. 2. There was a difference in severity between a prison (*Zuchthaus*) and a jail (*Gefängnis*).
32. *BJFB*, January 1926, p. 3.
33. Helen Boak, "Die Frau gehört ins Haus: Traditional Attitudes among Middle-Class Women in the Weimar Republic" (paper delivered at SSRC Research Seminar on Modern German Social History, Summer 1981, pp. 12–13).
34. *BJFB*, January 1926, p. 4.
35. See Gisela Bock, "Racism and Sexism in Nazi Germany," in this volume.
36. *AZDJ*, May 28, 1915, supp., p. 2; *AZDJ*, May 14, 1915, supp., p. 1; *BJFB*, April 1936, pp. 9–10.
37. *BJFB*, August 1926, p. 4.
38. *Israelitisches Familienblatt*, December 15, 1927, supp., p. 8.
39. *BJFB*, November 1931, pp. 4–6.
40. *BJFB*, August 1926, p. 4. Interview with Dora Edinger, former member of the JFB, 1975.
41. *Israelitisches Familienblatt*, October 28, 1920, p. 3.
42. See Schönewald memoir; also, interviews with Lilli Liegner, Klara Caro, and Dora Edinger (all former JFB leaders).
43. Schönewald collection, ALBI, IV, 14 (written in 1957 or 1958).
44. *AZDJ*, December 26, 1919, supp., p. 1.
45. *BJFB*, November 1931, pp. 4–6.
46. *BJFB*, December 1931, pp. 7–8.
47. *BJFB*, December 1930, p. 7.
48. *BJFB*, December 1930, pp. 5–7; September 1932, pp. 4–5.
49. This was the case as late as June 1932, when members of the BDF executive committee, including Zahn-Harnack, insisted on challenging only Nazi attacks on women. The majority, however, agreed with Emma Ender, "National Socialism has grown big in its fight against Jews and women," Evans, *Feminist Movement*, p. 255.
50. *BJFB*, March 1933, p. 1.
51. Reinhard Rürup, "Jewish Emancipation and Bourgeois Society," *LBIYB*, 1969, p. 80.
52. Niewyk, *Jews in Weimar Germany*, p. 80.
53. Ibid., pp. 86, 112.
54. Ibid., p. 55.
55. Rahel Straus, *Wir Lebten in Deutschland: Erinnerungen einer deutschen Jüdin, 1880–1933* (Stuttgart, 1962), p. 266.
56. *BJFB*, December 1930, pp. 5–6.
57. Hackett, "Politics," pp. 176–87; Evans, *Feminist Movement*, pp. 200, 243–44. Evans suggests that many BDF members voted Nazi even though the organization officially opposed the party (see pp. 254–55).
58. *Israelitisches Familienblatt*, November 5, 1908, p. 11.

59. Bund Deutscher Frauenvereine, Archives, 3 Abt. No. 5.
60. *AZDJ*, April 4, 1913, supp., p. 5, and April 24, 1913, supp., p. 14.
61. Hans Muthesius, ed., *Alice Salomon: Die Begründerin des Sozialen Frauenberufs in Deutschland* (Cologne, 1958), p. 85.
62. *BJFB*, February 1931, p. 13. On Jewish political allegiances, see Niewyk, *Jews in Weimar Germany.*
63. *BJFB*, July 1933, pp. 1–2, quoting *Central Verein Zeitung*, October 1931. By understanding criticisms of the feminist movement as also aimed against Jews, Jewish women were not being overly sensitive. The Nazis had always drawn a connection between feminism and the "Jewish Bolshevik conspiracy."
64. *BJFB*, June 1933, pp. 11–12. Despite its "regret," the BDF, insisting on its "national" and "social" character, did not dissolve itself as an act of ideological defiance (Evans, *Feminist Movement*, pp. 256–59).
65. Paula Ollendorff collection, ALBI, 3060, #15.
66. Schönewald collection, IV, 8.
67. Ibid.
68. Ludwig Holländer, executive director of a German-Jewish defense organization, as quoted by Peter Gay in "Encounter with Modernism: German Jews in German Culture, 1888–1914," *Midstream*, February 1975, p. 60.
69. *Israelitisches Familienblatt*, February 7, 1918, p. 10; *AZDJ*, September 16, 1921, supp., p. 2; Adolf Asch, memoirs, ALBI, p. 3.
70. Schönewald collection, ALBI, II, 11.
71. "Letters from Berlin," *LBIYB*, (1957), p. 312.

# Part 2
## Women in Nazi Germany

# The Competition for a Women's *Lebensraum,* 1928–1934

## Claudia Koonz

*Most German women, even those who identified with the women's movement, accepted gender roles based on biological differences between the sexes and spoke of complementary spheres for women and men, rather than of an integrated society with equal access to power and to resources for all. Claudia Koonz shows that Nazi women took this heritage to new extremes, hoping to enlarge and administer women's space in public life in the new Nazi state and to open a hierarchy of female careers in that female sphere. Before Hitler came to power, they operated freely in autonomous organizations, unsupervised by Nazi men, whose misogyny led them to neglect female recruitment. After Hitler came to power, however, the early leaders were dismissed and their organizations dismantled. Under the obedient new head of the women's division, Gertrud Scholtz-Klink, new organizational forms with more docile administrators recruited women from a broader base. A separate sphere was indeed created, but without any illusion of autonomy, such as the early converts to Nazism had held.*

The surest, and often the only way by which a crowd can preserve itself lies in the existence of a second crowd to which it is related. . . . Given that they are about equal in size and intensity, the two crowds keep each other alive. The superiority on the side of the enemy must not be too great, or, at least, must not be thought to be so. In order to understand the origin of this structure we have to start from three basic antitheses. The first and most striking is that between men and women; the second that between the living and the dead; and the third that between friend and foe.

—Elias Canetti

The wonderful thing about nature and providence is that no conflict between the sexes can occur as long as each party performs the function prescribed for it by nature.

—Adolf Hitler

Since the Third Reich, the term *Lebensraum* has brought to mind Hitler's pretext for making war against the "racially inferior" Slavic peoples who inhabited Central Europe's rich agricultural lands. In what must rank as one of the shabbiest pretexts for war of all time, Hitler claimed that the German *Volk* needed more "space" in which to "live." Before Hitler used *Lebensraum* to popularize conquest in the East, however, the term was ambiguous. Besides serving as a code word for bellicose expansion in Hitler's vocabulary, it also meant to contemporaries "a space in which to live," or "living room" inside Germany—a social space where domestic tranquillity and traditional values reigned. In this sense, women commonly used the term to describe a space beyond the materialist and abrasive "masculine" world of business, class struggle, and high politics. The leading spokeswoman for the middle-class women's rights movement, Dr. Gertrud Bäumer, captured this meaning in her book *The Woman in the New "Lebensraum,"* in which she outlined women's responsibilities for bringing order and humanity to public life in times of hardship and chaos.[1]

Historians have investigated the appeal of Hitler's expansionist rhetoric as well as his oath to purge German society of "racially inferior" people and Marxist revolutionaries. The attractiveness of Hitler's vision of a gender-differentiated society—bifurcated into the male realm of production and the female sphere of reproduction—has remained virtually unnoticed.[2] *Lebensraum* provides a useful metaphor for analyzing the variety of competing views on how women ought to enter the modern world. Whatever their views about men and politics, middle-class women generally believed they could establish their own harmonious "living room," cleansed of diversity and dissent within national life.

Virtually all civic, occupational, and religious women's organizations in Weimar Germany shared a commitment to nineteenth-century notions about women's "separate sphere." They differed, however, about how to delimit that sphere, how to coordinate "womanly" activities with the masculine sphere, and how to determine which values and roles ought to be appropriate to each sex. Generally speaking, middle-class associations endorsed women's entry into political and economic life as representatives of women's interests. In addition, they argued that women could enrich previously male spheres by contributing their superior morality and human concerns. The Nazi movement, by contrast, saw little overlap at all between masculine and feminine worlds and endorsed a strong separatist policy on the "woman question." Nazi women both admired and disdained the brutal male world, which, they believed, would corrupt any woman who entered it. Relinquishing any influence over men, they carved out instead their own distinctive network and demanded a socially separate world divided between "more masculine men" and "more feminine women." Nazi policy staked out men's claim to public spaces and posted "No Trespassing" signs at the borders—thus avoiding the contradictions that bedeviled liberals and conservatives.

In this essay I will summarize the aspirations of the major national organizations of middle-class women and contrast their views about woman's place with the opinions of the numerically much smaller Nazi organizations of women before Hitler seized power.[3] I will then contrast the responses of non-Nazi, middle-class women and Nazi women to the National Socialist state after 1933. Besides addressing questions such as which women joined the Nazis, this essay will add to contemporary debates about feminine morality, feminism, and political reaction.

## "Separate Spheres" in Women's Politics during the 1920s

Women's deep attachment to the ideal of a separate sphere during the 1920s resulted not only from the heritage of nineteenth-century women's movements, but also from women's experiences during World War I and the defeat in 1918, which had, in the popular mind, done the work of women's emancipation by uprooting women from domestic life and recruiting them into volunteer activities and, more disturbing to contemporaries, into previously masculine occupational areas (heavy industry, higher education, transportation, medicine, communications, and mining and metallurgy). Shibboleths about "natural" feminine weakness dissolved in the face of clear evidence that women could perform men's jobs with only minimal training. War made the antifeminists' worst nightmares come true: as men marched off to die, women "stole" their jobs. Thus, "progress" for women occurred in the context of death for men and (in Germany) starvation, deprivation, social dislocation, and defeat. Small wonder that trade unions, the state, and industry cooperated immediately after the war to expel the women they had lured into men's work, even as the writers of the new constitution held out the promise of emancipation.

After the suffrage victory, hundreds of women entered the Reichstag, local legislatures, and even a few law courts and ministries.[4] Inspired to prove their worth to the nation by elevating the spiritual level of public debate, women from the prewar women's movement plunged into their new tasks and turned their backs on the exclusively women's organizations that had fought for suffrage. They brought their "conciliatory spirit, . . . steadiness, . . . and love" to a political sphere torn by conflict, as one former woman opponent of women's suffrage declared in 1919.[5] Such sentiments emerged nationally out of the middle-class campaign for women's rights, which had based its claims to equality on the proposition that women, if emancipated, could offer invaluable services to the national community. Instead of threatening men in areas conventionally designated "masculine" (as they had during wartime), women promised to carve out their own public sphere.[6] By reinforcing, in other words, the status quo in role division, they hoped to win rights without a battle against a male-dominated system. Strategically, women's rights advocates expected to cooperate with, not fight against, masculine hegemony. Equality, they assured their audience, did not mean "sameness." Helene Düvert put it simply: "We do not want to push the man aside, but to stand next to him."[7] Anxiety about "masculinization" loomed at least as large as longing for emancipation.

A handful of women in politics did not, of course, manage to usher in an age of idealism or humanity, but women did succeed in more pragmatic tasks. All major parties endorsed women's emancipation, and they followed through by running women candidates (Socialists and Catholics chose the highest percentages), expanding social welfare, passing protective legislation, and drafting electoral appeals for the female vote. During the 1920s, women organized on an unprecedented scale in special-interest organizations which were avowedly apolitical, and often religious or oriented to single issues. In the Reichstag, where between 7 and 10 percent of all delegates were women at any given time, women delegates introduced women's concerns and participated on committees concerned with women's issues.[8] A few experienced women leaders led the crusade for emancipation within the political context. But what happened to the masses of women who, they expected, would eagerly seize the potential for further reform?

Veterans of the women's rights movement anticipated that the suffrage victory would galvanize previously apathetic and uninformed women into action. Women, they hoped, would mobilize for action in the public sphere and introduce into politics their uniquely "feminine" concerns. As women demonstrated their trustworthiness, political leaders would admit them to full participation in the system. In fact, woman suffrage did release women into public life—but not in the way the early women's movement leaders had anticipated. The cry for "women's renewal" eclipsed the demand for emancipation. Conservative, traditionalist women organized in defense of the roles they had been raised to accept as natural and feminine. The broad coalition of middle-class organizations that had crusaded for women's rights before the war, the Federation of German Women's Associations (Bund Deutscher Frauenvereine; BDF) continued to exist, but the last signs of radicalism vanished from its program.[9] The millions of women who joined organizations after 1919 saw their public roles in terms of traditional religious, civic, or occupational activities. Thus, when searching for women's public record, historians cannot look in the political archives that provide evidence about men in public life. Women "went public," but they did so within the context of institutions that typically defined themselves as apolitical.

This means that the church or community *(Gemeinde)* provided for women roughly the same outlet that the political party did for men. Although they claimed to have no political preferences, middle-class women's organizations explicitly opposed Marxism and usually displayed preferences for one or another of the nonsocialist parties. The BDF shared historical ties with the Democratic Party, and its leaders made no secret of their hatred for socialism and fear of what Marianne Weber (a Reichstag delegate and widow of the well-known sociologist) described as the "propertyless masses" who had sunken into a deplorable moral state.[10] Protestant women displayed a considerably more conservative preference while Catholic women favored the Catholic Center Party, and Jewish women's organizations actually "played by the rules" and kept the pages of their publication free of politics.

### Bourgeois, Non-Nazi Organizations

The major bourgeois women's organization (BDF) from prewar days did not disband once the vote was won, but carried on its work under new leadership. It published the monthly *Die Frau (The Woman)* and  lobbied for strict laws against pornography, abortion, and venereal disease; during the French occupation of the Ruhr, it protested against black soldiers stationed on German soil; and in the first years of the Weimar Republic it boycotted international women's conferences because it did not want to associate with Germany's enemies. By the mid-1920s, however, it reconsidered its stance and joined international associations. The Federation dedicated its efforts to middle-class politics—shunning both socialists and feminists (who distinguished themselves from the BDF by their radical stance on pacifism and sexual morality)—and underwriting the status quo. As the result of concerted effort and political lobbying, the BDF managed to push several laws through the legislature that benefited women: strict laws for punishing  carriers of venereal disease, protection for mothers and all women who worked for pay in domestic settings (either women in the putting-out system or servants), public care for mothers, and expanded welfare service for youth. The rightward drift of the organization, which had begun long before the war, continued apace during the 1920s. A glance at membership statistics illuminates one source of this tendency. Of the approximately 750,000 members of the Federation of German Women's Associations, most belonged to occupational associations. The National Federation of German Housewives' Associations (Reichsverband Deutscher Hausfrauenvereine; RDH) for example,

counted over 100,000 members by 1931—with the second-place white-
collar women workers' union claiming over 100,000 members. Approximately 40,000 teachers belonged to the women teachers' union, and
20,000 to the Catholic women's teachers union.[11]

A tiny minority of feminists held their ground against the predomi-
nant trend favoring biologically based glorification of women. Led by
stalwart pacifists from World War I, they remained faithful to the
egalitarian and libertarian origins of the suffragist movement. In cooperation with international organizations, such as the Women's International League for Peace and Freedom (WILPF) and the Open Door
Movement (which opposed protective legislation), they worked for
women's full equality as a human right. Lida Gustava Heymann and
Anita Augspurg, feminists from the prewar era, found themselves outflanked by the overwhelmingly conservative majority in the BDF.[12]
Although opposition to World War I and continued commitment to
pacifism isolated them from their former co-workers, they continued to
work for women's equality, arms reduction, and feminism. As the
middle-class women's rights organization marginalized them as
"radicals," these feminists turned to international organizations for support.[13]

Since the late nineteenth century, the BDF had been led by a coalition of liberal women, many of whom were teachers. But after 1919 a
transformation of the teaching profession exerted a moderating influence on the new generation. The old guard found itself outflanked
by a more cautious younger generation that was plagued by unemployment and a highly organized backlash among male teachers.[14]

Another source of organizational strength from prewar days also
underwent a conservative transformation. In 1914 nearly 100,000
women belonged to the nation's first all-woman union, the Trade and
Office Workers' Association (Verband Weiblicher Handels- und
Büroangestellte; VWA).[15] As conservatives they avoided strikes, but
also lobbied for improvements in wages and working conditions and
sponsored courses to upgrade members' skills. After the war, a new
generation made other demands related more to the quality of life than
to material conditions. To attract younger members, the VWA founded
a special magazine, *Junge Kräfte (Youthful Workers)*, which featured
articles on the organization's tours, vacation houses, and cultural projects. Whereas the regular magazine stressed office and selling skills
designed to interest women who saw themselves as permanently employed, younger women emphasized their ladylike skills and docile
good nature—even in the face of longer hours, lower wages, and
rationalization. While urging young women to take up the professions
of office work or merchandising, the new generation stressed that such
a background harmonized well with marriage and family.

The RDH, by far the largest occupational grouping,[16] took even more reactionary stands—against women's emancipation and against the poorer and often younger women whom they employed as servants. While most women's organizations endorsed expanding educational opportunities for girls, the housewives tied their educational proposals to a frankly conservative purpose. For example, a local leader of the RDH wrote to the leadership of the reactionary Fatherland Party:

> Home economics, training of future wives and mothers, is the most important, most effective, and cheapest weapon in the fight against the general economic and moral need. All welfare funds (where there are any these days) will remain sterile unless economically astute, motherly and self-sacrificing women in *all* classes protect the household from misery.[17]

Housewives, like the millions of small businesspeople, artisans, nonunionized workers, and office workers who joined conservative protests, organized a powerful offensive to save their domestic workplaces, complete with employees, servants in this case. They turned conventional language upside down and spoke of "liberating" women from occupations outside the home and expanding their opportunities within domestic roles. Other occupational organizations within the BDF emphasized (in different and often contradictory ways) a special feminine contribution to political and economic life. They cared little about rights, and worked to upgrade their status using the rhetoric of responsibility.

Conservative as the BDF may seem by our standards, the organization created broad opposition among women with still more traditional views. The very fact that the BDF supported expanding educational opportunities for women, endorsed international women's organizations, and debated proposals to reform family law made them suspect in the eyes of women who saw their identity entirely in terms of motherhood. Such women saw the suffrage reform as a threat to their traditional *Lebensraum,* and they flocked to organizations that pledged to oppose further reforms—the religious and charitable organizations that had always attracted middle-class women. Only the national organization of Jewish women remained committed to the cause of women's rights and remained within the BDF.[18]

### Protestant Women's Organizations

The largest single women's organization in Weimar Germany was the German-Evangelical Women's League (Deutsch-Evangelischer Frauenbund) with over a million and a half members in the mid 1920s. In 1897, at the behest of Protestant bishops, a group of women broke away from older women's associations in order to found a women's movement that would offset the growing popularity of women's rights organizations.[19] Although the German-Evangelical Women's League joined Bäumer's federation (BDF) in 1908, they withdrew in 1918 because they objected to its radical stance—by which they meant support for woman suffrage. In a "great phalanx of helping love," Protestant women defended women against modernity.[20] This meant, in the 1920s, not only opposition to feminism, but support of the family— with programs for overworked mothers, rescue missions for "endangered" young women who left home, and marriage counseling centers to combat "mixed" marriages (i.e., between Catholics or Jews and Protestants). These strong-minded and conservative women hesitated, however, when they confronted topics such as family law and abortion reform. The majority opposed changes related to either— but a progressive minority of social workers wondered publicly if liberalized divorce and abortion laws might not indeed strengthen the family. Unable to arrive at a consensus, they often admitted they envied Catholic women because at least they received their orders from above and did not have to wrestle with troublesome alternatives.

Protestant teachers generally reached agreement about girls' education, however, and opposed teaching science, Greek, mathematics, and other "masculine" subjects in girls' schools. While fearing masculinization, Protestant women leaders actually did decide that certain careers might be appropriate and even necessary for women. Besides education and childrearing, social work seemed especially rewarding from two standpoints. "Like the wife and mother in the family, the social work agency remains a living example of the female principle in the larger family which one calls welfare, or police, or health care supervision."[21] Two points of view alternated. When Protestant social workers felt confident, they saw themselves as angels of mercy, saving endangered girls from sexual and economic exploitation by evil men. When, however, they were overwhelmed by recalcitrant clients and funding cutbacks, they increasingly viewed *themselves* as endangered and acted like police officials protecting society from unregenerate "fallen" women. As frustrations mounted, their definition of the victim shifted away from the innocent country girl exploited by greedy men to the society as a whole, which risked being polluted by fallen women. In this context, eugenic solutions began to replace love and mercy in their thinking. The Christian mother became the scientific policewoman.[22] As political leadership defaulted and the economy collapsed, the organization placed its trust in religion and science.[23] Protestant women's organizations expanded their membership from 1929 to 1934 by a third, which may indicate that the crisis atmosphere mobilized previously apathetic women.

## Catholic Women's Organizations

Catholic women, likewise, joined women's associations in unprecedented numbers, and, at the time of the Great Depression, just under 1 million women worked in charitable, educational, religious, and occupationally oriented associations. Since the eighteenth century, the church had sponsored organizations for women and published a special magazine for housewives, *Haus und Herd (House and Hearth)*. By the late nineteenth century, however, church leaders recognized the need for special organizations to cope with unprecedented problems connected with Germany's rapid industrialization. At the behest of the hierarchy, Catholic women in 1905 founded "our own women's movement," in the form of the League of Catholic German Women (Katholischer Deutscher Frauenbund; KDF). Catholic women, more than their Protestant counterparts, explicitly stressed the all-encompassing nature of their religious community: "The Catholic Women's League is not merely a defense [*Abwehr*] against the other women's movement (even though it staunchly opposes Socialism and liberalism), it is also a deepening [*Vertiefung*] of the Catholic way of thinking in all women . . . designed to shape the total woman in intellect and emotional life."[24] They spoke in terms of carving out a space for Catholics apart from mainstream Protestant and liberal life. Gerta Krabbel, leader of the KDF, continuously asserted women's needs for expanded horizons. "We see that women still do not have genuine space [*Raum*] in which to create a community . . . that people still do not respect the contributions which only women can make to a community."[25] Another Catholic leader, a state representative, used the metaphor in an opposite sense, but with the same goal in mind. She urged women to depart from their traditional *Lebensraum* in their own homes. Economic conditions, she said, mandated that women carry their private virtues into the public arena and save the nation from moral collapse.[26] As women were uprooted from their familiar environments, Catholic volunteers strove to "restore their lost homes."[27] Catholic women, more than Protestants, saw themselves as working completely within the religious community and fighting for Catholic women's position, as opposed to benefits for women as a whole.[28]

With the Depression, Catholic women, too, felt the crisis of declining budgets and escalating need. Two questions dominated their concerns: women's roles and the politics of reproduction. On both issues, the papacy had provided clear guidelines. Leo XIII, in *De Rerum Novarum*, had issued unambiguous guidelines for women's proper roles: "Women again are not suited to certain trades; for a woman is by nature fitted for home work and it is this which is best adapted at once to preserve her modesty, and to promote the good upbringing of chil- ·

dren and the well-being of the family."[29] In 1930, in the encyclical *On Christian Marriage*, Pius XI expressed his staunch opposition to any form of eugenics, from abortion to sterilization.[30] While supporting the pope's views on reproduction, leading Catholic women quietly ignored his opinions about employment and women's roles. Women had a right (and sometimes even a duty) to seek jobs, male unemployment notwithstanding. The KDF and various organizations under the umbrella of Catholic Charities (Deutscher Caritasverband) organized associations to foster the interests of working women, white-collar workers, students, and teachers, as well as rural and urban housewives. Like the Protestants, they developed a vast network of facilities to aid unmarried mothers, overworked housewives, and homeless girls. Far more than the Protestants, however, Catholic women defended the dignity of women who did not marry and of married women who worked outside their homes. But they did so in Catholic terms: women did not work to fulfill their own egotism (a notion that, in their view, would have reflected a feminist opinion); rather, economic necessity drove them to work to support their families. Such altruism deserved praise and material support, not condemnation.[31] From this, however, it did not follow that Catholic women workers ought to strike for better pay or working conditions (that would have presumably been "egotistical") but ought to accept their lot and cultivate, instead, a genuine commitment to their work, however humble or ill paid.[32] Helene Weber, representative to the Reichstag, assured women that a general weakening of religious faith, not capitalism, caused the Depression.[33] Catholic women juggled two sets of competing values—the family and women's right to paid work—within the context of an overtly misogynistic church. Not surprisingly, they found themselves in the midst of confusion.

## Jewish Women's Organizations

Unlike Catholic and Protestant women's organizations, the League of Jewish Women (Jüdischer Frauenbund; JFB) worked within the BDF throughout the Weimar Republic and, in fact, exerted a liberalizing influence on it. The pages of the organization's magazine indicate a concern for women's religious equality and participation in religious life and more general involvement with social work, welfare, culture, and homemaking. Unlike the Protestant and Catholic magazines, which professed an apolitical stance while spreading the cause of antisocialism and fostering the interests of the Conservative and Center parties, the *Jewish Women's Pages* really did abstain from political involvement. Instead of warning about Nazism and anti-Semitism in their publications, the members of the JFB worked through "enlightenment committees" in which they invited non-Jewish women to discuss the "Jewish Question" in small gatherings.[34] Perhaps these efforts seemed minor on a national scale, but this strategy was intended to mobilize non-Jewish women on behalf of their friends. The local chapters in the Rhineland, for example, offered to send individual members to the homes of any Christian family who invited them in order to discuss Jewish tradition. One participant in this effort recalls that Jewish women probably had no chance of influencing hard core anti-Semites, but they could raise the consciousness of potential friends and alert them to Jews' already endangered position.[35] Jewish women's organizations faced an impossible situation in which they simultaneously defended Jewish traditions and a more liberal view of women's emancipation than that of their non-Jewish colleagues.

Thus it can be seen that the dozens of liberal and conservative women's organizations surveyed in this essay all argued simultaneously for women's rights and for women's special mission. Women ought, in their view, to integrate themselves into mainstream political life as representatives of womankind, or a sort of "woman's lobby." This meant entering the Reichstag and serving in high bureaucratic positions; entering the university and pursuing hitherto male professions; and participating in economic decision making at the local and national levels. But these sweeping goals (which directly affected the life choices of only a few women) contained two implicit limitations. First, women admitted into previously male situations ought to resist masculinization, that is, to avoid being materialistic, ambitious, petty, or power hungry. Second, the numbers of women who entered into masculine preserves would be limited to non-mothers because mothers must not shirk their primary obligations to their families. Hitler remained consistently within that tradition when he swore to remove women entirely from the masculine sphere. The question therefore arises: why did some middle-class traditional women find religious and civic women's organizations lacking? Why did they follow the Führer?

### Women in the Nazi Movement prior to 1933

Hitler spoke of his following as a "movement," not a mere "party," and the distinction is crucial in understanding women's attraction to the Nazi cause. A party, guided by a coherent ideology and material self-interest, seeks to realize its goals by mobilizing followers at election time. The National Socialist *movement,* by contrast, offered its members a total world view (*Weltanschauung*), laying out codes of behavior and thought for every aspect of life and maintaining an intense schedule of activities between elections. Nazis built what their enemies called a "state within a state," and backed it with their own paramilitary force. Women in the movement complemented men by providing a broad range of social services and by solidifying the movement as a way of life, or subculture, apart from mainstream German society. In addition, women contributed a "spiritual" and "pure" image that offset the stormtroopers' brutality. Women's organizations in the Nazi movement functioned, in other words, as much like a secularized church as a state. Because Hitler's spectacular voter mobilization owed at least as much to the Nazis' infrastructure as to national propaganda campaigns, women Nazis contributed a vital (if unnoticed) role in the spread of Nazi ideas.

The most visible difference between middle-class women's associations and Nazi women's groups lay in official statements about women's roles. Non-Nazi women at the very least paid lip service to ideals of women's equality, though this often led them into contradictions as, for example, advocating unmarried women's rights to careers and education while insisting on mothers' special responsibility to their families. Nazi policy, by contrast, proceeded from a clear denunciation of women's emancipation and an unequivocal defense of "traditional" female roles. Because the Nazi Party, alone of all major parties, had not endorsed woman suffrage, it would not be accused of hypocrisy. National Socialists unambiguously endorsed collective over individual values and swore to eliminate women from masculine turf. Joseph Goebbels's feathered metaphor said it simply.

> The mission of women is to be beautiful and to bring children into the world. This is not at all as rude and unmodern as it sounds. The female bird pretties herself for her mate and hatches the eggs for him. In exchange, the mate takes care of gathering the food, and stands guard and wards off the enemy.[36]

Alfred Rosenberg, party ideologue, underscored his hatred of women's emancipation when he blamed democracy for liberating women and Jews.[37] Already in *Mein Kampf* Hitler declared, "The German girl belongs to the state and with her marriage becomes a citizen," and added as an afterthought that the woman who never married but performed important services to the state might also receive citizenship. In either case the principle was clear: women were not endowed by birth with rights but gained them by service to men.[38]

Before I discuss Nazi women's organizations, a few generalizations about the individuals who joined the cause before 1933 are in order. Nazi women, like their male counterparts, were on the whole younger than women in middle-class associations and, therefore, less likely to have had the opportunity to assume leadership roles in the older women's organizations.[39] Party records for the pre-1933 period are rare, and the published records commonly list all women as "housewives" or "without occupation." We must be content with scanty evidence about personal backgrounds of Nazi women. A three-year run of applications from Hesse indicates that of women whose occupations are listed, none were defined as factory workers, and virtually all considered themselves sales personnel, office workers, tailors, teachers, or housewives.[40] It may well be that some of the self-definitions mask working-class origins, but even if that is true, it seems clear that women applying for membership in the Nazi Party wanted to emphasize their claim to at least petty-bourgeois identification.[41] A collection of forty-five autobiographies of Nazi women (collected in the 1930s) indicates a strong tendency for these women to identify with middle-class families, occupations, and values.[42]

Autobiographical accounts suggest that the women who "converted" to Nazi candidates before 1933 came overwhelmingly from Protestant backgrounds, and national voting statistics reinforce this conclusion. While it is not always clear just which Germans voted for Nazism, there is no doubt about two categories who did *not* vote Nazi. Marxists often switched allegiance between Social Democracy and Communism, but their principles immunized most of them against the Nazi contagion. Similarly, Catholic voters did not "go over" to Nazi candidates, even under the severe intimidation of the March 1933 elections. What traits did these two groups (which so bitterly opposed one another) have in common? Both can be considered "movements" more than parties because they offered to their members more than a political platform. Dense organizational networks provided their adherents with leisure-time activities, educational facilities, an international network of like-minded believers, a vision of justice in the future, a social hierarchy, and an array of social services. Socialists and Catholics partook in a way of life and a community that offered them a defense against the ravages of economic depression. Protestants, by contrast, lived in a decentralized and fragmented world. Without an international network, political party, educational system, or minority consciousness, they operated in a secular society. When disoriented by economic depression, Protestant voters turned away from liberalism and staid nationalist parties to a vigorous movement that offered them a secular framework within which to reintegrate *all* aspects of their lives: work, family, faith, and community.[43] It is worth noting as well that Protestants, who were not only numerically in the majority but also enjoyed the privilege of belonging to the state church, experienced a loosening of ties within their community.

Besides investigating statistical data, which because of its fragmentary nature is problematic, we can also turn to the archives and published writings of early Nazi women to reinforce these generalizations. A major theme in women Nazis' rhetoric prior to 1933 was the call for a sisterhood among all German women. For them biology—in other words, sex and race—replaced "artificial" divisions (read "class") among people. They bitterly decried socialists and feminists for organizing on the basis of class and for maintaining contacts with women from other nations. Nazi women demanded a society in which "every German woman will call other women 'sister'" and boasted that within their world "the Frau Minister or Frau Doctor treat their like-minded sisters equally."[44] A second common theme concerned women's loss of femininity. Nazi supporter Hertha Braun, in a pamphlet published in 1932, accused the women's movement of selling out to the "masculine spirit" and deplored the fact that Gertrud Bäumer embraced a French representative to an international women's convention.[45] Beneath the rhetoric of harmony, however, we hear strains of intergenerational warfare. The League of German Girls (Bund Deutscher Mädel; BDM), no less than the all-male Hitler Youth, enjoyed strong peer-group solidarity as against adults in general and parents in particular.[46] Melita Maschmann, for example, recalled the appeal of Nazism when she was young. Secretly she admired her mother's tailor, who believed ardently in Hitler's cause. "My mother was displeased . . . but it was the very fact that this woman was one of the common people that made her attractive to me. I felt myself drawn to her for the same reason that I often inwardly took the maids' part against my mother."[47] Christa Wolf described the pleasure she found in gathering around the BDM leader "together with all the others, at the end of the evening, forgetting one's own shyness, to grasp her hand, to enjoy the extraordinary familiarity. And on the ride home to become familiar with a new word by repeating it to herself: 'comradeship.'"[48] Despite and because of their mothers' disapprobation, girls sought new forms for their own need of community. For Maschmann and hundreds of Nazi followers, the claim for an interclass solidarity provided a format for attacking mothers, community leaders, teachers, and snobbish neighbors.

Alongside tensions between young and old, we also read in early Nazis' writings about deep resentments against more "respectable" women who scorn Nazi women as lower-class "riff-raff." Nazi women retaliated by calling BDF members "blue stockings" and "social snobs." Nazi women displayed as much anger at their social "betters" as anxiety about slipping down into the ranks of their "inferiors"—workers or poor peasants. A woman reported from a small town: "The Queen Louisa League here is and will remain hostile to us. You should just see the executive committee! You cannot believe the condescension with which these ladies treat us Nazi women! You can just hear them whisper a hundred times, 'I would NEVER sit on the same bench as a Nazi woman!'"[49] In their autobiographies, Nazi women recalled wearing swastika armbands in the streets of their home towns or neighborhoods and hearing taunts of "Hitler whore!" "brown goose!" or "Nazi pig!" Often they compared themselves to the Christians in the catacombs and spoke of their joy at being able to participate in a genuine community. "What did it matter that we were nearly always ridiculed and stoned by Communists lurking in the shadows. . . . We were so despised in our neighborhoods that we hardly dared to walk alone in the streets."[50] Scorn and ridicule forged a unity among them that in itself overcame the feelings of alienation and helplessness that they experienced before joining the movement.

Nazi women before 1933 made an important contribution to Nazis' belief that they belonged to a movement rather than a mere party. Whereas women's associations based on occupation, religious conviction, a particular social cause, or other single issues all remained powerless in the context of national politics, Nazi women believed they played a vital role within a revolutionary subculture. They converted social scorn into an advantage and saw themselves as an embattled and virtuous group operating in an area beyond the reach of ordinary Christian women. Because Nazi leaders generally ignored them, women Nazis falsely believed they enjoyed a considerable amount of autonomy from Nazi men, as well.

Nazi women could fight for their concerns as women and still enjoy the thrill of belonging to a massive national movement. Thus, Nazi Party membership brought the advantages of a movement and a party, combined with the emotional appeal of a religion.

Instead of demanding equality, Nazi women called for "more masculine men" and "more feminine women." While their enemies accused them of throwing themselves into male control, they planned to expel men from their female sphere.[51] Restoring "proper" roles would  leave women free to assume control over areas they deemed feminine, such as social welfare, education, culture, health care, and community organization. "We want more than the three K's," wrote one Nazi woman, "besides *Kinder, Küche, Kirche* [children, kitchen, church], we want two more—*Krankenhaus und Kultur* [hospitals and culture]." In a collapsing social structure, a woman needed, according to a woman psychologist with Nazi sympathies, a secure sense of identity. And that could be achieved only by reinforcing her sense of her own sex and race.[52] Emancipation, she feared, would blur people's identity and melt everyone into one democratic mass. Class lines, in other words, should give way to a biologically demarcated society.

Throughout the early years of the party, women remained not only outside the official party organization, but ignored by male leaders.[53] This proved to be an advantage in that women enjoyed considerable freedom from male scrutiny. Nazi leaders' apathy gave ambitious and often angry young women the chance to pioneer in the creation of new organizations independent of established women's associations and male supervision. Despite Hitler's boasting about "iron will" and the "leadership principle," Gregor Strasser, the mastermind of party organization, knew that the real secret of Nazi success lay in a very different reality. It was precisely the absence of fixed dogma or clear chains of command that provided ambitious young local leaders with sufficient scope for their energies. The less important the suborganization, the greater the latitude it enjoyed.[54] Women fell into a very unimportant category. Until late 1931 they remained "miscellaneous," along with physicians, automobile drivers, and veterans. The idea of a women's paramilitary group, discussed briefly in 1927, was dropped at once. As a result, Nazi women could link their own particular ambitions and aspirations to the amorphous Nazi movement with little fear of censure or scrutiny. A brief survey of nationally prominent and local leaders illustrates the diversity of opinion that counted as "national socialist" before Hitler's takeover.

The oldest pro-Nazi group, Guida Diehl's Newland Movement, predated the Nazi Party by at least six years. Diehl, a conservative and a professional social worker in her forties, had founded this patriotic association recruited from the conservative, well-educated, Protestant "establishment."[55] In florid prose and trinitarian metaphors, she preached that "truth, purity, and love" could not survive without women's protection. Germanic "air, light, and sunshine" had fallen under the cloud of "humanism, individualism and Romanticism." "Americanism, materialism, and mammonism" threatened to overpower "*Volk*, God, and Fatherland." Men, as soldiers and statesmen, fought for territory; but only women bore the responsibility for preserving life-giving values, for loving, and nurturing. "We women are in much closer touch than men with the hidden secrets of life."[56] In the early 1920s she founded her own newspaper and built a national conference and educational center, called the New Land House, in Saxony. While supporting National Socialist goals, Diehl did not form any tie with the party organization. In her post–World War II memoirs, she wrote fondly of her first impressions of Hitler in the mid-1920s. "Serious, warm, and natural—he set out his goals. He brought nothing new, just a summary of the very best of our national tradition. He offered a dynamic organization where others relied on uninspired party politics."[57] By the late 1920s, she boasted over 200,000 followers.

Diehl openly praised women in Protestant organizations and appealed to the most anti-Semitic, conservative members of the BDF. Gertrud Bäumer and other early advocates of women's rights, according to Diehl, addressed genuine needs, but had been misled into thinking that these needs could be met by adapting to masculine rational values in a liberal state. Diehl argued that women's social emancipation had produced an unhealthy preoccupation with sexuality and the search for personal pleasure. The national spirit, as well as women themselves, suffered in a social milieu dominated by rationality and sexuality. At fault for this "chaotic inner life" were women themselves. "If women sink, the entire nation sinks; and if the whole *Volk* declines, then women bear the largest guilt." Behind their guilt, however, lurked a more sinister culprit: the Jew, luring women into rational thinking and sexual pleasure.[58] Incidently, this sort of "coded" anti-Semitism was standard in Hitler speeches. This enabled his rabidly anti-Semitic followers to know that he still hated Jews, but his more respectable and probably more recent followers could more easily ignore the overtones.

Throughout the 1920s Diehl and her devoted followers (who called her "Mother Guida") preached a spiritualist, quasi-Christian, and nationalist message. On occasion, Diehl could display more down-to-earth concerns. When she advocated removal of women from all employment outside the home, for example, she insisted on state subsidies for women whose husbands could not provide for them. Although she advocated the end of woman suffrage in Hitler's state, she proposed a female legislature that would take charge of legislation directly related to women's sphere.[59]

A very different sort of woman rallied to the strident tone of the "Order of the Red Swastika," founded by Elsbeth Zander, in 1926. Zander deputized herself as the female equivalent of Hitler—and indeed she resembled him in many of her personal traits. Like him, she remained somewhat of a hermit and never married. She came to life, however, when facing an audience—terrifying people with dire predictions or filling them with joy at the thought of a new Reich. The masthead of her newsletter bore a megaphone emblazoned with the words "Elsbeth Zander Speaks!" Devoted followers wrote adoring poetry and pledged obedience to her every wish. While Hitler called on men to march in the SA, Zander recruited women to defend their community by aiding mothers, caring for unemployed stormtroopers, and organizing charity for Nazi families. Moody and emotionally unstable, she drove her associates to distraction by extravagant spending, temper tantrums, and bureaucratic ineptitude.[60] At one point in 1931, complaints about Zander's irresponsibility flooded party headquarters, but Gregor Strasser ordered a full investigation and ultimately defended her.[61] Although it is difficult to ascertain precisely who joined the Red Swastika, from the simplistic language of Zander's speeches and letters, it would appear that she recruited women with little formal education from small towns and rural areas. Unlike Diehl, Zander vigorously attacked the snobbishness of the bourgeois women's organization and said virtually nothing about Christianity.

Twenty-six-year-old Lydia Gottschewski offered Nazi women still another alternative. This dynamic and forceful organizer called on women to form their own fighting union—to close ranks and march against the enemy. Men, she believed, would "clean up the streets" while women would undertake the more arduous task of doing missionary work among the unconvinced. Forming the Nazi personality, in her view, presented a far more exciting challenge than street brawling. She traveled throughout Germany, wrote articles for the popular press, and published a book in which she propagated her ideas about "male and female communities."[62]

A small group of women Nazi academics carried racial theory even further and proposed that while women of "lesser" races might be inferior to their men, Germanic women in prehistoric times had grown to equal size and had performed equal work. Decadent "Western" civilization had degraded Germanic women; Nazi society alone would restore true equality between the sexes, they predicted. And from a practical standpoint, they added, Hitler would discover that his new state needed the most highly qualified personnel to replace incompetent Weimar officials. The need for talent would surely mean that women Nazis would be hired before non-Nazi men.[63]

Before 1933, all of these opinions coexisted. When friction did develop, it occurred between and among women's groups, not between Nazi women and their male superiors. A similar diversity flourished at the grass-roots level. While the national leaders did not have husbands, many local leaders did; some were Christian and others atheist; some admired the BDF and others hated it; some engaged in traditional "women's" work while a few marched in uniform just behind the men.[64]

The variety of Nazi doctrines preached by national leaders, however, tells only part of the story; because the strength of the Nazi Party lay in its dense network of local organizations, it is important to survey regional variations as well. Rallying their followers to contradictory slogans, regional leaders appealed to very different audiences. In the days when votes counted and male leaders worried about stormtroopers and rallies, no one at party headquarters bothered to outlaw any theme that attracted new women followers.

The types of women's activities varied as widely as the ideologies. Sewing circles gathered to listen as women read aloud passages of *Mein Kampf*; when members felt unable to comprehend Nazi ideology, they eagerly sought more education. "Since I had no political background, I was quite inexperienced," wrote one young woman who joined in 1925. "To my astonishment, I soon was transformed into a fanatical fighter for the German Freedom Movement. I even put up posters and held meetings in my house because no one would rent public rooms to

Nazis." She purchased a revolver to deter hostile neighbors from harming the swastika flag she draped in front of her house.[65] A local organizer in Westphalia adapted her tactics to suit local needs, establishing needlework circles, SA aid stations, projects to aid farmers' wives, or reading groups, as the situation demanded. "It was very difficult to attract a following here. Since everyone was Socialist or Catholic, they thought I was a fanatic."[66] "To this day, I don't know how I found the courage to join!" wrote another woman. Often the poorest women felt proud that they could pay party dues. "The membership dues were a real hardship for us, but our work was vital," recalled one early follower. "In the evenings we would paste up illegal posters and on countless occasions we would stake out sentries to be sure our SA Men were not intercepted by the police. When necessary, we carried weapons in our blouses for the SA."[67]

Women speakers prided themselves on activating previously apathetic women—telling them that they could offer their traditionally feminine skills, emotions, and experience in the service of a national movement. One woman orator, Irene Seydel, who drew hundreds of women to hear her speeches, reported after a tour of Westphalia in 1932:

> From my own experience I can tell you about women who have responded to our appeal and begun to see things clearly because they discovered they could once again serve the Fatherland. Women have something to offer their *Volk*—the purity of their hearts and the power of their spirits! Women long to hear that politics emanates from love, and that love means sacrifice. . . . The German woman's talents wither at the harsh sound of commands barked by northeastern (Prussian) trumpets. But she is eager to work for whomever sends a friendly ray of sunshine her way.[68]

Seydel developed a unique style, inspiring simple country women and factory workers alike and lavishing praise on women for just those womanly traits that men so often decried as "merely emotional" or "irrational." These qualities alone, she insisted, would restore unity to the badly fragmented national life. Seydel's superior, Elisabeth Polster, demonstrated her effectiveness at launching a very different type of appeal to the very women Seydel considered "upper class" and perhaps even snobbish. Polster established a network of charitable projects, imitating the activities of church women in her area. Since she had virtually no funding at her disposal, she relied on imagination and enthusiasm. Among her most publicized drives were giving children from industrial cities a chance to spend a month in the summer with Nazi farming families and collecting used bedding for working-class families in which, she claimed, the lack of sufficient single beds led to incest and sexual license.[69] Unlike Seydel, who depended on charisma,

Polster demanded order. "We need a sisterhood whose goal is unquestioning obedience to our movement. The movement needs the total person."[70]

Nazi women remained "independent"—free to either sew or wear brown shirts. In the chaotic days of the Depression and political disarray, male leaders cared little about women's activities; all contributions and ideas were welcomed. One rural group might gather to knit socks and sing Nazi songs; and in another village, women might run secret missions through police guards to smuggle illegal weapons to an underground stormtrooper cell. One early convert to Nazism relished the feeling of tranquillity after returning from an exhausting day of conflict with anti-Nazi demonstrators. As she rested sipping a cup of tea, she heard the family next door (also devoted Nazis) playing a Mozart string quartet. This, she recalled, is what she fought for—to save culture and virtue in a world polluted by materialism.[71]

Virtually all of these ideals and programs fell within the range of activities endorsed by the most conservative elements of non-Nazi women. What set Nazi women apart was a rebelliousness, a fanatical devotion to a closed and embattled community, and the belief in an extreme separation between male and female spheres. "We're not just a coffee-and-cake ladies club," as Zander once commented. Taking up the ubiquitous rhetoric of *Lebensraum*, women Nazis demanded their "*Lebensraum* for the woman in the state and the culture" of the Third Reich. Racist author Sophie Rogge-Börner appealed to Hitler that the "Germanic state may never be called 'men's territory,'" but must be regarded as "*Lebensraum* of the total human being, which includes man and woman."[72] Operating from their own base, women pledged to create a community of believers. Unlike women in religious organizations, who had to manipulate their male superiors into granting permission for every new project and approving every resolution, Nazi women had *carte blanche* to innovate as they saw fit; since virtually no funding from national headquarters was available to any regional organization, they raised their own funds and developed their own programs. This feeling of solidarity among women made it possible to ridicule and openly deride men in "their" sphere. For example, at an organizing meeting in Westphalia, the husband of the local leader of the women's group attempted to chair the meeting. He met implacable resistance. So did his wife, the district leader. "What are you doing here? Addressing us women! In a women's gathering, men have no place! If a woman leader has nothing to contribute to other women, then she must resign at once—and not turn over the meeting to her husband."[73] In vain, the husband and wife sought to mollify their outraged followers; finally an eighteen-year-old member retorted to his threat to call in the SA by shouting, "The SA Men are all pricks

*(Gesocks)* anyway." Complaints about male Nazis filled local women's organization reports whenever men did attempt to interfere in women's affairs. These protests did not, needless to say, result in real victories for women, but served (like slave humor) to reinforce the boundaries of the women's world.

Thus, Nazi organizations did not simply lure women who wanted an "escape from freedom" or a secular savior.[74] On the contrary, they attracted women who longed to escape from male scrutiny—who sought a vent for their anxiety about women's status in the world. Paradoxically, too, women Nazis, while defending clearly demarcated traditional or natural masculine and feminine roles, enjoyed greater latitude than did their more traditional counterparts in apolitical women's organizations. The needs of the moment, in the revolutionary and chaotic atmosphere of the early 1930s, provided Nazi women with a rationale for "unwomanly" actions such as smuggling, law-breaking, and confrontation with hostile demonstrators. They took their fate into their own hands, and they typically described their organizations as part of the "German Liberation" or "Freedom" movement. The "System"—by which they meant Weimar democracy—enslaved them; their Nazi movement would make them free. "Democracy" connoted to them an impersonal, bureaucratized state over which they had no control—and from which they would receive little protection or recognition. Nazi women shared a hunger for community that would provide them with a secure social environment in which they thought they could be "free."

To a far greater extent than non-Nazi middle-class women, Nazi women leaders were willing to pioneer their own solutions in times of social crisis. When they formulated expectations about a Nazi future, they looked forward to close cooperation with state structures as a means of strengthening women's status in society. Middle-class women, by contrast, hoped to restore the husband's role in family life and worked for nongovernmental alternatives to improve women's pride.

### Backlash During the Depression

By the late 1920s, women in the bourgeois women's movement looked back on a mixed record. A decade of participation in *Realpolitik* had instructed them in the difficulty of transforming predominantly male structures. The Great Depression severely damaged their faith in a "man's world" to provide a stable society. When they surveyed the broader, nonpolitical scene, they had even graver reasons for despair.

Although officially women had retained their political rights through the 1920s, *outside* the domain of politics, a backlash gathered force.

"Experts" wrote books with such titles as *Psychopathology of the Women's Movement* and *Sexual Character and National Strength; Basic Problems of Feminism* or *Feminism and Cultural Demise; The Erotic Roots of Women's Emancipation.* Sociologists gave warning with *The Nation in Danger* and *The Declining Birth Rate and its Consequences for Germany's Future.* Political scientists offered *The Rule of the Inferior.*[75] The woman's movement, according to Professor Anton Schuecker, was really a brutal struggle for power, resulting from the "jealousy of lesbian souls." He analyzed women leaders' unfavorable characters according to Kretschmer's typology:[76] "And in their autobiographies, they mention no men; as young women they were tomboys and girltypes." These portentous voices resonated with the wartime memories of a topsy-turvy world where women stepped in as men marched away.

Women leaders from all branches of the middle-class women's movement sensed the mounting opposition not only to women's equality, but to women's claim to public status altogether. They met the charges by redoubling their promises not to usurp male prerogatives. While swearing loyalty to their special civilizing mission, they also defended "natural" values against male critics who equated nature with chaos. Implicit in their rhetoric, however, one detects a note of anger at men for defaulting on their major obligations to protect the nation and the home. As in wartime, women often lamented, "their" men were helpless, dishonored, and disarmed *(wehrlos, ehrlos, und heerlos).* Civilization—man-made, materialistic, and corrupt—brought war and economic crisis, they argued; a return to nature and women's values would restore social health. Alongside their disillusionment with the male state, many women leaders exalted their own female world, glorifying women's ability to save the day.

> Women are assuming a more dominant role in world affairs, according to the Baroness von Hindenburg, niece of the German President . . . German women today . . . constitute a bulwark upon which rests the present and future safety of Germany. Never before have the women of her country evinced such a cultural awakening of such an interest in science, art, politics, sociology, and education.[77]

Women who accepted such special responsibilties for maintaining the nation's cultural level and safeguarding family life set themselves up as potential targets for misogyny. However complimentary women may have found such praise, ultimately the women's movement suffered because it naïvely accepted such notions. Linking women to private, moral, and cultural health ascribed to women power and influence they did not possess. In many cases, they themselves deplored the cultural decadence of Weimar Berlin, the silver screen, and relaxed standards of behavior, and blamed themselves for not having done more to combat it. To many, it may well have seemed true (to quote one male critic) that "the high point of women's emancipation coincided with the low point of culture." When the backlash mounted, women had no weapons in their conceptual arsenal. Occasionally, they counterattacked by blaming the "masculine will" for its impotence. But they remained within a gender-differentiated scheme that separated women's moral purity from men's political efficacy. Both men and women could exchange recriminations without seeing their responsibility for a human solution to a national problem. On the other hand, interclass hostility precluded a broad-based women's alliance against the mounting threat of National Socialism. The Depression exacerbated these anxieties, and activated shibboleths about women's duty to sacrifice in times of national emergency. Defending against backlash and feelings of helplessness, advocates of women's rights relied even more heavily on the nineteenth-century argument of separate spheres to vindicate their claims. Despite the contradictions inherent in this approach, it seemed the only possible tactic to reassure opponents (and perhaps supporters of emancipation as well) that the family would survive—and with it the stable moral world that depended on feminine virtues. Women insisted on their equal rights but did not abandon their commitment to their special nature.

Both Nazi and non-Nazi women's organizations saw as their primary goal the strengthening of the woman's world by encouraging solidarity among women and also by enlisting male support. However, at this point the similarity ended. Nazi women envisioned that an authoritarian state would, after the "revolution," provide them with funds and leave them as autonomous as they had been throughout the 1920s. Non-Nazi women, by contrast, expected little aid from the state and saw the problem in individual terms. Husbands, they believed, ought to be tied more tightly to their family obligations, and religious institutions ought to provide the spiritual context for what they called "women's renewal."

## Women's Organizations and the Creation of the Nazi State

In the immediate aftermath of Hitler's seizure of power in the spring of 1933, feminists and socialists left the country for exile or withdrew totally from public life to either "wait out" the Third Reich or to cooperate with resistance against Hitler. The League of Jewish Women, preparing for the worst from the Hitler state, appealed for solidarity in the face of anti-Semitic attack and debated defense strategy in an increasingly hostile environment. Stalwarts from the BDF and Protestant and Catholic women's organizations, by contrast, published joyful proclamations welcoming the new state.

The positive reaction to Nazi power had already been presaged by editorials in religious periodicals. Despite pretensions at being apolitical, women from many backgrounds had, before Hitler became chancellor, expressed the hope for some form of authoritarian government. Paula Mueller-Otfried, president of the German-Evangelical Women's League, expressed her political views in New Year's messages in 1933 and 1934. In 1933 she castigated Weimar democracy:

> Are we on the brink of collapse? Is the *Volk* to become extinct? Even against the background of Christmas and New Year's bells, we can hear a warning, menacing, dull, subterranean, rumble. . . . What can we do? We must remain faithful and pray, confident that God is at the controls. . . . He will send us a steel-hardened man, without weaknesses, who makes no compromises and places his entire personality at the service of a single goal: the salvation of Germany.[78]

One year later she rejoiced. "We prayed and the answer arrived. . . . Now we only hope that the man of steel for whom we waited . . . will be granted enough power."[79] At last, she rejoiced, Protestant women could cast off their promise to remain apolitical; with a state that inspired their confidence, they could wholeheartedly pledge cooperation. Within months, the editor of the Protestant women's magazine *Mutter und Volk* joined the Nazi Party, cut her ties with the church, and worked directly with the Nazi welfare bureau. This meant divorcing her Jewish husband, which she did, apparently, with few regrets.[80] Magdelena von Tilling, another national leader, swore full support for the new state and pledged total cooperation with its women's bureau. These women did not wait to be invited, they asked to be admitted. When it became clear, by the summer of 1933, that they would have to cast out women with Jewish ancestry, their enthusiasm waned only slightly.[81]

Catholic women had long endorsed socially and politically conservative views, and some leaders had spoken cautiously in favor of an antidemocratic solution to Germany's problems within the framework of the Catholic Center Party. For example, in a newsletter to all regional Catholic Women's League branches in January 1933, women were exhorted to support an "authoritarian democracy" and to allow women to assume full responsibility for "reconciling authority and freedom" under a new political system. During the early months of the Nazi state, Catholic women preserved a cautious silence. Perhaps it resulted from their skepticism; or maybe they merely awaited orders from the hierarchy. Once the concordat between Hitler and the Vatican had been signed, however, Catholic women adjusted to the new state despite strong reservations about eugenics. The themes publicized in their periodicals reflected the new emphasis on motherhood and nationalism; defense of unmarried women and women in the labor force disappeared. Catholic authors did their best to make their religious faith compatible with political acceptance of Hitler's state.

For Catholic and Protestant women, the Nazi state had a minimal impact on daily operations and plans for the future.[82] Jewish women realized at once the magnitude of Nazi power. The Christian women with whom they had worked for years made it clear that lifelong ties of friendship and shared ideals could not survive the new *Weltanschauung*. When the BDF suggested that continued association might not be expedient in the spring of 1933, Jewish women complied. "Cooperation under the present circumstances seems impossible. . . . Internally, we remain committed to the women's movement. . . . This decision is not easy . . . and we depart with deep pain."[83] Jewish women wondered how they could have trusted their non-Jewish friends. But they concluded, "We must rely entirely upon ourselves in this trial by fire. Until now we have noted no success in our efforts to obtain the cooperation of the great Christian religions. With few exceptions, intellectual leaders have also remained silent."[84] Women Christians behaved no worse than men; nor did they display a shred of the superior humanity and morality of which they had so often boasted.

Gertrud Bäumer (who even before 1933 had written of the "narrow, asphalt democracy, the Jewish atmosphere of Weimar")[85] lost no time in declaring she had been a National Socialist long before Hitler had heard of the term and called on women to continue their fight for equality under the new political circumstances.[86] "We do not oppose National Socialism as a party, but only its position in relationship to women," she declared.[87] Articles in *Die Frau* praised the new state, with reservations only regarding women's status. One author, who had long belonged to the BDF and had joined the Nazi Party, exulted at the extraordinary "wave" of national enthusiasm that washed over the nation after Hitler's destruction of Weimar democracy. At last, "the intellectualism which had become so sterile" gave way to the "revived powers of the soul, of German blood, of our own home soil, and of religious consecration [*Vertiefung*]." Here was the beginning of a true "renaissance" in women's *Lebensraum*, which could be purged of useless women whom she called "luxury plants" of the middle class. She closed with a strong appeal for women to force their concerns to the forefront of the new Nazi regime.[88] Bäumer did not protest when her name was removed from the masthead of her magazine, and *Die Frau* continued to appear in the same format, featuring sentiment extolling the virtues of motherhood. But its authors also continued to report regularly on the status of women's rights and employment. Even after paper became scarce during World War II, *Die Frau* received its allotment and did not miss an issue until shortly before the German surrender. This continuity resulted from compromises on both sides. Bäumer retreated to her country castle and devoted her energies to writing on historical topics unrelated to women. The Nazis, within a few months of capturing power, realized that women could not be dismissed wholesale from the labor market. Minister of the Interior Wilhelm Frick hastened to reassure women that their employment would be secure. Somewhat later they also realized that Bäumer could turn out to be an asset, so they allowed her freedom to travel the nation on speaking tours and participate in conferences, and began officially to celebrate her birthday after 1938.[89]

Meanwhile, the BDF had decided to disband during the first months of Nazi power. The directors refused to submit to "Nazification" (or *Gleichschaltung*), which would have entailed expulsion of all women with Jewish ancestry. Its thirty-six affiliated organizations, however, did not dissolve. Nor did they protest against any Nazi measure—with one exception. When, in February 1933, Bäumer was dismissed from her post in the Ministry of Culture, hundreds of women and organizations telegraphed their indignation to the new Nazi leaders. Bäumer, of course, was not reinstated, although eventually she was offered a post in the Ministry of Education (which she did not accept). The various former member organizations of the BDF agreed to submit all policy decisions to Nazi officials for approval; to cooperate closely with the Nazi women's organization at a local level; to guarantee that at least one-third of their members became Nazi Party members; and to submit lists of their officers for Nazi approval. And, with as much delicacy as they could muster, women leaders requested their non-Aryan members to step into the background for the time being.[90] Not surprisingly, the housewives' associations joined the general celebration and eagerly signed up for service in the new regime. The extent to which they cooperated with the order to sever ties with members who had non-Aryan ancestry varied widely. The women white-collar workers eventually integrated themselves into the Labor Front. (Until the records are discovered, however, we cannot say whether this process was simple.) As a whole, teachers displayed considerable skepticism and even hostility to the women's division of the Nazi Teachers Union.[91] However, their exceedingly precarious employment situation rendered them ineffective as a group.

In exchange for cooperation, the state promised Nazified organizations the right to continue to exist. Thus the women's movement, hailed in its day as "the fortress of German feminism" by Kirkpatrick[92] and admired by feminists everywhere, opted for cooperation within the Nazi regime. Middle-class organization women, for decades accustomed to operating within alien, male-controlled structures, regarded the Nazi victory as merely a new variation on an age-old political reality. A heritage of cooperation conditioned them to expect to win advantages for women in exchange for concessions. This strategy had not prepared them for withdrawal from (much less resistance to) Nazi rule.

Hitler's seizure of power, seen from the vantage point of organized middle-class women, appeared as a salvation from the anxieties about which they had complained throughout the Weimar Republic. Weak men in church and state had defaulted in their masculine responsibilities; perhaps a new male order would succeed. No doubt calculations of self-interest also hastened the decision to underwrite the Nazi state. Many women explained their cooperation by saying that their voluntary pledge of support would earn them special privileges later on. They anticipated, in other words, winning autonomy in exchange for early surrender.

Against this background of non-Nazi women's enthusiasm, the Nazi women's rather less joyful response seems paradoxical at first. After an initial burst of euphoria in the winter of 1933, Nazi women fell at once into despair and often into opposition. When Hitler took power, his Nazi women followers received public endorsement for their own separate sphere. Indeed, they were charged with the crucial task of carrying the Nazi faith into the "hearts and minds" of the millions of unbelieving Germans who did not vote Nazi. One of the earliest newsletters for women leaders underscored the importance of women's missionary work in the Third Reich. In her book, Gottschewski had predicted a vital role for women, and during the spring of 1933 she became their national leader.

> The New State would remain a fantasy, if it failed to create a new human type. . . . Our calling will be to inculcate into the new generation this deep transformation [*Erschütterung*] of the soul. . . . One must either belong entirely to the National Socialist cause or drop out completely. The individual "I" [*ich*] must become smaller, so that the "we" [*wir*] can expand . . . men will construct the state, we women will create the atmosphere, new morality, and purity.[93]

However, after an initial wave of rejoicing, Nazi women began to express grave doubts about their new masters. Nazi women, unlike their non-Nazi counterparts, had endorsed strong state intervention into women's affairs. Naturally, given their experience of the pre-1933 era, they anticipated that this would mean high positions in the bureaucracy for women and considerable autonomy. They wanted, in short, government support without state control. Gottschewski complained about women's status, and Seydel ridiculed local leaders' incompetence. Rogge-Börner opposed attempts to expel women from wage labor, and called for new solidarity *(Gebundenheit)* among women.[94] Zander and Siber conformed to the party line on "the woman question," but both women expected to create a powerful women's bureaucracy. In different ways, these leaders from the "old days" displayed traits that might theoretically have equipped them to become administrators in the new state.[95] Nazi men leaders did, indeed, intend to organize regiments of faithful women behind tightly organized male elites. But their contempt for women and distrust of any rival factions within the Nazi Party quickly eclipsed their need for competence. Women leaders, to be effective, needed to retain control over organizations they had created before Hitler's takeover. The Nazi state, however, proscribed this autonomy. Within a year of Hitler's takeover, no woman leader from the "old days" had survived in any major office. Guida Diehl, shortly after Nazifying her motherhood school, found herself demoted; Zander was fired within months of Hitler's takeover; and party leaders felt that putting the youthful Gottschewski in charge was "like turning the mothers over to their daughters' power."[96] Sophie Rogge-Börner continued to publish her newspaper, but did not occupy an official office. Paula Siber publicly supported women's retreat from paid employment and avoided any display of independence, but her protector, Minister of Interior Frick, could not buffer her against his rivals' attacks. Even after she sued the director of national welfare on grounds of slander and won, she was outlawed; but she continued for years to fight for reinstatement in the party.[97] Having edged all women out of national prominence, the party leaders turned in desperation to one Herr Adolf Krummacher for help in organizing the female half of the population. Under the slogan "German culture will survive only if men are willing to die for it and women are willing to live for it," the new leader took office without the slightest evidence he could do the job.[98] Krummacher's own unwillingness to play a forceful organizational role combined with complaints from his women subordinates led to his resignation in early 1934. At the local level, too, old-timers faced impossible odds. Seydel's oratory had roused audiences to action; but it was Polster's charitable projects that were designed to attract the "right" sort of middle-class respectable woman.[99] The message seemed clear: no form of women's autonomy could be tolerated—even when accompanied by the most fanatical loyalty to Hitler or Nazi ideology. Stalwart, idealistic "old-time" Nazi women leaders withdrew or were subtly expelled from the very organizations they had helped to create. They saw themselves replaced by more "respectable" and docile women—many of whom had not even supported the Nazi Party before 1933. The days of charisma had passed; the era of organization had begun.

Because Nazi leaders had neither established guidelines for women nor groomed a woman leader before Hitler seized power, chaos reigned for the first year of the Third Reich. Where could they find a perfect woman leader? Was the concept itself not a contradiction in terms? A married woman would provide an ideal role model, but would owe obedience to her husband above the state; but an unmarried woman who could devote full time to the job projected a sterile image. Moreover, an energetic leader capable of inspiring her followers would threaten masculine control. Finally the conundrum was solved when the national director of welfare found a thirty-six-year-old blonde, blue-eyed widow, with no record of independent action whatsoever. Her account of how she joined the Nazi Party highlighted her perfect image. Although her husband had long been a Nazi stalwart, she had devoted her time to raising her children and keeping house. However, one day he suffered a heart attack and died during an SA rally. Grief-stricken and enraged, Gertrud Scholtz-Klink pledged to replace her dead husband in the "freedom struggle." This mother without a husband turned out to be the perfect woman leader who followed every order.

## Conclusions

World War I and Weimar democracy shifted the image of woman dramatically without altering very much the real conditions under which most women lived. In the Weimar Republic something had appeared to be wrong with the balance between what Elias Cannetti called the "size and intensity" of the female and the male "crowds." Men, in the wake of war, economic depression, and political reform frequently felt insecure; often, too, they blamed their discomfort on women's emancipation from traditional roles. Despite a relatively brief encounter with new roles during the war, by far the overwhelming majority of all German women never in fact strayed from the conceptions of womanhood by which they had been raised and resented being linked with a few unusual women in masculine roles. These women organized massive national networks to preserve their endangered *Lebensraum* within the context of the strong family. Appealing to a special "womanly" nature, they reaffirmed their commitment to a social world in which male and female spheres rarely overlapped. This instinct had portentous consequences, which they could not have foreseen in 1933. Biological thinking—based on race and sex—made its adherents vulnerable to doctrines that dehumanized "the other." Social rhetoric during the Third Reich did indeed preach a realignment of all citizens along new lines, based on the national community instead of class. Social policy, however, demonstrated that Nazi leaders wanted merely a change in consciousness, not a new reality.

Hitler's state purged the ranks of Nazi women of independent leaders and incorporated "respectable" middle-class and ambitious women. Organized middle-class German women—by working within their own sphere of activity and outside the formal political system—had long cultivated the habit of ignoring the world they defined as masculine. Following traditional women's dictums, Nazi women epitomized the everyday "banality of evil." Carrying out traditional women's roles (reinforced by lavish praise from the state), they cooperated with war, genocide, and terror by ignoring it and helping to create an image that all was well. Along with broad sections of organized middle-class women, Nazi women believed in their spiritual superiority and saw their mission in terms of purifying their own social *Lebensraum* of alien elements. Even when not overtly anti-Semitic, this habit of thinking, in itself, eroded the ability to oppose racist politics. The masculine principle that so many traditionalist women had hoped would restore the family was removed from the father and vested in the state. Women leaders, under strict state supervision, organized millions of women and girls into a social network that remained remote from the realms of male power. Natural biological divisions by race and sex provided the framework within which Nazi leaders undermined independence, morality, and tradition.

This bifurcation of human nature according to sex severed women (together with the moral purity they were supposed to preserve) from any access to political effectiveness. While Nazi men brutally murdered their political, racial, and national enemies, Nazi women organized motherliness so the world would appear normal and virtuous to average German citizens and to the most murderous SS men. Thus, women became not leaders of their separate sphere, but raw material for the propaganda offensive that glossed evil with the healthy glow of motherly virtue.

## Notes

1. Gertrud Bäumer, *Die Frau im neuen Lebensraum* (Berlin: Herbig, 1931); Emma Witte, "Die Frau im Lebensraume des Mannes," *Nationalsozialistische Monatshefte* 4 (1933): 29. Male authors also used the term as a warning against an invasion of women, for example, Josef Rompel, *Die Frau im Lebensraum des Mannes* (Darmstadt, 1932). Joseph Beeking, in *Die katholische Frau im Lebensraum von Familie, Volk, und Kirche* (Freiburg: Jugendwohl, 1934), wrote a chapter entitled, "Die Frau im Lebensraum des Mannes," warning men of impending danger.
2. Richard Evans documented in his concluding chapter the continuity between the conservative women's movement and the Nazi state (*The Feminist Movement in*

*Germany* [London: Sage, 1976]), and, more recently, Christine Wittrock has described leading Nazi women within the tradition of Gertrud Bäumer, *Weiblichkeits Mythen. Das Frauenbild im Faschismus und seine Vorläufer in der Frauenbewegung der 20er Jahre* (Frankfurt a.M., 1983). See also Barbara Greven-Aschoff, *Die bürgerliche Frauenbewegung in Deutschland 1894–1933* (Göttingen: Vandenhoeck Ruprecht, 1981), 158–95; Maria-Antonietta Macciocchi, *Jungfrauen, Mütter und ein Führer* (Berlin: Wagenbach, 1976); cf. Jane Caplan, "Introduction," *Feminist Review* 1 (1979): 72–80. Irene Stoehr, by contrast, defends middle-class women's organizations for their perseverance under Nazi oppression in "Frauenbewegung Machtergriffen?" *Courage* (February 1933): 23–32.

3. The powerful Socialist and Communist women's networks remain beyond the scope of this essay because Nazi ideas gained little support in those circles and because Hitler outlawed all Marxist organizations immediately after imposing his dictatorship.

4. Moreover, since they saw it as their duty to represent women's special concerns in the "male" world, their mission epitomized traditional views of gender relations. See Gabrielle Bremme, *Die politische Rolle der Frau in Deutschland* (Göttingen: Van den Hoeck and Rueprecht, 1956); W. Phillips Shively, "Party Identification, Party Choice, and Voting Stability: The Weimar Case," *American Political Science Review* 66 (December 1972); 1203–225; Hans Beyer, *Die Frau in der politischen Entscheidung* (Stuttgart, 1932).

5. A comment by a Conservative delegate to the National Assembly in 1919. "Rede von Frl. Julie Velde, gehalten auf der ersten Nationalversammlung der deutschen Volkspartei," BA Koblenz, ZSg 1 42/45; Maria Schlueter-Hermkes, "Die Frau und die geistige Kulturentwicklung," in *Die Kultur der Frau* (Berlin: Herbig, 1929), p. 191. The author spoke in the name of the German Association of University Women. "The spiritual mission of the woman is to transmit culture, to be the container *(Gefäss)* . . . Men may create, but it is only the women who really understand them" (p. 195).

6. This dilemma, from which German middle-class women never emerged, has its parallel on the left in Social Democrats' inability to decide if their goal was to make capitalism more just and effective or to demolish it entirely.

7. Helene Düvert, *Die Frau von Heute,* 1933, p. 58. She continued, "Beneath chic professional clothes and a cool smile live untold numbers of genuinely female women, . . . who protect their individuality from the corrosive environment that would destroy it" (p. 67). Women's special talent was to "create *Raum* for the Germanic spirit" (p. 126). Or, as the ubiquitous slogan put it, "Equal in value but not equal in nature."

8. An excellent example of this is found in Regine Deutsch, *Parlamentarische Frauenarbeit* (Stuttgart: Perthes, 1924), 2nd ed. She divided women's speeches and committee activities into the following categories: women's rights, youth, education, population politics, motherhood benefits, women civil servants, nutrition, etc. Although women delegates occasionally spoke out on foreign policy, their participation in discussions of national political policy was extremely rare.

9. On the subject of the failure of German feminism, see Evans' excellent account in his *Feminist Movement,* chap. 8, "The Bitter End," and Bridenthal and Koonz, "Women in Weimar Politics and Work," in Berenice A. Carroll, ed. *Liberating Women's History* (Urbana: University of Illinois, 1976), reprinted in this volume as the first article; Rita Thalmann, *Être Femme dans le Troisiéme Reich* (Paris: Robert Lafont, 1981); and Greven-Aschoff, *Die bürgerliche Frauenbewegung,* pp. 183 ff.

10. Marianne Weber, "Die Besondere Kulturaufgabe der Frau," *Frauenfragen und Frauengedanken: Gesammelte Aufsätze* (Tübingen, 1919), p. 252. Only women's contribution as the "bearers of culture" could "reconstruct the general ethical level *(Volksgesittung),*" she maintained.

11. Evans, *Feminist Movement*, pp. 175–201. Rural and Urban Housewives' associations often combined their totals to enhance their impression of large size. These totals exclude other conservative women's associations, such as the elitist Queen Louisa League with 150,000 members (Buch to Krummacher, September 29, 1933, Berlin Document Center, [hereafter referred to as BDC]). Cf. Agnes von Zahn-Harnack, *Die Frauenbewegung: Geschichte, Probleme, Ziele* (Berlin, 1928), pp. 20–28, for a breakdown of 60 supposedly nonpolitical women's organizations.

12. Greven-Aschoff, *Die bürgerliche Frauenbewegung*, pp. 180–81, notes that only 3,000 women belonged to the radical *Staatsbürgerinnenverband* and that after the war, Heymann and Augspurg directed their energies entirely toward activities unrelated to the BDF.

13. Particularly in the context of the contemporary tendency to pluralize and hyphenate feminism, it is important to insist that these women were not "radical" feminists—a term that marginalizes them in the international long-term struggle for women's emancipation. The term "feminism" itself refers to a radical movement of women who fought and still fight for women's rights in the context of universal, human liberation and who envisioned a radical transformation of women's roles in society. On the historical accuracy of this, cf. Ellen DuBois' remarks on the origin of the term in *Elizabeth Cady Stanton and Susan B. Anthony, Correspondence, Writings, Speeches* (New York, 1981), p. 193. After the American women's movement had opted for "reliance on the simple fact of gender to unite women politically, . . . no longer understood itself primarily as a part of a larger political effort to transform society and achieve true democracy," and "no longer connected itself with the radical transformation of the sexual order and the emancipation of women from coercive sexual stereotypes," the *new* term "feminism" emerged to "distinguish the small minority who called for radical transformation of women's lives." In other words, feminism in its very nature *is* a radical movement.

14. Erika Said, "Zur Situation der Lehrerinnen in der Zeit des Nationalsozialismus," and Doris Kampmann, "'Zolibät—ohne uns!' Die soziale Situation und politische Einstellung der Lehrerinnen in der Weimarer Republik," in Frauengruppe Faschismusforschung, ed., *Mutterkreuz und Arbeitsbuch. Zur Geschichte der Frauen in der Weimarer Republik und im Nationalsozialismus* (Frankfurt, a.M.: Fischer, 1981), pp. 79–104. On the history of the Catholic Women Teachers movement, see Maria Elisabeth Backhaus, *Probleme des Frauenbilds der katholischen Frauenbewegung Deutschlands seit 1900* (Paed. Hochschule, Aachen, 1979).

15. "Der VWA 1929," *Junge Kräfte* 5 (1930): 50–52.

16. Renate Bridenthal, "Class Struggle Around the Hearth: Women and Domestic Service in the Weimar Republic," in Michael N. Dobkowski and Isidor Wallimann, eds. *Toward the Holocaust: The Social and Economic Collapse of the Weimar Republic* (Westport, Conn.: Greenwood Press, 1983).

17. Hannover Hausfrauenverein to Oberst Leut. Feldmann, Hannover (Chairman of the local Fatherland Party) May 26, 1932, Hann/320 I/69.

18. Marion Kaplan, *The Jewish Feminist Movement in Germany: The Campaigns of the Jüdischer Frauenbund, 1904–1938* (Westport, Conn.: Greenwood Press, 1979), and idem, "Sisterhood under Siege: Feminism and Anti-Semitism in Germany, 1904–1938," in this volume.

19. Fritz Mybes, *Geschichte der Evangelischen Frauenhilfe in Quellen* (Gladbeck: Schriftenmissions-Verlag, 1975), pp. 56–57. In 1928, 600,000 German women belonged to the *Frauenhilfe* alone (in 5,000 local associations); by 1933 all women's branches of church organizations totaled over two million (Helmut Talazko, "Frauenbund und Frauenhilfe," typed manuscript, Innere Mission Archiv [hereafter IMA], Berlin).

20. Olga Friedemann, "Noch einmal Hausfraufragen," *Evangelische Frauenzeitung* 32 (October 1930): 8–9.

21. Niederschrift, G. F. Fachgruppe, December 13, 1929. IMA, CA/GF 1353. The imperialistic aims in the female *Lebensraum* appear under the thinnest of veils in this article.

22. Since the early nineteenth century, Protestant women had participated in charitable programs to aid women in prisons, poor families, and "endangered" women. On the early history, cf. Dr. Ellen Scheuner, *Die Gefährdetenfürsorge* (Berlin: Heymanns, 1930). By 1899 over 5,000 branches of the women's association devoted to rescuing young women had been founded—with 528 regional offices and over 200,000 members. On the general issue of the eugenics movement during the period, see Loren Graham's excellent article "Science and Values: The Eugenics Movement in Germany and Russia in the 1920s," *American Historical Review*, December 1977, pp. 1133–164; and Atina Grossmann, *The New Woman, the New Family and the Rationalization of Sexuality: The Sex Reform Movement in Germany, 1928–1933* (diss., Rutgers Univ., 1984), esp. chap. 3.

23. "Die Frau in der Wohlfahrtspflege der Inneren Mission, 1893–1945," CA/GF1353/ Archives of the Inner Mission, Berlin, and "Fachgruppe der Gefährdetenfürsorge des Verbandes Ev. Wohlfahrt, 1929–1933." CAGF/1415/1/IMA.

24. Dr. Amalie Lauer, "Katholischer Deutscher Frauenbund." It should be noted that the Catholic Center Party ranked second only to the Socialist Party in the numbers of women it included in its slates of candidates and legislative representatives.

25. Gerta Krabbel, speech to the 1927 Convention of Catholic Women (*Freiburger Tagespost*, 159 [June 14, 1927]: 2).

26. Dr. Katharina Herkenrath, "Die Heimat der berufstätigen Frau," *Die Christliche Frau*, January 1933, p. 21.

27. "Fünfundzwanzig Jahre Deutscher Nationalverband der katholischen Mädchenschutzvereine," Deutsche Caritas Verband—Archiv (hereafter DCV-A), 172.m.2.; and Heinrich Auer, *Geschichte des Katholischen Fürsorgevereines für Mädchen, Frauen, und Kinder. 1889–1924* (Freiburg: Kath. Fürsorgever, 1925). Women's charity associations were founded to "combat the political confusion and struggles of the present day" (in 1893) and create new communities.

28. Doris Kaufmann, "Vom Vaterland zum Mutterland. Frauen im katholischen Milieu der Weimarer Republik," in Karin Hausen, ed., *Frauen suchen ihre Geschichte* (Munich: Beck, 1983), pp. 250–73.

29. Quoted in F. S. Nitti, *Catholic Socialism*, trans. Mary Mackintosh (London: Sonnenschein, 1895), pp. 409–410.

30. Cited in Don Dietrichs, "Euthanasia and Anti-Semitism: Catholic Theology in the Third Reich" (paper delivered at the 1983 meetings of the American Historical Association in San Francisco).

31. Protokolle der Tagung der Bildungs-Kommission des KDF, Bensdorff, November 8– 9, 1903. Typed minutes in KDF Archive, Cologne (hereafter KDF-K); "Katholischer Deutscher Frauenbund," *Kölnische Volkszeitung* 380 (June 3, 1929).

32. Antonie Hopmann, "Berufswahl ohne Beruf," *Frauenland*, February 1931: 40–42. She blamed women for their "feelings of inferiority," which impelled them to accept low pay; and she worried about "a weakening of self-confidence and a clear impact of spiritual pressure." All this drove women to a dangerous exaggeration of the capacity for fantasy and emotional life. (Speech from the Essen Congress.)

33. "Kultur und Wirtschaft," *Frau und Wirtschaft*, 11th Generalversammlung. KDF-K.

34. Kaplan, *Jewish Feminist Movement*, pp. 200–205.

35. Interview with Lilli Kretzmir, Worcester, Massachusetts, December 2, 1983. She recalled with amusement that when she appeared on the doorstep of "her" Christian family as invited, the lady of the house could not understand what she was doing there because she had never realized that Kretzmir was Jewish.

36. Joseph Goebbels, *Michael. Ein deutsches Schicksal in Tagebuchblättern* (Munich: Eher, 1929) p. 41.

37. A. Rosenberg, *Der Mythos des XX. Jahrhunderts* (Munich: Hoheneichen-Verlag, 1930), p. 512.

38. Hitler, *Mein Kampf*, trans. Ralph Mannheim (Boston: Sentry, 1962), pp. 412–414, and 441.

39. Karl Dietrich Bracher, *The German Dictatorship: The Origins, Structure and Effects of National Socialism*, trans. Jean Steinberg (New York: Praeger, 1970). Party members were seven years younger than the national average; leaders in 1934 were on the average eight years younger than the national elite; and "the average age of the Cabinet members was forty, while in the United States it was fifty-six" (pp. 273–274). "In 1931 almost 40 percent of the members were under thirty, compared with a bare 20 percent in the SPD" (p. 146). See also Hans Gerth, "The Nazi Party and Its Leadership and Composition," *American Journal of Sociology* 14 (1940): 517–45; and Daniel Lerner, *The Nazi Elite* (Stanford, 1951).

40. Hessisches Hauptstaatsarchiv, Wiesbaden, Darmstadt, Rep. G 12/B, "Neuaufnahmen," 1931–33, May 6, 1932 (Bl. 483–596); May 12, 1932, July 1, 1932 (Bl. 66–74); Nov. 10, 1932 (Bl. 1–232); and March 20, 1933 (Bl. 232–259), April 13, 1933 through May 15, 1933. Cf. Eberhard Schoen, *Die Entstehung des Nationalsozialismus in Hessen* (Meisenheim am Glan, 1972), p. 100.

41. This tallies with Thomas Childers, "The Social Bases of the National Socialist Vote," *Journal of Contemporary History* 11 (1976): 17–42; for a different interpretation, see Richard Hamilton, *Who Voted for Hitler?* (Princeton: 1982), pp. 9–36, 309–61. See also Alexander Weber, *Soziale Merkmale der NSDAP Wähler. Eine Zusammenfassung bisheriger empirischer Untersuchungen und eine Analyse in den Gemeinden der Länder Baden und Hessen* (diss., Freiburg, 1969), esp. pp. 159–64, 176–77; and Robert Ley, ed., *Parteistatistik 1935*—2,387 women who were leaders in 1935 had joined the party before 1933, and *Parteistatistik II*—5,536 women leaders had joined prior to 1933 (pp. 146–47).

42. Theodor Abel, *The Nazi Movement* (New York: Columbia University Press, 1938) and the more recent reanalysis by Peter Merkl, *Violence under the Swastika* (Princeton: Princeton University Press, 1975), pp. 152–53. Abel collected 683 autobiographies, and Merkl analysed 581 of them.

43. Hamilton, *Who Voted for Hitler?*, p. 364.

44. Seydel, "Die Frau als Hüterinnen deutscher Volkskraft," typed manuscript, n.d. (pre 1933), Staatsarchiv Münster [hereafter SAM], W-N/ NSF 268.

45. Hertha Braun, *Die Frauenbewegung am Scheidewege!* BA Koblenz/ NSD 47/14, 6, 9. It is worth noting, however, that the author cites no members of the mainstream women's movement (BDF) as evidence, but uses instead Martha Vaerting and other individual feminists.

46. Dagmar Reese, "Bund Deutscher Mädel" in *Mutterkreuz und Arbeitsbuch.*

47. Melita Maschmann, *Account Rendered*, trans. G. Strachan (London: n.d.), p. 10.

48. Christa Wolf, *Model Childhood* (New York: Farrar, Straus and Giroux, 1980), p. 189.

49. "Bericht," Bocholt, September 15, 1933, SAM/W-N/ NSF 74., and Ahaus to Polster, December 12, 1933, ibid., NSF 525.

50. Dornberg, interviewed by Frau L. Koller, 1940, SAM/ W-N/ NSF 128. For example, see the autobiography of Helene Radtke, in the Theodor Abel collection at the Hoover Institution, Stanford University (hereafter HI). Similar expressions occur in about half of the Abel biographies—all would have agreed with Maria von Belli (212) who recalled, "In those days there were only two types of people—those who followed Hitler and those who did not" (Frau Dornberg, interviewed by Frau Koller in 1940 in / SAM/ W-N/ NSF / 495.

51. Erich Fromm, *Escape from Freedom* (New York, 1956), pp. 235, 237, on the relationship of sadomasochism to Nazism.

52. Anna Zuhlke, *Frauenaufgabe und Frauenarbeit im Dritten Reich*, special issue of

*Das Dritte Reich: Bausteine zum neuen Staat und Volk* (Leipzig: Quelle Meyer, 1934), pp. 9–12.

53. Oddly, this obvious fact has attracted notice but little comment: for example, see Bracher, "The first point of interest is the 'male movement', the elimination of women from the new leadership" (*German Dictatorship*, p. 273). Some excellent studies have appeared recently: Annette Kuhn and Valentine Rothe, *Frauen im deutschen Reich*, 2 vols. (Düsseldorf: Schwann, 1982); *Frauen unterm Hakenkreuz* (Berlin: EP 94, Elefanten, 1983); Dorothee Klinksiek, *Die Frau im NS-Staat* (Munich: Institute für Zeitgeschichte, 1982); and Jill Stephenson, *The Nazi Organization of Women* (London and Totowa, N.J.: Croom Helm and Barnes Noble, 1980).

54. Gregor Strasser, letter dated August 12, 1932, noted the unique nature of Nazi propaganda and stressed the importance of "organization forms which are not dictated from the conference table, but grow organically out of the necessity of daily struggles and the goals which grow up from underneath" (Bundesarchiv Koblenz [hereafter BA Koblenz], NS22/ 348, "Geleitwort"). Hitler noted in *Mein Kampf* that "the function of propaganda is to attract supporters, the function of organization is to win members." In the day-to-day work of recruiting Germans into the Nazi subculture women played a key role.

55. From a nationalist and anti-Semitic family, Diehl boasted of her father's exploits as a German colonialist in Southern Russia before 1914. As a young woman she attended social work school and later worked as a teacher of social work in Frankfurt. Her thoroughly conservative outlook inspired her to seek out Adolf Stoecker, the anti-Semitic Chaplain to Kaiser Wilhelm II, for guidance (Guida Diehl, *Christ sein heisst Kämpfer sein: Die Führung meines Lebens* [Giessen: Brunne, 1960?], p. 166). For a less biased account, cf. Press Release, July 22, 1933, EZB/ B 3/ 441.

56. Guida Diehl, *Die deutsche Frau und der Nationalsozialismus*, 5th ed. (Eisenach: Neuland, 1933), pp. 17, 19, 54, and 129.

57. Diehl, *Christ sein*, pp. 219–20.

58. "Behind it all stands Mammon, scornful and cold. He recognizes his success and ascertains quickly where money can be made. By the search for pleasure, the easy life, and overheated eroticism . . . he enriches himself most quickly wherever he discovers laziness. Wherever he sees an open wound in the body politic, he inserts his bacteria. . . . Therefore we must fight against the origins of the evil. That means against Mammon which causes materialism and naturalism" (Diehl, *Erlösung vom Wirrwahn wider Dr. Mathilde Ludendorff und Ihr Buch, Erlösung von Jesu Christo* [Eisenach: Neuland, 1931]). In *Die deutsche Frau*, Diehl accused the mainstream women's movement of being dominated by Jewish women (pp. 61 ff.). For similar evaluations of the BDF (without the anti-Semitism), see Gertrud Baumgart, *Frauenbewegung: Gestern und Heute* (Heidelberg: Winters, 1933).

59. Guida Diehl, *Deutscher Frauenwille* (Gotha: Klotz, 1928), pp. 134–37, 143–51, and 191–98.

60. Zander to Hitler, May 28, 1926, BA Koblenz, Sammlung Schumacher, 230. On March 24, 1925, Hitler invited women to join in the "most masculine of fighting movements."

61. Dr. Hadlich, open letter to Zander accusing her of inability to provide leadership, Beilage to the *Völkischer-Beobachter* 4 (January 23, 1926). Rogge Börner to Zander, April 20, 1931, and Frau Beyer, DFO, p. 7, Breslau, 1931. BA Koblenz/ NS 22/ vorl 349. 79; Dr. Conti to Strasser, June 3, 1931, BA Koblenz, Saml. Schu. 230. cf. Jill Stephenson, pp. 41 ff.

62. Lydia Gottschewski, *Männerbund und Frauenfrage. Die Frau im neuen Staat* (Munich: Lehmans, 1934).

63. L. Kuehn, "Natürlicher Aristokratismus," and Sophie Rogge-Börner, "Denkschrift an den Kanzler," pp. 7–13, in I. Reichenau, ed., *Deutsche Frauen an Adolf Hitler*, 3rd ed. (Leipzig: A. Klein, 1933), pp. 36–37; and Pia Sophie Rogge-Börner, *Am*

*geweihten Brunnen. Die deutsche Frauenbewegung im Lichte des Rassegedankes* (Weimar, 1926?), and *Die innere Gestalt der Nordischen Frau* (Berlin, 1938).

64. Paula Siber to G. Strasser, "Düsseldorf, 20 September 1932, BA Koblenz/ NS22/ 355 appealed to women's Christian faith, while Hildegard Passow in Bavaria, by contrast, saw Christ as the first Socialist and praised Hitler as his successor (Hildegard Passow, "Geschichte, Blut und Boden," and "Sozial oder Sozialistisch?" *Nationalsozialistische Frauenkorrespondenz,* June 24, 1932, [Mimeograph]). Socialism, she said, meant not Marxism but sacrifice for the common good (BA Koblenz, NSD 47/ 37–39).

65. "Mein Kampf als Nationalsozialistin," HI Reel 13, 254. See also *Das war unser Anfang. Aus den Jahren des Kampfes und des Aufbaues des Berliner BDM,* (Berlin: BDM, n.d.). HI Archives. Eva Maria Wisser Wellmann, *Kämpfen und Glauben: Aus dem Leben eines Hitler Mädels* (Berlin: Steuben, 1933).

66. Frau Dornberg, Münster, interviewed by Frau L. Koller, in 1940, SAM/ W-N/ NSF/ 128.

67. History of the Steinfurth NSF, compiled on February 20, 1934, SAM/W-N/NSF 232.

68. Seydel to Hitler's Sister, December 27, 1933 SAM/ W-N/NSF 393. Cf. a speech given April 17, 1935, "Verstand und Herz," ibid., NSF 313. Seydel typified early Nazi leaders who traveled through the nation electrifying audiences with charismatic, homespun oratory. Goebbels once commented, "We have the worst writers and the best speakers" (Weber, *Soziale Merkmale,* p. 176).

69. El Polster to local group leaders in Westfalia-North, 27.9.1932. BA Koblenz/ NS22/ 355. She urged kindergartens to offset the "damaging influence of Catholic and Protestant schools," and (despite her imitation of religious women's charity) spoke not a word about religion.

70. "Mutterhaus," March 4, 1933. NSFS.

71. Maria Weibe, "Mein Lebenslauf," Abel biography 456. HI. See also "Nationalsozialistische Frauenschaft," *Hochschule für Politik-Berlin-Schriften* Abt. 2, 12–20 (Berlin: Junker and Dünnhaupt, 1937), pp. 5–6, for account of Schubert evenings.

72. Leonore Kühn, "Lebensraum für die Frau," *Die Frau* 40 (June 1933); Emma Witte, "Die Frau im Lebensraum des Mannes," *NS Monatshefte* 4 (1933): 29; Rogge-Börner, "Denkschrift," p. 13.

73. "Bericht," Hervest-Dorsten, SAM/ W-N/ NSF 265.

74. Fromm, *Escape from Freedom,* p. 237. Fromm compares Nazis to women, and cites Hitler to prove his point (pp. 246–247).

75. Anton Schuecker, *Zur Psychopathologie der Frauenbewegung* (Leipzig: C. Kabitsch, 1931), pp. 37, 49; E. F. W. Eberhard, *Geschlechtscharakter und Volkskraft. Grundprobleme des Feminismus* (Darmstadt and Leipzig: Ernst Hoffman, 1930); idem, *Feminismus und Kulturuntergang: die Erotischen Grundlagen der Frauenemanzipation* (Vienna and Leizpig: Braumueller, 1927), 2nd ed.; and Otto Helmut, *Volk in Gefahr. Der Geburtenrückgang und seine Folgen für Deutschlands Zukunft* (Munich: Lehmanns, 1933); also Edgar J. Jung, *Die Herrschaft der Minderwertigen* (Berlin: Verlag der Deutschen Rundschau, 1930).

76. Cf. Hugh Wiley Puckett, *Germany's Women Go Forward* (New York: Columbia University Press, 1930), pp. 308–13, and Annemarie Tröger, "The Creation of a Female Assembly-Line Proletariat," in this volume.

77. The American delegate to the congress at which Hindenburg spoke declared that the day of "the hunter and the soldier had passed. Today the other element in life that hitherto has been subordinate is emerging. It is the spirit of the woman, the spirit of nurture." ("Looks to Women to Save Germany," *The New York Times,* Tuesday, January 19, 1932).

78. Paula Mueller-Otfried, "Rückblick und Ausblick," *Evangelische Frauenzeitung* 34, no. 1 (January 1933): 49–50.

79. Ibid., January 1934, p. 50.

80. The woman in question was Klara Schlossmann-Loennies, "Stand und Aussichten der Müttererhohlungsfürsorge," 1932. Landesarchiv Berlin/Pr. Br./57/852 (Mutterdienst der evangl. Frauenhilfe; hereafter LB). See also her file in the Berlin Document Center (BDC), Evangelisches Zentralarchiv Berlin (hereafter EZB) /C 3/ 186, B1. 439–443; Jochen-Christoph Kaiser, "Das Frauenwerk der deutschen Evangelischen Kirche: Zum Problem des Verbandsprotestantismus im Dritten Reich," in Dollinger, Gründer, and Hanschmidt, eds., *Weltpolitik, Europagedanke, Regionalismus* (Münster, 1982), pp. 483–507.

81. During the winter of 1933–1934, Agnes von Grone requested that she be allowed to delay expelling "non-Aryan" women, but she made the demand of the National Bishop who, in any case, was a Nazi pawn; there is no record of either an answer or a repetition of the request (von Grone, 11 October 1933, IMA/ I 241, Bd. dv. Frauen im soz. Dienst.).

82. Kaiser, "Das Frauenwerk," pp. 484–91, and Michael Phayer, "Challenges Met and Opportunities Missed: Catholic Women in Nazi Germany" (paper delivered at the AHA Convention in San Francisco, 1983).

83. Bertha Pappenheim, Bettina Brenner, Paula Ollendorff, Dr. Marg. Berent, and Hannah Karminski, letter dated May 20, 1933, BJF XI (June 1933), 12. See also Kaplan, *Jewish Feminist Movement,* pp. 145–65 and 200–05. Cf. Else Ulich-Beil, *Ich ging mein Weg* (Berlin: Herbig, 1961), pp. 142–146.

84. "The attitudes of my most intimate group of fellow workers . . . most of whom were Protestant in predominantly Protestant Berlin, were typical of educated women. . . . Some came out of the battle with finer and stronger personalities, others lost whatever moral poise they had ever possessed. Long before Aryans were forbidden to talk to the "wrong" people, it was painful for me to see them because with every word they felt a nervous urge to declare their new faith" (Salomon, "Character is Destiny," unpublished manuscript at the Leo Baeck Institute, New York, pp. 234 or 243).

85. Quoted by Greven-Aschoff, *Die burgerliche frauenbewegung,* p. 186.

86. "Lebenslauf," BDC.

87. Gertrud Bäumer, "Umwege und Schicksal der Frauenbewegung," *Die Hilfe* 39, no. 9 (June 1933): 385–87.

88. Leonore Kuehn, "Lebensraum für die Frau in Staat und Kultur," *Die Frau* 40, no. 9 (June 1933): 515. Although the author published in the women's periodical *Die Frau,* she belonged to the Nazi women's organization.

89. Reber-Gruber to Anna Frank, December 5, 1938, "Bericht," December 3, 1938 about Reber-Gruber's protest. Staatsarchiv Munich (hereafter SM) /NSDAP. When asked about this protest, Scholtz-Klink admitted she did come to respect Bäumer, adding that during her first years in office she had been "naïve" in not appreciating her more (interview with the author, Tübingen, June 1981). Letters of March 7, 1936, and March 19, 1937, B1. 57–58, K1. Erw. 267/1 / BA Koblenz.

90. Helene Nicker Nylhoff, "Erklärung," 4 July 1933, Hannover 320 I/ 72. Hindenberg-Delbrück to Wilhelm, 14 September 1933, Hannover 320 I/ 72 I.

91. Papers of Reber-Gruber. Staatsarchiv Munich/ NSLB/ 1004 and BA Koblenz / NS12/ 1315 and vorl. 844. Clifford Kirkpatrick, *Nazi Germany: Its Women and Family Life* (Indianapolis and New York: Bobbs-Merrill, 1938), p. 89, notes that 25,000 women joined the ranks of the new Frauenwerk, or Women's Bureau.

92. Kirkpatrick, *Nazi Germany,* 43.

93. Gottschewski, *Männerbund,* p. 8. She quotes Hitler's speech at Reichenhall on July 1, 1933.

94. "Frauenwirken am Wiederaufbau Deutschlands," *Soziale Praxis* 42, no. 49 (7 December 1933): 1426; Lydia Gottschewski, "Neue deutsche Frauen!" *Teutonia,* Dortmund, 262 (September 22, 1933) in DCV-A/CA VIII/a) B.13; Seydel to Koch, May

23, 1933, SAM/ W-N/ NSF 393; Rogge-Börner, "Kein Abbau erwerbstatiger Frauen die Ernährerinnen sind," *Die Deutsche Kämpferin* (March 1934).

95. Siber, "Rundschreiben," May 8, 1932, SAM/ W-N/ NSFS/ 326. "Freiheit fur unsere Frauenbahn!" and dozens of letters on Zander, NS 22/ vorl. 349 and 355/ BA Koblenz.

96. Memos and letters from early 1933, BA Koblenz/ NS 22/ vorl. 342 reporting on harassment of Gottschewski.

97. Siber File, BDC, and records of the Oberste Parteigericht, BDC, especially Scholtz-Klink to Hess, Dec. 20, 1934, bl 357.

98. Krummacher "Die Organisation. Aufgaben und Pflichten der Nationalsozialistischen Frauenschaft," *Amtliche Frauenkorrespondenz*, October 25, 1933, p. 1. He opposed women's entry into the labor market.

99. Of the prominent early Nazi women leaders, only Guida Diehl seems to have been disloyal to the Nazi regime. During the war she was accused of maintaining contacts with Jewish friends and sheltering a Jewish child (BDC Diehl personnel files with the letters typed up while her mail was censored, esp. Grete from Leipzig to Diehl, June 29, 1940). Zander, Gottschewski, and Siber remained faithful to the state, which condemned them. Rogge-Börner, for reasons which are not clear, continued to publish her periodical, which had a circulation of about 2,000, until 1938. Seydel eventually relinquished all claim to office and sullenly withdrew from public life.

# The Creation of a Female Assembly-Line Proletariat

## Annemarie Tröger

*The Nazi agenda required control over women because of their pro-*
*ductive and reproductive powers. Annemarie Tröger shows how the*
*ideology of biologism was used to move women into, out of, and around*
*the workforce as needed. Rationalization had already created a labor*
*market segmented by sex. The Nazi state added political coercion to*
*market forces in order to ensure a hierarchical classification of jobs*
*with women at the bottom. This hierarchy depended on the notion that*
*women's primary occupation should be motherhood. Monotonous and*
*exhausting "gender-suitable" work, justified by technocrats on pseudo-*
*scientific grounds, was supposed to "free" women's minds and hearts to*
*ruminate on their "true" responsibilities at home. Thus they could be*
*paid less, kept unskilled, and, by being considered temporary, be made*
*ineligible for much social insurance. Such an elastic ideology of femi-*
*ninity met the demands both of the capitalist economy and the Nazi*
*state.*

### The Significance of National Socialism for Female Employment

The period between the two world wars was marked by repeated
government interference regulating and limiting female employment.
This was necessary because the normal mechanisms of the capitalist
labor market no longer sufficed to reproduce a sex-specific division of
labor. The historical facts are these: In Germany during World War I,
women were placed in "men's jobs" in industry to an extent previously
unknown. Furthermore, "rationalized" mass production was then introduced for the first time in armament industries on a large scale.
Both processes transformed the sexual division of labor, which had
existed since the second third of the nineteenth century, undermining
traditional skill hierarchies. The demobilization campaign of 1918–
1919 represented the first massive government intervention for the

restoration of the traditional division of labor. But other pressures pulled in the opposite direction. The great number of single women, divorcées, widows—especially war widows—now dependent on permanent jobs, contrasted with the stagnant number of available jobs. Massive unemployment, annually averaging at least 1 million from the time of the Weimar Republic until far into the 1930s, undermined sex lines in industrial and other areas. The wave of rationalization during the second half of the 1920s confused the demarcation between male and female work even more thoroughly and more lastingly than had World War I.

Although the sexual division of labor is nothing new in history and state interference to help "free enterprise" and to regulate the "free forces of the market" has been quite common in Germany, the Nazi regime is of special significance in this regard. Historically it is partly the product and certainly the heir of the rationalization of industry, which was followed by economic depression and mass unemployment. The attraction to fascist concepts of separate worlds for men and women—which we find rather peculiar nowadays—becomes more understandable in view of the far-reaching changes in production and the resulting insecurity, especially for men but also for women. For the first time in recent history, a government came to power with an ideology that made sex-specific employment an integral part of its program. It did not return sporadically to legal means to restore the old "balance," as had many previous governments. Rather, it used a whole arsenal of instruments:

—direct intervention in the size and structure of the labor market: the campaign against married women's employment,[1] marriage loans,[2] forcible employment at the beginning of World War II
—guidance of the labor market for juveniles: besides the much expanded Job Counseling Service, obligatory since 1936, a variety of services existed: Labor-Service, Agricultural Year Service, Obligatory Service Year, Home-Economics Year, etc.[3]
—the replacement of paid with unpaid workers, mainly in social welfare tasks;[4]
—the ideology of the "innate differences between men and women" and of "sex-specific work," which became something like an official doctrine

Almost all measures had a multiple function; accordingly, the political effect on the labor market was diffuse. But, except for the campaign against the employment of married women, none aimed at eliminating women from employment altogether. Rather, the general direction was for deskilling. Here, the interests of various partially competing pressure groups converged:

—that of industry, which wanted a cheap and disciplined labor reserve for assembly-line work and typing

—that of middle-class men, who wanted to get rid of female competition for middle- or higher-level white-collar jobs

—that of middle-class housewives, who wanted domestics

—that of agriculture, which wanted laborers with no other choice of work

—that of the regime, which wanted a female population that could reconcile the major goal of childbearing with readiness to perform diverse and vital tasks whenever men were in short supply

## The Two Models

Two kinds of patterns or models for female labor emerge from the jumble of regulations, group interests, and economic changes in the twelve years of Nazi rule. I would call them the "Blood and Soil Model" and the "Social-Engineering Model."

The Blood and Soil Model is the conglomeration of misogynist beliefs and reactionary social concepts generally regarded as the original or real fascist ideology about women. It is a product of the fascist movement—as opposed to fascism in power—and it appears in similar forms in other fascist movements, as in Italy or Spain or in right-wing populism to this day. Fascist movements are—among other things—an expression of a deep crisis of traditional male identity. The crisis is a result of large-scale economic change. However, the ideologies about and models of women depicted by the male-dominated movements have, first of all, a psychological function. They are intended to patch up the crumbling male identity and to define—*ex negativo*—a "new," splendid, male self-image. Only secondarily is there an economic goal attached to the female models. When they have had the chance to be put into practical labor-market policies, as in Germany, Italy, or Spain, they have achieved only awkward and contradictory results.

The point of departure of the Blood and Soil Model was the concept of the "two separate worlds" (spheres), the female one being the house and the (farm) yard, where the concept of "yard" was expandable according to economic necessity. The only legitimate role was that of mother or one of its derivatives in "social motherhood" (social worker, teacher, nurse, etc.). The type of women projected was earthbound, "barefoot and pregnant." Everything urbane and intellectual in a female was seen as a sign of "Jewish decadence" and "bolshevist and feminist excrescences of the liberal system,"[5] which the Nazis promised to eradicate.

The Blood and Soil Model had its major function in the years before 1933, when the Nazis were building their movement. It was a rallying point especially for middle-class males, who were anxiety ridden about

Jewish and female competition in a situation of high academic and white-collar unemployment, and for farmers whose daughters and female farmhands had run away in masses to the cities after World War I. This model served also as a guideline for the cleaning-up process in the labor market in 1933. It focused on the expulsion of women from all qualified jobs and professions, including factory work, until 1935. On the other hand, women were to be "returned" permanently and in sufficiently great numbers to miserably paid jobs in agriculture and households. But its success was rather mixed, even under conditions of unemployment, as I will show later. As soon as the economy picked up and the female workforce was in demand again, the Blood and Soil Model proved to be completely inadequate. Yet it was never officially renounced.

Unlike the Blood and Soil Model, the Social-Engineering Model was originally not part of National Socialist ideology. The technocratic elite of the regime developed this pseudo-scientific theory using conventional and fascist wisdom about "the nature of women," drawing on Social Darwinism and concepts of industrial psychology from the Weimar Republic. During the boom in arms production, it was perfected to provide detailed guidelines for female employment in industry and trade. These branches of the economy needed flexible availability of female workers: after an education in their "real" profession of housewife and mother, women had to work in industry and trade for some years. After marriage they would disappear into their homes, but not forever; they had to be available whenever needed. The programmatic inclusion of married women is new. Until then their employment had been considered a social evil, its elimination an urgent task for the Nazis. The economic and social background for the second model is the increase of assembly-line work in almost all industries as well as the increase in unskilled jobs for white-collar workers. Government officials and industrialists had already agreed in the Weimar Republic that the few relatively skilled jobs had to be reserved for German males, who should not be expected to spend a lifetime with meaningless work. This implied two goals for the vocational guidance of girls: first, to attract girls and women to the assembly line, and second, to prevent them from wanting better work than that at conveyor belts or typewriters. The Social-Engineering Model was conceptualized by Nazi technocrats at the beginning of World War II. Yet we do not find its full-fledged application until after the war: in the period of the "recovery" and the "economic miracle" of West Germany it is a fundamental and integral part of a new and more differentiated hierarchy of job classifications and wage differentials. Today, we are only too accustomed to this model, assuming it to be much older and an outgrowth of a "natural social development." But first, a brief account of the fate of the Blood and Soil Model.

*From Ideology to Policy*

The sexual division of labor was certainly not a Nazi invention. Nevertheless, the impact of numerous laws and governmental regulations combined with official propaganda about the different nature of women was more powerful than at any preceding time. On the other hand it would be wrong to assume that behind the propaganda stood a monolithic, centrally directed National Socialist policy for female labor in general. Rather, the function of Nazi labor-market policy was dramatically to single out a reactionary tendency from among several tendencies, to give it an official stamp of legitimacy, and then to leave further developments to a free play of forces. So the sexual division was promoted differently in various segments of the labor market, sometimes even in contradiction to the official ideology. Expulsions, dismissals, and demotions became most numerous in areas where women encountered status anxieties and fears of competition by a reactionary male majority, as in practically all academic professions and in the civil service. Dismissals from the civil service exceeded by far those of married women prescribed by law. The Law for the Reconstitution of the Civil Service Profession of April 7, 1933, also provided a handle for persecuting women who were politically undesirable or tainted with women's rights advocacy. The male colleagues moved so aggressively against their female co-workers that in the fall of 1933 the minister of the interior had to ask for moderation:

> In public service, I consider it basically correct to give preference to male applicants in case of equal aptitude among male and female employees. On the other hand, I have to indicate that in specific areas, such as juvenile care in welfare and parts of education, the service sector needs female personnel.[6]

By 1939 this preference had led to a decrease of female civil service employees by 5.5 percent and to an increase of males by 23.8 percent.[7]

By contrast, in the private sector of the economy, especially in industry, women were employed only in conformance with the actual interests of entrepreneurs—and that might be in total disagreement with National Socialist ideology. The Law to Decrease Unemployment (June 1, 1933) stipulated "employment of female factory workers in households, as far as possible, in order to replace them with men in the factories." State-Secretary Reinhardt hoped his "General Plan against Unemployment" would "effect a permanent shift [in the structure of the labor force] of our German women"; this "reassignment" was sup-

posed to cause a huge upswing in all branches of the German economy.[8] But neither carrot nor stick succeeded in transferring the still-
employed female laborers to the underpaid jobs in agriculture and
households that were considered important for the future war economy
and for the "battle for births." Neither the Nazi Party nor the state
bureaucracy was able to defeat a coalition of employers interested in
trained, cheap—that is, female—labor and women workers interested
in wages twice as high as those for agricultural laborers.[9] Men replaced
women in only a few cases. This was highly exploited for propaganda
purposes, for example, in the cigarette industry. But in these cases the
newly hired men gained a wage increase over the displaced female
workers at the expense of the already employed men, whose wages
were decreased in order to equalize them with those of their new
colleagues. The lack of success in "reassigning our German women"
only shows the naïveté of Nazi experts concerning the sexual division of
labor in industry and their ignorance about the fundamental importance of women's wages for the economic system. That does not prove,
however, that all these measures had no effect. Two were of great
importance for the troubled capitalist economy:

1. The Reinhardt plan combined with marriage loans created flexi-
bility in the female workforce: a faster turnover of female laborers as
well as of salaried employees *without* burdening unemployment insurance. Rationalized industry was especially interested in a faster turnover in order to get rid of "worn-out" workers. This was also true for
white-collar workers, where the number of years in uninterrupted
service automatically increased the wage. Greater turnover meant constant declassification in order to lower wages.

2. The "cleaning-up" of the social security system was more urgent
in the short run. This was achieved by pressuring women into undesirable jobs. In the Great Depression the unemployment insurance
budgets were in great difficulty.

In 1933, 942,000 women were listed officially as unemployed, and
the crisis in consumer goods industries did not bottom out until 1936.
These industries employed two-thirds of all female labor. Many were
skilled women who would not easily let the labor administration cheat
them of their support claims. And it was well understood that women
factory workers in particular could hardly be "persuaded" to work in
sex-determined jobs as household servants or farm laborers. Since
there were not enough marital or parental households above poverty
level into which these women could be absorbed, the pressure
mounted, especially on unmarried women, to accept one of those miserable "naturally female" jobs—or to marry. The National Socialist
government facilitated this way out of the existential dilemma by paying a "marriage loan" (to the husband!). Between 1933 and 1936 more

than 617,000 marriage loans were disbursed on condition that a woman relinquish her job or have lost it after 1931.[10] Between 1933 and 1934 the number of officially *un*employed females decreased by 445,000. In the same period the number of employed wage-earning women increased by only 300,000.[11] The remaining 145,000 can be assumed to have settled for marriage loans.

The first years of the Nazi regime are marked by the partnership of big business with government to structure the labor market. Such collaboration was not new in Germany, but was considerably refined compared with the drastic "demobilization" at the end of World War I, which caused politically dangerous social disturbances.

The propaganda for "innately female work" became a farce very soon because of the unorganized but massive resistance by employed as well as unemployed women against this proposed sexual division of labor. A separate study would be worthwhile on their protracted, bitter warfare against administrators in employment offices who were only too happy to agree to a sex-segregated labor market. Even in a poor district like Jena, where women could scarcely have been tempted by the "tinsel and sham" of a big city and where they never could have had a choice of attractive jobs, an employment official complained in 1934:

> The reeducation of female employees towards jobs which correspond to the nature and talents of women—the state's basic goal for the female labor force—encounters . . . resistance. This stems more from the personal views of today's generation of women than from factual or economic causes. Members of the "National Socialist Women's Group" should be expected to be the first to follow the demands of the state. Yet, despite physical aptitude for such work even they refuse opportunities for work in homes and countryside. This proves first, that it is almost impossible for the present generation to overcome personal dislike for real "women's jobs"; and secondly, that the wanted change will be possible only through use of force.[12]

However, force didn't help much either: despite stricter laws against leaving agricultural work, 61,000 women laborers still succeeded in moving to the cities. Even the younger generation of women did not conform to the earthbound ideal of "German Womanhood" despite socialization in the Third Reich. Indeed, this generation had only limited choice. But the urbane and relatively independent secretary remained a popular goal—as in the Weimar Republic. Between 1933 and 1939 the number of white-collar female employees increased by 19 percent (from 1.6 to 1.9 million). In 1940 the distribution of female apprentices signaled an even more obvious refusal to conform with a National Socialist type of woman, with 72 percent apprenticed in commercial, clerical, and administrative jobs. The remaining quarter subdivided into: 14 percent tailors, 5 percent hairdressers, 3 percent household help, and—even the officers of the Labor Department could not deny this irony—"We are glad to be able to indicate that at least a little more than 1 percent of female apprentices can be found in the category 'agricultural professions.'"[13]

The Blood and Soil Model was not a complete failure, despite its unpopularity among German women, especially of the lower classes, and despite its mixed results for the capitalist system. As a reactionary campaign with popular male support it was in general too erratic and noisy and too overtly political to guarantee a smooth functioning of the labor market in difficult times. Nazi technocrats understood that a highly complex system like modern capitalism needs built-in social mechanisms instead, which prevent or solve certain problems *before* they become politically volatile. But a number of "originally fascist" ideological concepts, political measures, and mass prejudices were worth absorbing into modern "scientific" social management. This is the real success story of the Blood and Soil Model.

Earlier I mentioned two major problems faced by the capitalist state and its planning agencies: (1) providing a sufficiently large and flexible (i.e., female) labor force for the growing number of rationalized work-places in factories and offices; and (2) preventing women from wanting anything better than work on assembly lines and at typewriters. The first presented no problem so long as there were sufficient numbers of unemployed women (and men) who were forced to accept any kind of work for economic reasons. This was the case in Germany from the end of World War I until 1937–1938. When labor became scarce with the beginning of World War II, foreign workers were brought in. The second goal, however, had already constituted a problem in the Weimar Republic, especially in the realm of white-collar work. An increasing number of women had managed to work themselves into permanent jobs as lower- and middle-level civil servants or into academic positions. This interfered with the unstable sexual division of labor in two ways: they took these privileged places away from men, and they served as models for the vocational goals of many young women. The Blood and Soil campaign against "double-earners," that is, against the employment of married women, had given only a few of these places back to men, since most female civil servants were unmarried anyway. Many more were downgraded, and new internal regulations made it nearly impossible for a woman to attain a permanent position against even the most unqualified male competitor. But stopgap measures like these caused too much trouble and political awareness among women and lowered their "work morale."

A successful regulating social mechanism had to begin in school, before girls developed a specific vocational desire. Here fascism offered a whole arsenal of ideas and measures. The Nazis expanded home economics and sports (so that women would bear many healthy children!) at the cost of mathematics and Latin. The fascist notion of work as "service" was applied much more consistently to the work of women: whatever a woman did at home or in the factory, was *for* somebody— for her husband, her family, the "fatherland," or the Führer. Wherever "he"—whoever "he" was—put you, you were part of a higher entity, such as the national community [*Volksgemeinschaft,*] and of a higher mission. But an average young man, unless he was part of an elite formation like the SS, could easily differentiate between his military service and his job or career, because of the awkward contradiction between this nostalgic concept and the practical values that governed his job-life: efficiency, achievement, and output. By contrast, the life and work of an average mother and homemaker bore more than a superficial resemblance to servitude. Why not extend it to everything else she did? Since no "higher meaning" or value could be offered in repetitive work, serious attempts were made to cast it in the light of service.

The obligatory service year for young women in their "natural spheres" of household and agriculture was an integral part of the Blood and Soil Model. It was vigorously supported by agriculturalists and by the National Federation of German Housewives' Associations, which had demanded it long before 1933. But the various services for girls— household year, labor service, agricultural year, and the obligatory service year, to name just a few—never got off the ground effectively before 1937–1938, after full employment had been reached and female labor came into great demand in all parts of the economy. At this point, the Blood and Soil Model had long been buried as actual policy. Although business and the military pressured to get a bigger share of the super-exploitation of young women, the focus of the services remained household and agriculture until the last year of the war. So it is fair to say that one of the major functions of the prescribed services was to create a substitute vocational ethic in order to prevent girls from setting their minds on professional careers.

One has to distinguish, however, between manual and clerical workers: the substitute ethic was aimed primarily at young women from families of the middle class and at skilled workers who looked forward to clerical jobs. Education for housewifery and motherhood meant no high-level positions and thwarted any wishes for upward mobility from the outset. Even discharge from jobs was programmed beforehand— with marriage. Under no circumstances would large numbers of females be allowed to become independent unmarried women living solely for a career, a role created by the pre-Nazi women's movement. This strategy of family orientation for white-collar workers is assumed to have been successful by Timothy Mason, who writes:

Among the female working population of the 1930's white collar workers were the fastest growing group. From an economic perspective these women became unproductive much earlier [in their lives] than any other group of workers. They represented a new type of house- or apartment-bound housewife or mother. This was the kind of family life promoted by the national socialist regime.[14]

However, for women workers, regardless of age, education in housework was primarily training for carrying the double burden of work inside and outside the home, which enables women to adjust their care for the family to the political and economic situation."[15] As always, women were burdened with housework and a job simultaneously. Economic necessity was an obvious motivation to seek a job. The sexual division of the labor market was not endangered from this point of view. The problem here was rather to find a substitute motivation to keep women working at the assembly line for low wages. The rest of this essay will deal with that problem. The mixture and blending of fascist concepts with economic rationality and modern social techniques will be shown in detail.

The class-specific strategy for the labor market corresponded clearly to the differentiated population policy of the regime. Its main goal was to lead middle-class women from the two-child family to a four-child family. They were expected to produce "inherently healthier" and "racially more valuable" offspring than women from the lower strata.

### The Search for an Assembly-Line Proletariat

With its takeover of power, the Nazi Party had also taken over certain key problems, probably without understanding them. Rationalization was one of these problems.[16] The unions, with the German Metalworkers' Union (Deutsche Metallarbeiterverband; DMV) in the lead, had accepted assembly-line production almost euphorically during the 1920s. Yet a little-known study by the DMV published in 1933 closes with the following sentence: "The machine has become a curse, whose ill effects can only be overcome by completely restructuring the economy.[17] It must be assumed that the continuing process of rationalization would have encountered great difficulties without the Nazi regime's violent suppression of the labor movement. In Germany, rationalization had been anything but a rational and systematically planned action. Instead, it was a headlong rush for increased production that produced unforeseeable and dangerous consequences. A contemporary observer noted:

The labor problem has been handled in much the same way as the problems of mechanization and technical reorganization have been treated; that is to say, in a piecemeal and disorderly fashion, without regard to or understanding of the numerous cost, efficiency, and human variables involved, and without any notion of the bearing of changes made in any one sector upon the solution of problems affecting the industry as a whole.[18]

In the context of the world economic crisis of the 1930s, this created strong antimodernization feelings in wide circles of the population. Opportunist as on many vital issues, the Nazi Party incorporated this one, too, into its hodgepodge of ideologies by proposing a simpleminded agrarian romanticism. The Blood and Soil Model has to be seen in this context. The primitive but popular antimodernization propaganda of the party may have contributed significantly to its electoral success. Once in power, however, it was plainly told by industry and the Defense Department that warfare simply called for a "modern" arms production. While some party leaders continued to espouse the old ideology, subdivisions of the party apparatus, like the Institute for Labor Research of the German Labor Front (Arbeitswissenschaftliches Institut der Deutschen Arbeitsfront; AWI), specialized in helping industry by getting workers to accept rationalizing measures.

> Workers, whether of National Socialist persuasion or not, still hold on to the Marxist and union position of rejecting criteria of productivity. . . . Controls over individual achievement are rejected. Therefore they resist all attempts to time them.[19]

The undue haste with which rationalization had been carried through in the 1920s had left the capitalist economy with many social and political problems, including changes in the structure and ranking of the labor force, the sexual division of labor, and the wage hierarchy. Underlying these problems were—and are—two fundamental issues: (1) In the 1920s, the International Labor Office stated that the "natural attraction of satisfying work is disappearing and has to be replaced with material incentives";[20] (2) at the same time, it was common knowledge and also scientifically proven that stress and monotony rapidly lead to human deterioration. The international community of labor researchers advised breaks, vacations, and sports to prevent this. But in Germany, the problem had to be dealt with more seriously, since the "impairment of health" had lifelong consequences for a worker. German industrial psychologists had argued in the early 1920s that the Taylor system of scientific management could not be taken over unaltered from the United States.[21] Such prudent concern for the worker seems not to have been caused by greater humanistic tendencies among the German technical intelligentsia nor by the fear of a labor shortage, as the amount of unemployment during the Weimar Republic proves. Rather, *it stemmed from the existence of the social security system.*

The German social security system had been introduced step by step in Prussia in the 1880s. Then and later, the German labor movement was very powerful compared with that in other industrial countries. In order to reduce the influence of social-democratic ideology, of "Marxism," labor had to be pacified and channeled. It was tied to the state by a social security system that remains outstanding to this day. Its four main pillars were (and still are) health insurance, disability insurance, retirement pensions—all dating back to 1881—and unemployment insurance, introduced in 1927. Half of the dues were paid by the company, the other half were deducted from the worker's paycheck. Under these circumstances, prematurely worn out or disabled assembly-line workers were very expensive burdens. During the world economic crisis, the financial limits of the social security system became painfully clear.

In the face of ongoing rationalization, German capital had three options in the long run: to do away with social security, to modify the processes of rationalization, or to exclude segments of the working class from social security. Doing away with the social security system altogether was a solution favored by the conservative part of the business community. Small shopkeepers, especially, hoped the destruction of the labor unions would pave the way for the "recovery of our fatherland." But it was wishful thinking, because no government would have dared to abolish the social security system, and certainly not the National Socialists. The populist element in their ideology and much of their constituency called for more social security, not less. Their elementary concept of a single, powerful, and responsible leader implied that he would also provide for those in service to him. Here National Socialism was in a bind.

In their twelve years of rule, the Nazis did a lot to undermine the social security system but they did not abolish it. They transformed social security into something like a bonus system, which could eliminate the racially "impure" and political opponents, thereby abolishing the principle of legal claim. By thus narrowing the *Volksgemeinschaft*, the Nazis fulfilled one of the most ardent desires of its populist constituency. At the same time, it diminished social expenditures—the urgent demand from capital. Yet the politicization of the social security system was insufficient and structurally inadequate to keep out the masses of workers that Taylorism would wear out in the future.

A second option would have been a "German rationalization," as was tentatively proposed by the AWI. That meant less splitting up of the work process and allowing for individual variations of speed. Industry reacted to these attempts to "humanize" the workplace as it does today: by pointing to its need to compete on the world market.

Third, the social-technical solution was proposed: government must create certain categories of workers who have no, or only partial, access to the social security system; these would then be channeled into the worst part of rationalized production. This is the option that was realized. In Germany, the fascist regime determined such groups biologically: working-class women, Jews, and foreign forced labor. Yet there were different ways of making these determinations. Preexisting social mechanisms, such as popular prejudices and attitudes, were mobilized and assisted by various administrative measures in order to create the desired labor pool. When German, Polish, and Jewish women worked at conveyor belts—all involuntarily—they did not get there by the same coercive forces nor were they kept there by the same mechanisms.[22] German working-class women did not undergo the brutal and coercive treatment reserved for Jews, forced foreign labor, or Gypsies. The policy of "extermination through work," applied, for example, to Jews, could hardly be applied to a group that was to bear and raise the next generation of workers and soldiers. German women, at least, had to be worn down slowly enough to carry them beyond the childbearing years. More subtle forms of coercion had to be developed. In other words, social techniques and ideology were called for.

## Producers of Ideology

Now I will characterize in more detail the particular groups of "producers of ideology" referred to previously. Most of the evidence given in this essay stems from the Institute for Labor Research of the German Labor Front. The German Labor Front was created by the regime as a substitute for the labor unions abolished in May 1933.[23] (The political organizations of industrialists, as well as their research institutions, remained by and large untouched.) Every employed person was forced to become a member of the Labor Front, with dues automatically deducted from the paycheck, making it the largest mass organization in the Nazi era. Employers and managers were also part of the Labor Front, thus supposedly demonstrating that class divisions and struggle had been overcome. The political position of the German Labor Front was unique in the spectrum of Nazi organizations because it claimed to represent workers' interests, and many of its lower functionaries at the shop level sincerely believed they were doing so. The populist element was stronger here than in any other fascist organization.

AWI, created in 1935, officially only advised the national leadership of the Labor Front; unofficially, however, it was probably its most influential suborganization. On the one hand, AWI worked closely with industrialists, providing them with studies and general economic information. On the other hand, it produced educational material for middle- and lower-level functionaries of the Labor Front, thereby having direct ideological influence on the mass organization at large. From its start, AWI regarded its major mission as the dismantling of the ideological and emotional barriers among Nazi leaders and followers against rationalization and Taylorization. In 1936, one year after its establishment, the AWI published guidelines on this tricky subject for party and Labor Front functionaries, rehabilitating the notion of a "genuine" rationalization.[24] Thus from early on it represented the modern wing within the spectrum of Nazi organization.[25] Although there were older and more experienced institutions, such as REFA and the German Institute for Technical Education (DINTA), which continued to work during the Nazi era, the AWI quickly gained more political influence than any other organization of the technical intelligentsia.[26] This resulted from its strategically favorable position as part of the political power structure, supposedly defending the interests of the working population, in direct contact with activists in the plants, while at the same time siding with capitalists on concrete questions. It would be too simple, however, to portray the AWI as a mere mouthpiece of entrepreneurs. For instance, the AWI was overtly critical of capitalists on the wage question.

AWI's publications did not present a consistent ideological line or political position. This is not surprising since it served so many masters. The cynical opportunism of these labor experts can be seen in the way they transformed their concepts of technocratic efficiency and their drive for smooth exploitation into populist, paternalistic, racist, fascist, or even socialist language. This cynical mixture was then "sold" to the lower functionaries of the Labor Front under the label of "German Rationalization," "German Socialism," or simply "organic" or "indigenous."

The AWI's influence on academic youth, especially in economics, business administration, and the social sciences, manifests itself in dissertations from 1938 on, in which the AWI is quoted diligently. This is predictable, since its publications were the only halfway coherent and intelligent utterances authorized by the Nazis, especially when compared with the stupid and contradictory statements on social and economic issues in the speeches of the *Führer* and other officials. Without overstressing its importance, one could say that the AWI influenced a whole generation of the technical intelligentsia and the managerial class—the generation that became active in postwar reconstruction and influential in the period of West Germany's economic miracle.

"Social technicians" and other experts in the Weimar Republic realized how inhuman the work was that they had created. Most studies of the 1920s reveal astonishment that people even lifted a finger under the new conditions. Industrial psychology of the 1920s had failed to provide conclusive evidence about personality types that would best endure stress, monotony, and meaninglessness. Even less had they found a specific aptitude for Taylorized work. Besides, the psychological approach had two economic disadvantages: the massive amount of psychological testing required would have been too costly for the individual company, and, more importantly, psychological selection was bound to stray into all layers and groups of the work-force, thus aggravating instead of solving the problem of social security by including German males in the pool of potential claimants. It seems that the heyday of industrial psychology ended with the world economic crisis. Sociological, or rather sociobiological, solutions were called for to solve the economic problems of rationalization.

The German Institute for Technical Education, which was controlled by heavy industry, reflected in general terms the rather simple-minded patriarchal social concepts of German industrialists. DINTA presented a dual-labor-market model: male workers were subdivided into two groups, an elite of skilled workers closely attached to management (the "company family") and a main body of free-floating workers not so firmly rooted in their jobs.[27] The AWI disagreed with this model for eugenic and social reasons. It would have destabilized many German families to the detriment of the capitalist system as a whole. According to the National Socialist experts, German Rationalization meant elimination of most skilled workers with their two to four (and sometimes six) years of formal training. The majority of male workers would be trained in very specific areas for several months and be called specialists. Subdivision of jobs and occupations was basically approved, indeed, even intensified, but only to a point where the newly created jobs still had some meaning and carried some occupational characteristics. An occupational ethos had to be established for every German male, even for the unskilled. The latter could qualify either as unskilled specialists servicing various different automats, or as an unskilled generalist, doing everything, including sweeping floors. That it was not pure empathy and identification with the German male that governed National Socialist experts, but also sociobiological considerations, is shown by the following quotation:

> One could regard the unskilled as a group of fellow Germans to whom fate has denied the blessings of an education. . . . Right from the outset such a point of view is mistaken; it is materialistic. It underestimates the natural drives within human beings . . . and the biological basis which determines qualification. . . . Lower qualifications of the unskilled have a biological basis . . . and cannot be changed by vast improvements in the quality of education. They are linked to the problem of race and the question of spouse selection.[28]

The occupational ethos was supposed to guarantee a motivation to work hard. It was combined with a more differentiated hierarchical system offering "advancement." The latter could easily be achieved by subdividing the formerly skilled jobs. Fascist dreams about a "new work order," which included far-reaching goals, such as a new nation-wide ranking of all occupations and professions, or an abolition of white-collar privilege, aimed to solve real problems in the capitalist system. But these goals were mostly unrealistic because they would not have elicited a maximum profit in a short time. Business did not take them seriously. Only when they gained a "hard economic core" were they put into practice—mostly after 1945. In 1940, when wages "exploded" because of the shortage of labor, the Labor Department pointed to the economic kernel of the AWI model described above: "Until now wage categories have been: skilled, trained, and unskilled. This is no longer satisfactory. . . . Experience shows . . . that the wage level can be maintained only through further differentiation of wages."[29] However, the AWI model of German Rationalization had the distinct disadvantage of not providing guidelines for assembly-line work. Its experts had been so preoccupied with the future of the German male that this vital part completely slipped out of their theoretical model. Yet, they were probably not so unrealistic as to believe that their German Rationalization would stop extreme Taylorization altogether or reverse the trend. As a matter of fact, the institute provided feasibility studies for management on the exact location and kind of manpower needed for assembly-line production.[30] Part of the problem might have been that there was little to be said about assembly-line work, other than that it was a health hazard.

The few experimentally validated results of aptitude research even contradicted the sociobiological theories of the new regime. The 1920s research about differences in aptitude among German males was mainly oriented toward and expressed in terms of the current biologically anchored "typologies of personality," best exemplified by Ernst Kretschmer's work.[31] If an experimentally validated result existed at all, it was that introverted personalities tolerate monotony easily while extroverted personalities do not.[32] But according to Kretschmer's original theory, women overwhelmingly belong to the extrovert type and would therefore be extremely intolerant of repetitive, monotonous work. Similar difficulties resulted from connecting race with assembly-line work. On the one hand, Nazi experts asserted that as a rule "Eastern and East-Baltic" people were well suited for the assembly line, especially for conveyor belts, whereas "Nordic" or "Faelic" people were less well suited for it. This, however, contradicted their own race theory, according to which Nordic people are introverted and Eastern people are extroverted. Logically, then, the "precious" Nordic people (men) would have belonged at the conveyor belt.[33]

The AWI experts did not even go to the trouble of trying to resolve these contradictions, since the social groups suitable for the assembly line were already predetermined by economic necessity. This corresponds to a general trend in sociobiological studies in the Nazi period: relatively little research went into finding out the different aptitudes of the various "races," compared with massive amounts of skull and bone measuring. That is, it was more important to place a person "correctly" and with "scientific proof" into a specific "race." Everything else followed from that: aptitudes, skills, personality traits. These remained untested and were simply ascribed to the races according to their value to fascists. Thus it was only consistent that, during the war, foreign forced laborers were paid according to their race and not according to their qualifications or the difficulty of the job. A minutely hierarchical scale of food rations and money payments was ordered, with the French (Western race) at the top and the Poles (Eastern race) at the bottom, and the other nationalities ranked in between.

Equally superficial and contradictory were the AWI's theoretical and scientific grounds for the lesser abilities of females. The favorite explanations of the nineteenth century, such as the lower brainweight of females, had long been proven untenable. Although these theories remained popular, the Nazi intelligentsia deliberately did not use them. After all, they had to uphold the fame of "German science" after it had been cleansed of "Jewish decadence." Thus, they tried their luck with the concept of "energy" fashionable in the humanities during the early twentieth century: the female body "consumes more energy for maintenance than men's despite equal nutrition. Through menstruation alone a woman loses twice her body weight in 27 years."[34] Consequently, it should have seemed necessary to accord women a larger share of food rations, not a fourth or a third less, as was the case. This was dismissed: "By nature women need less nutrition." Indeed, their digestive system was even considered incapable of dealing with a larger amount. In any case, women supposedly had less energy left for work. This in turn purportedly resulted in greater ups and downs in women's disposition in comparison with the stability of men's energy for work. The experts did not draw the logical conclusion that in that case women would be best suited for work whose speed they could control themselves, whereas the fixed pace of the conveyor belt corresponded to men's "stable" energy. Instead, they stated that the steady speed of the conveyor belt met working women's wishes.

The AWI principles on female labor convey the impression that the experts did not care to prove anything or to convince anybody; indeed, that they themselves did not even believe their own ideological nonsense. The point was only to establish a new sexual division of labor. In 1940 this was very urgent because the danger existed that large numbers of female factory workers would take over (unchanged) male jobs.

The shock of World War I still haunted the AWI. Crowds of "uppity" women had learned from experience that men's jobs were not only not harder than women's jobs but generally more interesting. Next time it would probably be more difficult to return them to their conveyor belts. Still worse: women had demanded men's wages then—and they were doing it again! Therefore, the Nazis had to fear for their still shaky and inconsistent division of labor. With war production speeding up, it was necessary to act fast. There was no time to work out an intricate scientific theory. Employers were repeatedly urged to "feminize" the workplaces—that is, to split up tasks—before taking women into war production. Under no circumstances should a woman be allowed to look into the inside of a machine.[35]

Everything the AWI experts said about female aptitudes had already been conventional "wisdom" among labor experts in the Weimar Republic. But National Socialism marked a particular stage in a longer-term historical development of justifications for women's employment at the conveyor belt. Before World War I, they had been purely and simply economic. For example, the metal industry had stated its needs clearly: "We prefer girls without education, in any case those who did not yet work in another branch of our industry so that we can train them precisely for the demands of our specialty."[36] In the 1920s, industrial psychologists hunted for noneconomic criteria, specific aptitudes and abilities in men and women to match the requirements of the new workplaces. Such authorities as the psychologist Fritz Giese[37] and the Viennese industrial physician Richard Hofstätter[38] influenced a whole generation of intellectuals, progressives included. The question of whether differences stemmed from education or inheritance had remained open. Under National Socialism, finally, the relationship was reversed: technocrats insisted that workplaces employing women be Taylorized because that allegedly best suited "female nature."[39]

Race- and sex-based work allocation is merely a means for enforcing a division of labor. If it works well, it becomes a self-sustaining mechanism for channeling the labor supply. Women no longer think of searching for any jobs other than those provided for them. Yet, while this may be an excellent way of forcing certain people to work at conveyor belts, it does not guarantee that these people will do their best. This leads to the issue of motivation, another problem left unsolved by the wave of rationalization.

## Mothers on the Assembly Line

Background "musak", storytelling, and pink walls had already been tried, but apparently they had not proven successful in counteracting alienation and instilling motivation. It was only in the late 1920s that social technicians realized that a completely different—an external—

motivation was required. They concluded that only a worker with strong nationalistic, political, family, and religious ties endured the new type of work well.[40] However, National Socialist experts were realistic enough not to rely on German workers' politics and nationalism as the motivation for work. They insisted with uncompromising rigidity on traditional work and traditional work orientation for the German male: "A man relates to his job best if he is allowed to work on a product from the beginning to the end. Therefore he is mostly dissatisfied on the assembly line."[41]

When the Opel plant gave older workers with heart ailments "easy work" on the conveyor belt (which exemplifies the urgent need for an assembly-line proletariat in the thirties), the managers were admonished by the AWI to let the elderly perform more than just one hand motion "in order to give them the opportunity to get involved and to remain aware of the meaningfulness of their work."[42] How simple it was, comparatively, to provide meaningfulness for women. Hofstätter had already concluded in 1929:

> Women endure jobs well that lack any personal involvement if they have sufficiently strong psychological ties independent of the job. Their natural ties are the family, love and care for their husband, their children, their parents. Within such an environment everything becomes "profession," the most noble profession for a real woman.[43]

The AWI elaborated on this idea because it seemed realistic enough. Not that they trusted the familial drive of young working-class women—especially of the generation that had grown up in the Weimar Republic—any more than the politics of male workers. But they knew perfectly well that the overwhelming majority of employed women remained economically dependent on their marital or parental families. Harnessing the family role of women to the requirements of rationalized production had the mark of genius. At least it was new and inventive for the social technology of the time, in contrast with the old-fashioned sexism of social biology. Everything in the AWI's major article on female labor was couched in a haze of patriarchal benevolence, so that the underlying formula is hard to establish.[44] This is another sign of intelligent ideology—production for practical purposes; in this case it was for managers, foremen, and installers on the shop floor.

The article began with guidelines for the recruitment of female labor. This had to be oriented toward home life since, for women, jobs were only means for securing typically female ideals in home and family life.[45] Women were so deeply rooted in their little community of the family that a general and long-lasting training could not be economically justified. Besides, they themselves supposedly shied away from extensive training. Under no circumstances should women be allowed to loosen their roots in family life because of their jobs; rather, employers should provide workplaces "which correspond to mind, feelings and different attitudes of women toward their jobs."[46] Above all the job must provide "freedom of thought." How could that be better assured than by the "most fragmented work, especially at a conveyor belt"?

> Because so little thinking is involved, the unskilled task ties a woman only loosely to her job and *above all only loosely to its purpose.* In her fantasy she enjoys visions of her children's happy faces while she is toiling for them, etc.[47]

Thus, the troublesome problem of monotony had been finally "solved": "The assembly line offers women the opportunity to reflect on their personal lives without any effect on their achievement, which automatically loosens the attachment to a specific (meaningful) job, characteristic for men."[48] Women could enjoy their fantasies at monotonous work so much that they would become captivated and would not leave, even at the prospect of better pay. This eliminated the need for promotion, a constant problem when restructuring men's jobs. Quite the contrary, since women had full responsibility at home, they were burdened enough. One could not burden them additionally with decision making at the workplace.[49] Another problem of rationalization, automatic tempo, was also solved to everybody's satisfaction. Because of women's abundant initiative in the home,

> the fixed speed at the belts corresponds to the desires of women who are employed in industry; they are spared responsibility for initiative on a job which has no meaning for them. Therefore, they gladly forgo control over the pace of their work.[50]

However, experts were still plagued by doubts if children's happy faces would suffice as motivation for the "biologically justified employment of women."[51] Thus, they also recommended to management strictest control over training, tool upkeep, accident protection, waste, achievement, and health. A whole battery of male trainers, foremen, mechanics, time controllers, and supervisors had to be available everywhere and at all times. (This facilitated promotion for males.) Obviously, women needed specific training methods "which are based less on systematically teaching a whole work process than on an actual drill of specific work motions."[52] Pavlov's experiments with his dog seemed to be of good use in training females:

> Women, more than men, want to see results of their work immediately; once that is achieved for a simple segment, training for the following operation is easier to accomplish.[53]

> It is useful to point out their progress and to praise them when an occasion arises because they themselves are not always capable of judgment.[54]

For the work with a machine, it is important to train her to service it correctly. . . . An explanation of its elements and functioning is not necessary.[55]

Even the oiling of the machine should be done by a man, whereas a woman could be entrusted with the external care of a "beautiful" machine in order to increase her motivation—and perhaps also not to break her habit for domestic order and cleanliness. A few pages later, the lack of technical knowledge, thus produced and maintained, is explained: "The internal laws of machines and tools are in principle alien to a woman."[56]

Of course, it was evident that the adjustments and drill necessary for such maximum simplified work caused "damage." This was to be treated with appropriate "recreational measures" in the case of males who were "biologically ill equipped." However, for women even this was superfluous: "Her 'innate' vocation is the best compensation as well as the best recreation when it is given sufficient time."[57] Even permanent injuries did not need to be considered because her innate vocation exempted the state from disability insurance expenditures.[58]

The need for a division of labor that forced certain groups of the work force into extremely Taylorized work must be discussed in terms of workers' access to social insurance, especially to the disability and pension funds. In the case of disability, the rationale behind social engineering is quite simple. It was already clear in the 1920s that no human being would be able to endure Taylorized work for a full, normal work life from age fifteen to sixty-five without major damage to the nervous system. So a workforce was needed that would either quit by itself, like women of childbearing age, or could be thrown out without unemployment and welfare benefits, like foreign and especially forced labor. In any case, it was necessary that a worker leave before the impairment showed or could be connected directly to Taylorized work.

In the case of old-age pensions, the rationale was somewhat more complicated. The amount of a pension depended first on the wage, of which a certain percentage was deducted from the paycheck with the same amount paid by the employer. Thus, the lower the wage, the lower the pension and the higher the direct savings for the employer. Second, it depended on the number of years employed, with a minimum of fifteen. A portion of women and especially of foreign workers fell behind this demarcation line. Third, the pension depended on the years of the life cycle during which contributions to the pension funds had been made. Generally, the early years carried the most accumulated interest. Combined with the wage level, which is usually highest for an adult, the years between twenty and forty are the most fruitful pension years for the average male worker. But those are exactly the years in which the average woman is most likely to withdraw from the labor market. Social engineers aimed to reinforce this trend, for instance by the required household year, in order to create the ideal, that is, the cheapest assembly-line proletariat. A double saving was involved: smaller (or no) pensions over the long run and lower wages for actual production costs.

## Women's Wages under the Nazis

Wages were the central issue of female labor. Women's wages were a determining factor in the restructuring of work processes and places. The same changes simultaneously destroyed the traditional "god-given" models for a sexual division of labor and eroded the ideological basis for women's wages. The painstakingly constructed edifice whereby division of labor, ideology, and depressed wages supported each other had already been thoroughly shaken by the massive employment of women in male jobs during World War I. But the problems created by rationalization were incomparably more difficult to solve. It did not suffice to force women back into female jobs as in the demobilization after World War I. Rather, completely new tasks and workplaces had to be designated as "higher" or "lower," and then defined as "male" or "female." It was an overwhelming task, considering that the old criteria and ideologies of skill no longer applied. Rarely before in the history of capitalism had the complete arbitrariness of job and wage hierarchies and the irrationality of wage differences been so blatant.

To complicate things even more, changes in production continued at an erratic pace, even in the same plant and in the same branch of production. In their narrow-minded rush for profits, employers first assigned the cheapest labor force they could find to the new workplaces and machines, without considering any kind of consistent division of labor. New general wage guidelines were still more difficult to establish because they would have been contested immediately. As long as labor unions existed—until May 1933—they were not even discussed. Government and industry themselves were puzzled by the overall development and were certain of only one thing: that the sum total of wages was not to increase under any circumstances, and that the share of labor costs in production costs was to decrease. From the outset it was clear that the redistributed wage pie would not offer a bigger piece to those who needed additional motivation and compensation for inhuman work that was threatening to their health. What finally happened, relatively late, was that wage earners were subdivided into innumerable groups paid differently according to either their political strength or other social or technical considerations. Meanwhile, the tasks ahead for the Nazis were enormous indeed. A system of frictionless task assignment was needed as were the ideological reasons for it. New concepts of work evaluation had to be found to provide a technical-ideological tool to restructure the work hierarchy. This in turn had to fit and legitimize the new division of labor.

In fact, as with many truly difficult questions, the Nazis did not do anything.[59] After taking power, they had no better policy than to freeze the wages of 1932, thus freezing all structured irrationalities and inconsistencies that capitalism in general and rationalization in particular had produced. But under the cover of the freeze, employers did whatever they wanted. They reduced wages even more as long as unemployment lasted, and increased wage offers arbitrarily to attract workers when the labor shortage became acute. This left the wage system—or whatever had been left of it—in total shambles even before World War II. A young temporary helper could earn more than an old skilled worker who had been with the company for years. New, fantastic wage forms sprang up to circumvent the official wage freeze, for example, lunch for the whole family in the canteen. During the war, when heavy industry could practically dictate the price of armament to the regime, it "swallowed" most of the labor force left, to the detriment of consumer industries and agriculture. A complete breakdown of the economic system was retarded by the import of forced labor—7 million at its peak—whose distribution and wage was dictated by the state. Women's real wages developed as one would expect. The average wage gap between women and men decreased somewhat in the continuing depression, since women's wages were so close to the bottom anyway that there was little left to depress. The gap widened again in the economic upswing of 1936 when men's wages rose faster than women's.[60]

Much more interesting than the immediate concrete development— and more important in the long run—were the debates in the upper echelons of the technical intelligentsia about a new wage system, and their models and experiments. One theme ran through the numerous publications of the AWI on the wage problem: the traditional principle of wages paid for skill and education had to be discarded altogether. It had to be replaced by the performance principle. Here the social experts continued a debate from the Weimar Republic. The performance principle was considered the only adequate concept for wages in modern industry. As motivation for work and for efficiency, it had to be unquestioned and all-inclusive. And it had to include women. In their relentless mission for the performance principle, they had probably overlooked all the ramifications of the problem surrounding women's wages. The performance principle, if consistently applied, would have been gender-neutral. The specificity of women's wage work became a political issue only as the war approached. However, the wage differential was needed as badly as under the old system, because a number of vital social functions were attached to it. Both the sexual wage differential and the wage based on skill had been mechanisms by which a certain stratum of the workforce—skilled male workers—had once gained a family wage. On the one hand, the AWI rightly pointed out that the old argument, that men support women, became more and more unacceptable as an explanation for wage differences according to sex. On the other hand, however, the family wage (for men) and the economic mechanisms securing it could not be discarded completely. First of all there were eugenic reasons; nearly the whole party leadership stood firmly behind the principle of lower female wages, because women's primary concern was supposed to raise a healthy family.[61] But it was also a basic precondition for their labor-force stratification. As has been shown, family, home, and children, largely supported by a husband's wage, formed an integral part of their concept of a female assembly-line proletariat, both for the type of work and for the periodic form of employment.

The AWI "solved" the contradiction between family wage and performance principle theoretically by one of its grandiose populist dreams: it prescribed a "basic biological wage" appropriate for the average performance of *all* workers. This was supposed to provide a livelihood for a family of four. It would have meant an enormous increase in wages. Therefore, it was to be paid only to "full workers"— that is, full-time, male, adult Germans. Young workers' wages had to be decreased through taxes and enforced savings. No clear directive was given for decreases for married women.[62] In any case, wage differences according to sex were to remain. The problem was how to present the concept *ideologically* without abandoning the performance principle.

Since social ideology was insufficient as a reason for women's lower wages, the reason had to be related again to the work itself. In order for the wage differential to persist, it had to be derived from and "proven" by the type of work. But 1940 was no time to fool around with populist dreams of a "new work order." Social technicians—the AWI in the forefront—had opened a can of worms with their performance-wage. They got support from quarters with which they themselves were probably uncomfortable. For instance, women functionaries and activists of the Women's Bureau of the German Labor Front, a kind of sister institution of the AWI, had put great hopes on the performance-wage to bring about wage justice, that is, equal wages for women. Suddenly, equal wages were a public issue again, in the worst conceivable moment, when equal work had become a reality not only in Taylorized production but also in the realm of traditional skilled work. How dangerous the notion was is shown by the following example: the metal industry, the major war producer, asked the Department of Labor for permission to pay equal (i.e., male) wages to women who had taken over men's jobs. The industry wanted to do this in order to attract women workers, and could have easily afforded it. But even protagonists of the performance principle like the Labor Front and the Labor Department were afraid to allow equal pay for equal work even in this relatively circumscribed area. The Labor Department warned mainly against two consequences: first, female colleagues who remained stuck in lower-paid women's jobs would necessarily become dissatisfied; second, men in industries with lower wages—and that was almost all of them—were even more likely to rebel against such high pay for women. An avalanche of wage demands would be dislodged and bury the whole national wage hierarchy.[63] In other words, the performance principle could be established only when there was a guarantee that equal work no longer existed. The only way out of the dilemma was to create "unequal" work.

As a matter of fact, unequal work, or a new sexual division of labor, became something of a panacea in the AWI's publications for all the problems and contradictions that had arisen with regard to women's wages. It was supposed to save the wage differential and the family wage, to provide an ideological explanation, to be a safeguard against real equal wages, and to solve the ideological contradiction between the leveling performance-wage and the sexual wage differential. Short-sighted and resistant industrialists were instructed by the AWI on how to apply the performance principle faultlessly without sacrificing cheap female labor. The example of clerical workers was used. Since the end of the nineteenth century, male employees *(Angestellte)* had always managed to leave female colleagues behind by means of a skillful pattern of task allocation and promotion. They had surprising success. The average income difference between the sexes was (and still is) greater here than for manual workers *(Arbeiter)*.

> The salary difference for male and female employees is a result of the fact that female employees are not promoted to better paid positions, or only in exceptional cases. But this is merely caused by the type of activities most of them [must] perform. In accordance with performance evaluation they can only classify for lower salaries. This does not mean that performance as such is evaluated differently.[64]

In principle, this model could be transferred to manual labor: "Most men rise to a higher level from modest work. Women, however remain with the simple occupations. They don't work in a lifelong job but leave when they marry. . . . Therefore, general performance principles for wages are unquestionably applicable."[65] Labor experts assured management in almost comforting words: "If women's wages continue to be lower in the future . . . it is because women usually prefer unskilled or semiskilled jobs, apart from specifically female professions."[66] In practical terms however, the experts offered only one piece of advice on how to install a sexual division of labor: repetitious, monotonous, subdivided work was by definition for females. This was inadequate for the armament industries, as we have seen. But even for Taylorized and semiskilled work it was not specific enough. After all, men had to be employed there too, since skilled jobs became scarce and avenues for upward mobility could not be provided in sufficient numbers. The silence of experts had deeper reasons. They had gotten stuck in constructing their own wage models. This has to be explained in some more detail.

The economic core of the performance principle was that rationalization, especially Taylorization and Fordism (standardized work processes) equalizes jobs and tasks. What would be left as a basis for wage difference and hierarchy was the simple output per time unit. But this especially has to be kept in very narrow limits to maintain a smooth flow of production. In order to get any wage differentiation at all, minute differences in performance have to be found and, if necessary, constructed. They could be found in the work process itself only in the case of skilled and semiskilled jobs: for example, five versus fifty different motions involved in a task. Yet even here the complexity kept diminishing. Second, the concepts of measurement have to be the same or comparable from one job to the next, and, if possible, quantifiable, to "instill the feeling of justice in the laborer," as the AWI put it. So the concepts of measurement had to be found in the human psycho-physical apparatus itself: physical endurance versus speed, constant attention versus fast reaction, output of energy required, and so forth. Here we find a tendency toward "biologizing," that is, internalizing external working conditions and requirements of the workplace, which was parallel and related to the ideological reason given for a female assembly-line proletariat. Most of the psycho-physical concepts had already been worked out by labor experts in the Weimar Republic, but no attempts had been made, at least not publicly, to bring them into an integrated scheme of wage evaluation. It was up to the Nazi experts or rather to the labor experts in the Nazi era (since most of them had remained in their jobs) to present models of integrated job-evaluation schemes.

Two problems remained to be addressed. First, a wage hierarchy does not follow automatically even from the most differentiated catalogue of psycho-physical concepts of job evaluation. Therefore a "value" had to be attached to the different psycho-physical performances (in technical language: they had to be "weighted"). Whether constant attention or fast reaction, whether endurance of monotony or decision making has a higher value—that is, is paid better—is essentially a political question, as the AWI remarked correctly. Second, even the most perfect new wage hierarchy would not have produced a division of labor according to race, sex, and age by itself. On the contrary, since the new wage criteria had to be derived from the human body, young people, not yet worn out, were bound to earn more than experienced fathers of families. This had already been a major concern of unions in the 1920s. And since the psycho-physical apparatus is rather equal in all human beings, especially on the level demanded by Taylorized work, many women and foreigners would appear on *all* levels, even the highest, of a new wage hierarchy. This in turn would have resulted in equal wages for women on the average, in spite of a wage hierarchy.

The AWI put the problem quite bluntly: wage differences according to sex, age, and family status

> cannot be derived from the work itself; they have to be derived from a value-system outside the sphere of work, by society and social politics. . . . Whether women or youth should earn the same or less for equal work and equal performance can . . . only be decided by popular sentiments and not by statistical comparisons [of work performances].[67]

One could have barred women and other unwanted people from access to middle or higher levels of the new wage hierarchy by a simple formal decree. (This stopgap measure had been applied against women in the civil service, but it had, as we have seen, too many undesirable side effects.) However, such a crude procedure would have undercut the incentive value of an achievement wage hierarchy—one of its major purposes—thereby condemning the whole scientific enterprise to futility and public ridicule.

Thus, the whole technologic process of establishing a new wage system—setting up categories of work evaluation or psycho-physical performance, weighting them, putting them into groups of equal value, coming up finally with a hierarchy—got stuck in a sociopolitical corner. It was like squaring the circle: one could not attach a value to any category of work evaluation or psycho-physical performance before knowing which social groups of the workforce would benefit from the valuation most and which the least.

National Socialism, with its blatant racism and sexism, helped social technicians to square the circle. One simply had to put the cart before the horse: by putting certain "low" people, said to be of less "biological value", into certain workplaces and tasks, one could eventually attach the label "low" and "of less value" to the workplaces and tasks themselves. Or, put in economic terms, by forcing people with low wages—

women by tradition, foreign labor by physical force—into certain undesirable and dangerous jobs, one automatically defined the wage level of these jobs.

This explains the contradiction of why, on the one hand, AWI experts insisted that women belonged in Taylorized workplaces, even if this meant creating them, while, on the other hand, fighting for a humane German Rationalization. Even the ridiculously petty race–wage differentials, which distinguished forced laborers according to their nationality, thus acquire a certain rationale. Meticulous differentiations like this did not stem only from popular hatred and prejudice; they came from bureaucratic brains. From industrialized countries like France or Belgium, mostly experienced industrial workers were deported, desperately sought by German industrialists, while from Poland and Russia masses of rural male and female population were deported. So it was generally foreseeable at what type of workplace the different nations would end up. Their "compensation"—below a minimum of subsistence—had to reflect the (desired) wage hierarchy of the Germans, though the difference be only a matter of pennies! Seen from this perspective, the AWI's theoretical reasonings gain a chilling realism: wages were no longer to represent a payment for extended labor power or work performance. Instead they were an "expression of the value of a working compatriot within the German community."[68]

On the assumption that the division and distribution of labor could be solved, by physical force if necessary, the labor experts could proceed to the next step of ideological production. In 1940 the AWI submitted its "System of Work Evaluation," which claimed to be a scientifically objective "ranking order for all workers using uniform criteria."[69] Not surprisingly, despite uniform criteria, assembly-line work gained a very low value on that scale. All depended on a "careful selection and examination of criteria," the AWI remarked. For example, only one of four main criteria of evaluation dealt explicitly with the specific burden of extremely detailed and monotonous work, "stress," which was subdivided into "endurance" and "responsibility." A woman at the conveyer belt could score a relatively high point value for endurance (3 out of 4 points) but she lost this advantage again because of less responsibility in relation to other work.[70]

The AWI system was not applied in the Third Reich. Yet this Nazi expertise contributed to the establishment of scientific job evaluation and corresponding wage scales in many industries shortly after World War II. They were pushed through by employers without major resistance from the unions, which were still in the process of reconstructing their organizations. A pioneering job had been accomplished with the scientific evaluation of assembly-line work. Criticism about the content and consequences of such work, widespread and massive at the end of the Weimar Republic, had now subsided. The experts had succeeded in defining work as "female and therefore easy" or vice versa. Wage categories for this work are still so defined today.

### Conclusion: From Hitler's Reserve Army to the Psycho-Trained Mother

The economically efficient use of the double burden—motherhood to regulate the labor market, housework to be a recreation for assembly-line workers, a meaningful family life to substitute for meaningless work—showed its full effect only after 1945. In the 1960s, researchers found that women with lesser qualifications and job opportunities were more family oriented, and that young female assembly-line workers were more inclined to marry with each year that their hope for vocational change dwindled. This means that the scheme of the Nazi technocrats worked. Driven into marriage by monotonous work, returned to the labor market by the narrowness and dependence on the nuclear family and by economic need, women provide the desired flexible assembly-line proletariat that never could qualify for full social security protection.[71]

Ideology and the image of "women's role" was modernized too. It now encompassed both motherhood and some notion of vocation. Depending on the economic situation, one or the other received a stronger emphasis: from a soldier's heroic mother turning out hand grenades for the war through the 1950s' efficient partner in reconstruction and modern mother, to the smart and aggressive career woman of the 1960s and 1970s and, finally, to today's psychologically trained mother who retires from the strained labor market to devote herself fully to the emotional needs of her overworked husband and nervous children. Thus, the Nazi period had an absolutely modernizing effect on working women, if that means an effective exploitation of workers, rather than a quasi-automatic road to freedom, equality, prosperity, and democracy, as some of its theoreticians at least imply.

Marx had recognized that industrial capitalism contains a tendency toward leveling and equalizing work. But the system carries this contradiction like a burden, rather than consciously encouraging or tolerating its development. Instead, its survival and the security of its economic and political system require differentiation and a hierarchy of the workforce. However, capitalist production cannot spontaneously produce consistent hierarchies and coherent groups of exploitable pariahs. Yet consistency and coherence are necessary in a fully developed capitalist system with well-organized and centralized labor unions; otherwise the hierarchies would not be effective. Therefore traditional models of former hierarchies, consistent patterns of racial

266    *When Biology Became Destiny*

and other prejudices in the population at large, and/or the help of state bureaucracies are needed. Developments for the sexual division of labor give evidence of this with particular clarity.[72]

Yet the question remains: Why was German capitalism incapable of dealing with the problems of rationalization without the help of a fascist regime? This cannot be answered outside of the historical context. A whole constellation of historical, cultural, and economic factors specific to Germany have to be taken into account. These include a long tradition of state intervention in the economy, one form of which was a comprehensive social welfare system; the absence of colonies (due to World War I losses) for cheap materials and labor; and the absence of exploitable minorities or "internal colonies." All of these factors joined to put Nazi biologism in the service of capitalist profit. In addition, the Nazi approach and organization had an edge over other parties in that it was willing to smash the labor movement forcibly. The desperation engendered by the crisis of the 1930s gave the Nazis the opportunity to realize their schemes.

—Trans. Liselotte Wolff and Annemarie Tröger;
ed. Renate Bridenthal.
Notes trans. Renate Steinchen and Renate Bridenthal

### Notes

This is a revised version of an article that appeared in *Mutterkreuz und Arbeitsbuch*, ed. Frauengruppe Faschismusforschung (Frankfurt/Main: Fischer, 1981).

1. Dismissal of women with employed husbands and of unmarried women, who could be supported by their parents. This campaign against double income was mainly carried out in the Civil Service. Compare Jill Stephenson, *Women in Nazi Society* (London, 1975); *Mutterkreuz und Arbeitsbuch. Zur Geschichte der Frauen in der Weimarer Republik und unterm Nationalsozialismus,* ed. Frauengruppe Faschismusforschung (Frankfurt/M., 1981), especially the contributions by Claudia Ossami-Said and Doris Kampmann.
2. The law to increase the number of marriages was part of an overall law, issued in July 1933, aiming to minimize unemployment. In effect, young couples planning to get married could obtain a subsidy of up to 1,000 marks, provided they were politically and eugenically "reliable." For each child born to that marriage, a quarter of the subsidy was forgiven. These aids were given on condition that the (future) wives had been employed prior to their marriage and would give up their jobs afterward. From August 1933 to July 1936, 617,390 such marriage subsidies were granted (*Statistisches Jahrbuch* 57 [1938]: 48).
3. The various "services" and "years" required before vocational training proper had more of a tracking—and for that matter, disqualifying—impact on the professional opportunities of girls than it had for boys. Since most parents were generally less willing to pay for their daughters' vocational training—because, so convention had

it, "they would get married anyway"—an additional year without pay may well have contributed to many parents' decision against such a training. On the different kinds of services, see Lore Kleiber and Dagmar Reese in *Mutterkruez und Arbeitsbuch.*

4. Unpaid or underpaid programs of social welfare, which particularly aimed to mobilize housewives into the labor force, were mainly organized by the Nazi Women's Group (NS Frauenschaft) and carried out by the Women's Bureau (Frauenwerk). See Susanna Dammer in *Mutterkreuz und Arbeitsbuch.*

5. In Nazi jargon, the Weimar Republic was the "period of the system."

6. Letter from the Reich's Secretary of the Interior Frick to the Supreme Administration Departments (Obersten Reichsbehörden), to the Federal Governments and the Reich's Governors of October 5, 1933. Quoted from Ursula von Gersdorff, *Frauen im Kriegsdienst 1914–1945* (Stuttgart, 1969), pp. 279.

7. See Dörte Winkler, *Frauenarbeit im "Dritten Reich"* (Hamburg, 1977), p. 64. Cf. also Stephenson, *Women in Nazi Society,* and Hahn, in *Mutterkreuz und Arbeitsbuch.*

8. Fritz Reinhardt, "Generalplan gegen die Arbeitslosigkeit," (Lecture, Oldenburg, 1933).

9. The average weekly wage of a skilled woman worker in the textile industry in 1936 was 22.48 marks and of a woman farm worker in 1937, approximately 13 marks.

10. Renate Zimmermann-Eisel, "Die soziale Stellung der Frau und ihre Einschaltung in den Arbeitsprozeß als Problem der Ideologie und Praxis des Dritten Reiches." (M.A. thesis, Ruhr University Bochum, 1976), p. 42. In the meantime, the deadline for applications had extended to June 1, 1938. With this, all unmarried women who had lost their jobs as a result of the Depression became potential candidates for marriage loans.

11. Comparison made of employment data according to the health insurance companies and the employment offices (*Stat. H.,* pp. 474 and 484).

12. Fritz Junghans, "Der weibliche Arbeitsmarkt des Arbeitsamtsbezirkes Jena" (Ph.D. diss., Jena, 1934), p. 78.

13. Census of Employment Records, July 5, 1940, p. 86. Analyzed by the Reich's Department of Labor, Berlin.

14. Timothy Mason, "Women in Germany, 1925–1940: Family, Welfare, and Work." *History Workshop Journal,* nos. 1 and 2 (1976), p. 165.

15. *Arbeitswissenschaftliches Institut der Deutschen Arbeitsfront, Jahrbuch* 1940/41, Vol. 1, p. 417 (hereafter *AWI, Jahrbuch*). A thorough presentation on the subject is given by Carola Sachse, "Hausarbeit im Betrieb, Betriebliche Sozialarbeit unter dem Nationalsozialismus," in Carola Sachse et al. *Angst, Belohnung, Zucht und Ordnung. Herrschaftsmechanismen und Nationalsozialismus* (Opladen, 1982).

16. Hereafter, I use the term "rationalization" in the inclusive sense normally used today: a subdivision of work processes, technological changes, assembly-line work, etc., including related matters of labor performance, such as psychological aptitude tests. During the Weimar Republic, rationalization was more often an economic concept connoting various processes related to the accumulation of capital.

17. The attitude of the Free Trade Unions (Freie Gewerkschaften) toward rationalization was actually much more complex and it changed with the business cycles. "Fordism" (serial mass production and assembly-line work) was very much favored, as the unionists assumed that it would provide the laborers, too, with a higher standard of living. On the other hand, scientific management (Taylorism) and the selection of workers by means of psychological aptitude tests was harshly criticized at first, especially by the rank and file.

18. Robert A. Brady, *The Rationalization Movement in German Industry* (Berkeley, 1933), p. 101.

19. *AWI, Jahrbuch* 1937, p. 206.

20. International Labor Office, "Die sozialen Auswirkungen der Rationalisierung," in *Studies and Reports*, Series B, (Economics and Labor), No. 18 (Geneva, 1932), p. 355.

21. This criticism of Taylor led to an idiosyncratic "German School" of labor research, particularly in the beginning of the 1920s. In contrast to Taylor's goal of maximum productivity, the German School strove for an average standard of productivity. Additionally, "differentiated labor research" was popular in Germany. It sought qualitative performance differences primarily through career aptitude tests.

22. A biological fixation on grounds of gender, race, age, and physical or social characteristics in the first instance only reflects ideological patterns and sets of social behavior. Those in power cynically reckon with those mechanisms because they make continuing political interventions unnecessary. However, the ideological patterns and social mechanisms with respect to women, Jewish and Polish forced labor, convicts, etc., are different. In most cases, the existing control mechanisms do not suffice to enforce the desired rate of productivity. Additional means have to be introduced and they are different for each group in question. Direct physical violence was applied to forced laborers, while German women were mainly subject to social control mechanisms (threats, social pressure) and economic pressures.

23. A general assessment of the German Labor Front in the Nazi state can be found in Franz Leopold Neumann, *Behemoth: Struktur und Praxis des Nationalsozialismus 1933 bis 1944* (Frankfurt/M., 1977). Timothy Mason gives a detailed study of the organization in *Arbeiterklasse und Volksgemeinschaft* (Opladen, 1975). A specific examination of the Arbeitswissenschaftliche Institut (AWI) does not exist as yet.

24. *AWI, Jahrbuch* 1936, p. 189.

25. Later on, other modern deviations from the agrarian romanticism and right-wing populism of the Nazi Party arose, for instance among the younger SS officers of the Organization Todt.

26. REFA: Reichsausschuß für Arbeitszeitermittlung (official name: Verband für Arbeitszeitermittlung REFA e.V.) was founded in 1924. It worked, and continues to do so, under the RKW (Reichskuratorium für Wirtschaftlichkeit), which was an umbrella organization of different institutions and groups concerned with the rationalization of industry. It was set up in 1921 on the joint initiative of the Ministry of Economics and the Federation of Technical and Scientific Associations. At times it had a more or less token representation of labor unions. For DINTA, see note 27.

27. DINTA (Deutsches Institut für Technische Arbeitsschulung) was established and controlled by coal and steel industrialists. Brady, comments that "of all the attempts to influence the workers, perhaps the most extensive, and certainly the boldest, is that of DINTA. Its purpose is that of 'utilizing human motive force to the best advantage' of the owners of productive equipment" (*Rationalization Movement*, p. 82).

28. *AWI*, "Zur Frage der Ungelernten," *Jahrbuch* 1940/41, Vol. 1, pp. 334 and 341.

29. The Reich's Minister of Labor in an address to the Reich's trustees of labor, February 9, 1940, Bundesarchiv Koblenz: R 41/57, Sheet 4, quoted from Tilla Siegel, "Lohnpolitik im nationalsozialistischen Deutschland," in Sachse et al., *Angst, Belohnung, Zucht und Ordnung*.

30. *AWI*, "Die Einsatzfähigkeit von Arbeitskräften für Fließbandarbeiten," *Jahrbuch* 1939, Vol. 1, p. 450.

31. The theories of typology—having undergone a variegated history from the times of the ancient Greeks—had a renaissance during the Weimar Republic. Their underlying idea is to systematize certain affinities between physical appearance and character traits and to put them into a theoretical framework. (Their attraction for "race theoreticians" is obvious.) The psychiatrist Ernst Kretschmer became one of their most outstanding exponents with his book *Körperbau und Charakter* (1921). To the

researchers on labor—who derived from the Behaviorist tradition—typology offered a method of bringing psychotechnical data into a reasonable and practical context.

32. Cf. Herbert Wunderlich, "Die Einwirkung einförmiger zwangsläufiger Arbeit auf die Persönlichkeitsstruktur," in *Schriften zur Psychologie der Berufseignung und des Wirtschaftslebens*, Vol. 31 (Leipzig, 1925).

33. AWI, "Die Einsatzfähigkeit von Arbeitskräften für Fließbandarbeiten," *Jahrbuch* 1939, p. 447.

34. AWI, "Zum Arbeitseinsatz der Frau in Industrie und Handwerk," *Jahrbuch* 1940/41, Vol. 1, pp. 373ff.

35. This warning appears often and vehemently in fascist literature. It can be assumed that it is more than a simple social technique to prevent women from learning to master machines. The general woman/machine phobia among men seems to be especially strong among fascist men. In the last years of the war, the shortage of skilled labor was so desperate that the National Socialist government even offered money to employers to train women for skilled jobs. Industrialists mostly refused, preferring foreign male workers. However, this does not prove that the regime had given up its principle of a sexual division of labor and even less that part of the Nazi elite was more progressive in this regard than business, as has been suggested (see Dörte Winkler, *Frauenarbeit*). Rather, it demonstrates different assessments of the actual situation. The Nazi regime clung to every straw to bring about the "final victory," whereas industrialists, like the majority of the population, were already preparing for the "final defeat." Why should they, at the last minute, increase the potential for social unrest, which their experience at the end of World War I had taught them to fear? Foreign workers were expected to go home, but women workers would stay, "overqualified" and dissatisfied with their women's work, needed but spoiled for the business of reconstruction.

36. Elisabeth Altmann-Gottheiner, *Die Entwicklung der Frauenarbeit in der Metallindustrie. Schriften des Ständigen Ausschusses zur Förderung der Arbeiterinneninteressen*, Vol. 8 (Jena, 1916), pp. 8 and 18ff.

37. Of the vast amount of literature during the Weimar era dealing with the "psychology of gender differences," I mention only Fritz Giese, because he was also rated as one of the labor research experts at the time. See his *Psychologische Beiträge*, Vol. 1 (Halle, 1916). Idem. *Körper, Seele* (Munich, 1924), and *Die Frau als Atmosphärenwert* (Munich, 1926).

38. Richard Hofstätter, *Die arbeitende Frau* (Vienna, 1929).

39. AWI, "Zum Arbeitseinsatz der Frau," *Jahrbuch* 1940/41, p. 399.

40. Hofstätter, *Die arbeitende Frau*, p. 5.

41. AWI, "Arbeitseinsatz," *Jahrbuch* 1940/41, p. 398.

42. AWI, "Berufsschicksal und Arbeitsbeanspruchung," *Jahrbuch* 1940/41, Vol. 2, p. 208.

43. Hofstätter, *Die arbeitende Frau*, p. 5.

44. AWI, "Arbeitseinsatz," p. 373.

45. Ibid., p. 385.

46. Ibid., p. 386.

47. Ibid., p. 399. Emphasis added.

48. Ibid., p. 399.

49. Ibid., p. 392.

50. Ibid., p. 399.

51. Ibid., p. 406.

52. Ibid., p. 378.

53. Ibid., p. 378.

54. Ibid., p. 390.

55. Ibid., p. 393.

56. Ibid., p. 395.
57. *AWI*, "Arbeitseinsatz, p. 400.
58. *AWI*, "Die Einsatzfähigkeit."
59. On the attempt to restructure the wages, see Siegel.
60. The most important works concerning wage progression of women industrial workers are as follows: Theoretical analyses: Hans Sperling, *Die ökonomischen Gründe für die Minderbezahlung der weiblichen Arbeitskraft* (Berlin, 1930):, Elisabeth Oehlandt, *Deutsche Industriearbeiterinnenlöhne 1928–1935. Hamburger Wirtschafts—und sozial—wissenschaftliche Schriften* 10 (1937).
    Statistical data: Henry Braunwarth, *Die Spanne zwischen Männer-und Frauenlöhnen* (Cologne, 1955); Gerhard Bry, *Wages in Germany 1871–1945*, National Bureau of Economic Research 68, General Series (Princeton, 1960).
    See also one chapter in Angelika Meister, "Die deutsche Industriearbeiterin. Ein Beitrag zum Problem der Frauenerwerbsarbeit" (Ph.D. diss., Jena, 1939).
61. Several alternatives to the family wage were proposed during the Nazi era, especially by population experts. They ranged from state subsidies through "family insurance" (comparable to the social security system) through a heavy taxation of unmarried wage earners. which succeeded because it was the least costly. It is in use to this day.
62. This problem is dealt with in several publications of the AWI concerning wage policies. See *AWI*, "Zur Problematik einer Reichslohnordnung."
63. Winkler, *Frauenarbeit*, p. 75.
64. *AWI*, "Das Problem der Arbeiter und Angestellten." *Jahrbuch* 1940/41, Vol. 1, p. 297.
65. Ibid.
66. *AWI*, "Zur Problematik," p. 184.
67. *AWI*, "Die politische Aufgabe der Lohnordnung," *Jahrbuch* 1940/41, Vol. 1, p. 175.
68. *AWI*, "Politische Maßstäbe der Lohnbildung," *Jahrbuch* 1937, p. 22.
69. *AWI*, "Entwicklung und Begründung eines Systems der Arbeitsbewertung," *Jahrbuch* 1940/41, Vol. 1, p. 220. The political background that furthered the development of such a system was not so much related to women's wages as to the general disorder of wage levels due to the rapid growth of the armament industry. Primarily, however, it came about through the wage rises due to a shortage of laborers. Cf. Siegel. In 1942, the iron and metal wage classification catalogue was introduced into some of these industrial sectors. The AWI and the Ministry of Labor in conjunction with the industrialists' organization designed it. It was the first attempt to create a wage system based on evaluations of productivity. I cannot say how much of an impact the AWI's system of productivity measurements had during the postwar period.
70. Ibid., pp. 239ff. An exact study of implicit sexism in the scientific analyses of productivity would have to be based on concrete data of how sexism was reflected in wages, which do not exist for this AWI system. A critical feminist evaluation of contemporary systems of a similar kind does not exist as yet either.
71. Cf. E. Pfeil, *Die Berufstätigkeit von Müttern* (Tübingen, 1961); Elfriede Höhn, *Das berufliche Fortkommen der Frau* (Bad Harzburg/Frankfurt/M., 1964). These works are criticized in SOFI/RKW, *Frauenarbeit und technischer Wandel* (Göttingen, 1973).
72. Cf. Ute Gerhard, *Verhältnisse und Verhinderungen. Frauenarbeit, Familie und Rechte der Frauen im 19. Jahrhundert* (Frankfurt/M, 1978), p. 52. Concerning job opportunities in the nineteenth century, Gerhard comes to the conclusion that the inequities for women in this field can be understood only as a result of juridical discrimination of various sorts and prevailing ideologies concerning the family.

# Racism and Sexism in Nazi Germany: Motherhood, Compulsory Sterilization, and the State

## Gisela Bock

*If Annemarie Tröger shows an elastic, even hypocritical, ideology of femininity in Nazi Germany, Gisela Bock shows an increasingly rigid ideology of racism, used to the same ends: social control, social cohesion, and relief from the expense of maintaining an increasing number of "undesirables" in the welfare system. The Nazi state extolled and materially supported motherhood and housework as the proper fate of certain "well-bred" Aryan women, while mandating sterilization and forced labor for the economically "unfit" and the racially and morally "deviant." The mere threat of sterilization enforced acceptable behavior. Furthermore, hierarchies of "valuable" and "valueless" life were used to justify euthanasia and, finally, extermination. On the other hand, "pro-family" measures for the racially, morally, economically, and politically acceptable groups also oppressed women, though in different ways. Race hygiene and a sexism that denied all women control over their own bodies were first used in class politics. They heralded the mass murder of Jews and non-Germans.*

### "Alien Races" and the "Other Sex"

By presenting some largely unexplored features of women's lives under National Socialism in Germany, this essay considers larger questions about the complex connections between racism and sexism. It does not presume to exhaust the issue, or even touch on all its aspects. Instead, it approaches it through the perspective of one part of women's lives affected by state policy: reproduction or, as I prefer to call it, the reproductive aspect of women's unwaged housework. It can be no more than a contribution for two reasons. First, dealing with racism in Germany during this period involves considering an unparalleled mass murder of millions of women and men, an undertaking beyond the scope of any single essay. Second, this analysis is a first approach, for neither race nor gender, racism nor sexism—and even less their connection—has been a central theme in German social historiography.[1] When historians deal with women in modern Germany, they generally do not consider racism or racial discrimination against women,[2] while the literature dealing with anti-Jewish racism and the Holocaust generally does not consider either women's specific situation or the added factor of sexism.

The extent to which the racist tradition was concerned with those activities that then and now are considered "women's sphere"—that is, bearing and rearing children—has also not been recognized. Perhaps we might argue even further that a large part of this racist tradition remained invisible precisely because the history of women and of their work in the family was not an issue for (mostly male) historians and theoreticians.[3]

To make the issue of motherhood and compulsory sterilization the center of discussion places the focus not so much on anti-Jewish racism, on which we have an extended literature, as on another form of racism: eugenics, or, as it was called before and during the Nazi regime and sometimes also in Anglo-Saxon literature, race hygiene.[4] It comprises a vast field of more or less popular, more or less scientific, traditions, which became the core of population policies throughout the Nazi regime.

Beyond the plain yet unexplored fact that at least half of those persecuted on racial grounds were women, there are more subtle reasons for women's historians' interest in the "scientific" or eugenic form of racism. The race hygiene discourse since the end of the nineteenth century deals with women much more than do most other social or political theories, since women have been hailed as "mothers of the race," or, in stark contrast, vilified as the ones guilty of "racial degeneration." Then, too, definitions of race hygiene made at the time show some conscious links between this field and women's history, describing it, for instance, as "procreation hygiene" *(Fortpflanzungshygiene).*[5] In fact, we might consider that most of the scientific and pseudoscientific superstructure of eugenic racism, especially its mythology of hereditary character traits, is concerned with the supposedly "natural" or "biological" domains in which women are prominent—body, sexuality, procreation, education—the heretofore "private" sphere.[6]

For a third reason, eugenics and racism in general are significant to women's history. After a long hiatus, the result in part of Nazism, interest in the history of women in Germany has seen a revival during the past half decade or more. However, this interest has focused almost exclusively on the historical reconstruction and critique of those norms and traditions that underlined women's "natural" destiny as wives, mothers, and homemakers whose work was not paid. Those with this perspective see National Socialism as either a culmination of, or a reactionary return to, belief in women's "traditional" role as mothers and housewives; motherhood and housework become essential factors in a backward, premodern, or precapitalist "role" assigned to women.[7]

Thus most historians seem to agree that under the Nazi regime women counted merely as mothers who should bear and rear as many children as possible, and that Nazi antifeminism tended to promote, protect, and even finance women as childbearers, housewives, and mothers. It seems necessary to challenge various aspects of this widely held opinion, but particularly its neglect of racism.[8] Printed and archival sources on Nazi policies, passages from Hitler's writings, other often-quoted sources like the Minister of Agriculture Walter Darré's breeding concepts, and documents from the lower echelons of the state and party hierarchy[9] show quite clearly that the Nazis were by no means simply interested in raising the number of childbearing women. They were just as bent on excluding many women from bearing and rearing children—and men from begetting them—with sterilization as their principal deterrent. It is true that the available literature does not altogether lose sight of these latter women. However, they are at best briefly hinted at, between quotation marks and parentheses, as mere negations of the "Aryan," the "racially and hereditarily pure"; the general conclusions on "women in Nazi society" usually neglect them further.[10]

Although the desirability of a new perspective seems clear, the historical singularity of the Holocaust and the need for more research before models can be constructed qualify the extent to which we may compare the interaction of racism and sexism under Nazism and under other historical conditions.[11] Yet specific comparative approaches seem possible and necessary: first, to compare the eugenics movements internationally in the first half of this century both with international population policy today and with the new sociobiological "biocrats";[12] and second, in accord with new approaches in the United States, stimulated largely by women of color, to conceptualize the connection between racism and sexism not as the mere addition of two forms of exploitation—as a double oppression—but as a manifold and complex relationship.[13]

### Value and Worthlessness: Women in the Race Hygiene Tradition

In the late nineteenth century, a theory of the possibility, even necessity, of eugenic, race hygienic, or social hygienic sterilization emerged, which argued that those considered transmitters of hereditary forms of "inferiority" *(erbliche Minderwertigkeit)* should be prevented from having children. Presumably lacking in social value and usefulness, they and their offspring were seen as not serving the interest of the folk or the "racial body."[14] By the end of World War I, when German aggrandizement and stability seemed at its lowest, such sterilization was widely and passionately recommended as a solution to urgent social problems: shiftlessness, ignorance, and laziness in the workforce; deviant sexual behavior such as prostitution and illegitimate births; the increasing number of ill and insane; poverty; and the rising costs of social services.[15] Recommendations for sterilization came from elements of the right and of the left, from men and women, from those leaning toward theories of heredity and from those with a more environmental orientation.[16] Criteria of what constituted inferiority were elaborated not only by political ideologists, but also by anthropologists, medical doctors, psychiatrists.

This type of reasoning, with all its subtle appeal to naïve belief in modern science, social rationality, and planning, has been called *scientific racism*, which transcends the more traditional and more overt *gut racism*.[17] Based on a polarity between "progress" and "degeneration," its criteria of inferiority had at their center concepts of "value" and "worthlessness" (*Wert* and *Unwert, Minderwertigkite* and *Höherwertigkeit*) that were related to the social or racial "body" and its productivity. The use of eugenic sterilization was intended both to control procreation and, by defining and proscribing what was unacceptable, to impose a specific acceptable character on women and men: the hard-working male breadwinner, his hard-working but unpaid housewife, and children who were a financial burden to no one but their parents. This was the "valuable life": a gender-specific work and productivity, described in social, medical, and psychiatric terms. Or, in the more flowery language of gut racists: "German-blooded, Nordic-raced beings: right-angled in body and soul."[18]

What were the social motives behind these policies and their wide acceptance? The principal and most haunting spectre for the race was seen not only in the women's movement and in the lower-class uprisings between the turn of the century and the 1920s, but in a phenomenon that seemed to encompass both: the unequal propagation of the "talented" and the "untalented," the "fit" and the "unfit," the rich and the poor, the deserving and the undeserving poor, those of social value and the "social problem group."[19] The better-off, the fit, those thinking rationally, the upwardly mobile, those pursuing or competing for hard and honest work, and women seeking emancipation all limited the number of their children. The decline of the birthrate after the 1870s, reaching an international low point in 1932 and perceived as a "birth-strike" after about 1912, was attributed mainly to women.[20] On the other hand, the mentally and financially poor and the restless were seen as copulating and propagating indiscriminately, as in a "witches' sabbath,"[21] transmitting to their offspring, by the mechanism called heredity, their poverty and restlessness and their search for income from public welfare funds.[22]

Whatever the historical reality of this differential birthrate may have been,[23] its social interpretation came to be the double-edged essence of what was defined as "racial degeneration" or "race suicide." It was charged that the problem stemmed from women, possibly associated with the women's movement, who preferred to have fewer children than their mothers, and from women or couples who raised their children against prevailing norms and at the expense of community and state.[24] The proposed remedy was to reverse both trends: to impel the "superior" to have more children and the "inferior" to have fewer or none. The first aim was to be achieved through a heightened public concern as well as financial and social incentives; the latter through sterilization or, more generally, the eugenic use of just those means by which certain women or couples had limited their fertility.[25] This policy was sexist in its demand for state control of procreation, and racist in its differential treatment of superior and inferior procreation. It can therefore be seen as a dual attack against the birth-strike of the desirable people and against the social maladjustment of those not trained to orderliness and to the work ethic, the natural task of valuable mothers. Thus special concern was given to women. "If we want to practice race hygiene seriously, we must make women the target of our social work—woman as mother and not as sexual parasite," urged the main race hygiene review in 1909. In 1929, a widely known book, *Sterilization on Social and Race Hygienic Grounds,* suggested that "the number of degenerate individuals born depends mainly on the number of degenerate women capable of procreation. Thus the sterilization of degenerate women is, for reasons of racial hygiene, more important than the sterilization of men."[26]

## "Kaiserschnitt" *and* "Hitlerschnitt": *Nazi Body Politics*

Along with discrimination and segregation of Jewish women and men, Nazi sterilization policies were the main strategy of "gene and race care," as eugenics or race hygiene was now called, from 1933 to 1939. Sterilization policy was one form of comprehensive Nazi racism. Jews, those eligible for sterilization, were defined as inferior. Along with the Jews, National Socialism had a second scapegoat held responsible for the degeneration of the race: millions of non-Jewish, inferior women and men, who supposedly were a "burden" to the state. Like Jews, they were seen as "ballast" and "parasites" to the "body" of *Volk* and race, though Jews were seen as threatening this body from the outside, and other inferior beings were seen as threatening it from the inside. For Jewish as for non-Jewish inferior people, one decree or law followed the other from 1933 on. Among other things, they served to identify them. Thus, having a Jewish grandmother defined a Jew or a Jew of "mixed blood," and a schizophrenic episode—one's own or that of one's grandmother—served to define a sterilization candidate. The identification of human beings as valuable, worthless, or of inferior value in supposedly hereditary terms was the common denominator of all forms of Nazi racism. Birth strategy was one of these forms.

Nazi pronatalism for desirable births and its antinatalism for undesirable ones were tightly connected. On May 26, 1933, two pieces of penal legislation preceding the 1926 reforms were reintroduced, prohibiting the availability of abortion facilities and services. More important was the stricter handling of the old antiabortion law, resulting in a 65 percent increase in yearly convictions between 1932 and 1938, when their number reached almost 7,000.[27] From 1935 on, doctors and midwives were obliged to notify the regional State Health Office of every miscarriage. Women's names and addresses were then handed over to the police, who investigated the cases suspected of actually being abortions.[28] In 1936 Heinrich Himmler, head of all police forces and the SS, established the Reich's Central Agency for the Struggle Against Homosexuality and Abortion, and in 1943, after three years of preparation by the Ministries of the Interior and of Justice, the law entitled Protection of Marriage, Family, and Motherhood called for the death penalty in "extreme cases."[29]

The corollary measure was race hygiene sterilization. Along with the new antiabortion legislation, a law was introduced on May 26, 1933, to legalize eugenic sterilization and prohibit voluntary sterilization.[30] Beyond this, the Cabinet, headed by Hitler, passed a law on July 14, 1933, against propagation of "lives unworthy of life" (*lebensunwertes Leben*), called the Law for the Prevention of Hereditarily Diseased Offspring. It ordered sterilization for certain categories of people, its notorious Paragraph 12 allowing the use of force against those who did not submit freely.[31] Earlier, on June 28, the Minister of the Interior Wilhelm Frick had announced: "We must have the courage again to grade our people according to its genetic values."[32]

Before we turn to the outcome of such value-grading, it is important to understand some laws that aggravated this policy, enabled its realization, and linked it closely both to antiabortion policy and to future race hygienic extermination. Beginning in January 1934, on the initiative of the "Reich's Medical Doctors' Leader" Gerhard Wagner, abortion of "defective" pregnancies on the grounds of race hygiene was secretly practiced with Hitler's approval; it was introduced by law on June 26, 1935.[33] It was legal only with the consent of the woman, but after being declared of inferior value, she was sterilized, too, even against her will, and after 1938 she could not even decide to revoke her initial consent.

In 1933, the government passed a law against "habitual delinquents" that provided for castration (i.e., took sterilization one step further to the destruction of the gonads) in specified cases.[34] While this law concerned men only (2,006 up to 1940), castration of women by destruction of the gonads (beyond tubal ligation: ovarectomy) was introduced in 1936, when sterilization by X-rays was included in the sterilization law.[35] Later, officials favored this procedure as an easy method for mass sterilization of camp inmates without their knowledge.[36]

The law that provided for the enactment of all these policies was passed in July 1934. It created a centralized system of State Health Offices with Departments for Gene and Race Care. Numbering 1,100 and staffed by 1943 with 12,000 State Medical Officials, they became, from 1934 on, the main agents of sterilization proposals and marriage approvals.[37] They also were the pillars of another huge enterprise: a centralized index of the hereditary value of all inhabitants of Germany *(Erbkartei)* to become the basis for all state decisions on the professional and family life of its subjects.[38]

Popular vernacular expressed the situation pungently. Eugenic sterilization was called *Hitlerschnitt* (Hitler's cut), thereby linking it to an antiabortion policy that refused abortions even to women who had gone through two previous *Kaiserschnitte* (caesarean operations). Only after three caesareans did a woman have the right to an abortion, and then only on the condition that she also accept the sterilization.[39] Transcending older political partnerships, prohibition of abortion and compulsory sterilization, compulsory motherhood and prohibition of motherhood—far from contradicting each other—had now become two sides of a coherent policy combining sexism and racism. Only for descriptive purposes do the following sections deal with them separately.

### Forced Labor for Mothers or Children of Confidence?

Nazi population planners liked to register the gradual rise of the extremely low birthrate after 1933 (the birthrate of the years 1934–1939 was, on average, a third above the level of 1933, thus reaching again the level of the mid-twenties) as "a completely voluntary and spontaneous proof of [the] confidence of the German people in its Reich, its Führer, its future, a confession which could not be more beautiful" than in the form of "children of confidence."[40] Sometimes (and not only in the past) this increase has been considered a proof of the suspicion that women favored rather than rejected the regime and that they redirected themselves toward *Kinder, Küche, Kirche* (children, kitchen, church) after their emancipation in the 1920s.[41] Such an argument, however, confusing as it does childlessness and liberation, motherhood and backwardness, does not seem an adequate instrument for the historical analysis of women's lives. What was the real effect of the pronatalist aspect of Nazi population policy on women specifically as well as on the whole society?

Nazi and non-Nazi demographers agree on the limited extent of the rise in the birthrate.[42] More importantly, from the limited evidence we have on women's motives for contributing to its rise, none seems to be the result of Nazi policies and goals. Voluntary births clearly increased as economic conditions improved. Wives of party officials and SS men, who may have been close participators in Nazi goals (but who, as part of the upper class, had easier access to voluntary birth control), had extremely few children.[43] From the outbreak of war in 1939 when, mainly under the command of Fritz Sauckel, unemployed (mostly middle-class) women were encouraged or forced to join the war effort in the munitions industries and employed (mostly lower-class) women were forbidden to quit their jobs, hundreds of thousands of women used the only alternative to forced employment open to them: pregnancy. Popular wit called these women *Sauckelfrauen* and their children *Sauckelkinder*, while Nazi leaders accused them of "lack of comprehension of the necessity of war."[44]

However, while women's positive response to pro-natalism seems limited, we must also try to relate the rise of the birthrate to the one directly coercive measure of pro-natalism: forced labor for mothers through the prohibition of abortion for "valuable," "German-blooded" women. Antiabortion policies are sometimes considered the main reason for the rise in births. In fact, there is some evidence, though locally limited, that after 1932 the rise in births nearly equalled the decline in abortions.[45] This argument could be decisive, if it were measurable. Fortunately for those women who resorted to abortion it is not; the relationship between known and unknown abortions and that between spontaneous and induced miscarriages is controversial, not only in democratic societies, but even under the tight control and supervision of the Nazi regime.

While abortions are estimated at one-half to 1 million per year between 1930 and 1932, a gynecologist in 1939 counted 220,000 miscarriages in hospitals, of which he estimated 120,000 to be abortions. Criminal police experts estimated that the number of unknown abortions equalled the number that came to their attention.[46] In the 1930s, very much as in the 1920s, various documents tell of regional "abortion epidemics" in which abortions were performed by pregnant women themselves or by "old shrews."[47] In 1937 Himmler gave various estimates in secret documents ranging from 400,000 to 800,000 abortions per year.[48]

These numbers seem high, particularly if measured against the rising number of trials and convictions for abortion. Taken together, they permit conclusions that may well question women's easy compliance with Nazi pro-natalism. Nonetheless, those who were denied abortion or who did not want to risk prosecution, even if they did not want children or were endangered by childbirth, had to accept motherhood as forced labor: the labor of childbirth in its modern misogynist form and the labor of additional unpaid housework.[49]

A last consideration helps to answer our initial question. The qualitatively neutral birthrate does not tell us about the proportion of undesirable children to the desirable ones so dear to Nazi population politicians. Although it makes little sense to try through numerical count to match one against the other and thus as a women's historian to repeat the favorite eugenics game called "differential birthrate of the inferior and superior," we should definitely not assume that all children were welcome to the state.[50] While on the one hand, around 1937, the Nazis became worried about something they called *Erbangst*—people's fear of having children because there was so much talk about unworthy genes[51]—on the other hand there were German (though not "German-blooded") women who succeeded in conceiving during the time lag between their sentence of sterilization and its actual enforcement.[52] Most important, Nazi pro-natalism excluded from the ranks of honor and allowances every large family found to be undesirable because it was "hereditarily defective or racially mixed or asocial, alcoholic, lacking an orderly family life, and one in which children [are] a burden."[53]

## "Lives Unworthy of Life"

The sterilization law, meant to prevent "lives unworthy of life," came into force on January 1, 1934. It listed nine diagnostic causes whereby a person could be sentenced by a specific genetic health court to sterilization; five categories were related to psychiatric "invalidity," three to physical "invalidity," the last to alcoholism. Authorities gave differing estimates of how many should be sterilized, somewhere between 5 and 30 percent of the population; the minister of the interior recommended 20 percent in his speech of June 1933.[54] During the nearly five and one-half years preceding the outbreak of World War II, about 320,000 persons (nearly 0.5 percent of the population) were sterilized under the terms of this law. This figure included some 5,000 eugenic abortions with subsequent sterilizations (under comparable laws in thirty states of the United States, 11,000 persons were sterilized between 1907 and 1930, and 53,000 more by 1964). While men alone determined sterilization cases in court, the victims were divided evenly between women and men. Three-quarters were sterilized under the law's first two categories: 53 percent (with a somewhat higher share among women) for "feeblemindedness," 20 percent (with a somewhat higher share among men) for "schizophrenia."[55] Between 1934 and 1937, about 80 men and 400 women died in the course of the operation.

One of the reasons why men also became subject to eugenic sterilization, in contrast to the period preceding the legislation when it had been practiced only in birth clinics frequented by poor women, was the new and efficient bureaucracy established for this purpose. Between 1933 and 1936, about 250 special sterilization courts were established as parts of the judiciary, and race hygiene experts along with judges decided on the desirability of sterilizations. Directors of institutions such as hospitals, schools, prisons, workhouses, and concentration camps, as well as welfare authorities, were responsible for selecting candidates for sterilization from among their charges. But the bulk of applications to the courts came from the newly established State Medical Officers, who got their information from the above-mentioned institutions, from mayors and private doctors, and, more rarely, from employers and neighbors of the candidates, as well as through the medical and eugenic examination of all recipients of state funds. Hardly anybody applied to be sterilized him- or herself.

The reactions of the victims were bitter and complex, as can be seen from their letters to the courts and from contemporary investigations. A medical student, checking up on sterilized women in 1936, observed that some of them

> were morally so inferior, that they welcomed sterilization. . . . Other women saw sterilization as a relief, because they were in such financial straits. In these cases, moral indifference and economic need are so great that they dominate their thoughts and attitudes toward children and toward the sterilization law. . . . On leaving, I often heard behind me scornful and mocking laughter at the idea that childlessness was a sacrifice. Many said bitterly "that children only cost money; only the rich can afford them." . . . Others viewed the loss of motherhood as a loss of purpose in life and, moreover, as a devaluation of their humanity, a source of shame and disgrace. . . . For them, the only solace could be the conviction that their sacrifice had not been in vain, but had been made to the German people.[56]

The actual criteria for sterilization can be deduced from the meticulous records kept by the courts. These criteria include mentally and physically defective kin—a broad spectrum of deficiencies ranged from quarrelsome aunts, alcoholic grandparents, and spendthrifts to sexual deviancy, particularly alleged promiscuity of women and the resulting illegitimate births. Intelligence tests examined for the ability to read, write, and do arithmetic, as well as for a knowledge of geography, history, and the names of Nazi leaders. The category "general ethical concepts" asked:

> Why does one study? Why and for whom does one save money? Why should one not burn even one's own house? If you won the lottery, what would you do with the money? How do you plan your future? What is the meaning of fidelity, piety, honor, modesty? What is the opposite of bravery?[57]

A ghastly crowd of people who did not live up to the social expectations voiced by these questions populated the voluminous official commentary to the sterilization law. They included currently ill and recovered schizophrenics, backward students, so-called promiscuous women, "asocials," and prostitutes.

Resistance came early and took various forms. Examination questions and answers were passed on, rendering the standardized intelligence tests useless. Poorly educated Nazi supporters were hauled into sterilization courts. Some victims, mostly men, hired lawyers and sometimes succeeded in protracting their cases for years. The combined resistance led to renewed debate over the criteria of inferiority in 1936–1937 and to modification of the intelligence test and its use. The individual's proof of social worth (*Lebensbewährung*) was now officially established as the decisive criterion, thus bringing into the open the contents of the medical rhetoric of eugenic psychiatry. A 1936 government decree to the sterilization courts described such "proof":

> If a person has a profession demanding achievement based on independent judgment, we can assume there is no feeble-mindedness. However, if a person performs only steady and repetitive mechanical work, shows no inclination to change or to become more efficient, and also seems unintelligent, we will be close to a diagnosis of "feeble-mindedness." . . . We almost certainly find it in people unable to earn a steady livelihood or otherwise unable to adapt socially. Such feeble-minded persons are morally underdeveloped and unable correctly to understand the order of human society.[58]

An attempt to identify the actual victims of race hygienic sterilization may help to illuminate not only their lives and social situations, but also the forms and functions of reproductive racism and some links with racism's better-known historical "solutions." The majority of those sterilized under the law were not (as in the United States) asylum inmates, or ethnic minorities, but noninstitutionalized persons of German ethnicity. The poorer strata of the population had the highest share (unskilled workers, particularly agricultural laborers), and three categories of women were far overrepresented: servants, unskilled factory or farm workers, and jobless housewives, especially those married to unskilled workers. Many prostitutes and unmarried mothers were among them.[59] "Deviancy from the norm," from "the average," was the crucial criterion in the courts. The norm itself was elaborated even more clearly as demonstrable through adherence to the work ethic, self-sacrifice, parsimony, and through the resulting upward mobility: the "German work character." For women, this ideal was represented by the worker who performed ungrudging housework and efficient labor in outside employment; her antithesis was the slut, the prostitute.

The other sterilization victims between 1934 and 1939 were inmates or ex-inmates (searched out in the old files) of institutions, mainly of psychiatric clinics and of psychiatric departments of regular hospitals. More precisely, they were all those discharged from the clinics as recovered, but whose recovery did not, according to race hygienic thought, involve their "genes," which they might pass on to posterity. It is well known that most inmates of psychiatric institutions came from a background of poverty. Patients in specified, sexually segregated "closed institutions" were not sterilized if they stayed there at their own expense.[60] A considerable number of people used this loophole and entered such an institution if they could afford one. However this option was closed by the "euthanasia" project "T 4," in which from 1939 to 1941 up to 100,000 inmates of these institutions were killed outright as "useless eaters"; after August 1941 many more were killed through plain starvation. In another way, race hygienic sterilization was a direct prelude to mass murder: the prohibition against bearing "unworthy" children was expanded into the mass murder of about 5,000 such children, sixteen years and under, between 1939 and 1944. In order to get control over these children, the government would often force their mothers into the war industry so that home child care was impossible.[61] For both sorts of mass murder, a secret and elaborate machinery was set up, resembling in its procedures the publicly acknowledged sterilization bureaucracy.

The transition to still another form of mass murder is clearly visible. T 4 was meant to be kept secret, but the news spread rapidly, arousing fear and the suspicion that sterilization of the "useless" was just a first step. Public opinion and pressure—which was, in 1941, largely led by women, children, and old people—in fact forced Hitler and his SS doctors to stop T 4 and the planned murder of three million "invalids." But the gas chambers, used for the first time in this enterprise, were transported with their entire staff to occupied Poland, where they were installed for the "final solution."[62] The terror that had met resistance within Germany was exported beyond its frontiers to work more smoothly.

These links between race hygiene inside and outside the death-and-work and death-by-work camps suggest that only the merger of gut racism with the more scientific, bureaucratic, and planned approach of eugenic racism was able to bring to reality a bureaucratic, scientific, and faultlessly efficient genocide on the scale of the Holocaust.

Connections between these two expressions of racism are evident not only in their methods but also in their victims: along with the "deviant" groups already mentioned, ethnic minorities such as Gypsies and the few Germans of black color were targets for sterilization. In 1935, people of the Polish minority of Upper Silesia protested against sterilization of members of their group. German Jews, defined out of the German *Volk* from 1933 on, were not defined out of it through "negative race hygiene," that is, sterilization. While sterilizations of Jewish women and men were common in areas with a substantial proportion of Jews, and especially of poor, often eastern Jews, such as in Berlin, and while in 1938 abortions were "permitted" to Jewish women, by 1942 it was declared that "no more applications for sterilization of Jews need to be made."[63] The reason was that at this time Jews were being killed in concentration camps. The division between those who were and were not eligible for race hygienic sterilization according to the 1933 law coincided to a large degree with a prior division within the lower classes: between the subproletarian strata including part of the ethnic minorities on the one side and, on the other, the proper and orderly German workers hailed by many Nazis as the hard and hard-working core of racial superiority. Predominantly unskilled, the former were not integrated into the stable norm of waged work for men and unwaged housework for women; the official labor movement, which had largely excluded them, had during the 1920s taken a position toward the unskilled and toward ethnic minorities very much like that of the American Federation of Labor.

However, we should not disregard the number, though limited, of middle- and upper-class victims of racist psychiatry and sterilization.[64] To some extent, race hygiene crosses class lines, as do, to a larger degree, sexist and gut racism (most visibly in the case of anti-Semitism). To the extent that it does, it can be seen as a policy directed against those who deviate not just from general social norms but from the norms and expectations of their specific class. Its purpose is to "select" against those who do not fit into the class or the class-specific sex role to which they supposedly belong. In this way, race hygiene contributes to a confirmation of the class structure not just at its lower level, but at all its levels. Thus race hygiene carries over the attitudes and implementation of racism from the social conflicts between ethnicities into social conflicts within an ethnicity. From the perspective of its victims, the terms *ethnic racism* and *social racism*[65] might denote the connection as well as the difference between both expressions of racism.

Moreover, scientific (and gut) racism had a decisive function in the spread and confirmation of two sexual double standards: assignment of typically modern, sexually differentiated roles and labors to women and men,[66] and assignment of different roles and labors to superior and inferior women. According to theoreticians of race and race hygiene, the difference and polarity between the sexes (reason/emotion, activity/passivity, paid work/housework) is fully developed only in the superior, and Nordic, races; among inferior races, including those of low hereditary value, the sexes are less differentiated—and thus heavy and cheap labor is good for both.[67] These assignments might both appropriately be called aspects of *sexist racism*.

## "Value" of Race and of Sex: Nazi Money Politics

Financial population policy was another form of racism and sexism practiced by the Nazi regime. Historians have usually examined it as an instrument of population increase, by which, it has been argued, women were bribed back into the home, became grateful adherents of the regime, and were bought off in order to reconcile them to Nazi antifeminism.[68] However, while demographic evidence (referring to the number of births in families receiving state support) remains inconclusive at best, it suggests that the rise in births was not due to such incentives. The economic aspect of Nazi population policy is more significant to questions of racism and sexism. It can be shown by comparing the intentions and effects of state investments in births, their racist and sexist distribution, and some of the social struggles around them.

All family subventions were given to husbands, and only under strong eugenic restrictions to unwed mothers. Mothers themselves received only the nonmonetary Mother Cross, introduced in 1939. Equally important, both financial and honorary entitlements were tied to race hygienic qualifications. This was most visible in the case of marriage loans and child allowances.[69]

The June 1, 1933, Law to Reduce Unemployment, in its section "Promotion of Marriages," provided for marriage loans up to one thousand marks for those men whose wives gave up their jobs (there were similar loans in France, Italy, Spain, and Sweden); in fact, only half of this sum was paid. Three weeks after the law was passed, a new provision forgave one-fourth of the debt with each childbirth, popularly seen as "paying off in children" *(abkindern)*. It was argued that the marriage loans would reduce female pressure on the labor market and give jobs to male heads of households. It did not have this result, since men rarely took up "women's work," and the condition of female nonemployment was soon abrogated, when the employment of both sexes increased. The real aim of the marriage loan was to allow men to marry at an earlier age by helping them to establish a household, and to increase the number of births. However, the loan recipients practiced family planning despite reduced access to birth control: between 1933 and 1943, two million husbands "paid off" their loans with an average of just 1.1 children each.[70]

The distribution of financial family subventions was not only sexist, since it privileged men, but also racist, since people with "defects" considered hereditary were excluded: people eligible for sterilization (even if the sterilization tribunal had absolved them) included Jews, Gypsies, and other "alien races" as well as asocials whose "aggregate hereditary value" was considered to be below average. The latter category included "those with police records, shirkers, those with behavior problems, uneconomical persons or those on welfare, and those unable to conduct an orderly household or to raise their children to be useful citizens."[71] Ultimately, about two-thirds of all couples marrying did not apply for the loan in the first place, largely because of the eugenic restrictions, and it was denied to about 3 percent of the applicants.[72] Thus, while most loans went to working-class heads of households, they failed to reach many couples who really needed help. The main purpose of the loans was met: discrimination between the hereditarily pure and those with no or low race or hereditary value.

Child allowances, introduced in 1936, were similarly used. They consisted of a one-time benefit of 65 marks for each child and 10 marks monthly thereafter for children after the fifth, and later after the third, child; unlike in contemporary Sweden, they were given not to mothers, but to fathers. Moreover, race hygienists distinguished between "full families rich in children" and "asocial large families," between those with desirable and those with undesirable children. The latter were denied allowances, along with those of alien races and of unwed mothers with more than one child, especially if the father was not known.[73] In 1940, when these restrictions were sharpened, crowds of women and children harassed city officials demanding what they thought was rightfully theirs.[74] What had been hailed by hopeful race hygienists as the "quiet struggle of mothers for Germandom"[75] became instead a vocal resistance of mothers against discrimination against inferior women.

### "Birth-War" in the World War

With the declaration of war in 1939, another stage of the "birth-war"[76] was inaugurated, exacerbating previous trends. Only a few of its features can be presented here. A decree of August 31, 1939, ruled that the sterilization law was to be applied only in those cases "where a particularly great danger of propagation is imminent."[77] While this change in policy may give some insight into the earlier handling of this "danger," its principal rationale lay in the war. Sterilization candidates could not be counted on to be compliant war workers, and the old race hygiene personnel were needed for other purposes.[78] In fact, the number of sterilization trials was drastically reduced.

Simultaneously, however, sterilization policy was extended and radicalized in three dimensions beyond the 1933 law. First, mass sterilizations were executed in concentration camps, mostly on Jewish women and Gypsy women and men. Gypsy women and men were sterilized outside the camps also, sometimes with a "choice" between camp and sterilization. Future mass sterilizations were planned for those Jews who, defined as of mixed blood *(Mischlinge)*, were not transported to the camps. Sterilizations of Jewish and Gypsy people in and outside the camps were done both for the sake of medical experiments and for population control, that is, in order to prevent inferior offspring.[79] Second, many women from the conquered and occupied territories in the east—about 2 million women had been deported as forced labor into Germany—were subjected to compulsory abortion and sterilization for the sake, again, of population control and in order to maintain an efficient workforce unhampered by the care of children. Little as yet is known about their lives. It is clear, however, that abortion was "allowed" to them, and that from 1942 on, an eastern working-woman's pregnancy was reported—via management and regional labor offices— to a special regional SS officer who tested her racially and decided about the outcome of her pregnancy.[80]

Less is known about the third dimension of the new policy, the birth-war against the asocials. Asociality had been an important criterion in the sterilization courts; many persons had been sterilized and asocials, including prostitutes, had been proportionately high among those deported to concentration camps during the second great wave of imprisonment from 1936 to 1941.[81] However, this criterion still had smacked too much of the "social" instead of the "biological," and it had not always been easy to classify such persons under one of the four psychiatric categories of the 1933 law.[82] Meanwhile, race hygiene theory had established the hereditary character of the disease "asociality" with such efficiency that it had become a central category of racism. After 1940, when many asocials were released from the camps to answer an urgent shortage of labor, a new law was being elaborated that provided for their sterilization. In terms of contemporary psychology, the definition of asocial was extended from the psychotic to the psychopathic and the neurotic, while the bill called them simply "parasites," "failures," "itinerant," "good-for-nothing." The legislation was to be enforced right after the war, and many high and low government and party agencies continued to discuss it throughout the war.[83]

Among women, the good housewife and industrious mother could be sure to evade sterilization. Unwed and poor mothers with "too many" children, women on welfare, and prostitutes could not be so sure. Ever more obviously, the birth-war applied typically racist measures that violated the bodily integrity of those considered socially deviant and linked ever more closely the various forms and victims of racism. In an official, though secret, decree of September 1940, the "Reich's Health Leader" Leonardo Conti granted the State Health Offices permission to perform eugenic sterilization and abortion on prostitutes, on women of inferior character, and on those of alien race.[84] The sterilization law planned for the future was anticipated in practice.

## Conclusion: Sexism and Racism

One should not assume, as is often done, that Nazi sexism concerned only superior women and Nazi racism concerned only inferior women. Both Nazi racism and sexism concerned all women, the inferior as well as the superior. The "birth achievement" demanded of acceptable women was calculated carefully according to the numbers of those who were not to give birth.[85] And the strongest pressure on such acceptable women to procreate, to create an orderly household for husband and children, and to accept dependency on the breadwinner perhaps came not so much from the continuous positive propaganda about "valuable motherhood," but precisely from its opposite: the negative propaganda and policy that barred unwelcome, poor, and deviant women from procreation and marriage and labeled either disorderly women or single women with too many children inferior. Thus, racism could be used, and was used, to impose sexism in the form of increased unwaged housework on superior women.

On the other hand, women who became or were to become targets of negative race hygiene tended also to be those who did not accept, could not accept, or were not supposed to accept the Nazi view of female housework, whose main features can be traced back to the late eighteenth century. Sexism, which imposed economic dependency on superior married women, could be used, and was used, to implement racism by excluding many women from the relative benefits granted to desirable mothers and children and forcing them to accept the lowest jobs in the labor-market hierarchy in order to survive. In fact, modern sexism has established, below the ideological surface of theories on "women's nature" and the "cult of true womanhood," two different though connected norms for women. The demand was made of some women to administer orderly households and produce well-educated children, the whole enterprise supported by their husbands' money; others, overburdened and without support, were obliged to adopt menial jobs that paid little or nothing, while their children, like themselves, were treated as ballast. Racist-sexist discourses of various kinds have portrayed socially, sexually, or ethnically alien women as nonwomen, and thus as threatening to the norms for all other women, or as threatening, and there again as nonwomen: thus a racist view of Jewish or Gypsy women as prostitutes, the eugenic sexologists' view of lesbians as pseudo-men, the race hygienic view of prostitutes as asocial and infectious to the "racial body,"[86] the fantasy of Polish or feebleminded women "breeding like animals." But of course, much more is involved here than (predominantly male) images and symbols,[87] influential though they may be in determining women's very real treatment and self-image. Women's history needs to concentrate on the lives of those "non"-women without marginalizing them as (male) history has done.

Precisely because of the complex links between sexism and racism and, therefore, because of the relevance of reproductive racism to all women, we should be careful not to term simply "sexism" the demand placed on ethnically or socially superior women to have children they may not want, and not to term simply "racism" the ban against ethnically or socially inferior women having children, even though they may want them. More strictly speaking, we might call the imposition on the first group of women *racist sexism,* since their procreation is urged not just because they are women, but because they are women *of a specific ethnicity or social position declared superior.* Accordingly, we might call the imposition on the second group of women *sexist racism,* since their procreation is prohibited not just on grounds of their genes and race, but on grounds of their real or supposed deviation, *as women, from social or ethnic standards for superior women.* Establishing in such terms the dual connection between racism and sexism does not (as may be evident from the context) give different weights to the experiences of racism and sexism, or suggest that racism is primary in one case and sexism primary in the other. Precisely the opposite is true: where sexism and racism exist, particularly with Nazi features, all women are equally involved in both, but with different experiences. They are subjected to one coherent and double-edged policy of *sexist racism* or *racist sexism* (a nuance only of perspective), but they are segregated as they live through the dual sides of this policy, a division that also works to segregate their forms of resistance to sexism as well as to racism.

Attempting to look at the situation of all women from the perspective of "non"-women may help to analyze and break down the boundaries of such segregation. As far as the struggle for our reproductive rights—for our sexuality, our children, and the money we want and need—is concerned, the Nazi experience may teach us that a successful struggle must aim at achieving both the rights and the economic means to allow women to choose between having or not having children without becoming economically dependent on other people or on unwanted second and third jobs. Cutbacks in welfare for single mothers, sterilization abuse, and the attacks on free abortion are just different sides of an attack that serves to divide women. Present population and family policy in the United States and the Third World make the German experience under National Socialism particularly relevant. In Germany, new attacks on free abortion, the establishment of a university department of "population science," sterilization experiments on women and sterilization of welfare mothers without their knowledge, pressure on Gypsy women (especially those on welfare) not to have children, xenophobic outcries against immigrants "breeding like animals" and sometimes asking for their castration or sterilization, all-too-easy abortions and sterilizations on Turkish women, the reduction of state money connected to human reproduction, both private and public, have all occurred during the last two years.[88] It is an open question what will follow from these—still seemingly unconnected—events in the course of the present economic crisis.

## Notes

This is a revised version of the essay that appeared in *Signs: Journal of Women in Culture and Society* 8, no. 3 (1983).

1. The more progressive new generation of social historians in Germany since the 1960s has tended to present racism as a mere ideology, its application as more or less economically/politically "rational" or "irrational," often as merely instrumental, and mostly as an appendage to more important developments, "political" or "economic." See, for example, Peter M. Kaiser, "Monopolprofit und Massenmord im Faschismus: Zur ökonomischen Funktion der Konzentrationslager im faschistischen Deutschland," *Blätter für deutsche und internationale Politik* 5 (1975): 552–77.
2. A rare exception is Marion A. Kaplan, *The Jewish Feminist Movement in Germany: The Campaigns of the Jüdischer Frauenbund, 1904–1938* (Westport, Conn.: Greenwood Press, 1979).
3. However, three conferences of women historians on women's history have taken place: "Women in the Weimar Republic and under National Socialism," Berlin, 1979; "Muttersein und Mutterideologie in der bürgerlichen Gesellschaft," Bremen, 1980; and "Frauengeschichte," Bielefeld, 1981. Some of the workshops of the latter are documented in *Beiträge zur feministischen Theorie und Praxis* 5 (April 1981). Thus, women's history has been exploring this and similar themes in recent years, but much work still needs to be done, and many questions cannot yet·be answered in a consistent way.
4. A good overview of the American and international eugenics movement is Allan Chase, *The Legacy of Malthus: The Social Costs of the New Scientific Racism* (New

York: Knopf, 1977). Although there had been, at the beginning of this century, a debate among experts on distinctions between "eugenics" and "race hygiene," I use these terms interchangeably, as does Chase, for I believe the issue dealt with in this article requires my doing so. On this debate see Georg Lilienthal, "Rassenhygiene im Dritten Reich: Krise und Wende," *Medizinhistorisches Journal* 14 (1979): 114–34.

5. See Alfred Grotjahn, *Geburten-Rückgang und Geburten-Regelung im Lichte der individuellen und der sozialen Hygiene* (Berlin and Coblenz, 1914; 2d ed., 1921), p. 153, and the chapter "Birth Regulation Serving Eugenics and Race Hygiene"; and Agnes Bluhm, *Die rassenhygienischen Aufgaben des weiblichen Arztes: Schriften zur Erblehre und Rassenhygiene* (Berlin: Metzner, 1936), esp. the chapter "Woman's Role in the Racial Process in Its Largest Sense."

6. Good examples are the classic and influential books by Grotjahn, *Geburten-Rückgang* (1914) and *Die Hygiene der menschlichen Fortpflanzung* (Berlin and Vienna: Urban and Schwarzenburg, 1926); Erwin Baur, Eugen Fischer, and Fritz Lenz, *Grundriss der menschlichen Erblichkeitslehre und Rassenhygiene*, Vol. 2, *Menschliche Auslese und Rassenhygiene* (Munich: Lehmann, 1921). These volumes had many interestingly divergent editions. I have used Vol. 1 (1936) and Vol. 2 (1931). For a scientific critique of the pseudoscientific theory of character traits see, e.g., Chase, chap. 8.

7. For a preliminary critique of this view, analyzing housework as no less modern and no less capitalist than employment outside the house, see Gisela Bock and Barbara Duden, "Arbeit aus Liebe—Liebe als Arbeit: Zur Entstehung der Hausarbeit im Kapitalismus," in *Frauen und Wissenschaft: Beiträge zur Berliner Sommeruniversität für Frauen, Juli 1976* (Berlin: Courage Verlag, 1977), pp. 118–99. Parts of it have been translated as "Labor of Love—Love as Labor," in *From Feminism to Liberation*, ed. Edith Hoshino Altbach, 2d ed. (Cambridge, Mass.: Schenkman, 1980), 153–92.

8. Dörte Winkler, *Frauenarbeit im "Dritten Reich"* (Hamburg, Hoffmann und Campe, 1977), esp. pp. 42–65, revised this picture by showing that under Nazism, employment of lower- and middle-class women was not reduced. This is confirmed by various authors in the anthology edited by Frauengruppe Faschismusforschung, *Mutterkreuz und Arbeitsbuch: Zur Geschichte der Frauen in der Weimarer Republik und im Nationalsozialismus* (Frankfurt a.M.: Fischer, 1981). Leila J. Rupp, *Mobilizing Women for War: German and American Propaganda, 1939–1945* (Princeton: Princeton University Press, 1978), esp. pp. 11–50, revised the current view of the Nazi image of women. It was more diversified than usually assumed and did not simply stress home and housework, but any "woman's sacrifice" for the state and "the race," including employment. See also Leila J. Rupp, "Mothers of the *Volk:* The Image of Women in Nazi Ideology," *Signs: Journal of Women in Culture and Society* 3, No. 2 (Winter 1977): 362–79. In relation to racism, I have tried to revise the picture in "Frauen und ihre Arbeit im Nationalsozialismus," in *Frauen in der Geschichte*, ed. Annette Kuhn and Gerhard Schneider (Düsseldorf: Schwann Verlag, 1979), pp. 113–49; and " 'Zum Wohle des Volkskörpers': Abtreibung und Sterilisation unterm Nationalsozialismus," *Journal für Geschichte* 2 (November 1980): 58–65.

9. Clifford R. Lovin, "*Blut und Boden:* The Ideological Basis of the Nazi Agricultural Program," *Journal of the History of Ideas* 28 (1967): 279–88, esp. 286.

10. Cf. Hans Peter Bleuel, *Das saubere Reich: Theorie und Praxis des sittlichen Lebens im Dritten Reich* (Bern-Munich-Vienna: Scherz, 1972), p. 273; Jill Stephenson, *Women in Nazi Society* (London: Croom Helm, 1975), pp. 64, 69, 197.

11. Obviously, approaches exclusively or mainly based on ethnic women's labor-force participation are not useful to the issue of reproduction: e.g., Diane K. Lewis, "A

Response to Inequality: Black Women, Racism and Sexism," *Signs* 3, No. 2 (Winter 1977): 339–61.

12. For a critique of the new sociobiology, see Ruth Hubbard, Mary Sue Henifin, and Barbara Fried, eds., *Women Look at Biology Looking at Women: A Collection of Feminist Critiques* (Cambridge, Mass.: Schenkman, 1979); Chandler Davis, "La sociobiologie et son explication de l'humanité," *Annales*, E.S.C. 36 (July-August 1981):531–71. For the international dimension of older eugenics, see Chase, *Legacy of Malthus*; Loren R. Graham, "Science and Values: The Eugenics Movement in Germany and Russia in the 1920's," *American Historical Review* 82 (1977): 1133–64; G. R. Searle, *Eugenics and Politics in Britain, 1900–1914* (Leyden: Nordhoff International, 1976); and Anna Davin, "Imperialism and Motherhood," *History Workshop* (1978): 10–65. It is important to note that in fascist Italy, race hygiene did not take hold. Of course, present policies in the United States and women's campaigns for reproductive rights are immediately relevant to the issue and approach of this essay: Committee for Abortion Rights and Against Sterilization Abuse, *Women under Attack: Abortion, Sterilization Abuse, and Reproductive Freedom* (New York: CARASA, 1979).

13. Such new approaches have been presented at the Third National Women's Studies Association Conference, "Women Respond to Racism," Storrs, Connecticut, May 31-June 6, 1981. Of particular significance seemed to me the presentations by Vicky Spelman, Arlene Aviakin, and Mary Ruth Warner on "Feminist Theory and the Invisibility of Black Culture." See also Bonnie Thornton Dill, "The Dialectics of Black Womanhood," *Signs* 4, Vol. 3 (Spring 1979): 543–55, and Cherríe Moraga and Gloria Anzaldúa, eds., *This Bridge Called My Back: Writings of Radical Women of Color* (Watertown, Mass.: Persephone Press, 1981). For a different version of the double-oppression approach, see Gerda Lerner, "Black Women in the United States: A Problem in Historiography and Interpretation" (1973), in *The Majority Finds Its Past: Placing Women in History* (New York and Oxford: Oxford University Press, 1979), pp. 63–82; and *Teaching Women's History* (Washington, D.C.: American Historical Association, 1981), pp. 60–65.

14. For early sterilization practice and theory, see Otto Krankeleit, *Die Unfruchtbarmachung aus rassenhygienischen und sozialen Gründen* (Munich: Lehmann, 1929), pp. 41–45; Hans Harmsen, *Praktische Bevölkerungspolitik* (Berlin: Junker & Dünnhaupt, 1931), p. 84; Baur, Fischer, and Lenz, *Grundriss*, p. 270.

15. There was a extensive writing on this subject in the 1920s, and Chase (*Legacy of Malthus*, p. 349) seems to underestimate the German roots of the movement. Compare, as examples, note 6 above.

16. Marielouise Janssen-Jurreit, "Sexualreform und Geburtenrückgang," in Kuhn and Schneider, eds., *Frauen in der Geschichte*, pp. 56–81.

17. Chase, *Legacy of Malthus*, pp. xv–xxii and chap. 1.

18. *Die Sonne: Monatsschrift für nordische Weltanschauung und Lebensgestaltung* 10, No. 2 (1933):111.

19. The latter term is taken from the address of the president of the British Eugenics Society at the Third International Congress of Eugenics, New York, 1932, cited in Chase, *Legacy of Malthus*, p. 20.

20. In 1913, 4,000 working-class women assembled in Berlin to hear about the "birthstrike" and attracted huge attention. See Anneliese Bergmann, "Geburtenrückgang—Gebärstreik: Zur Gebärstreikdebatte in Berlin," *Archiv für die Geschichte des Widerstands und der Arbeit* 4 (1980); 7–55. Cf. G. Ardersleben, *Der Gebärstreik der Frauen und seine Folgen* (Lorch: Rohm, 1913); and Ernst Kahn, *Der internationale Gebärstreik* (Frankfurt: Societäts-Verlag, 1930).

21. Gustav Boeters, "Die Unfruchtbarmachung geistig Minderwertiger," *Wissenschaftliche Beilage zur Leipziger Lehrenzeitung* 28 (August 1928): 217.

22. *Von der Verhütung unwerten Lebens-Ein Zyklus in 5 Vorträgen* (Bremen: Bremer Beiträge zur Naturwissenschaft, 1933), pp. 15, 52, 61.

23. The differential birthrate is a main issue in all books on eugenics. On social differences in fertility, see John Knodel, *The Decline of Fertility in Germany, 1871–1939* (Princeton: Princeton University Press, 1974), pp. 223–45; Chase, *Legacy of Malthus*, pp. 403–05.

24. E.g., Roderich von Ungern-Sternberg, *Die Ursachen des Geburtenrückganges im europäischen Kulturkreis* (Berlin: Schoetz, 1932), esp. pp. 63–75, 174, 203; Grotjahn, *Geburten-Rückgang*, pp. 316–17.

25. E.g., Grotjahn, *Geburten-Rückgang*, p. 187: "Indeed, we should not underestimate the danger, that the methods of birth prevention, which . . . are necessary for a future rational eugenic regulation of the process of the human species, are presently abused for limiting the number of children independently of their value." Therefore he wants "to turn the technique of birth control into the point of departure for an essential control of human reproduction" (p. 43).

26. Josef Grassl, "Weiteres zur Frage der Mutterschaft," *Archiv für Rassen- und Gesellschaftsbiologie* 6 (1909): 351–66, esp. 366; Krankeleit, *Die Unfruchtbarmachung*, p. 95. These and all other translations from the German are my own.

27. *Reichsgesetzblatt* 1933/I, p. 296 (hereafter RGB); *Wirtschaft und Statistik* 15 (1935): 737, and 19 (1939): 534.

28. RGB, 1935/I, p. 1035; Stephenson, *Women in Nazi Society*, p. 68.

29. Bundesarchiv Koblenz, R 18/5517, pp. 251–52 (hereafter BAK); RGB, 1943/I, p. 140.

30. RGB, 1933/I, p. 296; Eberhardt Schmidt, "Das Sterilisationsproblem nach dem in der Bundesrepublik geltenden Strafrecht," *Juristenzeitung* 3 (February 5, 1951): 65–70.

31. RGB, 1933/I, p. 529; Martin Broszat, *Der Staat Hitlers* (Munich: Deutscher Taschenbuch Verlag, 1969), p. 356; Kurt Nowak, *"Euthanasie" und Sterilisierung im "Dritten Reich": Die Konfrontation der evangelischen und katholischen Kirche mit dem "Gesetz zur Verhütung erbkranken Nachwuchses" und der "Euthanasie"-Aktion* (Göttingen: Vanderhoeck & Ruprecht, 1980), esp. pp. 64–65.

32. Wilhelm Frick, *Ansprache auf der ersten Sitzung des Sachverständigenbeirates für Bevölkerungs- und Rassenpolitik* (Berlin: Schriftenreihe des Reichsausschusses für Volksgesundheitsdienst 1, 1933), p. 8.

33. Broszat, *Der Staat Hitlers*, pp. 356–57; Nowak, *"Euthanasie,"* p. 65.

34. Law of November 24, 1933, RGB, 1933/I, p. 995.

35. RGB, 1936/I, pp. 119, 122; BAK, R 22/943, p. 234.

36. Léon Poliakov and Josef Wulf, eds., *Das Dritte Reich und die Juden* (Berlin: Arani, 1955), p. 385; Alexander Mitscherlich and Fred Mielke, *Medizin ohne Menschlichkeit* (Frankfurt: Fischer, 1978), pp. 240–48; BAK, R 18/5519.

37. Law of July 3, 1934, RGB, 1934/I, p. 531; BAK, NSD 50/626, p. 10; Arthur Gütt, Herbert Linden, and Franz Massfeller, *Blutschutz- und Ehegesundheitsgesetz* (Munich: Lehmann, 1937). By the two laws described in the latter official commentary, marriage was prohibited with "alien races" as well as with the "defective" among the "German-blooded." In the "Blutschutz" (= Nuremberg) law, marriage prohibition concerned, besides Jews, "Negroes, gypsies, and bastards" (p. 16).

38. Gütt, Linden, and Massfeller, *Blutschutz*, pp. 9–10, 283–87.

39. Richard Grunberger, *The 12 Year Reich: A Social History of Nazi Germany, 1933–1945* (New York: Holt, Rinehart & Winston, 1972), p. 365; see also my article on sterilization and abortion, " 'Zum Wohle.' "

40. Friedrich Burgdörfer, *Geburtenschwund: Die Kulturkrankheit Europas und ihre Überwindung in Deutschland* (Heidelberg-Berlin-Magedeburg: Vowinckel, 1942), p. 80, and *Kinder des Vertrauens* (Berlin: Eher, 1942).

41. Bleuel, *Das saubere Reich*, pp. 21, 45; Grunberger, *12 Year Reich*, chaps. 16, 17; Tim Mason, "Women in Germany, 1925–1940: Family, Welfare, and Work," *History Workshop* 1 (1976): 74–113, esp. 87.
42. For demographic debate see David V. Glass, *Population: Policies and Movements in Europe* (1940; reprint ed., London: Frank Cass, 1967), pp. 269–313 on Germany and *passim* for other European countries; Knodel, *Decline of Fertility;* Bergdörfer, *Geburtenschwund;* Stephenson, *Women in Nazi Society;* Mason, "Women in Germany," *History Workshop* 1 (1976): 74–113, esp. 95–105, and 2 (1976): 5–32, esp. 12–14; Wolfgang Köllman, "Bevölkerungsentwicklung in der Weimarer Republik," in *Industrielles System und politische Entwicklung in der Weimarer Republik,* eds. Hans Mommsen, Dietmar Petzina, and Bernd Weisbrod (Düsseldorf: Athenäum-Droste, 1977), Vol. 1, pp. 76–84.
43. K. Astel and E. Weber, *Die Kinderzahl der 29,000 politischen Leiter des Gaues Thüringen der NSDAP* (Berlin: Metzner, 1943); Heinrich Himmler, *Geheimreden 1933–1945,* ed. Bradley F. Smith and Agnes F. Peterson (Frankfurt-Berlin-Vienna: Ullstein, 1974), p. 91.
44. Leila J. Rupp, "I Don't Call That *Volksgemeinschaft:* Women, Class, and War in Nazi Germany," in *Women, War and Revolution,* ed. Carol R. Berkin and Clara M. Lovett (New York and London: Holmes and Meier, 1980), p. 43; Bleuel, *Das saubere Reich,* p. 81; Winkler, *Frauenarbeit,* pp. 72–73. The quotation is from a high government official: Gitte Schefer, "Wo Unterdrückung ist, da ist auch Widerstand: Frauen gegen Faschismus und Krieg," in Frauengruppe, Faschismusforschung, ed., *Mutterkreuz,* p. 289.
45. Glass, *Population,* pp. 311–13.
46. BAK, R 18/2957; Atina Grossmann, "Abortion and Economic Crisis: The 1931 Campaign Against Paragraph 218 in Germany," *New German Critique* 14 (Spring 1978): 119–37, reprinted in this volume.
47. BAK, R 18/2957.
48. Himmler, *Geheimreden,* p. 91.
49. Adrienne Rich, *Of Woman Born: Motherhood as Experience and Institution* (New York: Norton, 1976), chap. 7.
50. Mason, "Women in History," p. 101; Bleuel, *Das saubere Reich,* p. 43.
51. Alexander Paul, "Ist Erbangst berechtigt?" *Volk und Rasse* 16 (1941): 130–35.
52. This is evident from the documents of the sterilization courts on which I am working. See also Theresia Seible (a sterilized German Gypsy woman), "Aber ich wollte vorher noch ein Kind," *Courage* 6 (May 1981): 21–24.
53. *Vom Sieg der Waffen zum Sieg der Wiegen* (Berlin: Reichsbund der Kinderreichen, 1942), p. 23. Space does not permit me to deal with an important financial corollary to the race-hygienic body policies: "incentives" such as marriage loans and child allowances given only to the "desirables" and only to husbands, not to wives.
54. Frick, *Ansprache,* p. 3.
55. For the social and historical significance of the first category see Chase, *Legacy of Malthus,* esp. chap. 7; of the second, see Thomas S. Szasz, *Schizophrenia* (New York: Basic Books, 1976). The precise number of sterilizations is unknown. Compare Nowak, "*Euthanasie,*" pp. 65, 118 n. 6. In 1967, an interstate commission of the Federal Republic of Germany investigated the number of "those unjustly sterilized under Nazism." While the number estimated (300,000 to 320,000) seems justified, this is certainly not true for the number of "unjust" sterilizations (83,000); the document has not been published. The other information is taken from BAK, R 18/5585, pp. 329–31. See Arthur Gütt, Ernst Rüdin, and Falk Ruttke, *Gesetz zur Verhütung erbkranken Nachwuchses vom 14. Juli 1933* (Munich: Lehmann, 1936). For the United States, see Chase, *Legacy of Malthus,* p. 350; Baur, Fischer, and Lenz, *Grundriss,* Vol. 2, p. 271.

56. Elisabeth Hofmann, *Körperliches Befinden und Einstellung von Frauen, die nach dem Erbgesundheitsgesetz sterilisiert wurden* (Heidelberg: 1937), pp. 14–17.
57. Gütt, Rüdin, Ruttke, *Gesetz zur Verhütung,* 1934 ed., pp. 73–78, and *passim.*
58. BAK: R 18/5585, p. 337. This official ruling corresponds to Gütt, Rüdin, Ruttke, *Gesetz zur Verhütung,* p. 125.
59. This is a preliminary evaluation of the records of the sterilization courts in three German cities; it agrees, generally, with the results of Gisela Dieterle (Freiburg), who is working on the records of another city, and with Wilfent Dalicho, "Sterilisation in Köln auf Grund des Gesetzes zur Verhütung erbkranken Nachwuchses, . . . 1934–1943" (Medical diss., Cologne, 1971), esp. pp. 160–65. There has been no research on the sterilization of male homosexuals, mostly performed outside the court procedure of sterilization law. Lesbian women are hardly ever mentioned in the court records (and very rarely in other archival documents from 1933 to 1945). We must assume, however, that they were strongly represented among the women in the asylums, and from reports given by women who were inmates of concentration camps, we know that many lesbians were among those incarcerated. See, e.g., Fania Fenelon, *Das Mädchenorchester in Auschwitz* (Frankfurt: Röderberg, 1980), chap. 21.
60. According to an addition to the law of December 5, 1933: Gütt, Rüdin, and Ruttke, *Gesetz zur Verhütung,* p. 84. For the general poverty of asylum inmates, see Klaus Dörner, *Bürger und Irre* (Frankfurt: Europäische Verlagsanstalt, 1969).
61. Klaus Dörner, "Nationalsozialismus und Lebensvernichtung," *Vierteljahreshefte für Zeitgeschichte* 15 (1967): 121–52, reprinted in Dörner, *Diagnosen der Psychiatrie* (Frankfurt and New York: Campus, 1975), pp. 59–95, esp. pp. 76–82; Dörner et al., eds., *Der Krieg gegen die psychisch Kranken* (Rehburg and Loccum: Psychiatrie-Verlag, 1980); Nowak, *"Euthanasie,"* pp. 77–85.
62. Mitscherlich and Mielke, *Medizin,* pp. 197–205. For the merger between gut and scientific racism in Germany, see esp. Chase, *Legacy of Malthus,* chap. 15. For the continuity of methods and means, see Gerald Reitlinger, *The Final Solution: The Attempt to Exterminate the Jews of Europe, 1939–1945* (London: Vallentine, Mitchell & Co., 1953), chaps. 6 and 7; Raul Hilberg, *The Destruction of the European Jews* (Chicago: Quadrangle, 1961), pp. 268–77, and chap. 9.1, esp. pp. 562–63, n. 21.
63. Decree of March 19, 1942, quoted in Werner Feldscher, *Rassen-und Erbpflege im deutschen Recht* (Berlin-Leipzig-Vienna: Deutscher Rechtsverlag, 1943), p. 123; BAK:R 43 II/720, p. 92; Stephenson, *Women in Nazi Society,* pp. 62–63; *Vom Sieg der Waffen;* Reiner Pommerin, "The Fate of Mixed Blood Children in Germany," *German Studies* Review 5/3 (1982): 315–23.
64. Dalicho, "Sterilisation," pp. 157–60 (12 to 20 percent).
65. These terms are, as might be obvious, not meant to mark the "ethnic" as "nonsocial" and therefore as "biological." Clearly what is meant by "biological" in the racist tradition is plainly "social" and often enough described in plainly social concepts. The above terms are meant to call attention to the links between different historical forms of racism. Moreover, "social racism" seems to me more accurate than "social Darwinism," as it is usually called, since Darwin certainly did not start it. Even though social history is more complicated than "Malthus started it all" (Chase, *Legacy of Malthus,* p. 12), it is true that the issues in question have older and/or different roots than Darwinism.
66. An illuminating example is the race hygiene classic by Baur, Fischer, and Lenz, *Grundriss,* esp. Vol. 2, and Bluhm, *Die rassenhygienischen Aufgaben.*
67. E.g., Paul Schultze-Naumburg, "Das Eheproblem in der Nordischen Rasse," *Die Sonne* 9 (1932), esp. pp. 20–25. Compare Karin Hausen, "Family and Role Division: The Polarization of Sexual Stereotypes in the 19th Century," in *The German Family,*

ed. Richard J. Evans and W. R. Lee (London: Croom Helm, 1981), pp. 51–83; Barbara Duden, "Das schöne Eigentum: Zur Herausbildung des bürgerlichen Frauenbildes an der Wende vom 18. zum 19. Jahrhundert," *Kursbuch* 47 (March 1977): 125–41.

68. Bleuel, *Das saubere Reich*, p. 178; Stephenson, *Women in Nazi Society*, p. 46; Winkler, *Frauenarbeit*, p. 49; Grunberger, *12 Year Reich*, chap. 16; Mason, "Women in History," pp. 87, 94–96, 100–02.

69. A list of further pertinent measures: Burgdörfer, *Geburtenschwund*, pp. 202–14.

70. *Monatsberichte über die deutsche Sozialordnung* 10 (1943), p. 6. These were, of course, not all children born in these families but just the ones that might be, if at all, linked to the "incentive." For the others, the general tendency is very similar to that described by Kälvemark for Sweden.

71. BAK: R: 18/3768; Gütt, Linden, Massfeller, *Blutschutz*, pp. 301–304. BAK: NS 19/ 1838; Uwe Adam, *Judenpolitik im Dritten Reich* (Droste Verlag: Düsseldorf, 1972), p. 169.

72. *Neues Volk* 1, no. 9 (1935): 30.

73. Burgdörfer, *Geburtenschwund*, p. 187. *Verfügungen, Anordnungen, Bekanntgaben*, ed. Parteikanzlei (Munich, 1942). Vol. 2, pp. 85–86, 93–103, 105–107 (decrees of the Minister of Finance from January 30, March 3, July 26, 1941); *Der Gemeindetag* 5/6 (1942).

74. Documents on this recurring event are scattered through the files of various large cities.

75. Burgdörfer, *Geburtenschwund*, p. 39.

76. Paul Danzer, *Geburtenkrieg* (Munich: Politische Biologie 3, 1939).

77. RGB, 1939/I, p. 1560.

78. Manfred Höck, *Die Hilfsschule im Dritten Reich* (Berlin: Marhold, 1979), p. 75.

79. See note 37 above, and Jan Sehn, "Carl Clausbergs verbrecherische Unfruchtbarmachungsversuche an Häftlings-Frauen in den Nazi-Konzentrationslagern," *Hefte von Auschwitz* 2 (Oswiecim, 1959), pp. 2–32.

80. On foreign women mainly from the east, see Ingrid Schupetta, "'Jeder das Ihre': Frauenerwerbstätigkeit und Einsatz von Fremdarbeitern und -arbeiterinnen im Zweiten Weltkrieg," in Frauengruppe Faschismusforschung, ed., *Mutterkreuz*, pp. 292–318; Franciszek Polomski, *Aspekty Rasowe w postepowanin z r robotnikami przymnsowymi i jeucami wojennymi III rzeszsy, 1939–45* [Racial Aspects in the Treatment of Forced Laborers and War Prisoners of the Third Reich] (Wroclaw: Ossolinskich, 1976); *Documenta Occupationis*, Vols. 9 and 10 (Poznan: Instytut Zachodni, 1975, 1976).

81. Frank Pingel, *Häftlinge unter SS-Herrschaft* (Hamburg: Hoffmann & Campe, 1978), pp. 69–80; Dalicho, "Sterilisation," pp. 54, 58, 60, 61, 63, 66.

82. Karl Ludwig Lechler, "Erkennung und Ausmerze der Gemeinschaftsunfähigen," *Deutsches Ärtzeblatt* 70 (1940): 293–97.

83. The documents are scattered in many files of such agencies.

84. The pertinent documents are scattered in various archives.

85. E.g., Burgdörfer, *Geburtenschwund*, pp. 136–47; G. Pfotenhauer, "Fortpflanzungspflicht—die andere Seite des Gesetzes zur Verhütung erbkranken Nachwuchses," *Der öffentliche Gesundheitsdienst* 2 (1937): 604–08.

86. For lesbian women and their presentation as "pseudo-men" by male psychiatrists since the last third of the nineteenth century, see Esther Newton and Carroll Smith-Rosenberg, "Male Mythologies and their Internalization of Deviance from Krafft-Ebing to Radclyffe Hall," and Gudrun Schwartz, "The Creation of the *Mannweib*, 1860–1900" (papers presented at the Fifth Berkshire Conference on the History of Women, Vassar College, June 16, 1981). For male views of prostitutes, see my article "Prostituierte im Nazi-Staat" in *Wir sind Frauen wie andere auch*, ed. Pieke

Biermann (Reinbek: Rowohlt, 1980), pp. 70–106; Judith Walkowitz, *Prostitution and Victorian Society: Women, Class and the State* (New York: Cambridge University Press, 1980), esp. chap. 10.

87. For an approach focusing on such symbols, see Elizabeth Janeway, "Who is Sylvia? On the Loss of Sexual Paradigms," *Signs* 5, No. 4 (Summer 1980): 573–89.

88. "Population Science" has been established in Bamburg and Bielefeld, while women have been, in vain, trying to get women's studies recognized and financed: *Beiträge zur feministischen Theorie und Praxis* 5 (April 1981): 119–27. For other information on immigrant women, sterilization, welfare, and state benefits, see the following issues of *Courage:* (March 1977): 16–29; 3 (April 1978): 14–29; 3 (September 1978): 11; 3 (October 1978): 44–47; 4 (June 1979): 39–40; 4 (September 1979): 27–29; 4 (October 1979): 12–17; 5 (April 1980): 12–13; 5 (May 1980): 12–13; 6 (March 1981): 5–8, 52; 6 (May 1981): 16–33; 6 (December 1981): 22–33; 7 (January 1982): 8–11. See also *Zu Hause in der Fremde,* ed. Christian Schaffernicht (Fischerhude: Verlag Atelier, 1981), pp. 74–75.

# Women and the Holocaust: The Case of German and German-Jewish Women

## Sybil Milton

*The same "racial hygiene" principles discussed by Gisela Bock were later used to justify extermination of the "unwanted," Jews in particular, as well as Gypsies, and "deviants" of various sorts. Sybil Milton provides the stark facts of the experience of German and German-Jewish women, both racial victims and political opponents, under the Nazi regime. In harrowing detail, she lists the stages of persecution (from jails to concentration and extermination camps) and the possibilities for survival outside the camps. Even under the extremes of German fascism, a situation many might suppose to be beyond the divisions of gender, Milton shows how women's experiences differed in some ways from men's. Indeed, women faced particular dangers and humiliations and drew on their own unique resources for day-to-day survival.*

The general subject of women and the Holocaust has received no systematic coverage in the growing literature on Nazi Germany and the Jewish catastrophe. Apart from memoirs, partisan literature, television productions, and token references, women have been largely invisible in the current historiography on the subject.[1] The classic secondary literature on the Holocaust is not sex-specific in language, referring to prisoners, victims, survivors, and perpetrators. This limits any analysis of gender-specific experiences and conditions. Recent literature, based mostly on the experiences of male perpetrators, male victims, and male survivors, has provided incomplete—and sometimes even biased and misleading—accounts of women's experiences under Nazi persecution. Although both men and women were victims of the organized state system of terror, the experiences that separated women from male prisoners have remained unexplored.

At the outset, two general premises must be stated explicitly. First, although Nazi Germany was in theory and practice a male-dominated society, this essay will not deal with the general victimization of women in that society, but only with women persecuted for racial, religious, or political reasons. Second, it is difficult and probably impossible to conceptualize these persecuted women as a unified group, since there are enormous and complex variations in their backgrounds. Thus this essay examines aspects of women's tragic odyssey between 1933 and 1945. It focuses, in particular, on German and German-Jewish women, both to conform to the subject of this book and because Nazi policies were developed and tested in their own homeland, Germany, before being exported throughout Nazi-occupied Europe. The subject of women and the Holocaust is moreover a field in its infancy, and it is too early to begin to understand the contours of this subject on a pan-European basis. Thus, we ought to explore the gender-specific experiences of German and German-Jewish women in German concentration camps and in hiding, flight, and resistance outside the camps. Their experiences should contribute to our understanding of the Holocaust in its entirety.

## *The Victims of Violence: German and German-Jewish Women*

Nazi coercion and violence against female political opponents began immediately after Hitler assumed power. Women socialist, communist, and moderate liberal parliamentary deputies on the national, state, and municipal levels were among the first targets. They were harassed by the Gestapo and the SA, who repeatedly searched their homes and offices; they were also often brutally interrogated and beaten. Many were held hostage for politically active male relatives in flight or in hiding. The women were arrested and confined in correctional and penal institutions; many were subsequently remanded to indefinite detention in concentration camps. A few were murdered.

Some examples will suffice to show the arbitrary brutality and calculated violence that the Nazis used equally against men and women to exact political revenge and enforce social control. Minna Cammens, former Socialist Reichstag deputy from Breslau, was arrested in March 1933 for distributing anti-Nazi leaflets and was murdered by the Gestapo during detention in protective custody.[2] Leni Rosenthal, Socialist ex-deputy in the Prussian State Legislature, was murdered by the Gestapo in October 1936.[3] The Communist Reichstag deputies Franziska Kessel and Helene Fleischer were also killed; Kessel was found hanged, probably murdered, in her jail cell in April 1934, and Fleischer died in the Moringen concentration camp for women in 1940, the result of seven years of brutal maltreatment while incarcerated.[4]

Vigilante SA thugs severely beat the Berlin Socialist municipal councilor Marie Jankowski in March 1933. This incident led to a formal protest to Reichstag President Goering by Jankowski's socialist friend and colleague Clara Bohm-Schuch. As a result, Bohm-Schuch was subjected to repeated house searches by the Gestapo and arrested for fifteen days in April 1934. Her death in May 1936 was attributed to the abuses she suffered.[5] The Communist Helene Overlach became severely ill after five years of mistreatment in the women's prisons of Aichach, Ziegenhain, and Gotteszell.[6] Even moderates, like the Democratic Party deputy Marie-Elisabeth Lüders and the Center Party's Christine Teusch, spent many months in Gestapo jails.[7]

The politics of intimidation and reprisal led to the arrest of wives, sisters, and daughters for the political activities of their absentee male relatives. The use of female hostages continued after the initial Nazi seizure of power in Germany, eventually extending to all of occupied Europe after 1940. When Gerhart Seger published his account in Czech exile in 1934 about his experiences and flight from the Oranienburg concentration camp, his wife and daughter were arrested in reprisal and released only after international protest.[8] Senta Beimler and her sister-in-law, Maria Dengler, were sentenced to indefinite protective custody in the Moringen women's concentration camp after her husband, Bavarian Communist deputy Hans Beimler, escaped from Dachau in 1933.[9] Similarly, Rudolf Meissner, a Jehovah's Witness, learned after emigrating in 1935 that his sister was arrested as a hostage for his behavior abroad.[10] Although the Socialist Franz Müller was safe across the Czech border, his wife was vulnerable. She was arrested in Chemnitz in June 1935 and held for over eleven months, despite the fact that their four children, aged six to twelve, were left bereft of parental support.[11] Else Steinfurth received a one-year jail term, soon extended for an indeterminate period, after her husband, an official of the Communist welfare organization Red Help *(Rote Hilfe)*, was shot in 1934 "while trying to escape." The official rationale for her continued detention was that her husband's death might cause "atrocity propaganda abroad" were she released.[12] At the end of 1935, 75 percent of the women in the Hohenstein jail—thirty-three out of forty-five women—were hostages for their male relatives.[13] Persecuted for either their own politics or as symbolic targets for their dissident male relatives, these women were vilified as traitors and blacklisted from public and professional employment in Nazi Germany.

Comparatively little historical attention has been focused on German prisons during the Nazi years, although they were the initial and primary place of detention for women until 1939. Precise statistics of the inmate population and its component groups are not easily available. It is estimated that 1,500 to 2,000 German women political opponents and hostages were confined in Nazi jails before 1939; this figure represented about 15 to 20 percent of all protective custody prisoners *(Schutzhäftlinge)* detained in prewar Nazi Germany. After 1935, this category for domestic subversives also included female Jehovah's Witnesses and Gypsies. The number of Jewish women detained in jails under protective custody cannot be established for these early years, although they probably represented less than 25 percent of the women held in *Schutzhaft*. The total female inmate population of the Nazi prisons between 1933 and 1939 was between 6,000 and 8,000 women, a majority arrested as so-called asocials (a category covering prostitutes, lesbians, vagrants, shirkers, and any person the police thought unfit for civilian society) and criminals (murderers, thieves, and violators of laws prohibiting sexual intercourse between Aryans and Jews).[14] Jewish women were incarcerated in the jails and concentration camps of Nazi Germany before 1939, *only if* they belonged to one of the other affected categories.

Jewish women were targets as Jews and not as women in the sporadic violence that accompanied the April 1933 boycott, the Nuremberg legislation in September 1935, the expulsion of Polish Jews in late October 1938, and the "Crystal Night" *(Kristallnacht)* pogrom in early November 1938. Vignettes from daily life before 1938 reveal that Jewish women were more vulnerable to verbal assaults than to physical violence in early encounters with Nazi vigilantes.[15] Normal social inhibitions still operative before 1939 prevented street violence against even Jewish women, despite their position as social pariahs.

After 1933, Jewish women were vulnerable to an unending barrage of insults and propaganda, including pressure exerted on their Christian husbands to divorce them. They were also subject to an "insidious creeping persecution" that legally excluded them from professional employment and inexorably banished them from the social, cultural, intellectual, and economic life of Germany.[16] Occasionally, they were also the targets of physical violence and sporadically of sexual assaults.[17]

Before "Crystal Night", ideological hostility was not immediately transformed into physical violence. Capricious and random acts of courtesy provided a small measure of protection even for Jewish women, who were otherwise ostracized and intimidated. Occasional acts of kindness did not prevent their ultimate deportation or murder, but it did show the limits of Nazi ideology and power during the early years. Neither racist propaganda nor government pressure could modify traditional behavior patterns towards "weaker" members of society (women, the elderly, and children of both sexes), nor could it always sever close social and personal ties between individuals. In the early years, this occasionally subverted or even ameliorated the excesses of Nazi behavior. Thus, for example, during the April 1933 boycott, local bus drivers in Pömbsen, Westphalia, were officially prohibited from carrying Jewish passengers between the railroad depot and the town business district. They nevertheless continued to transport vacationing Jewish school children and old women.[18]

During the expulsion of Polish Jews from Germany in late October 1938, 483 Polish Jews residing in Chemnitz were interned overnight in a local dance hall. The sudden expulsion meant that Jews left clothing, luggage, food, and other possessions behind. The interned Jewish women were treated with greater consideration and allowed to return to their homes under police guard in order to pack necessities for the trip to Poland.[19] Perhaps the police considered this concession to the incarcerated women a necessary expedient in order to pacify the frightened mass of prisoners, thereby ensuring an easier job of guarding the convoy on the journey to Poland. Packing household goods for the family was considered a woman's job, and women, intimidated by police presence, were less likely to smuggle valuables or escape custody. In Baden, women and minor children were left unmolested in their homes and only the men were expelled.

During the pogrom of November 9–10, 1938, 30,000 German-Jewish men were arrested and sent to concentration camps, but no women were arrested or deported to camps. Examples of correct behavior and practical assistance did occur,[20] but were probably exceptional, since vandalism, looting, theft, and rapes occurred during the excesses of "Crystal Night."[21]

Between 1933 and 1939 a large increase occurred in the ratio of Jewish women to men residing in Germany. In 1933, there were 1,093 Jewish women to 1,000 Jewish men; by 1939, this increased to 1,366 Jewish women to 1,000 Jewish men.[22] This relatively large increase in the number of Jewish women can be attributed to several factors: the excess number of German-Jewish women (including war widows) in the post–World War I population; the higher male mortality rate, since women usually outlived men and men were more vulnerable to confinement and maltreatment in Nazi concentration camps; and the substantial rise in international emigration by Jewish young and middle-aged single men after 1933. Thus the census of April 1939 recorded respectively 123,104 female Jews and 90,826 male Jews in Germany.[23] The comparatively large number of Jewish women meant that more German-Jewish women than men were deported and murdered after October 1941.[24]

As already mentioned, German-Jewish women found in concentration camps before October 1938 had been arrested as *individuals*. However, from October 1938 to October 1940, German and foreign Jewish women were treated as a *group* in a series of three experimental mass deportations. The first event was the expulsion of male Polish Jews and their family dependents (parents, wives, and minor children) on October 28 and 29, 1938. The expulsion pattern varied locally. In Bochum, Leipzig, and Dresden, whole families were deported together on "a freezing October day" in sealed trains guarded by the SS and police. "Most of the women and children herded into third class waiting rooms had been dragged out of bed without being allowed to pack."[25] In Frankfurt/Main and Nuremberg, women and children were expelled one day later than their spouses and were refused entry into Poland. Their return train fare was paid by local Jewish communities, who also negotiated the release of their sealed and sequestered homes and property. In Baden, only healthy male Jews above the age of eighteen were expelled, leaving wives and children impoverished, bewildered, and distraught. About 4,000 to 5,000 women and children from these last two groups were issued exit visas to Poland in June 1939, when some families were reunited.[26] About 6,000 of the 17,000 Polish Jews expelled in October 1938 were trapped in a primitive refugee camp near the Polish border at Zbaszyn, unable to return to Germany or to enter the interior of Poland.[27]

Two further trial deportations involving Jewish women occurred after the German occupation of Poland and northern France during 1940. The first occurred in February 1940, when 6,000 Jewish residents from Stettin, Vienna, Prague, and Moravian Ostrava were removed to Lublin in the General Government (the official name for Nazi-occupied Poland).[28] The last experimental deportation, in October 1940, dumped 7,000 German Jews from Baden and the Palatinate into internment camps in unoccupied southern France. Approximately 3,800 German Jewish women were among the Baden deportees sent to Gurs; they constituted 88 percent of the 5,000 German and Austrian women (predominantly Jewish) interned as enemy aliens in Gurs and other French camps after 1939. These women became vulnerable after 1941 to further deportations to the east.[29] After 1941, the deportations increased in size and frequency and systematically involved German-Jewish women as well as native Jews from every nation of occupied Europe.

### Camps for Women, 1933–1945

After arrest, administrative commitment, or judicial trial, women were sent to prisons, penitentiaries, converted workhouses, and concentration camps, where they were vulnerable to Gestapo whims and the arbitrary abuses of police power. Despite the presence of courts, the Gestapo had broad powers of interference in German jails. A pattern of indeterminate and indefinite sentences first in prisons and later in concentration camps became the norm. Women political prisoners were not sent to the early well-known concentration camps like

Oranienburg, Dachau, or Esterwegen. They were instead interned in six centralized protective-custody centers located after the spring of 1933 in penal and correctional institutions. These were: (1) Gotteszell prison near Schwäbisch-Gmünd in Württemberg; (2) Stadelheim prison in Munich; (3) the Barnim Street women's prison in Berlin; (4) Fuhlsbüttel prison near Hamburg; (5) the Brauweiler penitentiary in Westphalia; and (6) Hohenstein castle near Schandau in Saxony.[30] Women were also held in other local jails and improvised detention centers throughout Germany, such as the Aichach penitentiary in Upper Bavaria and the Moringen workhouse, located near Hanover in Lower Saxony.

Gotteszell was opened in March 1933 in a vacant convent. It initially held fifty-four women political inmates, who shared two small over-crowded cells. The first warden at Gotteszell was a lenient and proper administrator, schooled in the Weimar penal system.[31] The inmates were allowed material for knitting and sewing; they could also play chess and read books from the prison library. They even held an illegal May Day demonstration in 1933, improvising a flag from strips of red cloth torn from their clothing. Conditions at Gotteszell were atypical because of the absence of physical intimidation.[32]

The prison at Stadelheim was more typical, characterized by notoriously long detentions in solitary confinement for women politicals and miserably inadequate prison food.[33] Another typical jail was the penitentiary at Aichach in Upper Bavaria, which housed about 1,000 women; the majority were convicted criminals (thieves and prostitutes), who were involuntarily subjected to illegal sterilizations. A few of the prisoners at Aichach were political detainees.[34]

The jail facility at Hohenstein, located among the forests and isolated mountain peaks of Saxon Switzerland, was once a notorious sixteenth-century dungeon converted into a large and attractive youth hostel during the Weimar Republic. The Nazi commandant, his deputy, and the all male staff were exceedingly brutal. The facility housed between 25 and 40 women politicals in the same building with nearly 600 male prisoners.

New prisoners were greeted by taunts and humiliating dirty tricks on arrival. SA men tripped the marching women with night sticks and extended legs, threw water at their skirts and then teased them for "urinating," and insulted them as "slovenly sluts." The women lived in a single overcrowded cell, containing double-tiered bunk beds covered with thin straw mattresses. They sometimes spent both days and nights in this single cell, unable to sit or move about if even half of them were present.

The women were assigned labor inside the castle in the prison laundry, where they washed both guard and prisoner uniforms, linen, and towels, without the aid of washing and drying machines. Hanging huge lines of wet laundry in the cold damp air resulted in severe illness for many of the older and frailer women; inadequate prison clothing made even younger healthier prisoners vulnerable to the combined toll of undernourishment, forced labor, and exposure. The laundry faced the SA offices and women often inadvertently witnessed the interrogation of other inmates. Unlike the male prisoners, employed outside the castle on road construction crews affording them limited possibilities for escape and inside the castle in the prison kitchen, where they could secure better rations, the women's work assignments offered no possibilities for flight or improved conditions. The results of overcrowding, filth, and vermin were compounded by the lack of adequate medical care; the prison physician, a member of the SA, visited the facility only once a week for two hours. The women were also vulnerable to heterosexual rape by guards and criminal inmates.[35]

The regime at Hohenstein was capricious, brutal, corrupt, and incompetent; these conditions were duplicated in many other women's prisons throughout Nazi Germany. Before 1935 women's prisons resembled conditions in the "wild camps" for men (improvised places of detention run by individual local Nazis without rules for the settling of old scores and private vendettas; these temporary detention pens were dissolved after the first year of Nazi rule).[36]

The repressive apparatus of the state extended to the family life and child-care arrangements of arrested dissident women and Jehovah's Witnesses. As spouses were often already in flight, hiding, or emigration, children were involuntarily abandoned when the mother was arrested. Occasionally, the children could be sent to safety abroad or given to relatives and friends, who assumed temporary guardianship over them. Often, however, the children became wards of the Nazi state and were placed in Nazi foster homes, orphanages, and schools. This loss further eroded the morale of interned women, even more than the imprisonment itself.

A few women were released when their jail terms expired, none were paroled early, and many were subsequently detained indefinitely in concentration camps. The first centralized women's concentration camp was created during the winter of 1933; it was followed by a series of similar camps that co-existed alongside the Nazi prison system until 1945. The first camp was located in the former workhouse at Moringen, between Göttingen and Hanover. It remained in operation from October 1933 to March 1938. The second women's camp was Lichtenburg in Saxony, which opened in March 1938 and closed in May 1939. On May 18, 1939, a permanent installation for women was founded at Ravensbrück, located near the town of Fürstenberg in Mecklenburg.[37]

Very little is known about Moringen. Initially, from March to June 1933, the workhouse was used for the administrative incarceration of 300-400 male political enemies.[38] However, by the end of November 1933, Moringen held only a handful of women prisoners; the few Jewish women among them were nevertheless segregated in separate residential quarters. After the Prussian Ministry of Interior designated Moringen a women's concentration camp (*Frauenkonzentrationslager;* FKL) for women arrested in protective custody in all of Germany (order of October 28, 1933), the inmate population stayed between 26 and 70, except during the spring and autumn of 1935 when more women were paroled than detained. The categories of female prisoners did change: in 1933 most were political opponents (communists, socialists, and hostages) or Jehovah's Witnesses; after 1935, the inmate population included an increasing number of Aryan and Jewish women arrested for violations of the racial laws.[39]

New inmates at Moringen could not receive or send mail; after the first month censored mail was permitted once every two weeks. The combination of isolation from their families and the outside world plus constantly overcrowded surroundings resulted in many nervous breakdowns. Women worked inside the camp washing, sorting, and refashioning old clothing collected by the Winter Welfare (*Winterhilfe);* outside labor assignments for women involved physical labor in limestone quarries in all types of weather.

At first, Moringen did not operate according to the concentration camp model established at Dachau: inmates wore neither concentration camp uniforms nor triangular insignia denoting their arrest category. The director of Moringen, Hugo Krack, was a civil servant in the provincial penal and rehabilitation system. The SA and SS were not used as guards or administrators during the first years. The staff of women guards worked under male supervision and was recruited from the Nazi Women's Group (NS Frauenschaft). Two Nazi women physicians were assigned medical duty at Moringen. Nothing is known about the previous employment or training of women guards at Moringen or about personnel changes between 1933 and 1938. After several years, Krack was replaced as director by an SS-man, Cordes.[40] Moringen was dissolved as a women's camp in March 1938; it continued as a juvenile penal institution until the end of the war. The last twenty-five women imprisoned there on March 21, 1938, were transferred to the new women's concentration camp at Lichtenburg.

The second women's concentration camp, Lichtenburg, was located in Saxony near Prettin on the Elbe River. It was a dilapidated sixteenth-century fortress, still in use as a penitentiary in 1928. After June 1933, it became a men's concentration camp until the summer of 1937, when both the inmates and the SS guard units were transferred to Buchenwald. After a brief hiatus when the camp was closed in 1937–1938, it reopened as a women's camp from March 1938 to May 1939. It is not clear whether it was intended as an interim accommodation for housing the growing number of female prisoners arrested in 1937 and 1938, or whether it was to be a permanent FKL. The female inmate population consisted of 1,415 prisoners. This figure included a large number of politicals in protective custody and about 260 Jehovah's Witnesses; there were also large numbers of professional criminals, asocials, and violators of the race-defilement laws. Many prisoner categories included German-Jewish women. Lichtenburg was clearly larger and harsher than Moringen. Punishment for inmate infractions of the camp rules consisted of denial of food, being forced to stand at military attention for hours, and solitary confinement in unlighted cells. Unlike Moringen, the camp commandant and guards were members of the SS.[41]

The first two directors of Lichtenburg were trained at Dachau, the prototype of all later concentration camps.[42] The second, SS Captain Max Koegel, had served in Dachau from 1934 to 1937, assumed command in Lichtenburg on September 1, 1938, and was promoted to the rank of SS Lieutenant-Colonel as the first head of Ravensbrück from May 1939 to August 1942.[43] Although the women's camps were smaller in size and fewer in number than the men's camps before 1939, it is clear that many male and female SS made their professional careers within the camp system and—like the prisoners—were transferred between camps.

Koegel viewed his Lichtenburg inmates as "hysterical females" requiring strict discipline. In a letter of March 14, 1939, Koegel wrote to the Inspector of the Concentration Camps requesting the construction of thirty to forty detention cells at the new Ravensbrück facility. The letter shows his concept of order and authority.

> We will soon move into the new women's camp at Ravensbrück, where I have established the fact that detention cells have neither been built nor planned. Women have been placed in solitary confinement by Gestapo orders in the Lichtenburg camp. It is impossible to maintain order if the defiance and stubbornness of these hysterical females cannot be broken by strict confinement, since no more severe punishment can be used in a women's camp. Denial of food does not suffice for discipline and order in a women's camp.[44]

The solitary confinement cells were built, Koegel was promoted, and 860 German and 7 Austrian female prisoners were transferred to the new camp at Ravensbrück on May 15, 1939.[45] Koegel's letter is important for two reasons: it reveals first, that the worst punishment allowed for German female inmates was solitary confinement and *not* corporal punishment; and second, that the Nazis recognized the importance of camp friendships and bonding in women's resistance and survival. These bonds could be physical, occupational, intellectual, religious, or political, and were often effective in combating the depersonalization and disorientation caused by the camp regimen.[46] Corporal punishment for women inmates was introduced at Ravensbrück only in January 1940 after an inspection by Himmler, although it had existed in the men's concentration camps almost from the first.[47]

Ravensbrück, ostensibly a model camp, was constructed on reclaimed swamp land by male inmates from Sachsenhausen during the winter of 1938–1939. Designed to hold 15,000 prisoners, it eventually housed over 42,000 women from 23 nations. Over 130,000 women passed through Ravensbrück between 1939 and 1945. During the first two years, German and Austrian women inmates dominated the camp population; after 1941, they were outnumbered by new arrivals and categories of prisoners from every country of Nazi-occupied Europe. The average camp population by nationality during the war consisted of: 25 percent Polish women; 20 percent German; 19 percent Russian and Ukrainian; 15 percent Jews from all over Europe; and 21 percent representing several other groups (i.e., 7.3 percent French, 5.4 percent Gypsies, 2.9 percent Belgian, 1.9 percent Czech, 1.2 percent Yugoslavian, and 2.2 percent in other categories).[48] These groups included two barracks of prominent internees like Gemma LaGuardia Gluck, Geneviève de Gaulle, and Rosa Thälmann.[49]

Housing was initially allotted by prisoner category (identified by the color-coded triangles sewn on the inmates' uniforms) rather than by nationality, although this broke down during the massive overcrowding of 1944. Only Gypsy and Jewish women were segregated from the first. The inmate hierarchy placed the earliest arrestees—the politicals, professional criminals, and Jehovah's Witnesses—in a marginally better position for assignments to clerical jobs inside camp offices; Jews, Gypsies, and Soviet women prisoners of war were generally more exploited by the SS guards and rival inmate groups.[50] Ravensbrück was "like a circus, but one without clowns; a circus where crying was heard and no laughter."[51]

Ravensbrück had a similar administrative structure to the men's camps.[52] Until 1942, the inmate mortality among Ravensbrück women was the lowest among all concentration camp prisoners (ca. 84 deaths among 4,000 prisoners in 1941). Even in August 1943, the women's camp at Ravensbrück had a lower mortality than the male camp at Ravensbrück: .27 percent per month for women and .84 percent per month for men.[53] The low mortality rate among women until 1941 was attributed to the relatively uncrowded housing and somewhat better conditions during the early years at Ravensbrück. Later, women showed "greater ingenuity in many things touching directly on the simple preservation of life,"[54] such as nursing sick inmates, refashioning clothing from discarded items, and stretching limited food supplies. Traditional homemaking skills taught to women effectively lowered their vulnerability to death and disease, despite the obviously inadequate lavatory and sanitary facilities.[55]

Ravensbrück later included a separate men's camp, a children's camp at Uckermark, and an extermination installation for women that operated from January to April 1945, when the camp was liberated by the Soviet Army. Before early 1945, women prisoners were retransported to Auschwitz, Lublin-Maidanek, and Bernberg, where they were murdered. Women assigned to labor crews outside the camp worked in nearby factories sewing SS uniforms; manufacturing shoes, furs, airplane parts; and also working an old salt mine. Inside the camp, the labor details were assigned to the SS or to the prisoner laundries and kitchens, to the manufacturing of clothing, and to skilled labor, such as plumbing, carpentry, and masonry.

Ravensbrück was the site of notorious medical experiments on Polish women in 1942 and 1943. The victims of sterilization experiments were called "rabbits" by their SS medical experimenters. Some Ravensbrück inmates, generally referred to as *Schmuckstücke* (literally translated as pieces of jewelry), were the female counterparts to the male inmate *Muselmänner* (the emaciated walking corpses of Auschwitz and other camps). The Nazis used the term ironically and pejoratively, transmuting objective language into terms of contempt to describe the victims that their own policies and deeds had created. It seems probable that gender-specific usage was not peculiar to Ravensbrück, although since it was the largest and earliest major women's concentration camp, the usage probably began there.[56]

Although there has been no systematic study of the uniformed SS women guards (*Aufseherinnen*) assigned to the concentration camp system, some data are available. More than 3,000 women served as uniformed and supervisory guards (*Oberaufseherinnen*) in the network of main and auxiliary camps between 1939 and 1945. A few were volunteers; most were labor conscripts assigned to camp duty. They worked in many camps: 550 at Ravensbrück, 490 at Gross-Rosen, 150 at Neuengamme, 140 at Oranienburg, and 60 at Auschwitz.[57] The majority of these women supervised inmates in the subsidiary camps and labor details allotted to various industrial enterprises. A few worked as nurses and physicians in camp medical facilities. Their activities often included pseudomedical experiments.[58]

The camp at Ravensbrück was staffed by 500-550 uniformed SS women; 300 were assigned to the main camp and 200-250 supervised outside labor details. Just as Dachau served as a training center for men in the Death Head's units serving in the camps, Ravensbrück was a school for training women guards needed in the vastly expanded network of camps and labor centers where women were interned after 1940. Irma Greese and Maria Mandel, both infamous at Auschwitz, were trained in 1941 and 1942 at Ravensbrück.[59] Several women were notorious for their cruelty; they seemed to engage in a bizarre rivalry emulating the excesses and brutalities of their male superiors.[60] Other women guards tried to mitigate the worst extremes. For example, Johanna Langefeld, trained in the social welfare and penal institutions of the 1920s, served initially as a guard at Moringen and Lichtenburg during the 1930s. She was promoted to the post of chief warden at Ravensbrück in May 1939, a position she retained until April 1942. Her ambivalence toward her job was noticed by both inmates and superiors. It brought her into conflict with Camp Commandant Koegel, resulting in her forced reassignment to Auschwitz from April to October 1942.[61] Commandant Höss considered her "incapable of commanding and organizing the women's camp."[62] She was transferred back to Ravensbrück in October 1942. Langefeld was subsequently dismissed, arrested for dereliction of duty, and tried by an SS tribunal in the spring of 1943.[63] She was clearly an exception among the SS women assigned to Ravensbrück. Margarete Buber-Neumann, for example, described Langefeld in relatively complimentary terms, although she portrayed the other women guards as brutal, stocky, obese women in knee-high leather boots, with frizzy, overpermanented hair and too much makeup.[64]

Ironically, the SS women suffered sex discrimination on the job. Höss held the women guards in very low esteem:

> I must emphasize that the women I was sent from Ravensbrück were not the best. These supervisors had been thoroughly spoiled at Ravensbrück. Everything had been done to persuade them to remain in the women's concentration camp. . . . They were given the best accommodations, and were paid salaries they could never have earned elsewhere. . . . These supervisors were now posted to Auschwitz; none came voluntarily . . . From the very beginning most of them wanted to run away and return to the quiet comfort and easy life at Ravensbrück.[65]

Höss's contempt toward the women SS guards trained in crash courses at Ravensbrück and "let loose on the prisoners" appears to reflect the actual conditions that prevailed at Ravensbrück and Auschwitz.[66]

The camps created for Austrian and German women before 1939 became the models for the vastly expanded network of concentration and labor camps created after 1940 throughout occupied Europe. The size and number of camps grew with the increasing number of incarcerated women, now including new groups such as resistance fighters from western Europe, Poles caught in the "General Pacification" roundups, and Soviet women prisoners of war.[67]

After 1941, women were no longer restricted to Ravensbrück, but were found in fenced-off enclosures separated from men's camps in places like Gross-Rosen and Auschwitz-Birkenau. With increasing labor shortages as the war expanded, women were also assigned to labor details in satellite camps in larger numbers. A survey of the women interned at Mauthausen shows that apart from a small number of prostitutes, women were registered as transients until the autumn of 1944, when they were recorded in substantial numbers in Mauthausen and its satellites. In April 1942, four Yugoslav women were shot at Mauthausen and in June 1942, 10 prostitutes were selected from Ravensbrück for a minimum of six months' service in the Mauthausen and Gusen camp bordellos. Although promised release after six months, most of the women were returned to Ravensbrück. In October 1942, 130 Czech women were executed in Mauthausen and 189 Soviet women prisoners of war were shipped to Auschwitz via Mauthausen. SS statistics show that a permanent population of women internees existed from September 1944 until liberation in May 1945. In April 1945, approximately 3,077 women were found in the main camp and an additional 1,514 were incarcerated in the auxiliary camps.[68] In the last eight months of the war, women from Ravensbrück, Auschwitz, and Flossenbürg were evacuated to Mauthausen. They were employed as clerks; in agricultural labor, gardening, sewing, and laundry; in the armaments industry; and also as servants. Their heads were shaven on arrival and they faced the same brutal camp regime that the male prisoners did.[69]

By late 1944, as the fronts contracted from both east and west, large numbers of women were also recorded in other previously all-male camps.[70] During these closing chaotic months of the war, when forced marches and evacuations led to the dumping of exhausted prisoners of both sexes into the older German camps and their satellites, the rigid sex segregation of the earlier camps broke down completely. There is no complete statistical tally on the total number of women prisoners, nor are there any lists that establish all the places where they were detained.

Women were also sent to special police camps *(Polizeihaftlager)* and work camps *(Arbeitserziehungslager)*. The women's work "training" camps had mandatory minimum sentences of six weeks at hard labor. The camp at Rudersberg in Württemberg created in 1942 was typical. Although the total number of women interned there between 1942 and 1945 is not known, it appears that the camp initially held 200 women and girls transported from the Soviet Union, Poland, and France. About 80 women were assigned as woodcutters in the nearby Welzheim forest; 40 were rented to the Bauknecht Corporation in Welzheim; and others were assigned to local peasants as farm laborers. Political detainees were not permitted on outside work crews, and were assigned jobs in the camp laundry, kitchen, and tailor shops. Severe overcrowding, heavy labor, and inadequate food rations were common. The daily ration in 1944 consisted of 400 grams of bread, ersatz coffee in the morning, watery turnip mixed with acorn soup at noon, and small quantities of cottage cheese, margarine, and jam at night. Selections for transports to Ravensbrück and Auschwitz occurred once a week. After the prisons in Stuttgart were destroyed in Allied bombing raids in late 1944, many of the prisoners from there were transferred to Rudersberg.[71] Other women's labor camps existed at Radeberg in Saxony, Cologne-Deutz, and Hägerwelle in Pomerania.[72]

From August 1944 until the end of the war, a number of new satellite camps were created specifically for women evacuees from other already liberated eastern and western camps. Very little is known about these last transitory detention centers except for their names.[73]

### Survival Patterns Inside the Camps after 1939

The fate of the deported women depended less on nationality and the reason for arrest than on a variety of other factors: date of arrest, place of incarceration, and conditions of deportation. Survival also depended on luck, special skills, physical strength, and membership in a supportive group.[74] Women had significantly different survival skills and techniques than did men. Although there were neither killing centers nor ghettos in western Europe, German-Jewish women and those of other nationalities frequently used similar strategies for coping with unprecedented terror. Women's specific forms of survival included doing housework as a kind of practical therapy and of gaining control over one's space, bonding and networks, religious or political convictions, the use of inconspicuousness, and possibly even sex.

Women appear to have been more resilient than men, both physically and psychologically, to malnutrition and starvation. Clinical research by Jewish physicians in the Warsaw Ghetto confirmed the impressionistic accounts of contemporaries and brought proof to the assertion that women were less vulnerable to the effects of short-term starvation and famine.[75] Women in Gurs, Theresienstadt, and Bergen-Belsen reported that men "were selfish and undisciplined egoists, unable to control their hungry stomachs, and revealed a painful lack of courage."[76] Women also shared and pooled their limited resources better than did men. In Berlin, the Gestapo allowed small groups of Jewish women to provide food for the deportees at the railroad station. The women, experienced in trading for scarce and rationed food, performed this job until the end of 1942.[77] In the camps, women swapped recipes and ways of extending limited quantities of food. Men could be overheard discussing their favorite banquets and restaurants.[78] Since women had been primarily responsible for their families as housewives and cooks, there was some direct correlation between their own survival and previously acquired skills.

After the initial trauma of deportation in freight trains and cattle cars, women were separated from their husbands and children when they entered the camps. Entire groups were automatically sent to the gas chambers at Auschwitz on arrival: the old, the young, and the weak. Usually, mothers were not separated from their small children and, thus, perished immediately with them. Fathers were not linked to children in this way. Instead of the protection normally extended to these weaker individuals, women were more vulnerable and their chances of survival decreased if they were pregnant or accompanied by small children.[79]

Those who survived the deportations and selections faced great deprivations. Stripped naked, shorn of hair, and with all possessions confiscated, the women were shocked and numbed. At Auschwitz and Ravensbrück this scene was repeatedly enacted. France Audoul, deported from France to Ravensbrück in 1943, described being "skinned and shorn":

> One day the order came to go to the showers and there all illusions soon ended. Baggage, clothes, jewelry, letters, souvenirs, and even our hair disappeared under the hands of expert prisoners, hardened by this kind of work. Cries and tears only brought beatings. A hot shower was soothing, but only for a brief moment, for the distribution of shoes and bathrobes was made without any thought of size and height, and this horrible leveling, this ugliness was completed at the political office by the loss of all identity. Names were replaced by triangles with numbers on them. The concentration camp system closed over the terrified women.[80]

Religious Jewish women, who, once married, kept their hair covered in public under either a wig or scarf, felt both a physical and a spiritual nakedness, thus unprotected and exposed to the whims of their Nazi tormentors.[81] The initial trauma of loss and separation was compounded by isolation in quarantine followed by claustrophobically cramped living conditions in noisy overcrowded barracks, where sometimes as many as seven women shared one bunk or straw mattress.[82] The brutal separation of husbands from wives and parents from children only increased the sense of shock and despair. Even in the milder conditions of the Theresienstadt ghetto and transit camp, lack of space led to mass dormitory housing in separate men's, women's, and children's barracks. Many of the German-Jewish women were of middle-class origin; others came from small, close-knit rural communities; all were stunned by the noise of the overcrowded ghettos and camps.[83]

Epidemics also spread more quickly in the confined quarters, exacerbated by constant hunger and thirst. Inadequate sanitary facilities, latrines, and even water for drinking and washing reached unusual extremes in the women's camp at Auschwitz-Birkenau. In January 1943, one faucet served 12,000 women for drinking and washing. Charlott Delbo mentioned being unable to wash for sixty-seven days, unless it snowed or rained.[84] Even Camp Commandant Höss remarked that "general living conditions in the women's camp were incomparably worse [than in the men's camp]. They were far more tightly packed-in and the sanitary and hygienic conditions were notably inferior."[85]

Vignettes and diaries by women interned in Gurs, Ravensbrück, Auschwitz-Birkenau, and Bergen-Belsen revealed that women's traditionally domestic roles as wives, daughters, and mothers aided them under conditions of extreme duress. In Gurs, during the winter of 1940–1941, despite the increased overcrowding caused by the dumping of the Baden Jews, women fought against the primitive conditions. "They fought the dirt and lassitude with cleaning, scrubbing, and orderliness."[86] This cleaning apparently lowered the spread of disease and consequently decreased mortality in the women's barracks. Comparative mortality statistics by gender in Ravensbrück for August 1943 reveal a similarly lower death rate in the women's barracks. Survivors of other camps in western and eastern Europe reported similar experiences. In Bergen-Belsen, it was reported that "women revealed signs of a more practical and community-minded attitude, chiefly for the sake of the children. They steel themselves to find ways of remedying the situation and show real courage, even prepared, if necessary, to make sacrifices."[87] Cleaning not only prevented the spread of disease; it also functioned as did other familiar "housework" routines as a form of therapy enabling women to gain control over their own space.

Small groups of women in the same barracks or work crews formed "little families" and bonded together for mutual help.[88] Hanna Schramm reported that in Gurs "at first, the women were an undifferentiated mass; one did not recognize individual faces and personalities. Gradually, tentative friendships began."[89] These small families, usually not biologically related, increased protection for individual internees and created networks to "organize" food, clothing, and beds, and to help cope with the privations and primitive camp conditions. At the French jail at Rieucros, 360 refugee women pooled their pennies to buy a second-hand kettle, since the prison food was inedible and the water unsanitary to drink.[90]

Mutual support also came from membership in a religious, political, national, or family unit. Clandestine channels of communication existed in every concentration camp. Lone individuals, men as well as women, had a smaller chance for survival. Kitty Hart attributed her survival to the fact that her mother, deported along with her, was always in close contact.[91] Homogeneous religious groups like Jehovah's Witnesses retained a cohesiveness and comradeship that increased the emotional and physical will to survive. Depending on the situation, this could be either life-saving or very dangerous. Contemptuously nicknamed "Bifos, Bible-Bees, and Bible-Worms" by their SS tormentors, the Witnesses earned a reluctant and secret respect, which occasionally resulted in lighter work assignments as domestic servants in SS homes. But their religious scrupulousness sometimes proved dangerous; a small group of fundamentalists in Ravensbrück refused to eat blood sausage because of biblical injunctions and thus increased their risk of malnutrition and starvation as well as corporal punishment. [This refusal to eat prohibited foods also applied to some Orthodox Jews.] The Witnesses' pacifism led to their refusal to tend rabbits, whose fur was used in military clothing, resulting in the execution of several women for treason.[92]

Similar group cohesion existed among Orthodox Jewish women from Hungary and Subcarpathian Ruthenia. When Sabbath candles were unavailable they blessed electric light bulbs; their colleagues assigned to the Canada barracks at Auschwitz (the barracks where food, clothing, jewelry, and other goods taken from prisoners were stored) filched supplies for them to make Sabbath candles improvised from hollowed-out potato peels filled with margarine and rag wicks. During Channukah, *dreidels* (tops) were clandestinely carved from small pieces of wood.[93] Christmas was celebrated among the arrested French and Spanish women members of the resistance at the French camp of Les Tourelles "crouched on our straw mattresses, heads hidden under the covers, each sang whatever song she knew . . . through the night."[94] If caught violating camp prohibitions against religious observance, the women were punished by whippings or detention in dark, cagelike solitary confinement cells, and often "selected" for the gas chambers. Similar episodes of religious observant behavior also occurred in men's camps and barracks. Bonding because of religious or political convictions may not have been specific to women, but the degree of group cohesion and noncompetitive support available to women seems markedly greater than among men.

Survival frequently depended on a prisoner's ability to remain inconspicuous; reading a Bible or prayer book during roll call was a conscious risk. Religious Jewish women interned in Gurs during 1940 and 1941 sometimes refused to take advantage of Saturday releases from the internment camps, because of the traditional prohibitions against travel on the Sabbath. By staying, they were sometimes trapped and later deported to Auschwitz, where they perished.[95] Religious group cohesiveness among Orthodox Jews and fundamentalist Christians had both positive and negative implications for survival. During 1944 and 1945 it was tolerated, even in Auschwitz, whereas earlier in the war it often marked a prisoner for more rapid death.

Ability to withstand the extremes of winter made survival more likely. Almost all the memoirs refer to the miserable climate and swampy or clay soils that turned into seas of mud in Gurs, Birkenau, and Ravensbrück.[96] In freezing winter rains, this mud became as slippery as ice. Fetching food in Gurs during the winter was an acrobatic balancing act; prisoners sank up to their thighs in mud with arms filled with cauldrons of hot soup or ersatz coffee. Those women who were deported from the warmer and milder Mediterranean climates of Greece and Italy could not adjust to the harsh winters of eastern Poland; this increased their vulnerability to disease and death. Inadequate thin prisoner clothing and clogs were unsuitable for standing in rain, ice, and snow during roll calls, many of which lasted up to ten hours. Some of the women repaired their ragged garments and groomed themselves carefully despite the lack of water for washing; this imitation of normal behavior was a conscious and rational attempt at survival. A few prisoners with special skills, like the Communist plumber Charlotte Müller in Ravensbrück, enjoyed somewhat better living conditions. Favored labor brigades were plumbers, masons, and electricians; they received better barracks and rations, which increased their odds of survival.

A popular postwar myth, sometimes exploited and sensationalized, held that Jewish women were forced to serve as prostitutes in the SS bordellos and were frequently raped. Although such cases did undoubtedly occur, it was not the norm and reflects a macabre postwar misuse of the Holocaust for popular titillation. Kitty Hart calls these sexual fantasies of postwar literature and television "ridiculous misconceptions."[97] Sexuality, either heterosexual or lesbian, was most likely practiced by prisoners who were camp functionaries and therefore better fed.[98]

Still, clandestine heterosexual liaisons did occur, even in Auschwitz, where men were assigned to labor details in women's camps. Brief stolen moments were arranged in potato storage sheds, clothing depots, warehouses, laundry vans, the bakery, the canteen, and even in chicken coops. Despite the risks if caught, the border zone between the men's and women's subcamps in Ravensbrück and Auschwitz became a place for reassuring visual contact, signals, and covert messages. In Gurs, a limited number of passes were allotted to each barracks so that women could visit their interned husbands in the men's enclosure. Although privacy was hard to find, in Theresienstadt, for example, lovers met hurriedly in the barracks' coal bunker at night. Weddings also took place in Theresienstadt and other ghettos and transit camps where milder conditions prevailed; and if both spouses survived, these symbolic marriages were often legalized in postwar civil ceremonies.[99] There were also deep friendships between women that may have become lesbian relationships.[100] These have been difficult to document given the inhibitions of survivors and historians. Occasionally, flirtation and sex were used to buy food or a better work situation; even sex could have served as a strategy for survival.[101] Traditional anxieties and guilt about sex were not applicable in the world of total subservience reinforced by terror in the camps.

Every camp had an active resistance movement linked to the outside world. Women were observed to be more resourceful and skillful than men at passing messages between jail cells and barracks, on work details, and during roll calls. They were also more skilled at trading cigarettes and food to obtain essentials for their friends and prison families.[102] Inmate physicians in Ravensbrück saved many prisoners from selections; for example, the Yugoslav doctor Najda Persic wrote false diagnoses and the Polish doctor Maria Grabska tried to remove or change the tatoos on Austrian women slated for death.[103]

There were even open revolts in which women participated at Sobibor, Treblinka, Auschwitz, and possibly even Bergen-Belsen.[104] It is believed that French-Jewish women inmates revolted during October 1942 at the satellite camp of Budy near Auschwitz and were consequently massacred by those arrested as asocials and prostitutes together with SS officers. The only surviving evidence is from the memoirs of Perry Broad, an SS man in the Political Department at Auschwitz.[105] This event, if accurately reported in documents by the perpetrators, is unique, since there is no other instance of one category of prisoners massacring fellow prisoners on the same work detail.

Flight, escape, subversion of the rules, noncompliance, and sabotage on work details were common forms of resistance in every camp and ghetto of occupied Europe. Every camp had an active clandestine cultural life with concerts, theater performances, puppet shows, reading circles, music, and art.[106] Schools for children were also secretly organized. The care, supervision, and teaching of children were tasks that were frequently allotted to the interned women. Child care and education in the home were traditionally women's work and, after deportation, those children who survived were usually housed with the women. Hanna Lévy-Hass recorded in her Bergen-Belsen diary that she tried to teach 110 children of various ages ranging from three to fifteen.[107]

## Women Outside the Camps: Resistance, Hiding, and Flight

Very little systematic research has been done about women's resources for survival in resistance, hiding, and flight (including emigration). It is clear that there were two basic types of resistance: (1)
organized networks linked by a common ideology; and (2) autonomous
personal acts of noncompliance. It is important to remember that all
classes of German women participated in the resistance movement
between 1933 and 1945. Resistance meant opposing Hitler in the name
of socialism, communism, monarchism, Christianity, or democracy,
but not necessarily helping persecuted Jews in the name of
humanitarianism. Women were statistically overrepresented in many
resistance groups because of the severe demographic imbalance of the
sexes due to the huge demands of the war for males in the army and
war industries. Furthermore, many politically vulnerable men were
already in flight, hiding, or incarcerated in jails and camps, leaving
women as the mainstay of many anti-Nazi political groups. Women
previously employed in subordinate and ornamental positions in many
male-dominated political organizations suddenly assumed responsibility for directing and devising clandestine political strategies. They also
continued their traditional domestic chores. German women were actively involved in the White Rose movement in Hamburg and Munich,
the Lechleiter group in Mannheim, the Schulze-Boysen-Harnack
group, and the Red Orchestra.[108]

Although there were genuine limitations on what could be done to
thwart the Nazi aim of mass murder, many ordinary women and men
showed decency and compassion in helping Jewish and other victims of
Nazi terror. One form of resistance involved the clandestine publication and distribution of anti-Nazi literature. These pamphlets and
fliers, written and printed secretly in Germany and abroad, often contained eyewitness accounts of tortures and conditions in the men's and
women's concentration camps. This literature was distributed widely
in Germany and before 1939 was often smuggled across the borders.
There are no clear statistics of the number of German Jews or the
number of German-Jewish women among the organized anti-Nazi
groups (Communists, Zionists, Socialists, or dissident Christians). A
substantial number of the dissidents arrested for producing or distributing such clandestine political literature were German-Jewish
women and *Mischlinge* (persons of mixed blood defined as non-Aryans
under the Nuremberg Laws).[109] Public support for Nazi policies increased hostility and the risk of exposure, but anti-Nazi resistance
groups proliferated and slowly developed effective strategies to combat
the network of Nazi informers, collaborators, and police spies. These
political dissidents were never able to dent the general passivity and

indifference to the Nazi regime, nor could they develop effective strategies that combated mass deportations of Jews and rapid population transfers across Nazi-occupied Europe.

The fragmentary information currently available reveals that German-Jewish women used two distinctive types of resistance behavior: (1) open protest, exemplified by the female members of the Herbert Baum group; and (2) escape by evasion and improvisation, exemplified by the adolescent women in the Chug Chaluzzi (an underground Zionist Pioneer group).[110] The absence of data does not allow us to distinguish gender-specific behavior. It is possible that conditions in resistance and hiding were not different for men and women. Despite the obvious risks of capture and their isolated situation as Jewish compulsory laborers in the Berlin Siemens factories, the young women who worked with the Herbert Baum group openly distributed Zionist and Communist leaflets after 1939. They were captured because of their participation in burning down an anti-Soviet exhibition in Berlin in May 1942. After torture, interrogation, and trial, five women were executed in August 1942. Two surviving women, awaiting their execution in Berlin prisons, communicated secretly and sought to raise their respective morale: "In spite of everything, I always pull myself together and I am not giving in."[111] The male and female adolescents recruited by the Chug Chaluzzi continued training for an eventual emigration and survived despite their lack of identity papers and ration coupons. They improvised temporary shelters and slept on the subway's and night buses of the Berlin transit system; they also received food and warm clothing from their Aryan protectors, whom they nicknamed *Aufbewarier* (a combination of the two German words *aufbewahren* and *Arier*, meaning an Aryan who protected them).[112] Despite their lack of contingency plans, many survived the war with such help.

Often other autonomous individuals and groups provided temporary asylum, forged papers, and rations for Jews in hiding. Dr. Gertrud Luckner, head of the Catholic Charities (Deutscher Caritas Verband) extended financial help to Jews and non-Aryan Christians (converts and offspring of mixed marriages) in Germany; she was arrested and subsequently deported to Ravensbrück. Often members of the Confessing Church and their families and Jews in privileged mixed marriages helped others to safety after 1943. Their rescue work has been relatively well documented in memoirs and oral histories, although the story of the Jews who survived in hiding has received less systematic attention. There have been no histories of German-Jewish women surviving underground, and the limited and incomplete nature of the available sources does not yet allow analysis by gender.[113]

There were also unique and spectacular gestures of mass popular resistance inside Germany. In one instance, 200 to 300 Christian wives living in privileged mixed marriages demonstrated for a week outside several Berlin assembly centers after their Jewish husbands had been rounded up without warning at their workplaces during the so-called Factory Operation of late February 1943. The men had not been permitted to return home to pack their belongings and could not notify their wives and families. Despite police efforts to disperse the growing crowds of women, rumors spread and more women demonstrated each day in front of the assembly centers and police stations. They demanded the release of their husbands and attempted to ameliorate their situation by passing them packages with food and clothing. In a rare conciliatory gesture, possibly fearing the reactions of Christian relatives of the internees, the Gestapo released those men married to German non-Jews.[114] Jewish women with Christian husbands were also trapped in this raid:

> The loading of people onto SS trucks was carried out with such speed that most of the women, who were wont to sit at work in colored overalls, were taken as they were, without overcoats and without their breakfasts, which remained at their factory wardrobes.[115]

Jewish women in privileged mixed marriages were probably also released, although there is no evidence indicating that their Christian husbands joined in the demonstrations of late February 1943. Smaller similar protests occurred at a Jewish old-age home on March 6, 1943, resulting in a temporary cessation of the deportation of the residents.[116] These were the only demonstrations against deportations of Jews that ever took place in Germany.

Another demonstration, similar to a food riot, occurred when 300 women and children evacuated from heavily bombed mining towns in the Ruhr and Rhineland demonstrated in November 1943 in the town of Witten. The women protested about their new housing and the lack of ration cards for food, and expressed fears that their families would be split apart by the relocation. These German women, predominantly Catholic, also feared anti-Christian Nazi propaganda in the schools their children would attend. In Witten, the police called to disperse the demonstration refused to intervene, since they felt the women's protest was justified because the bureaucracy had withheld ration cards for the relocated women and children. Similar demonstrations occurred in Hamm, Lünen, and Bochum.[117] It is probable that these public demonstrations expressing discontent with the war were not unique, but there has been little systematic investigation of the forms of and participants in public protests in Nazi Germany.[118] Empathy, war weariness, and police hesitancy to arrest German women must be explored as possible explanations for the success of these two larger female demonstrations in February and November 1943.

More common than public protest and group resistance were private, often unrewarded, gestures by many individuals, whose decency and compassion helped Jews evade the increasing restrictions placed on their daily lives after November 1938. Restricted hours for food shopping (in Berlin from 4:00 to 5:00 P.M.; in Leipzig at three designated stores from noon to 12:30 P.M.) made buying essentials exceedingly difficult, especially when most Jews had to perform compulsory conscript labor for ten hours every day. After January 1940, Jews did not receive ration cards for textiles, shoes, and leather goods; and in September 1940, the range of prohibited items increased. Jews could not purchase fish, coffee, alcoholic beverages, sweets, tobacco, meat, eggs, fresh milk, ice cream, or cut flowers. Many of the essentials of daily life were confiscated: radios were seized on September 29, 1939 (the day of Yom Kippur); telephones, except for physicians', on September 30, 1940; and, in June 1942, German Jews had to surrender all privately held electrical appliances, phonograph equipment, records, typewriters, bicycles, and optical goods (cameras and microscopes). Many neighbors, friends, acquaintances, employers, and even strangers occasionally provided necessities for German-Jewish survival. Inge Deutschkron, a young Jewish journalist, reported that stores where she once regularly shopped held food until she could pick it up, blatantly disregarding the rules.[119] Another Berlin Jewish woman reported that her governess shared coffee and other rationed food when life in hiding without papers had left her impoverished and near starvation.[120] German-Jewish women in hiding or living discreetly on forged Aryan papers lost access to the accoutrements of respectability, such as hairdressers and laundromats. More significant was their loss of education and any professional life. These women had few support systems available to them and no outlet for amusement or resentment. Daily existence became a constant battle with fear of deportation and certain death if their deception was discovered. The price of nerve-wracking isolation was high, since before 1933 the majority of German-Jewish women lived in a relatively secure middle-class milieu.

Despite the risks of denunciation, many Germans aided Jews in finding underground escape routes and hiding places. In order to evade detection, the artist Valerie Wolffenstein moved eighteen times in two years.[121] In another case, a woman and her physician husband fled Berlin for southern Germany in 1943. Armed with two sets of bogus identity papers with the surnames of Günther and Perger, he assumed the identity and profession of a traveling salesman, his wife the traditional domestic jobs of cook and mother's helper. They were led to safe houses on an underground railway made up of ten pastors of the Confessing Church, including four women curates.[122] Warned of the intention of a Gestapo raid by fellow employees at a Berlin bakery, another couple went into hiding in Berlin from late 1942 until liberation. They survived without identity papers or ration coupons, sometimes sleeping with friends, but often living as homeless transients who slept in stairwells, railroad stations, and parks.[123]

Many German Jews who emigrated before 1938 found asylum in their adopted homelands.[124] Others, like Paula Littauer, fled from Berlin to Brussels in 1942 and survived with frequent changes of residence and constant identity changes, "so that I almost forgot my real name."[125] Fugitives lived a sub-rosa existence, successful if they could pass as local inhabitants in language, manner, and appearance—if luck was with them and their hosts. After 1941, they were colloquially called *camouflés* in France, *onderduikers* in Holland, and *U-Boote* (submarines) in Germany and Austria.

Despite the overwhelming odds, about 3,000 Jewish fugitives survived the war in Berlin, about 1,500 in other parts of Germany, and about 1,000 German Jews in other European countries. The Jews who survived in hiding were about 25 percent of the surviving 12,500 German Jews alive in May 1945 (out of the May 1939 population of approximately 240,000 Jews). There are no precise statistics available about the percentage of women among the Jews in hiding.[126] Systematic literature by region, class, or nationality, or about the background of the survivors and rescuers has not appeared. It is not yet clear whether women's experiences in hiding differed from men's in any substantial way.[127]

Many German-Jewish women sought to escape Nazi Germany after 1933 by emigrating to adjacent European nations or more exotic locations overseas. Although a substantial body of literature has already appeared about the odyssey of prominent political, literary, academic, and scientific professionals who fled abroad, there has been no systematic study of average emigrants nor has there been any focus on women forced to rebuild their lives.[128]

Although there are no conclusive statistics for the German and German-Jewish emigration of 1933–1941, it is believed that 270,000 to 300,000 Jews fled Germany; this figure was 80 percent of all emigrés from Germany.[129] The precise number of German and German-Jewish women is not known. However, it is clear that women formed approximately half of all refugees to the United States during these years. German-Jewish demographic trends were visible in the occupational profile of female emigrants; in the first period, until 1938, a majority of women were young or early middle-aged professionals and semiskilled workers. In the second phase, after 1938, the number of older women

When Biology Became Destiny

without job-related skills increased dramatically, as did the number of minor children. The number of single and married women was about equal between 1933 and 1941; there were few widows or divorcées.[130] Predominantly urban and middle class in pre-1933 Germany, these women already had certain distinctive career patterns before emigration.[131] In Nazi society, women's work outside the home was considered unnecessary and inappropriate; flight did not increase female status nor did it improve professional opportunities. The 1930s were the nadir of women's rights and the complex cultural and political forces of the Depression strengthened hostility to all alien job competitors. With few exceptions, this was reinforced for emigrant women by an ambiguous lack of support from male refugee colleagues and even within their own families, despite the dictates of economic necessity. Thus, the number of women domestics, cooks, and clerical workers increased dramatically among German-Jewish female refugees during the 1930s.[132] In one instance, Käte Frankenthal, a former doctor, supported herself as an itinerant peddler of ice cream during her periodic bouts of unemployment after arriving in New York.[133]

It is generally believed that although women and men faced similar difficulties in learning new languages and adapting to new milieus, women were faster and more proficient in acquiring new languages because they needed to communicate for shopping and child care. Female writers like Vicki Baum and Martha Albrand became widely known popular novelists in the United States, Helen Wolff a fixture in American publishing, and Lotte Lenya and Lili Palmer starred in English-language film and theater.[134]

The study of women and the Holocaust has barely begun, and the complexities and contours of the subject must be explored in future historical research. In order to stay within the framework of this volume, this essay has focused on German and German-Jewish women. Future work must include horizontal pan-European studies, focusing on different female prisoner categories and camps across occupied Europe and integrating the literature on western and eastern Europe. There will also have to be new vertical studies on women in German jails, on their underground experiences and their odysseys as refugees forced to rebuild new lives abroad. I hope this essay clears away some misunderstandings and opens the way for future investigations by scholars from many disciplines. The complexity of the subject will keep historians and other analysts occupied for many years.

## Notes

The author would like to thank Werner T. Angress, Henry Friedlander, Atina Grossmann, Marion Kaplan, Walter Peterson, and Joan Ringelheim for their advice and constructive suggestions in revising this essay, which was first presented at Southeastern Massachusetts University in June 1982 and again at the Stern College, Yeshiva University, Conference on Women and the Holocaust in March 1983.

1. For the general literature, see Raul Hilberg, *The Destruction of the European Jews* (Chicago, 1961); Martin Broszat, "Nationalsozialistische Konzentrationslager, 1933–1945," in *Anatomie des SS-Staates*, ed. Helmut Krausnick et al., 2 vols. (Munich, 1967), Vol. 2, pp. 11–133; Adalbert Rückerl, ed., *NS-Vernichtungslager* (Munich, 1977); and Falk Pingel, *Häftlinge unter SS-Herrschaft* (Hamburg, 1978). Two useful recent bibliographical surveys are conspicuous for their respective lacunae: a survey of Holocaust historiography fails to mention women's history, and a recent survey article on women's history omits all references to the Holocaust. See Konrad Kwiet, "Zur historiographischen Behandlung der Judenverfolgung im Dritten Reich," *Militärgeschichtliche Mitteilungen* 27, no. 1 (1980): 149–92; and Richard J. Evans, "Feminism and Female Emancipation in Germany, 1870–1945," *Central European History* 9, no. 4 (1976): 323–51. Two recent volumes are disappointing and occasionally misleading: Konnilyn G. Feig, *Hitler's Death Camps* (New York, 1979), pp. 133–90; and Hanna Elling, *Frauen im deutschen Widerstand, 1933–1945* (Frankfurt, 1978). Of greater value for the discussion of women in Nazi Germany and women as perpetrators are Dorothee Klinksiek, *Die Frau im NS-Staat* (Stuttgart, 1982); Maruta Schmidt and Gabi Dietz, eds., *Frauen unterm Hakenkreuz* (Berlin, 1983); Frauengruppe Faschismusforschung, eds., *Mutterkreuz und Arbeitsbuch: Zur Geschichte der Frauen in der Weimarer Republik und im Nationalsozialismus* (Frankfurt, 1981); Claudia Koonz, "Mothers in the Fatherland: Women in Nazi Germany," in *Becoming Visible: Women in European History*, ed. Renate Bridenthal and Claudia Koonz (Boston, 1977), pp. 445–73; and Michael H. Kater, "Frauen in der NS-Bewegung," *Vierteljahrshefte für Zeitgeschichte* 31, no. 2 (1983): 202–41. Several capsule biographies of Nazi women perpetrators are found in the valuable essay by Henry Friedlander, "The Nazi Concentration Camps," in *Human Responses to the Holocaust*, ed. Michael D. Ryan (New York and Toronto, 1981), pp. 33–69.
2. Bundesarchiv Koblenz [hereafter BA], Akte NS 10/66. See also Leo Baeck Institute, New York [hereafter LBI, NY], Wiener Library Press clippings microfilms, AR 7187/Reel 95 (Nazis and Women, 1933–1939), and 7187/Reel 109 (Nazis and Women, 1939–1945).
3. Elling, *Frauen im deutschen Widerstand*, p. 198; and Wolf Hammer, *Hohes Haus in Henkers Hand* (Frankfurt, 1956), p. 77.
4. For Kessel, see Elling, *Frauen im deutschen Widerstand*, pp. 57, 89; Hammer, *Hohes Haus*, p. 57. For Fleischer, see Max Schwarz, *MdR: Biographisches Handbuch der Reichstage* (Hanover, 1965), p. 648.
5. For the Marie Jankowski incident, see the emigré exposé *Braunbuch über Reichstagsbrand und Hitlerterror* (Basel, 1933), pp. 210–11; LBI, NY: 7187/Reel 95; and Käte Frankenthal, *Der dreifache Fluch: Jüdin, Intellektuelle, Sozialistin*, ed. Kathleen Pearle and Stephan Leibfried (Frankfurt and New York, 1981), pp. 126, 292. For Bohm-Schuch, see Marie Juchacz, *Sie lebten für eine bessere Welt* (Hanover, 1971), pp. 93–98; Franz Osterroth, *Biographisches Lexikon des Sozialismus*, Vol. I: *Verstorbene Persönlichkeiten* (Hanover, 1960), p. 32; and Hammer, *Hohes Haus*, p. 30.
6. For Overlach, see "Women Politicals in German Goals," *Manchester Guardian*, 29 January 1937 (also found in LBI, NY: E. J. Gumbel Papers).
7. For Lüders, see Hammer, *Hohes Haus*, p. 65. Hammer mentions that Lüders also hid Berlin Jews in her home between 1938 and 1942. For Teusch, see ibid., p. 93.
8. *Biographisches Handbuch der deutschsprachigen Emigration nach 1933* (Munich

and New York, 1980), Vol. 1, pp. 685–86. See also Gerhart Seger, *Oranienburg* (reprint; Berlin, 1979).

9. LBI, NY: E. J. Gumbel Papers, "Frauen als Geisel," *Sonderdienst der deutschen Informationen. Das Martyrium der Frauen in deutschen Konzentrationslagern,* No. 41 (11 June 1936).

10. Ibid.

11. Ibid.

12. Ibid.

13. Ibid.

14. There is almost no systematic literature on German jails and prisons in the twentieth century and in Nazi Germany. Some useful information on the prison conditions of Nazi women political opponents is found in two anthologies of memoirs: Gisela Dischner, ed., *Eine stumme Generation berichtet: Frauen der dreissiger und vierziger Jahre* (Frankfurt, 1982); and Gerda Szepansky, ed., *Frauen leisten Widerstand: 1933–1945; Lebensgeschichten nach Interviews und Dokumenten* (Frankfurt, 1983). Estimates of German women political prisoners are discussed in Schmidt and Dietz, *Frauen unterm Hakenkreuz,* pp. 158–67; and *Braunbuch über Reichstagsbrand und Hitlerterror,* pp. 274–76. For information on Jehovah's Witnesses, see Michael H. Kater, "Die Ernsten Bibelforscher im Dritten Reich," *Vierteljahrshefte für Zeitgeschichte* 5, No. 2 (1969): 181–218; and Christine E. King, "Strategies for Survival: An Examination of the History of Five Christian Sects in Germany, 1933–1945," *Journal of Contemporary History* 14 (1979): 211–33. See also LBI, NY: E. J. Gumbel Papers, "Die Zeugin Jehovas," *Beilage der Deutschen Information,* No. 6 (6 June 1936). For information on homosexuals, see Frank Rector, *The Nazi Extermination of Homosexuals* (New York, 1981); James D. Steakley, *The Homosexual Emancipation Movement in Germany* (New York, 1975); Hans-Georg Stümke and Rudi Finkler, *Rosa Winkel, Rosa Listen* (Reinbek bei Hamburg, 1981); and Rüdiger Lautmann, "Das Leben homosexueller Männer unter dem Nationalsozialismus," in *Terror und Hoffnung in Deutschland, 1933–1945,* ed. Johannes Beck et al. (Reinbek bei Hamburg, 1980), pp. 366–90. The literature on homosexuals contains only token references to lesbians. No literature about female asocials and criminals in Nazi prisons has been located.

15. See the memoirs of Marta Appel in Dortmund published in Monika Richarz, ed., *Jüdisches Leben in Deutschland: Selbstzeugnisse zur Sozialgeschichte, 1918–1945* (Stuttgart, 1982), pp. 231–33. Appel also tells of the growing social isolation of Jewish women, who met former Aryan women friends only infrequently even in public places (ibid., p. 233). German women guilty of racial misconduct under the Nuremberg Laws were photographed and their names and addresses published in *Stürmer* and displayed in the advertisement cases known as *Stürmerkästen.* Similar photos and lists of names and addresses appeared for Jewish men and women living in mixed marriages (see *Stürmer,* Nos. 37 and 40, 1935, reproduced in *Der gelbe Fleck* [Paris, 1936], pp. 197–218). This propaganda could misfire, producing sympathy for the victim and resulting in demonstratively friendly behavior to Jewish neighbors. See Ian Kershaw, "The Persecution of the Jews and German Popular Opinion in the Third Reich," *Leo Baeck Institute Yearbook* 26 (1981): 264–74.

16. The phrase "insidious creeping persecution" *(schleichende Judenverfolgung)* comes from Helmut Genschel, *Die Verdrängung der Juden aus der Wirtschaft im Dritten Reich* (Göttingen, 1966), p. 139. The persecution of Jews in Nazi Germany is documented in Uwe Dietrich Adam, *Judenpolitik im Dritten Reich* (Düsseldorf, 1972); and Helmut Eschwege, ed., *Kennzeichen J* (Frankfurt, 1979).

17. Hilberg, *Destruction,* pp. 28–29; and Christine E. King, "Strategies for Survival," pp. 216–19.

18. LBI, NY: Max Gruenewald Papers, Box 1, file 7: Simon Gruenewald, "Tante Emma," unpubl. ms., pp. 24–28.

19. LBI, NY: Celia Rosenzweig collection, AR 7128/1. This document is translated and annotated in Sybil Milton, "The Expulsion of Polish Jews from Germany, October 1938 to July 1939: A Documentation," *Leo Baeck Institute Yearbook* 29 (in press).

20. LBI, NY: Max Gruenewald Papers, "Tante Emma," pp. 26–28.

21. Three instances where mob violence was directed against German-Jewish women in rural small towns during the November 1938 pogrom are documented in Heinz Lauber, *Judenpogrom: Reichskristallnacht November 1938 in Grossdeutschland* (Gerlingen, 1981), pp. 110–14 and 221–33. Comparative statistics of violence against Jewish men and women during November 1938 are not available.

22. The 1939 statistics are based on Nazi racial definitions, regardless of actual religion, and thus include converts and *Mischlinge*. Furthermore, the figures include Jewish residents of annexed Austria and the Sudetenland. See Erich Rosenthal, "Trends of the Jewish Population in Germany, 1910–39," *Jewish Social Studies* 6, No. 1 (1944): 247–51; and Monika Richarz, *Jüdisches Leben in Deutschland, 1918–1945*, p. 61.

23. Fewer Jewish women were interned in the camps before 1938. They were also unable to emigrate and obtain visas in the same numbers as single Jewish men. See LBI, NY: Bruno Blau, "Die Entwicklung der jüdischen Bevölkerung in Deutschland von 1800 bis 1945," unpubl. ms. (New York, 1950), pp. 335–44; and Bruno Blau, "The Jewish Population in Germany, 1939–45," *Jewish Social Studies* 12 (1950): 161–72.

24. Complete statistics by gender and age for the deportation of German Jews between October 1941 and the last transport in April 1945 are not available. The problem of establishing statistics is discussed in Henry Friendlander, "The Deportation of German Jews: Postwar German Trials of Nazi Criminals," *Leo Baeck Institute Yearbook* 29 (in press). The Erich Rosenthal essay (see note 22) speculates that male Jews also participated more in internal migration to industrial and urban centers in Germany between 1910 and 1939. This may have had significant ramifications on survival by gender after 1941, since large urban centers like Berlin offered Jews more opportunities for survival in hiding than did small rural towns.

25. The quote is from Ottilie Schönewald's description of the expulsion in Bochum; see Martin Gilbert, *Final Journey* (New York, 1979), pp. 18–21.

26. H. G. Adler, *Der verwaltete Mensch: Studien zur Deportation der Juden aus Deutschland* (Tübingen, 1974), pp. 91–105.

27. For further information on Zbaszyn, see: LBI, NY: Wilhelm Graetz Collection, AR 4121/VI 15.

28. Adler, *Der verwaltete Mensch*, pp. 140–54.

29. Ibid., pp. 155–67; Michael R. Marrus and Robert O. Paxton, "The Nazis and the Jews in Occupied Western Europe, 1940–1944," *Journal of Modern History* 54, No. 4 (December 1982): 687–714; and Adam Rutkowski, "Le camp d'internement de Gurs," *Le Monde Juif* 36, No. 100 (October–December 1980): 131–33. The population of Gurs in November 1940 was 13,000 individuals, mostly German and Austrian Jews. Families were split up with men, wives, and children housed separately. There were 5,000 women and 450 children held in the camp, including many elderly Jews (2,500 people were older than sixty). Conditions in Gurs and women's strategies for survival will be discussed in a later part of this essay.

30. Elling, *Frauen im deutschen Widerstand*, pp. 23–37; and LBI, NY: E. J. Gumbel Papers, press clippings file, 1933–1936.

31. The first director at Gotteszell was Government Councillor Henning, who had previously served as director of the Moringen workhouse.

32. Julius Schätzle, *Stationen zur Hölle: Konzentrationslager in Baden und Württemberg, 1933–1945* (Frankfurt, 1974), pp. 25–27.

326    *When Biology Became Destiny*

33. LBI, NY: E. J. Gumbel Papers, "Die werktätige Frau unter der faschistischen Knute: Sechs Frauen als Geiseln in Stadelheim," *Die Neue Welt*, 31 October 1934; and *Deutsche Information*, No. 41 (11 June 1936). These appear to be the earliest illegal sterilizations in the Nazi period.
34. Elling, *Frauen im deutschen Widerstand*, p. 90 (interview with Maria Deeg).
35. "Frauen im Konzentrationslager," *Deutsche Freiheit*, 5 October 1934, containing an excerpt of the subsequently published refugee anthology about concentration camps issued by the Socialist Graphia Verlag in Czechoslovakia. See Otto Urban, "Burg Hohenstein," *Konzentrationslager: Ein Appell an das Gewissen der Welt* (Karlsbad, 1934), pp. 217–38.
36. Friedlander, "The Nazi Concentration Camps," p. 34.
37. For information about these three women's camps, including substantial data about Moringen, see Ino Arndt, "Das Frauenkonzentrationslager Ravensbrück," in *Studien zur Geschichte der Konzentrationslager*, ed. Martin Broszat (Stuttgart, 1970), pp. 93–129; Schmidt and Dietz, eds., *Frauen unterm Hakenkreuz*, pp. 140–48; Elling, *Frauen im deutschen Widerstand*, pp. 23–24; *Konzentrationslager* (Karlsbad, 1934), pp. 213–16; Hannah Vogt, ed., *KZ Moringen, Männerlager, Frauenlager, Jugendschutzlager: Eine Dokumentation* (Göttingen, 1983); Wolf-Dieter Haardt, "Was denn, hier—in Moringen?" in *Die vergessenen KZs: Gedenkstätten für die Opfer des NS-Terrors in der Bundesrepublik*, ed. Detlef Garbe (Bornheim-Merten, 1983), pp. 97–108; and Internationaler Suchdienst, *Vorläufiges Verzeichnis der Haftstätten unter dem Reichsführer-SS, 1933–1945* (Arolsen, 1969), p. 5.
38. Vogt, *KZ Moringen*, p. 15. The two women, Marie Peix and Hanna Vogt, were arrested for their Communist activities.
39. Arndt, "Das Frauenkonzentrationslager Ravensbrück," pp. 94–99.
40. For more data on Moringen, see ibid.; Elling, *Frauen im deutschen Widerstand*, pp. 23–24; and *Konzentrationslager* (Karlsbad, 1934), pp. 213–16. An explanation of the Dachau model is found in Friedlander, "The Nazi Concentration Camps," pp. 35–39.
41. Arndt, "Das Frauenkonzentrationslager Ravensbrück," pp. 99–101.
42. The heads of female camps were called *director;* those in the male camps carried the title of *commandant.* It is unclear whether this change in title implied any substantive difference in administrative organization or authority, or whether posting to women's camps had less prestige.
43. Berlin Document Center (BDC): Personnel Dossier of Max Koegel, SS no. 37,644. Koegel's predecessor at Lichtenburg, SS Colonel Günther Tamaschke, SS No. 851, was also trained at Dachau. Excerpts from both personnel dossiers at the BDC are used as facsimile reproductions in Elling, *Frauen im deutschen Widerstand*, pp. 33–36.
44. Facsimile of Koegel's March 14, 1939, letter is reproduced in the memoir by Charlotte Müller, *Die Klempnerkolonne in Ravensbrück: Erinnerungen des Häftlings Nr. 10787* (Berlin, 1981), illustration facing p. 48; my translation. For the pattern of corporal punishment against male and female prisoners, see *Trial of the Major War Criminals before the International Military Tribunal*, 42 vols. (Nuremberg, 1947–1949), Vol. 4, p. 201, and Vol. 29, pp. 315–16 (Nuremberg Document PS 2189). See also excerpt from Himmler's regulations for permitted punishments in the camps, 1941, ibid., Vol. 39, pp. 262–64 (Nuremberg Document USSR 011).
45. BA: R 58/1027, Gestapo circular of 2 May 1939. The inmate registration numbers at Ravensbrück continued with 1,415, showing a complete congruity and continuity with the registration numbers assigned prisoners at Lichtenburg.
46. I would like to thank Marion Kaplan and Joan Ringelheim for suggesting this connection. See G. Zörner, ed., *Frauen-KZ Ravensbrück* (Berlin, 1982).

47. Zörner, *Ravensbrück*, pp. 93–95; and Arndt, "Das Frauenkonzentrationslager Ravensbrück," pp. 112–13. Tuesdays and Fridays were designated for flogging, and a maximum of 25 blows with a leather whip were permitted, once Himmler and the camp physician certified an inmate "fit" to receive punishment. In 1942, the rules changed, allowing whipping on women's bare buttocks, and also permitting designated prisoner trusties to whip other prisoners. The latter rule was qualified so that German women could not be beaten by foreigners. This rule was designed to weaken any sympathy or solidarity between prisoners. It is believed that the formal rules were often violated with impunity.

48. Arndt, "Das Frauenkonzentrationslager Ravensbrück," pp. 119–20.

49. See Gemma LaGuardia Gluck, "LaGuardia's Sister: Eichmann's Hostage," *Midstream* 7, No. 1 (1961): 3–19. Geneviève de Gaulle was the general's niece and Rosa Thälmann was the wife of the imprisoned leader of the German Communist Party. No research has been done about the special barracks and somewhat preferential treatment accorded to the privileged prisoners and *Prominenten* in Ravensbrück, Auschwitz, Theresienstadt, or other camps.

50. The composition of barracks (called *Blocks*) with inmate housing is described in several memoirs: Margarete Buber-Neumann, *Als Gefangene bei Stalin und Hitler: Eine Welt im Dunkel* (Stuttgart, 1958); Germaine Tillion, *Ravensbrück*, trans. Gerald Satterwhite (Garden City, N.Y., 1975); Isa Vermehren, *Reise durch den letzten Akt: Ravensbrück, Buchenwald, Dachau* (Reinbek bei Hamburg, 1979); and the anthology edited by the Amicale de Ravensbrück, *Les Françaises à Ravensbrück* (Bordeaux, 1971). See also Arndt, "Das Frauenkonzentrationslager Ravensbrück," pp. 112–19.

51. LaGuardia Gluck, "LaGuardia's Sister," p. 5.

52. Arndt, "Das Frauenkonzentrationslager Ravensbrück," pp. 101–04; Tillion, *Ravensbrück*, pp. 67–71; and Friedlander, "The Nazi Concentration Camps," pp. 33–69.

53. Arndt, "Das Frauenkonzentrationslager Ravensbrück," p. 121.

54. Tillion, *Ravensbrück*, p. 39.

55. Ibid.; all memoirs report similar stories about women's experiences in Ravensbrück and other camps.

56. There have been no studies of the Nazi manipulation of language as applied to women, and the whole subject of gender-specific usage requires further analysis, as does the appropriation of that language by the prisoners themselves. This type of research is needed especially in light of Nazi sexual ideology stressing masculine superiority. An excellent introduction to this subject is found in Henry Friedlander, "The Manipulation of Language," in *The Holocaust: Ideology, Bureaucracy, and Genocide; the San Jose Papers*, ed. Henry Friedlander and Sybil Milton (Millwood, N.Y., 1980), pp. 103–13.

57. Statistics on women SS guards are found in Tillion, *Ravensbrück*, pp. 68ff., and Zörner, *Ravensbrück*, pp. 27ff.

58. Personnel dossiers of these SS women are available in the files of the BDC; the BA; the Ravensbrück Museum in Fürstenberg, German Democratic Republic; and the pretrial investigations and interrogations of the Nuremberg, U.S. Army war crimes trials, and British trials (see National Archives, Washington, D.C.: Record Groups 153 and 238). See BDC, typescript inventory of holdings, December 1970, 6 pages; also Robert Wolfe, ed., *Captured German and Related Records: A National Archives Conference* (Athens, Ohio, 1974), pp. 131–43. See also Gerhard Granier, Josef Henke, and Klaus Oldenhage, eds., *Das Bundesarchiv und seine Bestände.* 3d expanded ed. (Boppard am Rhein, 1977). The Association of Those Persecuted under Nazi Rule (Vereinigung der Verfolgten des Naziregimes; VVN) and their regional offices have archives on various camps and data revealed by trials; their

national newsletter is extremely useful in reconstructing the careers of SS women guards and other perpetrators. Similar relevant holdings exist with the Amicale de Ravensbrück and other survivors' umbrella organizations existing in every country once occupied during World War II. See also George O. Kent, "Research Opportunities in West and East German Archives for the Weimar Period and the Third Reich," *Central European History* 3, No. 1 (1979): 38–67.

59. Hermann Langbein, *Menschen in Auschwitz* (Frankfurt and Vienna, 1972), pp. 444, 447–49.

60. Conversations with Raul Hilberg and Joan Ringelheim.

61. Tillion, *Ravensbrück*, pp. 68ff.; Zörner, *Ravensbrück*, pp. 21–31. See also Buber-Neumann, *Gefangene bei Stalin und Hitler*, pp. 301–31; and idem, *Die erloschene Flamme: Schicksale meiner Zeit* (Munich and Vienna, 1976), pp. 30–42.

62. Jadwiga Bezwinska and Danuta Czech, eds., *KL Auschwitz seen by the SS: Höss, Broad, Kremer* (Auschwitz, 1972), p. 81 (Höss autobiography).

63. Bezwinska and Czech, *Auschwitz Seen by the SS*, pp. 79–82 (Höss); Buber-Neumann, *Gefangene bei Stalin und Hitler*, pp. 301–31; and idem, *Die erloschene Flamme*, pp. 30–42.

64. Buber-Neumann, *Gefangene bei Stalin und Hitler*, pp. 318–22, 325–32, 335–37; also Erika Buchmann, ed., *Die Frauen von Ravensbrück* (Berlin, 1960), pp. 7–22.

65. Bezwinska and Czech, *Auschwitz Seen by the SS*, p. 80 (Höss).

66. Ibid., p. 82.

67. Henry Friedlander, "Concentration Camps," in Janet Blatter and Sybil Milton, *Art of the Holocaust* (New York, 1981), pp. 136–37. The Soviet women POWs arrived in late February 1943, captured at the battle of Sebastopol.

68. The number of women in Mauthausen's satellites in April 1945 were: Lenzing—600; Amstetten—500; Hirtenberg—400; St. Lambrecht—20; Mittersill—15; and Gusen—14. See Hans Marsalek, *Die Geschichte des Konzentrationslagers Mauthausen* (Vienna, 1980), pp. 115–18.

69. In March 1945, several German prostitutes were drafted into a unit of women guards at Mauthausen, similar to the German and Austrian male criminal prisoners given arms during the Auschwitz' evacuation march or those drafted into military formations from Sachsenhausen. See Marsalek, *Mauthausen*, pp. 115–18; Kazimierz Smolen et al., *Auschwitz: Geschichte und Wirklichkeit des Vernichtungslagers* (Reinbek bei Hamburg, 1980), pp. 169–80; and Hilberg, *Destruction*, p. 623. The women who survived in Mauthausen and its subsidiaries consisted in April 1945 of the following subgroups: 1,453 protective custody prisoners; 608 Jewish women; 79 Gypsies; 62 "asocials"; 43 Jehovah's Witnesses; and 5 Spanish Communist women. More than half the surviving women were between 20 and 40 years old (Marsalek, *Mauthausen*, pp. ‹16, 137–39).

70. At the end of 1944, there were 5,000 women at Dachau; 14,600 at Flossenbürg; and 13,500 at Neuengamme. See Ernst Antoni, *Von Dachau bis Auschwitz: Faschistische Konzentrationslager, 1933–1945* (Frankfurt, 1979), pp. 30–38, 50–56; Fritz Bringmann, *Neuengamme: Berichte, Erinnerungen, Dokumente* (Frankfurt, 1981); Werner Johe, *Neuengamme: Zur Geschichte der Konzentrationslager in Hamburg* (Hamburg, 1981); and Barbara Distel and Ruth Jakusch, eds., *Concentration Camp Dachau, 1933–1945* (Brussels, n.d.).

71. Schätzle, *Stationen zur Hölle*, pp. 45–48.

72. The whole phenomenon of special labor camps in Germany for women, Jews, and other prisoner categories has not been adequately explored in the current literature. For treatment of forced labor camps for Jews, see Friedlander, "The Nazi Concentration Camps," pp. 43–50. See also Internationaler Suchdienst, *Vorläufiges Verzeichnis*, pp. VI–XLI.

73. A list of the last women's camps is found in Internationaler Suchdienst, *Vorläufiges Verzeichnis*, p. XIII.
74. Henry Friedlander and Sybil Milton, "Surviving," in *Genocide: Critical Issues of the Holocaust*, ed. Alex Grobman, Daniel Landes, and Sybil Milton (Los Angeles and Chappaqua, N.Y., 1983), pp. 233–35.
75. Leonard Tushnet, *The Uses of Adversity: Studies of Starvation in the Warsaw Ghetto* (London and New York, 1966).
76. Hanna Lévy-Hass, *Vielleicht war das alles erst der Anfang: Tagebuch aus dem KZ Bergen-Belsen, 1944–1945*, ed. Eike Geisel (Berlin, 1979), pp. 10–11. Also, LBI, NY: Eva Noack-Mosse, "Theresienstädter Tagebuch, January–July 1945," unpubl. ms. (1945); and Hanna Schramm, *Menschen in Gurs: Erinnerungen an ein französisches Internierungslager, 1940–1941* (Worms, 1977), p. 88.
77. Richarz, *Jüdisches Leben in Deutschland, 1918–1945*, pp. 429–31.
78. LBI, NY: Eva Noack-Mosse, "Theresienstädter Tagebuch," p. 85; and Hanna Lévy-Hass, *Inside Belsen*, trans. Ronald Taylor (Great Britain and New Jersey, 1982), pp. 6–7, 46–49.
79. Langbein, *Menschen in Auschwitz*, pp. 121–22.
80. France Audoul, *Ravensbrück: 150,000 femmes en enfer* (Paris, 1968), unpag.
81. Daniel Landes, "Modesty and Self-Dignity in Holocaust Films," in Grobman, Landes, Milton, eds., *Genocide*, pp. 11–13.
82. H. G. Adler, Hermann Langbein, Ella Lingens-Reiner, eds., *Auschwitz: Zeugnisse und Berichte* (Frankfurt, 1962); and Olga Lengyel, *Five Chimneys* (London, 1981).
83. Lévy-Hass, *Inside Belsen*, pp. 14–15; Adler, Langbein, and Lingens-Reiner, *Auschwitz*, pp. 111–62; and LBI, NY: Eva Noack-Mosse, "Theresienstädter Tagebuch," pp. 74–75.
84. Charlotte Delbo, *None of Us Will Return*, trans. John Githens (Boston, 1978).
85. Bezwinska and Czech, *Auschwitz Seen by the SS*, p. 75 (Höss).
86. Schramm, *Menschen in Gurs*, p. 88; Lévy-Hass, *Inside Belsen*, pp. 28–35 (entry for 22 October 1944); and Vermehren, *Reise durch den letzten Akt*, p. 26. Although this particular quote is from Schramm, almost identically worded descriptions are found in other memoirs; see also Buber-Neumann and Tillion.
87. Lévy-Hass, *Inside Belsen*, p. 8.
88. Joan Mariam Ringelheim, "The Unethical and the Unspeakable: Women and the Holocaust," *Simon Wiesenthal Center Annual* 1 (1984): 69–87; and *Proceedings of the Conference Women Surviving the Holocaust*, ed. Esther Katz and Joan Ringelheim (New York, 1983), pp. 22–26.
89. Schramm, *Menschen in Gurs*, pp. 14–16; see also Kitty Hart, *Return to Auschwitz* (New York, 1982), and Anna Pawelczynska, *Values and Violence in Auschwitz: A Sociological Analysis*, trans. Catherine S. Leach (Berkeley and Los Angeles, 1979).
90. American Jewish Joint Distribution Committee Archives, New York: "Germans in France," *Friday* 1, No. 10 (17 May 1940), clipping in the 1940 files on French Refugees.
91. Hart, *Return to Auschwitz*, pp. 76–80, 104–09.
92. Buber-Neumann, *Gefangene bei Stalin und Hitler*, p. 227; and Bezwinska and Czech, *Auschwitz Seen by the SS*, p. 77 (Höss).
93. Naomi Winkler Munkacsi, "Jewish Religious Observances in Women's Death Camps in Germany," *Yad Vashem Bulletin* 20 (April 1967): 35–8.
94. France Hamelin, unpublished diary, Christmas 1943 (unpag.), by permission of France Hamelin, Paris; see Blatter and Milton, *Art of the Holocaust*, p. 251.
95. Schramm, *Menschen in Gurs;* and LBI, NY: archival collections on Gurs and the French internment camps.
96. Schramm, *Menschen in Gurs;* Blatter and Milton, *Art of the Holocaust*, interviews

of prisoner-artists interned in Gurs, Birkenau, and Ravensbrück; the memoirs of Tillion and Buber-Neumann; and the archives of the LBI, NY and the American Jewish Joint Distribution Committee, New York.

97. Hart, *Return to Auschwitz*, p. 122; also Langbein, *Menschen in Auschwitz*, pp. 450–63.

98. Langbein, *Menschen in Auschwitz*, pp. 457–58; and Bezwinska and Czech, *Auschwitz Seen by the SS*, p. 83 (Höss).

99. H. G. Adler, *Theresienstadt, 1941–1945* (Tübingen, 1960); and Buber-Neumann, *Gefangene bei Stalin und Hitler*, pp. 260ff. Also LBI, NY: Noack-Mosse, "Theresienstädter Tagebuch," pp. 74–75.

100. Lesbian relationships are mentioned in very few memoirs; see Lengyel, *Five Chimneys*, pp. 191–93 for a detailed analysis of lesbian relationships in Birkenau. The excerpts from Erna Nelki's memoir, "Eingesperrt im englischen Frauenlager," reprinted in Walter Zadek, ed., *Sie flohen vor dem Hakenkreuz: Selbstzeugnisse der Emigranten; Ein Lesebuch für Deutsche* (Reinbek bei Hamburg, 1981), pp. 120–26, describes life without men among 3,000 mostly German-Jewish women interned on the Isle of Man. The whole subject of sexuality, love, and friendships in prisons and camps requires further systematic investigation. The taboos of historical literature have limited discussion and investigation of these subjects in the past.

101. The swapping of sex for food is described in the memoirs of Lengyel, *Five Chimneys*, pp. 189–90; and Fania Fénelon, *Playing for Time*, trans. Judith Landry (New York, 1979).

102. Vermehren, *Reise durch den letzten Akt*, pp. 25–27; and Hermann Langbein, *Nicht wie die Schafe zur Schlachtbank: Widerstand in den nationalsozialistischen Konzentrationslagern* (Frankfurt, 1980).

103. Langbein, *Widerstand*, pp. 178, 336–39.

104. Blatter and Milton, *Art of the Holocaust*, pp. 136–37; and Lévy-Hass, *Inside Belsen*, pp. 25–26.

105. Bezwinska and Czech, *Auschwitz Seen by the SS*, pp. 163–68 (Broad). The Budy revolt is unconfirmed by prisoner sources and requires further research to fill the gaps. See Langbein, *Menschen in Auschwitz*, pp. 135–38, for skepticism about the existing source literature on Budy.

106. Blatter and Milton, *Art of the Holocaust;* and Adler, *Theresienstadt*.

107. Lévy-Hass, *Inside Belsen*, p. 7; LBI, NY: Noack-Mosse, "Theresienstädter Tagebuch," pp. 75–76.

108. Peter Altmann et al., *Der deutsche antifaschistische Widerstand 1933–1945 in Bildern und Dokumenten* (Frankfurt, 1977); and Günther Weisenborn, *Der lautlose Aufstand: Bericht über die Widerstandsbewegung des deutschen Volkes, 1933–1945;* 4th rev. exp. ed. (Frankfurt, 1974).

109. Helmut Eschwege, "Resistance of German Jews against the Nazi Regime," *Leo Baeck Institute Yearbook* 15 (1970): 143–80; idem, *Kennzeichen J*, pp. 299–322; and Konrad Kwiet, "Problems of Jewish Resistance Historiography," *Leo Baeck Institute Yearbook* 24 (1979): 35–57.

110. See footnote 109. Also Margot Pikarski, *Jugend im Berliner Widerstand: Herbert Baum und Kampfgefährten* (Berlin, 1978); Lucien Steinberg, *Jews against Hitler*, trans. Marion Hunter (London and New York, 1974), pp. 19–53; and Wolfgang Wippermann, *Die Berliner Gruppe Baum und der jüdische Widerstand*, Brochure 19 of the Informationszentrum Berlin Gedenk- und Bildungsstätte Stauffenbergstrasse (Berlin, 1981). For the *Chug Chaluzzi*, see Jizchak Schwersenz and Edith Wolff, "Jüdische Jugend im Untergrund: Eine zionistische Gruppe in Deutschland während des Zweiten Weltkrieges," *Bulletin des Leo Baeck Instituts* 12 (1969): 5–100. See also the 1968 conference proceedings on Jewish resistance published as *Jewish Resistance during the Holocaust* (Jerusalem, 1971).

111. Eschwege, "Resistance of German Jews against the Nazi Regime," pp. 176–77.
112. Schwersenz and Wolff, "Jüdische Jugend im Untergrund," pp. 51–58.
113. Information on Gertrud Luckner is in Adler, *Der verwaltete Mensch*, pp. 825–28. See also Sybil Milton, "The Righteous Who Helped Jews," in Grobman, Landes, and Milton, eds., *Genocide*, pp. 282–87; Philip Friedman, "Righteous Gentiles in the Nazi Era," in his *Roads to Extinction: Essays on the Holocaust* (New York and Philadelphia, 1980), pp. 209–21; and idem, *Their Brothers' Keepers* (New York, 1978). Case studies are found in the interviews reproduced in Jochen Köhler, *Klettern in der Grossstadt: Volkstümliche Geschichten vom Überleben in Berlin, 1933–1945* (Berlin, 1979); Gerda Szepansky, ed., *Frauen leisten Widerstand: 1933–45*; Ilse Rewald, *Berliner, die uns halfen, die Hitlerdiktatur zu überleben*, Brochure 6 of the Informationszentrum Berlin Gedenk; und Bildungsstätte Stauffenbergstrasse (Berlin, 1982); Inge Deutschkron, *Berliner Juden im Untergrund*, Brochure 15 of the Informationszentrum Berlin pamphlet series (Berlin, 1982); and Charles Whiting, ed., *The Home Front: Germany* (Time-Life Books, 1982), pp. 96–109.
114. Blatter and Milton, *Art of the Holocaust*, pp. 255, 258–9, 1980 interview with Mieke Monjau about the arrest and deportation of Julo Levin in the February 1943 "Factory Operation." Single Jewish males and females and spouses in all-Jewish marriages were not released in February 1943. See also Monika Richarz, *Jüdisches Leben in Deutschland, 1918–1945*, pp. 64, 414; Kurt Ball-Kaduri, "Berlin wird judenfrei," *Jahrbuch für die Geschichte Mittel-und Ostdeutschlands* 22 (Berlin, 1973), pp. 196–241; and Wolfgang Wippermann, ed., *Steinerne Zeugen: Stätten der Judenverfolgung in Berlin* (Berlin, 1982), pp. 59–70; and LBI, NY: Microfilm Reel 239: Anklageschrift in der Strafsache gegen Otto Bovensiepen et al. (1969) [the indictment of the Berlin Gestapo for the deportation of the Jews of Berlin].
115. Quote from the memoirs of Hildegard Henschel, wife of the last head of the Berlin Jewish community, Moritz Henschel, in K. J. Ball-Kaduri, "Berlin is 'Purged' of Jews: The Jews in Berlin in 1943," *Yad Vashem Studies* 5 (1963): 274–75; also Hildegard Henschel, "Aus der Arbeit der jüdischen Gemeinde Berlin während 1941–1943," *Zeitschrift für die Geschichte der Juden* (Tel Aviv) 9, Nos. 1–2 (1972): 33–52; see also LBI, NY: Wiener Library microfilms containing eyewitness statements and a list of women participants in the February demonstrations (AR 7187/Reel 600).
116. Goebbels reported in his diary entry for March 6, 1943: "Unfortunately there have been a number of regrettable scenes at a Jewish home for the aged, where a large number of people gathered and in part even took sides with the Jews. I ordered the SD not to continue Jewish evacuation at so critical a moment. We want to save that up for a couple of weeks. We can then go after it all the more thoroughly" (Louis P. Lochner, ed. and trans., *The Goebbels Diaries, 1942–1943* [Garden City, N.Y., 1948], p. 276). There is no information about the composition of the crowd that demonstrated in this incident.
117. Heinz Boberach, ed., *Meldungen aus dem Reich: Auswahl aus den geheimen Lageberichten des Sicherheitsdienstes der SS, 1939–44* (Neuwied and Berlin, 1965), pp. 445–55 (report of 13 November 1943).
118. Kwiet, "Problems of Jewish Resistance Historiography," pp. 37–57.
119. H. D. Leuner, *When Compassion Was a Crime: Germany's Silent Heroes, 1933–1945* (London, 1973); Kurt R. Grossmann, *Die unbesungenen Helden: Menschen in Deutschlands dunklen Tagen* (Berlin-Grünewald, 1957); Bruno Blau, "The Jewish Population of Germany, 1939–45," *Jewish Social Studies* 12, No. 2 (April 1950): 161–72; Deutschkron, *Berliner Juden im Untergrund*, p. 6.
120. Rewald, *Berliner, die uns halfen*, p. 10.
121. Whiting, *The Home Front*, p. 102.
122. Richarz, *Jüdisches Leben in Deutschland, 1918–1945*, pp. 429–42; and LBI, NY: Pineas Collection, AR 94/1–52, containing the bogus identity and ration cards of

the Pineas family between 1943 and 1945. See also Grossmann, *Unbesungene Helden*, pp. 159–61.

123. LBI, NY: Berthold Freundlich family collection, AR 3774/1–4.
124. LBI, NY: Hermann Haymann family collection, AR 3216/1–4.
125. LBI, NY: Max Kreutzberger Research Papers, AR 7183, Box 8, folder 1, Paula Littauer, "My Experiences during the Persecution of the Jews in Berlin and Brussels, 1939–1944," unpubl. ms. (mimeographed by the Jewish Central Information Office, London, October 1945).
126. Further, the subject of suicides needs more investigation. See Kwiet, "Jewish Resistance Historiography," p. 57; and Richarz, *Jüdisches Leben in Deutschland, 1918–1945*, pp. 65, 394–400.
127. See the recent popular survey of underground life in Berlin by Leonard Gross, *The Last Jews in Berlin* (New York, 1982); and Sybil Milton, "In Hiding," in Blatter and Milton, *Art of the Holocaust*, p. 124 (and the interviews and biographies of Leo Mayer-Maillet and Toni Simon-Wolfskehl).
128. Two systematic archival guides provide data about sources for emigrant institutions and prominent refugee personalities: Steven W. Siegel, comp., and Herbert A. Strauss, ed., *Jewish Immigrants of the Nazi Period in the USA: Archival Resources*, vol. 1 (New York and Munich, 1978); and John M. Spalek with Sandra H. Hawrylchak and Adrienne Ash, *Guide to the Archival Materials of the German-speaking Emigration to the United States after 1933* (Charlottesville, 1978). See also Herbert A. Strauss, "Jewish Emigration from Germany: Nazi Policies and Jewish Responses," *Leo Baeck Institute Yearbook* 25 (1980): 313–61; and ibid., 26 (1981): 343–409; and see Werner Röder and Herbert A. Strauss, eds., *Biographisches Handbuch der deutschsprachigen Emigration*, Vol. 1.
129. Herbert A. Strauss, "Jewish Emigration from Germany," *Leo Baeck Institute Yearbooks* 25 and 26. See footnote 128.
130. Sophia M. Robinson, *Refugees at Work* (New York, 1942), pp. 28–31. Only in the year from 1938 to 1939 did fewer women arrive in the United States. From 1933 to 1938, 89,553 female immigrants and 85,686 male immigrants were registered. Statistics of marital status between 1933 and 1938 show that 52 percent of all refugees were single, 42.6 percent married, 4.3 percent widowed, and 1.1 percent divorced. During the two subsequent periods of 1938–39 and 1939–40, the percentage of married immigrants increased respectively to 49.2 and 54.6 percent of all immigrants to the United States.
131. Marion A. Kaplan, "Tradition and Transition: The Acculturation, Assimilation and Integration of Jews in Imperial Germany; A Gender Analysis," *Leo Baeck Institute Yearbook* 27 (1982): 3–35.
132. See A. J. P. Taylor, *From Sarajevo to Potsdam* (London, 1965); and Renate Bridenthal, "Something Old, Something New: Women between the Two World Wars," in Bridenthal and Koonz, eds., *Becoming Visible*, pp. 422–44.
133. Frankenthal, *Der dreifache Fluch*, pp. 242–43.
134. Aggregate data for the study of German and German-Jewish refugee women is available for research, for example, the case files of the American Jewish Joint Distribution Committee held at the archives of the LBI, NY (AR 7196; 13½ linear ft. of case records); the HIAS, ORT, and OSE immigration records at the Yivo Institute for Jewish Research in New York; and the records of agencies like Self-Help and the American Federation of Jews from Central Europe or the Association of Jewish Refugees in Great Britain still held by the agencies themselves. Papers of prominent female refugees are readily available. The archives of the LBI, NY holds the literary estates or substantial fragments for Alice Salomon, Else Lasker-Schüler, and Gertrude Urzidil.

The story of German and German-Jewish women who fled to adjacent European nations after 1933 has received some attention in conferences and anthologies, like

Jarrell C. Jackmann and Carla M. Borden, eds., *The Muses Flee Hitler: Cultural Transfer and Adaptation, 1930–1945* (Washington, D.C., 1983). The story of women who fled to the Soviet Union and ended up serving time in the Siberian Gulag is told in memoirs like Buber-Neumann, *Gefangene bei Stalin und Hitler;* Susanne Leonhard, *Gestohlenes Leben: Schicksal einer politischen Emigrantin in der Sowjetunion* (Frankfurt, 1956); and in archival sources about Zenzl Mühsam in the LBI, NY: Erich Mühsam papers, AR 1806/IV and V. The story of double migrations is revealed mostly through biographical works. Systematic emigration investigation is still in its infancy where refugee women are concerned.

# The Story of Ruth

## Ruth Nebel

*Ruth Nebel's testimony, given to Sylvia Kramer, an author friend, is the personal memoir of a young German-Jewish woman who lived through the stages of persecution and horror detailed by Sybil Milton. She talks of specific female experiences, as well as the overriding one of being Jewish. Her odyssey gives a survivor's view of some of the same places described by Milton. Moreover, her close female friendships, as well as some of her other survival strategies, offer support for a gender analysis of the Holocaust.*

Life had been good in Fritzlar, Germany, where I lived with my parents and two younger sisters, surrounded by the companionship of forty other Jewish families. We enjoyed the fruits of our Orthodox way of life, and the Sabbath was received each week as a special gift. It was a time of quiet family dinners and walks with friends. The pace slowed; there was time to really listen to each other, to experience a veil of calm.

The sanction of no work was closely adhered to by all the family. Even our wristwatches were pinned to our dresses the day before, lest we forget and "burden" ourselves with wearing them. My father attended services on the Sabbath. . . .

I was 14 years old in 1935 when anti-Semitism slowly crept into our little town. If one chose, it could be ignored, made excuses for, or denied altogether. But insulting remarks were being spoken publicly. "Jew, we'll get rid of you; it's good we have a Hitler, he'll do the job right"; "Jewish swine." It became difficult for Jews to secure jobs, and eventually all the Jewish children were not permitted to continue their schooling.

For a while I attended a Catholic school, but this came to an end when one day a nun took me gently by the shoulders and said, "Ruth, I think it would be best if you did not come any more. I fear for your safety. There are only two Jewish girls here in our school, and I worry that the children might soon taunt and harass you."

I pleaded with my father to leave for a big city where it was said that life was better, but each time I asked, he would reply, "What would Hitler want of me? I'm a simple working man, not a scientist or professor. You'll see, things won't be too bad. Maybe soon they'll let you go to school again."

The atmosphere of hate frightened me. I longed for a place that would restore a peaceful life to us, and, at sixteen, being unable to convince my parents to go from our town, I told them I was leaving.

My father cried, "You've gone crazy, you're too young to go away from home." My mother, through her tears, said, "Ruth, we will suffer worrying about you. Don't go, don't go."

The last thing I wanted to do was cause my parents grief, but my mind was made up. My plan was to find a safe place and then convince them to follow me there.

I left for the home of an elderly Jewish lady in Greglingen near Würzburg, where I worked as a companion, but soon found life was no better there, since the town was rampant with anti-Semitism.

I was afraid to go out at night. Gangs would attack Jews, beat them and leave them bleeding in the streets. I missed my family terribly, and went to see them before making new plans for myself.

The sight of my parents shocked and frightened me. Within months they had aged years. My father, with quivering voice, described November 9, 1938, *Kristallnacht*. All the synagogues in Germany had been set afire, and all books and valuables belonging to Jews were confiscated.

"And one day, Ruth," my father said, "we were told that we would be part of a group going to Palestine. Mama and I were overjoyed, since we knew for sure Germany was no longer a place for Jews. You were right, my daughter. What you wanted to do for us, we thought we would do for you; settle in Palestine and get you out of Germany.

"We met in the square, according to orders, one sunny morning, full of hope, and were brought to a railroad station where we waited all night. No train came. Then orders were issued that we were to turn around and go back. When we saw our burned-out homes and destroyed synagogues, I thought I was seeing hell, that I had already died." He went on to tell me how he had gone into shock and had been hospitalized for weeks.

I heard about a Jewish South American family who lived in Hamburg-Altona. Since the daughter had to work, a companion was needed for the elderly parents, and they welcomed my arrival. I was promised that they would include me in their planned departure to

England in a short time, and I was very excited about this prospect. I assured my parents that I would find a way out for all of us.

Rita, a girl my own age with whom I now lived, became a dear friend to me. In fact, when the order eventually was issued that all Jews had to wear a Jewish star sewn to their outer garment, my precious friend insisted on doing the marketing so that I could remain inside where I would be less conspicuous. (Rita's family was exempt from this ruling, since they were South American citizens.)

My parents, at this time, were finding life more and more difficult. Wearing the exposed Jewish star made them frightened about going outside to shop for the little food they could get with their ration stamps.

Knowing they would starve rather than eat food that was not kosher, I tried to help. I would bake fresh fish, package it, and get it on the night train so that it could be received early the next day—no simple task, since there was an 8:00 P.M. curfew for Jews. A very kind German Gentile policeman, who was a neighbor in Hamburg, would escort me to the train station twice a week for nearly a year, endangering his own life, for had he been caught, he would have been shot by the Gestapo for aiding a Jew.

From time to time, I heard that my packages had been received, and I was overjoyed that in some small way I was able to assist my parents.

On December 12, 1941, a date I remember well, I received a letter telling me to report to the local school building at 11:00 A.M. and to leave everything behind except one hundred pounds of personal belongings. All things of value had been confiscated long ago, so I took only some warm clothing.

Sitting down to write, I broke down and wept. My tears, falling on the paper, made the ink run, so again and again I rewrote, "I do not know where I am being taken. I will try not to be frightened, yet I wonder whether I will ever see you again, Mama and Papa." I wrote the words but could hardly believe them. Oh, God, I thought, what will become of me?

My friend Rita walked with me to the square. It was difficult for each of us to speak, and so we walked in silence, fighting back our tears, trying to be strong for one another. She insisted on carrying my suitcase—the last act of kindness I would know for a very long time.

We clung to each other, and finally, losing all control, cried. Patting my hair, telling me everything would be all right, she turned and was gone.

Stormtroopers—tall, handsome men in black uniforms and boots—shouted orders as hordes of people were gathered in the confined quarters of the school building. There was excited talking and questioning, but no hysteria. Everyone responded to Rabbi Carlebach's request to remain calm, to have faith, to wait and see. . . . It gave us courage to have our beloved rabbi from Hamburg, together with his family, in our midst.

Suddenly, as though we had formed a new family, we were each concerned for the other. For three days we remained here sleeping in straw bunk beds, never changing clothing, eating whatever little food we had brought with us. We were given nothing.

The SS moved through the crowds, hitting babies, clubbing old people, pushing, screaming orders and curses. "You goddamn Jews, glad we have you together. Wait and see what we are going to do with you."

In spite of all the horror around me, I kept thinking that someone would come soon and save me. How was I to know that this was only the beginning? That I, Ruth Stern, would in time lose my entire family and nearly my sanity.

Buses took us to a railroad station on the outskirts of Hamburg, and we were herded into what was known as the poor people's train, old, with holes in the floor and ripped seats. Few found a place to sit, and the pushing and screaming soon turned into panic.

For one week we traveled with no food other than stale bread, terrified, weak, feeling forsaken.

The bathroom became stuffed and out of order the first day. The stench was revolting and I would vomit each time I approached it. Fighting to maintain some sense of dignity, we would try to find scraps of paper with which to clean our bodies.

Only the strongest survived. A woman, an old man, two today, six tomorrow, would jump from the speeding train, welcoming death as the only relief.

One morning we were given postal cards and told we could write to whomever we chose. My heart was momentarily uplifted as I wrote to my beloved family, "We're traveling; I don't know where; but I hope to see you again. I love you, Ruth."

When the last card was collected, the train slowed down and an SS jumped off. Peeking out of holes in the side of the car, we stared with astonishment as he lit a match to the whole bunch of cards, and, laughing, turned our love into a mockery as our words of affection and longing went up in flames.

Sometimes a head would fall upon my shoulder, and I would look down, only to see that someone had died. I would quietly move away. We had, it seemed, become immune to death, even I, who had suffered at the sight of a wounded bird.

At the week's end we arrived at Shareh Tawah. In silence we crept off the train. Our bodies, bent from days of not moving, refused now to straighten up, and like animals, we used our hands as feet.

Moving through a line of armed SS, we were stunned by the piercing cold. The snow was at least two feet high. It was as though nature had formed a pact with man to punish us. We had no coats, no sweaters.

Where were we, I wondered? Why were we brought here? How many more times I would ask unanswered questions!

Later I learned that all the Jews of Riga had been killed prior to our arrival to make room for our group of German Jews. The SS seemed to take delight in our falling down, our moans, our wounds. Slipping on the ice, pushed by the wind, we moved slowly until we arrived at the open barracks camp called Jungfernhof.

Thousands of Jews were already there, pacing in circles in the deep snow, shivering and stooped, with bony faces and staring eyes. Whispers could be heard, more like groans, "It's no good here for anyone, no hope."

We whispered, "Where are you from?" and weak voices replied, "Frankfurt, Berlin, Würzburg" and every other major city in Germany.

Suddenly an order was shouted, "Let all personal possessions fall from you." Slowly my hand moved to my blouse as I released the precious pictures of my family that lay hidden near my bosom from the moment I had been ordered to leave Hamburg. As they fell, I whispered, "Good-bye, Mama and Papa and little Hertha and Erna." I stood dumbfounded as several troopers tore my photographs into tiny pieces. I winced, as though my loved ones could actually feel their faces being torn.

One Gestapo ran the entire camp that held about 5,000 prisoners, and Latvians acted as guards under the supervision of the SS.

Each morning at about six, an *Appell* was held, a time of counting and selecting. We were carefully inspected, since only the healthiest, most attractive young people were chosen to develop a model farm.

The commandant's eyes would travel over our bodies, studying faces, shapes, and legs. Those who displeased him would be called out of line, put against the closest wall, and shot.

During one inspection, he came up to me, touched my cheek, and said, "Tell me, what is your wish, to live or die?" Tears rolled down my face as I shuddered and replied, "Live, I want to live." He looked into my eyes for minutes and then slowly moved away saying, "I won't pick you yet."

The three groups who, in normal times, would have been the most honored in society—children, pregnant women, and the elderly—were now declared "rejects." They were put into old trucks and taken away.

The children were packed in twenty or thirty at a time, and the SS would say something like, "You are being taken to a nice place where there are toys and good things to eat."

To the pregnant women—"We have nice, clean houses for you to stay in while you await the birth of your babies."

Never was it enough for the Nazis to simply kill. They played sadistic games, always offering hope, a last promise of better times.

Those of us who remained thought these people were taken to another camp, but weeks later I learned that what looked like sirens on top of the trucks were actually gas tanks, and that the prisoners had been killed right in the trucks.

After weeks of living under the worst disease-infested, overcrowded conditions, it seemed as though the camp was nearly empty. What had been a camp for over 5,000 now held the chosen few, and it was my destiny to be one of the 200 young people kept alive to do labor.

Each morning we raked the unyielding earth, carried away rock and debris, preparing the ground for planting. None of us had ever done this kind of hard work before, and our bodies cried out in pain at the end of each day.

I thanked God that my parents could not see nor even know of my infected fingers, emaciated body, eyes swollen from crying. . . . I prayed for their safety and that they would never know the many punishments I was made to endure.

Twelve hours a day we labored with our waning strength, craving food as much as life itself. Our ration was a small piece of stale bread, half a teaspoon of bitter marmalade, or horsemeat from sick horses. If we were able to hide a carrot or turnip from the fields; we did so.

Latvian workers, who lived in surrounding areas, often sneaked bits of food to us, endangering their own lives. As starved as we were for food, so we hungered for news of the outside world—to know at least the month, the year. These merciful people brought us information as well as food.

Regardless of the danger of accepting food, hunger prodded us again and again. One day a Jewish prisoner was caught taking food from a worker. The entire camp had to witness his hanging as one of our own group was forced to pull the rope.

I watched a life snuffed out for the taking of a piece of bread. I was a witness, yet I did not believe what I saw. "God, God, where are you?" I asked with bitterness.

One morning a new order was issued. A potato field had to be planted. Arriving at the site with shovels and sacks of potatoes, we started to dig long rows.

Suddenly there seemed to be an undulating motion in the earth. I thought the heat had made me dizzy. The ground was moving! I watched in disbelief, frightened, searching the faces of my fellow prisoners to see whether one of them understood. Someone whispered, "Prisoners were buried alive under this ground."

As I lowered my shovel into the dirt, a leg was exposed, then an arm.

I moaned and threw up, screaming, "Don't make me do this, please, please, I can't."

The commandant shouted back, "If you don't, you'll join them, you idiot." Raising his wooden club, he yelled, "Work, you goddamn Jew."

As I touched the ground with the point of my shovel, I wept as I whispered to the Jews under my feet, "Forgive me for what I do."

After almost two years of confinement in Jungfernhof, we were ordered one day into open trucks. "Where are we going, are they going to kill us?" I asked of my fellow inmates huddled together. Their eyes returned my questions.

While we rode, I thought about all the things I had looked forward to doing as a young girl, the books I wanted to read, the places I longed to see. In my small town of Fritzlar, all the young people went to dances and concerts and sometimes fell in love. . . .

It was only a short ride before we were brought to a concentration camp called Kaiserwald. Herded into a small barracks, we were immediately ordered to get completely undressed. This time the woman in charge was a Jew whose name was Carola. I asked, "Why do we have to undress?" "Ask no questions, do as you're told," she shouted.

Moments later we were marched naked in front of a group of SS. When they approached me, looking my body over closely, my flesh burned with embarrassment. I bit my gums and stared ahead. Always, the thought of possibly staying alive gave me strength to endure still another act of degradation.

Although circumstances seemed to spin a web of humiliation, starvation, and ultimately death, there was a corner of myself that kept thinking, "I'll get out, something will save me." Being young, I just couldn't bury all my dreams of some day experiencing joy and laughter and love. . . .

Prison dresses were issued, dresses of grey and blue stripes. The material was rough, like burlap, and it hurt my skin instantly. We were permitted no underwear or stockings, and were given wooden shoes that cut our feet.

I followed the line of prisoners. As we were counted, No. 1064 was called out and the matron pasted a strip of cloth imprinted with that number on my prison dress. No longer was I Ruth Stern, daughter of Abraham and Friedel Stern, but a number, simply a number. I felt robbed. Without a name I felt just part of a mass, like one of a herd of cattle.

Looking at myself with bulky shoes, shapeless dress, and naked legs, I felt clumsy and ashamed. It still mattered somehow, even though I was surviving in the bowels of the world.

I begged Carola to let me keep my bra. She whispered that I might be severely punished. I said, "I don't care. I'm a woman, not a cow.

Please, I beg you." She told me she would bury it beneath a certain tree and what I did after that was my own business. I dug it up one day when no guards were around, and wore it unwashed, full of lice, all through the years of my imprisonment.

Living in wooden barracks, we slept in lice-ridden straw beds piled three or four high. There was little ventilation, and the odors from the unwashed bodies kept me in a constant state of nausea. I chose to sleep in the highest bunk, hoping for a bit more air, but I paid for this "luxury" each time I had to drag my weak body up the sides of the beds below.

Our ration of foul-smelling soup and stale moldy bread was given us once a day in the evening.

Our days were always the same. An *Appell* was held, we were mocked and cursed and made to stand absolutely still for hours. Sometimes the SS would walk over, tap the shoulders of six or seven prisoners, and as the Jews turned in response, they would be shot in the face.

As each week passed, I found it more difficult to hold onto my thoughts. My mind wandered and sometimes I hardly knew who or where I was. Holding my head in my hands, rocking in *davening* (praying) fashion, I would whisper, "God, why am I punished; why is this happening? God, where are you?"

Without calendars or clocks time could not be calculated. Time—the very rhythm of life, was stolen from us. We knew night because of darkness and day only when it arrived clear and bright.

Neither weeks nor months could be measured. We women thought that we could keep track of the passing of each month, but nature had been tampered with and malnutrition canceled out our menstrual cycle.

I couldn't count my passing birthdays, and I didn't know when a Jewish holiday was approaching. If only I knew when Yom Kippur came, so that I could deny myself even the stale bread! I yearned to honor these special days in my heart.

From time to time I found myself craving death. I would lie on my bunk and think of ways to commit suicide, but in the morning, I would lose my nerve. When I overheard rumors that trucks were entering the camp and removing women, I hoped that I would be selected. If the trucks were taking us to our death, good. Better death than beating, hunger, terror. . . .

I was shoved into a truck where I found myself pressing against a girl about my own age. We whispered to one another and discovered that we had been brought up in nearby towns. This gave me a sense of closeness, and I felt as though my sister were with me.

We held hands the entire trip to Riga, careful to keep our heads down. Those who did raise their heads were clubbed.

There was not a part of my body that did not itch beyond what I thought I could endure. Pus oozed from uncovered sores. I craved cleanliness as I did life itself. Many times, in fact, instead of getting in line for bread, I would take a shower, even though the water was either freezing or scalding. Soap was something I hadn't seen for four years.

I would beg a prisoner to bring my portion of bread back to me, but invariably she would eat it herself.

When the SS woman became bored, she would think of ways to tantalize us. The simple act of eating an apple brought us pain. She would munch on one slowly, allowing the juice to drip down her chin, making a sucking noise of delight.

Another SS woman would make us stand outside in rain, snow, howling wind, with no coats, no shoes, only prison dresses covering our skinny bodies. "If you move, you'll stay out two more hours, you Jew bastards," she would scream from her window above.

Being half insane from hunger, fatigue, and fear, we could release our frustrations no place except on each other, and most of the inmates became nasty to one another. The patience we had at the beginning of our imprisonment had left us.

If someone pushed against my sores, I would yell, "You clumsy fool. Can't you see me?" I never pushed anyone out of line to grab my piece of stale bread, but others did. Each would use whatever means might lead to her own survival. . . .

Most days my thoughts went no further than the stale bread in my hand and when I would get another. Each day I sank deeper into depression. As I awoke each morning, the realization that I was still alive struck even before my eyes opened, followed by the question, the constant question, "Will I live out this day?"

The matron reported to the commandant that we were all covered with lice, and she was instructed to cut our hair. "Now all your black hair will come off your head, Jew." When I heard these words, I froze. A clipper came toward me and quickly went down the center of my head, then another row and another until all my hair lay at my feet.

Feeling like a sheep shorn, I moved off into a corner and cried without control. One of the inmates, who had been an opera singer in Vienna before this hell swallowed her up, came to me and said, "Child, don't cry, this is not the worst. Hair will grow back if they let us live."

"Kill me," I sobbed, "kill me, I want to be dead." I kept running my hand over my bald head in disbelief. When I looked up, I recognized no one. We all looked identical with our prison dresses and bald heads. Many nights tears wet my cheeks, awaiting the release of sleep, but this night I wept until dawn as I kept thinking, "I must have died already, this cannot be life."

After having counted us one morning, the commandant shouted, "A group of you will be chosen to work in a factory; come forward, swine, as I call your number." . . . I was selected, and together with about sixty prisoners, was taken across the street to a factory that manufactured cables. Labor was so desperately needed that even our feeble assistance was necessary.

It was my good fortune to work side by side with my dear friend Sonya, whom I had met on the truck when we left Kaiserwald. We worked with Gentile employees who had great compassion for our lot, and at the risk of their own lives, hid sandwiches for us. They knew the danger, but chose to ignore the warnings of the SS that anyone caught either offering or accepting food would be instantly killed.

Sonya and I shared every bite of food we were able to get. Stealing into the tiny toilet, we would gobble it and rush back to work again. Our hunger was never appeased and stomach cramps always resulted, but we never refused something to eat.

The German soldiers who supervised our work often tried to get us bits of food. Without the same indoctrination of hatred for Jews that the SS had been given, they frequently took pity on us.

In the quiet of the night, rumors were whispered throughout the barracks that the Russians were coming closer and that there was a plan to ship us back to Germany to kill us. Fear, paralyzing fear, overwhelmed us anew. I prayed to die, and yet, when I thought death was close, I hoped to escape it. I used to think, "I can endure hunger if I can only live. I can ignore the curses, the threats, the insults, just let me live. I can survive as an animal, filthy, diseased, frightened, if only I remain alive."

Early in the spring of 1944 we were boarded onto trucks and taken to a river's edge where a ship was waiting. We were beaten and cursed at, but in spite of the confusion, we could hear shooting in the distance and realized that the Russians were probably close by.

For one week we traveled aboard the ship, lying in heaps over other weakened bodies, all of us just barely alive. . . . When the ship landed, I crawled out on my hands and knees, lacking the strength to stand on my quivering legs. SS guarded us with raised bayonets, a wasted gesture since not one of us could possibly have run. We were pushed down on the grass near the side of the pier, and watched well-dressed people in the distance walking freely. I couldn't believe normal people still existed in the world.

Stared at by those passing by, we ached to call to them and ask where we were, but, frightened by the guards, we remained silent. . . .

Walking through muddy, open fields for almost an hour, we came to another camp called Stutthof. Surrounded by electrified barbed wire, I saw stooped, shuffling bodies, groaning, mumbling, near the fence. I saw faces without flesh, mouths without teeth, and thousands of eyes— terror-filled eyes—staring.

I had a foreboding that my own end would be met here. There was death in the air. I could smell burned flesh. Turning, watching the prisoners behind the fence, I wept, struggling without success to stifle my tears.

Lice covered us. We cracked them with our nails as our hands scratched the already bleeding skin, looking for relief that never came. There were no toilets, no washing facilities. A woman standing close by read my eyes as I stared at the electric wire, considering the possibility of ending my misery. She put her bony hand on my shoulder and said, "Don't; you have time for that."

Day after day our numbers diminished. I craved death, longed for it, prayed for it. It seemed that my passion to live had burned itself out.

Then one cold, gray day we were ordered out of the barracks for another *Appell*. "Stand straight, you swine, heads up." I shivered so violently I thought I was having convulsions. The icy wind's whistles were all that could be heard, and when "1064" was bellowed from a distance, I thought my imagination was playing tricks. Then again I heard "1064." It was not the wind. My number was being called. I stood paralyzed. The moment I had feared every hour of these brutal years had come. I knew death had finally reached out for me.

There were about sixty women in the wagon that I was pushed into. Women did I say? They were merely bones and staring eyes. In terror we clung to one another, holding each other's waists, crying on one another's shoulders.

The SS driving the wagon screamed, "Idiots, what are you shrieking about, you are going to a factory to work." Dare we believe him?

Cattle had been removed from an open train, and we were transferred to it, and like the previous occupants, we stood packed together, smelly, mute. When the train arrived at its destination, we stepped down into deep mud in a forest and were brought to a small, unfinished barracks. The rain and snow came in, and there was no plumbing of any kind. We had to go into the deep snow to relieve ourselves.

The coarse fabric of my dress rubbing against my open sores made them bleed again. My arms and legs were covered with bumps of pus and dried blood. Of all the experiences I had endured these years, it was the itching that I thought would finally drive me mad. Night and day I ripped at my skin, seeking relief. The SS wanted us dead. The lice were glad we were alive.

We had no shoes, no foot covering of any kind, and our fingers were like red, brittle sticks, almost beyond feeling.

Like mice, we piled on each other for warmth, and lived like this for weeks with no work, absolutely nothing to do, on the edge of insanity. The guard would use his gun without provocation, handling his boredom by making sport of killing.

An order broke the silence one morning. "Let's go, line up for a march." Oh, God, I thought, it is now, they'll take us out into the snow and shoot us all. In the days ahead, I would pray for death, but now I was not ready. For one week we marched. I would try to keep up front since those who walked slowly were shot.

In the darkness I sank into deep despair, but always as the sun of a new day dawned, there would rise in me a bit of hope, and again I would pray to live, questioning God's existence one moment and praying the next.

The behavior of the SS women seemed strange. They were shaving their heads and removing dresses from dead prisoners, which they would hastily put on. Slowly the realization came that they were attempting to look just like us. They seemed frightened. Could it be that the Russian soldiers were really close by?

We were put in filthy stables where the stench made breathing difficult. "If one of you runs away, I'll kill you all, you Jew bastards," the commandant shouted. "I'll be right back."

After hours of fearful waiting, someone in our group said, "They've lied, they're never coming back, let's get out of here." We were terrified at the thought of doing what we had been told not to, having become first-rate order-followers. Cautiously we peeked around, saw no one, and sneaked out, running until we came to a farmhouse that had been left empty by fleeing Germans. There was food on the shelves and even some cooked food on the stove. Grabbing handfuls, we gorged ourselves, paying for our gluttony with severe stomach cramps and diarrhea.

A woman who seemed less scarred by her years of imprisonment gathered us around and said, "We must think and make some plans for ourselves in case the Russians really come." Most of us were dazed, drugged with pain and fear. Like idiots we stared back at her. Think? Make decisions? Orders are what we need; orders! Fortunately, well-educated Ilsa, who spoke German, Russian, and Polish, took charge.

Off in the distance we heard shooting, and we huddled together, looking at one another with terror in our eyes. Suddenly the door was forced open as six Russian soldiers burst in, filthy and wild looking, with guns pointed at us. They screamed, "You lousy Germans, you'll get it now."

Ilsa came forward, speaking in Russian. "Listen; just a moment, don't shoot, we are Jews. Jews, do you understand, Jewish prisoners! We've lived through so much," she cried, mixing Russian with German and Yiddish, "don't shoot us." Three soldiers pushed forward, hugged us and wept, whispering, "We too are Jews."

And so the day, a moment in time, that lived at the back of our consciousness as some wild fantasy had come, and we were finally surrounded by people who were not our enemies.

And yet, because they were men who had been at war for a long time and starved for female companionship, the soldiers forced girls to sleep with them, and were rough with those who refused. I was frightened anew, and realized that fear would probably live at my side for a long time. . . .

And so again I was a wanderer, seeking a place of safety. Sonya and I walked miles through muddy fields. Occasionally we were picked up by farmers in their small trucks. When asked where we were going, we would say, "Oh, just as far as you go." Panic never left us. . . .

Like vagrants, we wandered looking for food and a place to sleep. We followed some people who were crowded into a small room of a local inn, and remained there for several nights with other wandering prisoners from concentration camps. Without our dream that one day we might reach our hometowns and perhaps see our families again, we might have simply given up, succumbed to the running and starvation.

We were informed that we were now in the Russian zone and that there was some assistance being offered by a Jewish organization that had just recently been set up to help displaced people. When Sonya and I appeared there, we were welcomed with great warmth and joy. It seems we were the first young people to return. . . .They offered to house us in a nearby building temporarily, but I explained that it was my desire to get back to Fritzlar and try to find my family. . . .

Fritzlar was unrecognizable. Where was the little park I used to walk in with my friends on the Sabbath? Where was my school and my house? It was all rubble. I ran down streets screaming, "Mama, where are you?" Sonya held my arm tightly, trying to comfort me. I sat down on the ground, leaning on the scarred trunk of a tree, buried my head in my lap, and cried as I hadn't cried since the day they cut all my hair off.

The hope that I would someday get home and see my family, or at least learn of their whereabouts, is what kept me alive. The dream of holding them in my arms made the beatings bearable, the starvation bearable, the death of my fellow inmates bearable. . . .

As we walked around and through bombed-out buildings, we came to an area where the houses and stores were in fairly good condition. I walked into the grocery store where I used to shop occasionally with my mother, and just stood there. The owner glanced at me as he dusted his stock, and then, slowly putting his cloth down, he stared with a shocked expression.

"Is your name Ruth Stern?" he said. "Yes, I am Ruth," I muttered.

He greeted me as an old friend would, but when he touched my arm, my entire body broke into a sweat. Although he wore the typical grocer's white apron over his sweater and trousers, I could clearly see the black boots of the stormtroopers. Those he still wore.

I knew he had been one of them. It was in his manner, his movement. I did not live with them for four years without knowing the
personality that marked them all.

I asked about my family. He turned half away and said, "There are no
Jews here any more."

I knew this was no longer my home, and I asked Sonya what she
thought we should do. "Come with me to Eschwege, maybe things will
be better there," she said.

As we approached Eschwege, we read the sign simultaneously,
"American Zone. . . ."

Sonya and I shared the apartment with another girl just out of the
camps, whose name was Elie. We were the only German-Jewish girls
to return to Eschwege.

The American soldiers got us wholesome food and kept an eye on
us. . . . Doctors in Eschwege tended our infected sores, and I was
given medication for my nervous stomach, as well as a tonic to prompt
an appetite and build me up. . . .

Just as life had begun to look better and I was beginning to sleep and
gain weight, I was shattered by the news from a concentration camp
victim that he had seen my parents go to the ovens at Auschwitz
together with my two little sisters. . . .

Nightmares were to haunt me for many long years; I repeatedly saw
them coming toward me with flames shooting from arms and legs.
They never reached me, even in my dreams. Sleep was to become a
luxury. As much as I craved it, I feared it, for with sleep came the
torture of nightmares.

From time to time American soldiers would visit us in our apartment, enjoying home cooking and the company of three young women.
How lively the house would be for those hours! One day a young
German-Jewish man came with the soldiers and spent all of Sunday
afternoon with me.

This shy, tall, handsome man, named Hans Nebel, came to see me
every Sunday, always bringing fresh flowers. During the week he
worked for the American army doing tailoring. His gentle manner and
compassion comforted me, and I began to feel relaxed as I experienced, after so many years, great happiness. After several months
Hans asked me to marry him. . . .

On June 30, 1946, I, Ruth Stern, who never expected to live to this
day, stood with flushed face and joy. Twelve Hungarian girls dressed in
white held candles on either side of us as we approached the *chupah*
(marriage canopy), which had been made of fresh flowers.

The wedding was held in the garden in back of the house in which I lived where the flowers were in full bloom, lush and colorful. The perfumed air made me lightheaded, or was it the crowd of two hundred people, or my memories. . . .

There were no relatives, no family of any kind, only American soldiers and townspeople. Everyone was anxious to attend the first German-Jewish wedding since the beginning of the war.

## Note

Reprinted with the permission of Sylvia Kramer from a longer version that appeared in Sylvia Kramer, *Velvet and Stone* (Orange, N.J.: Heritage Publications, 1980). Another version of the story appeared in *The Jewish Exponent* (Philadelphia), from which permission was also received.

# Comrade—Woman—Mother—
# Resistance Fighter

## Katharina Jacob

*We still know much too little about the nature of resistance in the Third Reich; indeed, there is even intense debate about how to define and understand the term. Many of the accounts we do have focus on organized resistance efforts, either of the mostly upper-class and military conspiracy of July 1944, or of the Communist Party. That focus has tended to render invisible other forms of less-organized resistance, such as helping slave laborers, hiding hunted Jews, or just trying to hold the line against the encroachments of a National Socialist education on one's children. Ironically, however, we also know too little about those women who participated in the organized networks as independently functioning political women and as adjuncts to their activist men. This account is taken from an oral history of a heroic woman, Katharina Jacob, as told to a feminist historian, who recorded it in the present tense to preserve the sense of immediacy in the narrative. Jacob both supported her husband's underground work and was herself a committed Communist antifascist. Like the pieces on the Holocaust, it speaks to a certain universality of experience beyond gender, but also points to the ways in which women's experience—particularly in their relation to children and other women—was different from that of men. The narrative only goes to the point of Jacob's incarceration in a concentration camp—which she survived—because the remainder of the account essentially repeats material in the two previous essays.*

### The Girl from Kasper Street

Katharina, called Käthe, is born March 6, 1907, in Cologne on the Rhine. The little girl is particularly fond of her grandmother, whom she often visits in her home on Probsteingasse. Fascinated, she watches as the one-armed woman—who lost her right arm through blood poisoning—cuts potatoes with her left hand, slices and butters bread, cleans up and washes. The grandfather is a coachman who doesn't earn enough money; with four daughters to feed, Grandma looks for additional jobs outside the house to help support the family. She helps the farmers in the marketplace with packing and unpacking boxes. The oldest daughter (who is Katharina's mother) has to look after the three siblings and take care of the household. Therefore, she cannot attend school regularly and her teacher beats her with a cane if she has not done her homework, if she is late, or if she fails to keep her notebooks tidy. Even though she has had no opportunities to develop her talents, she writes perfectly and knows many songs and poems. Her easygoing, friendly ways are in stark contrast to Grandmother's belligerent fighting spirit, with its marked sense of justice, which Käthe has inherited.

With her parents, brothers, and sisters, Käthe lives in a tenement house on Kasper Street, in a working-class area in the northern part of Cologne. Her father, Jakob Emmermann, a mechanic working for the Cologne railway system, is a diligent and solid worker who never fails to bring home his wages punctually. In the evenings, Käthe sees him come home tired, have his dinner, read the paper, and go to bed early. Her mother, Wilhelmine, is thirty-six years old when Käthe, the youngest of five children, is born. The life of a working-class woman is not easy. In order to earn some extra money as a seamstress, Mother buys a sewing machine, which she pays off in installments. How long it takes before it finally belongs to her! All new purchases are acquired in this manner. It really gets bad if the weekly payment of one or two marks cannot be made. Everybody in the house is familiar with the sight of the city marshall. Whenever the partially paid merchandise is taken out of the house again, the women stand in the hallway shouting and crying, sharing the misery. . . .

### Pushing Doors Open

Käthe would like to become a teacher. She is a good pupil. Her teacher advises her to go to high school, but that is impossible, due to her financial situation. Finally, the pastor finds an apprenticeship for his confirmation candidate as a clerk in the *Kölner Frauen-Zeitung*, a small paper linked to the bourgeois women's movement. Her training there is remarkably bad. After two years she hasn't really learned anything that might be of use to her in a white-collar job. Knowing that she isn't dumb, it depresses her to realize that she hasn't acquired enough knowledge. She doesn't have the nerve to apply for another job and so she stays where she is.

She feels happy, however, in the youth group of the Trade Union Federation of White Collar Workers (Gewerkschaftsbund der Angestellten; GDA). Here she meets young people from other youth organizations, such as the Socialist Workers' Youth Group (Sozialistische Arbeiterjugend), the Communist Youth Group (Kommunistische Jugend), the Federated Youth Group (Bündische Jugend) and the "Wandervögel."[1] They take trips together, enjoy nature, and sit and talk until late at night. It is a wonderful time. Käthe falls in love with Walter Hochmuth, another member of the group, who has just arrived in Cologne from the Vogtland.

When her youth group is dissolved by the trade union administration because of its "leftist tendencies," Käthe, Walter, and other young people form another youth group by the name of "Florian Geyer." Using the name of a hero of the sixteenth-century peasants' rebellions is clearly a deliberate statement. Later, Käthe writes about these times:

> To me, the time in the Florian Geyer group was not only one of the happiest in my life, but also the most crucial. The Christian Youth group and the GDA-Youth organizations were certainly important, but in the "Florian Geyer," doors were pushed open. After our evening meetings in Cologne-Sülz, we continued our long discussions about "everything under the sun" on our way back home; seeing each other home, walking to each other's houses and then back and forth again, we talked on and on. I think, none of us shall ever forget these conversations. We all had our problems, also very personal ones. But what a young person needs and searches for, I found in this group: comradeship, learning about beauty, enjoying beauty, political discussions. And, finally, personal recognition. The latter, I needed—probably like everyone else—more than anything else. Kasper Street had provided me with inferiority complexes and shyness in abundance. The Florian-Geyer group helped me free myself from some of these inhibitions, if not all of them. But something started growing in those days that was to bear fruit in later years. And to a great extent the love of and for Walter Hochmuth contributed to that. . . . Much later, in Cologne, Helene Otto, a Communist teacher, said in one of her lectures, "We do not only want to drink wine, we want to drink it from beautiful glasses, too." She said something there that might have been meant especially for me. To a great extent, the realization that the problems of "little Käthe from Kasper Street" were the problems of most working-class children and that they were explicable and solvable, made me become a Communist. The theoretical foundation came much later.

In 1926 Käthe becomes a member of the Communist Youth Organization, and in 1927 she goes to Hamburg with Walter Hochmuth. They are married the same year. Both of them work as clerks in Paul Peiniger's large fabric store. In her career as well, Käthe finds herself, realizing that this is a place where she can apply her skills.

## *". . . the Sun Never Sets for Us!"*

In the critical year 1933, Käthe is a housewife. After her daughter Ursel's birth in 1931, she had given up her job. In the same year, her husband becomes a delegate of the Communist Party (KPD) in the City Parliament of Hamburg, at twenty-seven its youngest member. They have a vague idea of what lies ahead for them when Hitler comes to power, but reality soon exceeds their gloomiest forebodings in the most horrible way. One day after the Reichstag elections on March 6— Käthe's birthday—a man from the Gestapo (the secret police) and two young policemen knock on their door to arrest her husband. But Walter has already gone underground and only comes home to their apartment in Winterhude, Meerwein Street, from time to time. While their apartment is being searched, the entire library—Käthe's pride and joy—is looted. Among the pile of confiscated books are political books, works by socialist and progressive writers, but also works by Dostoevsky and Tolstoy. Käthe protests, "But that's great literature!" The Gestapo man makes a gesture of refusal, "Those names alone!" he says with contempt.

Käthe keeps a cigar box containing photos of the youth group's hiking tours on the bookshelf. When the Gestapo man takes them down, she has a bad conscience, realizing that she shouldn't have kept them at all. She knows that the Nazis have begun filing the names of all suspicious persons they can get hold of. So anybody might be incriminated one day.

After hours of searching they finally leave. When Käthe picks up the few books left, lying scattered all over the floor, the photos drop out at her feet. She doesn't quite understand how they got there, but she burns them immediately. Later on, a friend informs her: the two policemen were young Social Democrats who had deliberately put the photos back among the books. Käthe is glad to hear this, because the experience indicates to her that not all Germans had suddenly turned into Nazis.

Other than the *Hamburger Tageblatt*, the Nazi paper, there are now only middle-of-the-road papers in Hamburg, such as the *Hamburger Anzeiger* or the *Hamburger Fremdenblatt*, which have been subjected to the general party line. The entire progressive press has been smashed. The leftists are convinced that it is their duty to inform the population about the brutal injustice and crimes committed by this regime. Käthe, who has been a member of the Communist Party since 1928, volunteers to distribute illegal leaflets. She knows that if she is caught, imprisonment will be the mildest punishment. Later on, during the war, it would be penitentiary, concentration camp, or death. That is how seriously the Nazis take a leaflet, the dissemination of truth.

After the search of their home, Käthe warns her husband, who continues his work on an illegal newspaper in Hamburg until 1934, when he emigrates to Copenhagen. When Käthe is arrested in July 1933, she becomes acquainted with Charlotte Gross, who later becomes her friend. Some of her comrades have already been tortured or beaten to death, others have committed suicide for fear of making incriminating statements. She is imprisoned in the concentration camp of Fuhlsbüttel and in the pretrial detention center on the Holstenglacis. She is placed in solitary confinement. But even there, she learns of the other women's plans to protest the ever worsening conditions of their life in prison. Someone shouts into the cell, "Starting tomorrow, there's a hunger strike!" Alone in her cell, Käthe joins in the protest. Every day the cell door opens, a bowl of food arrives, but she doesn't touch it, feeling sure that the other women are doing the same. This goes on for eight days. The prison administration threatens to start force-feeding. When she is told that the hunger strike has ended, Käthe is suspicious. Another prisoner is called and she confirms that this is really true. The women come out of this joint action weakened by hunger, but with their morale strengthened.

After five months of pretrial detention, Käthe is released. The trial takes place in 1934. She is accused of "conspiracy to commit high treason." She is sentenced to one year imprisonment in the women's prison of Lübeck-Lauerhof. This time, she shares her cell with five others. The women try to make something even out of this kind of life and will not have themselves branded as criminals. Not letting themselves become demoralized is considered a form of resistance. Every day, large sacks of potatoes are put into their cells to be peeled. Usually, they do it in such a way that five of them do the peeling, while the sixth reads aloud, making sure that no one hears it, for this is, of course, strictly prohibited. Everyone is interested in reading. There is a prison library even though much that was offensive to the Nazis has been removed. But many good books are still there and, most importantly, the library is run by political prisoners. . . .

Often, Käthe thinks of her little daughter. Good friends are taking care of Ursel. Once, she comes to see her mother in prison. The four-year-old marvels at the prison uniform, an old-fashioned blue dress with a white apron and a white bonnet. Käthe may hold her on her lap. The little girl puts a piece of chocolate into her mother's mouth. The guard, seeing this, shouts at her and threatens to prohibit further visits if it happens again.

### Civic Courage

Even in 1933 Käthe could no longer afford her apartment. She stored her furniture with friends and went looking for a room. When she is released from prison, in December 1935, the agonizing search for a room starts anew. Finally, she finds a two-and-one-half room apartment on Jarre Street, provided she can come up with a sponsor. Käthe has not found a job yet; she lives on welfare and gets less than twenty marks a week. She finds a sponsor, her former coal dealer Rudolf Gieselmann. He not only guarantees the rent by giving his signature, but he also supplies her with cheap coal, for which she can pay in installments. This is one of those acts of solidarity that have an enormous impact on her and sustain her materially and emotionally. In order to be able to pay for the rent, Käthe has to sublet two of the rooms. She and her daughter sleep in the small one-half room and live in the kitchen.

In 1936, Käthe reads an advertisement in the paper: "Clerk wanted!" Despite her insecurity about her qualifications, she applies. Again, she is seized by the same old anxieties. "Will you be able to meet the requirements?" In her application letter she has written that she is separated from her husband. The manager asks her about that. Käthe thinks, "Now you tell him the truth and admit that your husband emigrated for political reasons." As a matter of fact, she gets the job. She soon realizes that the managers of this import-export firm aren't Nazis either. There is no portrait of Hitler to be seen and no one performs the "German salute." Käthe realizes now why she was chosen for the job.

Frequently, comrades come together in her apartment to exchange information. Sitting together in small groups, they listen to foreign radio stations; this is strictly forbidden and dangerous. Her head covered by a thick blanket, Käthe presses her ear against the radio and listens eagerly to BBC/London or Radio Moscow. On New Year's Eve 1938, Käthe, together with a number of friends, is arrested and imprisoned in the Fuhlsbüttel concentration camp. During this time, her marriage breaks up. Her husband Walter had gotten involved with someone else after 1933. "This was simply due to the circumstances," Käthe says. In prison she is confronted with another problem: the district court in Hamburg denies her custody of Ursel.

Käthe is very scared. They threaten to put the child into a Nazi boarding school. Luckily, Ursel's teacher, Gertrud Klempau, a Social Democrat, intervenes. . . . She used to work in an experimental school, whose entire staff had been dismissed by the Nazis. This woman had retained her civic courage even in those bad times. She agrees immediately to become guardian to Ursel Hochmuth, a child whose father lives abroad as an emigré and whose mother is imprisoned as an opponent of the Nazi regime. Käthe is relieved of an enormous mental burden. Later, Käthe writes about Gertrud Klempau:

> I was impressed by her progressive teaching methods, from which I, too, learned. My headstrong daughter had conflicts with her every now and

then. She didn't understand anything about the "protective hand" over
her. I remember the topic of an essay the children had to write, "How I
imagine the land of milk and honey." Ursel had created a childish
counter-image to National Socialist reality. Even though she got an A on
the paper, she was not allowed to read it aloud as was customary when
one got a good grade. She came home disappointed and angry. Frau
Klempau took the notebook away with her and did not return it until after
the war. The essay betrayed too much of the spirit of Ursel's home. She
feared for the child if the essay were to fall into the wrong hands, but she
kept it.

### Courage to Love and to Resist

Four months before the outbreak of the war, Käthe and her friends
are released from the Fuhlsbüttel concentration camp. She regains her
former position in the same firm. That means a lot to her. Ursel is sent
to Saxony for a year through an official program to send children to the
countryside.

Käthe's life takes a new turn. She is reacquainted with Franz Jacob,
whom she already knows from her work in the youth organizations. He
was also a Communist delegate to the City Parliament of Hamburg.
After three years in the penitentiary and four years in a Sachsenhausen
concentration camp, he had returned to Hamburg and soon started
contacting his old friends and comrades in order to organize a resistance group. He gets a job as a mechanic in a small firm, the BOCO
laundry. . . .

He had suffered terribly and witnessed terrible scenes. But he did
not despair, and, in fact, concluded that the fight against Hitler and the
war had to be pursued to the very end. Franz and Käthe met each
other again during meetings in Hamburg. Living in such a state of
permanent danger, they still have the courage to love, taking the risk
that their happiness might last only a short while.

Käthe and Franz wait for Ursel to return from Saxony. It is important
to them that she accept her new father. All three of them are happy
now, and the wedding takes place in 1941. Ursel's teacher, Gertrud
Klempau, is the witness at the wedding of these two former political
prisoners. Franz moves in with Käthe.

It turns out to be a time of great personal happiness. In 1941 Käthe
writes to Franz, "You make me very happy with your readiness to love
and understand Ursel. I always knew I could only love a man and share
my life with him if he accepts and loves the child. That this should
become true one day, I had dared not hope. I am not angry at Walter
anymore."

Together with friends, they manage to build up another organization, the large Bästlein-Jacob-Abshagen resistance group. Its center is
in the big factories and dockyards of Hamburg, branching out to Bre-

men, Kiel, and Lübeck. Käthe is her husband's closest comrade in struggle and works with him in the organization. She knows that a man on the front line needs a woman who supports and protects him as best she can, and also undertakes actions on her own. She organizes meeting places, finds shelter for those in the underground, collects money and ration cards to support persecuted comrades. She organizes discussions, which occasionally take place in her apartment. She types materials compiled by Franz or by others that explain the political situation to the comrades and thus help support the illegal underground in the factories. In the beginning, they had refrained from printing leaflets because of the risk involved distributing them. But in June 1942 they issue—among others—the "Information Leaflet for Construction Workers."

The typewriter they need so badly is with a friend who cannot keep it in his apartment anymore for security reasons. Franz and Käthe go to pick it up and take it to a small house outside of Hamburg, which they can use for their illegal work. Käthe starts getting nervous. She knows that her husband is well known; besides, he is conspicuous in appearance, very tall, with bent back and his shoulders drawn up. And now, there he is, carrying this typewriter around in his rucksack. She fears for her husband. It is clear to her that they cannot take the typewriter home. But where to put it? Käthe remembers an old friend . . . ; Fritz Bartsch immediately agrees to hide the typewriter.

By 1942, a large number of people hate the Nazis, are sick and tired of the war, and are willing to do something about it. The antifascist literature that the organization passes on to the illegal factory groups contains information and arguments to be disseminated among the workers. The comrades among the foreign workers translate them and pass on the news by word of mouth. The leaflets Käthe helps type contain challenges people could actually meet. The instructions in the leaflets during the British bombardment of Hamburg are: "When the alarm is over, go home instantly! Don't let yourself be drafted for extra clean up work in the factories. First, find out if your families and homes are still there!" Or: "Work slowly, sabotage Hitler's armament industry!" People actually followed these summonses, as was reported after 1945.

All goes well for approximately two years. Then, on October 18, 1942, the Gestapo comes to arrest Franz. Luckily, he had already been warned by a telephone call telling him that his brother has just been taken to the hospital. The word "hospital" always stands for the Gestapo and arrest. The day before, someone had not shown up for a rendezvous. A bad omen! Franz and Käthe think about whom in the neighborhood they might notify if the Gestapo should come again. They need a place where Käthe can leave messages for Franz. Finally, they remember Lidde Klingenberg, an old working woman and comrade who had always stood by Käthe's side and one from whom they might expect cooperation. It is absolutely clear to Käthe what a dangerous thing she is asking this woman to do, but she knows of her courage and her solidarity. Lidde agrees, but then, all of a sudden, disappears very quickly. Coming back, she says, "Whenever the political situation gets dangerous, I have to go to the bathroom first. But after that, I do anything. You can ask the craziest thing of me, if only it's against those damned Nazis."

How much Käthe fears for Franz in the following hours, how many thoughts go rushing through her head! The short good-bye may be a good-bye for ever. And all this in her condition—she is about to give birth. It doesn't take long before the Gestapo return. Franz isn't in and the men leave again. Käthe runs to Lidde's home, in order to warn Franz. She enjoins her daughter not to open the door if the bell rings. Ursel, by now eleven years old, obeys the instructions. The Gestapo come for the third time and search the apartment. Käthe keeps telling them that she doesn't know where her husband is, and that is the truth. Franz remains hidden for another two weeks with comrades in Hamburg and then manages to escape to Berlin with the help of Charlotte Gross.

Charlotte, Käthe's friend, is a Communist. A mother of two children, she is also an activist in the resistance movement. She maintains the contact between Hamburg and Berlin and acts as their courier, while Franz—against whom a warrant is out—and Anton Saefkow and others build up another large resistance group. This organization has members in the big Berlin factories and cooperates with Communist groups in other parts of Germany, as well as with Social Democrats, bourgeois critics of the regime, and some army members and foreign slave laborers.

Franz and Käthe maintain loose contact through Charlotte. She is also the one who tells him that on November 9, 1942, his daughter Ilse was born in the bomb shelter of a hospital during a heavy air raid on Hamburg. Gertrud Klempau, the good spirit of the Jacob family, puts a large bunch of roses on Käthe's blanket when she comes to visit her on the day after the delivery. "From Franz," she says. Käthe's thoughts revolve around her husband. "When will you see your child? I called her Ilse, Franz, just as you wanted me to." Like all mothers the world over, she hopes for a bright future for her child, but the gloomy present drives away all such hopes for future happiness. Back home, Käthe starts keeping a diary about Ilse, so that Franz can participate in his daughter's development. Charlotte will hand him these notes on one of her courier trips to Berlin.

After the heavy air raids in the summer of 1943, the connection with

Franz is temporarily interrupted. One night there is a knock on Käthe's door. It is Luise Hesse, who lives with her mother in the same building. Käthe knows them as good Christians and opponents of Nazism. Even though this woman's mother had been asked repeatedly to hoist the swastika flag on various occasions, the old woman refused, choosing to disappear on such days. She preferred to endanger herself rather than display the hated flag. Now her daughter stands in the doorway before Käthe, fumbling in her stocking. She produces a letter from Franz. Käthe's heart starts beating faster with joy. A sign of life! News of Hamburg burning and all the terrible things that were happening had also reached Franz and, alarmed, he had sat down to write. He addressed the letter to Luise Hesse's workplace, trusting in the courage and decency of a Christian anti-Nazi. Franz wrote to her how grateful he would be if she could give Käthe the enclosed letter but that he would also understand if she could not. She gives Käthe the letter on the very day of its arrival.

Käthe is constantly aware that she is dealing with an adversary who is determined to remain in power at any cost. She experiences this even in her own apartment. The Gestapo manages to turn Käthe's boarder into a spy by giving her money and promising to give her Käthe's apartment. . . . A Gestapo clerk reveals the details after 1945. The long years of living dangerously have made Käthe vigilant; she senses danger and acts cautiously. At first, she can hardly believe that this woman, who herself has children and grandchildren, who has shared in Käthe's life and Ilse's birth, is capable of doing such a base thing. At this time, Ursel and her schoolmates have been sent to the countryside. Whenever Käthe drops a letter to Ursel into the mailbox, the traitor immediately notifies the Gestapo, which then goes and fishes it out again. They hope thereby to locate Käthe's husband. Whenever Käthe gets ready to take Ilse out in the stroller, the woman signals by shaking a dustcloth out the window and Käthe's moves will be observed. Also, another Gestapo spy has taken quarters in the house across the street.

This vulgar boarder picks a fight over the most minute household details. Käthe cannot tolerate her petty nastiness. During one of their arguments, the woman smacks Käthe in the face. After that, Käthe tries to have her evicted, without success, needless to say. As a result, she cannot even feel at home in her own apartment.

## A Call from the Cell

On July 6, 1944, the Gestapo again arrest Käthe. She is in bad shape. Ilse has a bad case of whooping cough. . . . It is awful having to part from a sick child. Little Ilse, nearly two years old, speaks a few words, but they make sense only to her mother. "Will they understand her prattle?" she worries. Her downstairs neighbors immediately take care of Ilse and notify Käthe's mother-in-law, who comes to take her grandchild to Bergedorf. The Gestapo take Käthe away. On the way, they ask her in a malicious way if she doesn't know where her husband is. Later on, she learns that Franz and the other leaders of the group have been arrested in Berlin. There is a warrant out in Hamburg for Käthe's and Charlotte's arrest. Charlotte is away in Thuringia, where she is arrested.

Käthe is taken to the Fuhlsbüttel concentration camp for the night and is chained to the bed, despite the danger of air raids. The next morning, the policeman who is to take her to Berlin comes to pick her up and holds her with a long leash. . . . Käthe asks him, "What's the hurry?" "Well," he says, "the cell in Berlin is waiting for you, and if we don't get you there fast, we'll be in it ourselves."

Käthe spends the night in prison. In the morning, she is the first to be put into a prison van. At the next stop, two people are locked into the single cells in the front of the car. Suddenly a thought flashes through her mind, "Could that be Lotte?" She walks through the car, calling, "Lotte?" Unbelievably, it is. Käthe whispers the important news to her: that Franz, Bernhard Bästlein, and Anton Saefkow have been arrested and that the Gestapo knows all about her trips from Hamburg to Berlin. Then they have to get out of the car. Käthe wants to look at her friend again but is rudely pushed away. "Get out of here, quick!" someone yells at her. Käthe is relieved that she has had a chance to give her friend the message. That will be to her advantage.

All of the Saefkow-Jacob-Bästlein group prisoners are taken to the Gestapo prison in Potsdam. Käthe is there on July 20, 1944 (the day of the attempted assassination of Hitler). The commotion in the corridor and the swearing and the nervousness of the guards signify that something special must have happened. There are three women in a single cell. When they are led to the toilet the next day, Käthe notices a small corner of a newspaper sticking out from behind the large drainpipe. She hides the scrap of paper under her dress. Back in the cell, they wait for the time of day when the guards are normally not around. The paper clipping reports about the events of July 20 and the headline reads "Assassination Attempt on Hitler." But he survived, and they ask themselves, "How is this going to end?" The next time she goes to the toilet, Käthe puts the clipping back in its place for others to read. Käthe and Lotte are separated. Once, she sees Franz for a couple of minutes in the presence of a policeman. She feels happy and yet terrible. She can't say any of the things so close to her heart. . . .

They are transferred to pretrial detention in Berlin-Moabit. The guard asks her if she can mend shirts, and Käthe immediately says yes, even though it is not true. She takes the work as a welcome change in the daily prison routine. They put a sewing machine in her cell and a large pile of badly torn soldiers' shirts. Käthe gets discouraged and wonders how she can possibly manage to get it all done. Then she remembers what she learned in the needlework classes back in elementary school a long time ago. . . .

She doesn't stay in Moabit for long. The next stop is the womens' prison on Barnim Street. Käthe is interrogated about Lotte's activities as a courier. . . . At first, Käthe denies that Lotte ever brought her money or even a letter. She claims that someone else did that. In the meantime, however, the Gestapo had tortured Lotte by smashing her fingers. She confesses. After that, Käthe is not interrogated anymore.

At 6:00 in the evening, the guards change shifts. This is usually the time when the prison starts bustling with activity. Even though it is strictly prohibited, the women move close to the cell windows and shout out; they pass on news for an individual or for everybody. That is how they communicate. Everybody wants to know, for instance, where the front is. Maybe even more than those outside, they hope for a quick end to the war and the fall of the Nazi regime.

The windows are high, but if the women stand directly underneath them and shout with all their might, the others will hear. One evening in early September, one of those calls penetrates Käthe's cell and pierces her heart. "My trial was today," the voice shouts out. "Franz Jacob, Bernhard Bästlein, and Anton Saefkow were sentenced to death!" It is Judith Auer shouting, the mother of a little girl and sentenced to death herself. Standing by the window alone in her cell, Käthe learns that she has forever lost that which she loves most.

Several weeks later, Judith Auer dies on the scaffolds of Berlin-Plötensee, because she had smuggled illegal leaflets—among other things—to Thuringia and Saxony for the Saefkow-Jacob-Bästlein group. She had also temporarily sheltered Franz in her apartment in Berlin.

## Friendship

Käthe's and Charlotte's trial date is set for September 20, 1944. The indictment doesn't get to them until about a week earlier. No lawyer seeks them out. Käthe is charged with having known of her husband's whereabouts and political activities, without having reported him to the police. There is a law saying that anybody sought by the Gestapo has to be reported, no matter if he or she is one's mother, father, brother, sister, spouse, or child. To Käthe, these charges don't seem so serious. She will say, "I'd like to see the wife who reports her husband to the police." For Lotte, however, things look really bad. She is charged with having worked as a courier, smuggling money and leaflets, and having tried to organize people into joining illegal activities. Käthe is quite aware that Lotte's situation seems hopeless. Apart from Judith Auer—whose situation was even worse because she was Jewish—other women before Lotte had been sentenced to death with less evidence. Now, Käthe tries to figure out how she can help her friend. . . .

For Lotte it is particularly incriminating that some of the leaflets and the names of three old Communists (whom she had tried to organize) [for the resistance]) had been found on her. Käthe thinks it might be a good idea for Lotte to claim that she had written those names down because she had meant to ask these people if any of them could maintain the connection between Käthe and Franz, since she herself wanted to withdraw from political activities. In this manner, Käthe builds up the defense. The day arrives when they normally take showers. As always, they are led into the room in two groups, with Lotte in the first and Käthe in the second. Käthe walks straight into the wrong bathroom, clutching the tiny, densely written pieces of paper, which are small enough to swallow, if necessary. She is relieved to see Lotte standing under the first shower. The guard yells at her immediately, but at least Lotte gets her message. Will it be of any help?

The trial takes place on September 20, in the People's Court (*Volksgerichtshof*). Lotte testifies and follows Käthe's suggestions exactly. Then Käthe is led into the room and Lotte has to leave. Käthe's statements confirm Lotte's. Suspicious, the judge asks the policeman who brought them in, "Is there any possibility that these women had a chance to talk to each other?" For, in the files, there is a strict prohibition on any meeting between prisoners. "That is impossible," replies the policeman. The prosecutor demands the death penalty for Lotte and acquittal for Käthe. Then the court adjourns for deliberation. . . . Nothing can hold Käthe and Lotte back, now. Crying, they fall into each other's arms. They no longer believe in Lotte's rescue, even though they are afraid to say so. Käthe is angry about the lukewarm defense and yells at the lawyer, "This is a scandal! You never even mentioned the most important fact, that this woman has two children and a husband who is at the front.". . . At long last, the court returns. Its verdict: Käthe is acquitted for lack of evidence; Lotte gets a ten-year penitentiary term. But what does that matter, now, in September 1944? With the Allies coming closer every day, the prisoners . . . are already counting the days until their liberation! . . .

Käthe is immediately released from solitary confinement in the detention center and taken to another building in Barnim Street. As she sits waiting for her release papers and trying to formulate an application to see Franz, a prison clerk enters. "Is your name Käthe, by any

chance?" she asks. . . . "There is a letter for you." Käthe is startled at
the woman's strange look as she leaves the cell. She returns with a
letter from Franz. As she hastily tears it open, photos of their children
drop out. Then she knows that he isn't alive anymore. He was executed
on September 18. . . .

Käthe is taken to the police prison on Alexanderplatz. After the
silence of her solitary confinement, she feels completely overwhelmed
as she stands at the entrance of the large, overcrowded hall, with her
letter still in one hand and her small parcel in the other. Tears flow
down her face, blinding her. Two women come rushing toward her,
"Are you a 'political'?" they want to know. "Yes." "Who are you?"
"Käthe Jacob." "Martin's wife?" (Martin was Franz's assumed underground name.) Käthe just nods. The two women, Martha Paucka and
Mieze Krüger, belonged to the same resistance group and they take
Käthe to their corner. There she breaks down, able to cry at last and to
talk about her feelings. Then she is transferred to the prison on Kaiser-
damm, where she is now officially informed of her husband's
death. . . . In addition, she is informed in writing that it is strictly
against the law to make his execution publicly known.

### Going Through Hell

While she was still in Barnim Street, she had already been informed
that despite her acquittal, she was to be imprisoned in the
Ravensbrück concentration camp. Early one morning in mid-
November of 1944, a tram is waiting to take her and a group of other
women away. . . .

—Trans. Renate Steinchen

### Notes

Portions of this account appeared in *Frauen Leisten Widerstand, 1933–1945*, ed. Gerda
Szepansky (Frankfurt/Main: Fischer, 1983) and are reprinted with the permission of the
publisher.

1. Literally, "bird of passage," the name of a group that originated the German youth
   movement, mainly focused on hiking and camping.—Ed.

# Notes on the Contributors

*Gisela Bock* has published books and articles on women's history, early modern Italian history, and U.S. labor history. A book on *Forced Sterilization in National Socialist Germany: Studies in Race and Women's Politics* is forthcoming. She is a faculty member at the Historical Institute of the Technical University, Berlin.

*Renate Bridenthal* is co-editor of, and contributor to, *Becoming Visible: Women in European History* and contributed to *Household and Kin: Families in Flux.* She is associate professor of history at Brooklyn College, the City University of New York, and a co-founder of its women's studies program. She is currently writing a book on conservative economic interest groups among women in the Weimar Republic.

*Atina Grossmann* has published articles on the Sex Reform movement and the "New Woman" in Weimar Germany and is working on a book about *Women, Family, and the Rationalization of Sexuality: German Sex Reform, 1925 to 1935*. She is an assistant professor at Mount Holyoke College, where she teaches modern European and women's history.

*Amy Hackett* has written a dissertation on "The Politics of Feminism in Wilhelmine Germany, 1890–1918," as well as several articles on this subject. She is a member of the Institute for Research in History, New York City.

*Karin Hausen* has written books on the history of German colonialism in Africa, on the history of modern technology, and on the Paris Commune. She is the editor of an anthology on German women's history, *Frauen Suchen ihre Geschichte,* and has written articles on women's history and family history. She is professor of economics and social history at the Technical University, Berlin.

*Marion Kaplan* is the author of *The Jewish Feminist Movement in Germany: The Campaigns of the Jüdischer Frauenbund, 1904–1938* and edited, and contributed to, *The Marriage Bargain: The Dowry in European History* (forthcoming). She is currently at work on a book on the social history of Jewish women in Imperial Germany. She is associate director of the Leo Baeck Institute, New York City.

*Claudia Koonz* is co-editor of, and contributor to, *Becoming Visible: Women in European History.* She is the author of articles on German women's history and of the forthcoming *Mothers in the Fatherland: Women's Responses to Nazism.* She is associate professor of history at the College of the Holy Cross, Worcester, Massachusetts.

*Elisabeth Meyer-Renschhausen* has published articles on the history of feminism and women's work in Imperial and Weimar Germany. She is working on a dissertation about the women's movement in Bremen between 1810 and 1933, and teaches at the Sociological Institute of the Free University in Berlin.

*Sybil Milton* is co-author of *Art of the Holocaust* and co-editor of, and contributor to, *The Holocaust: Ideology, Bureaucracy, and Genocide* and contributor to *Genocide: Critical Issues of the Holocaust.* She is editor and translator of *The Stroop Report* and has written numerous essays on the history of the Holocaust. She is chief archivist at the Leo Baeck Institute in New York, and co-editor of the *Simon Wiesenthal Center Annual.*

*Annemarie Tröger* taught at the Free University in Berlin from 1975 to 1981 and now teaches social science methodology and oral history at Hannover University. She is co-editor of the journal *Feministische Studien* and has published widely on National Socialism, oral history, and women's studies.